THREE BASICS OF SIKH RELIGIOUS THOUGHT

Faith, Grace and Prayer

THREE BASICS OF SIKH RELIGIOUS THOUGHT

Faith, Grace and Prayer

SATNAM KAUR

Second edition

PRAGATI PUBLICATIONS
NEW DELHI

PRAGATI PUBLICATIONS
4382/4B, Ansari Road, Darya Ganj
New Delhi 110002
e-mail pragati1@ndf.vsnl.net.in

Second edition 2004

ISBN: 81-7307-094-6

Published by Vikas Kapoor for Pragati Publications
4382/4B, Ansari Road, Darya Ganj,
New Delhi 110002

TO THE MEMORY OF MY MOTHER

Sardarni Amrit Kaur

CONTENTS

PREFACE TO THE SECOND EDITION

In this second edition of the work, immediately before their translation into English, all extracts from *Sri Guru Granth Sahib* have been given in their original *Gurmukhi* form. This is its only difference from the first edition which has been very well received and for which I thank the readers heartily.

SATNAM KAUR

ACKNOWLEDGEMENTS

It was Dr. S Vahiduddin, sometime Professor of Philosophy at the University of Delhi, who first encouraged me to do some research in the field of Sikh religious thought. So my first impulse is to thank him sincerely.

However, as I set out to work for my research thesis, my regular supervisor was Professor S.K. Saxena of Delhi University. His help has been inestimable, and I take it as a privilege to acknowledge it.

As my work progressed, I had to leave my home and visit Professor Saxena's very often, for a detailed study of the Sikh scriptures with special reference to the concepts which form the crux of the present work. My husband and my children tolerated my absence ungrudgingly; and at Professor Saxena's residence, to both members of his small family—his son and wife—I was always welcome. I would be failing in my duty if I do not express my indebtedness to them all. My affection for my niece, Ritu, has also sustained me.

The typing of the manuscript has been the undivided responsibility of Mr. A.N. Sharma. Publishing has been done, quite well in my view, by Mr. Vinod Kapoor of Pragati Publications. I am naturally grateful to both these gentlemen.

I am also beholden to the various libraries from where I have borrowed books freely, namely, those that are located at the following centres of learning: University of Delhi, Mata Sundri College, Bhai Vir Singh Sadan, Guru Nanak Foundation, and Vidya Jyoti, where the kindly Father T. K. John, S.J. was always willing to give me all possible help.

Above all, I must thank the University of Delhi for giving me permission to publish my doctoral thesis on the Sikh view of faith, grace and prayer in the present revised form.

GUIDE TO TRANSLITERATION

अ — a	आ — ā	इ — i	ई — ī	
उ — u	ऊ -- ū	ऋ — ṛ	ॠ — ṛ	
ऌ — ḷ	ए — e	ऐ — ai	ओ — o	
औ — au	अं — aṁ	अः — aḥ		
क् — k	ख् — kh	ग — g	घ — gh	ङ् — ṅ
च् — ch	छ् — chh	ज् — j	झ् — jh	ञ् — ñ
ट् — ṭ	ठ् — ṭh	ड् — ḍ	ढ् — ḍh	ण् — ṇ
त् — t	थ् th	द् d	ध् dh	न् n
प् — p	फ् — ph	ब् — b	भ् — bh	म् — m
य् — y	र् — r	ल् — l	व् — v	श् — ś
ष् — ṣ	स् — s	ह् — h	ळ् — l	क्ष् — kṣ
त्र् — tr	ज्ञ् — jñ			

"... [Let us] try to understand the words of those whom we regard as men of God. Let them soak into our being ... so far as they appeal to the heart".

MAHATMA GANDHI

INTRODUCTION

This essay is a modest attempt to interpret three fundamental concepts of religion—namely, faith, grace and prayer—in the specific context of Sikh religious thought as embodied in its basic text, the *Ādi Granth*, which comprises the original writings of the Sikh *gurus*.

I am, of course, mindful of the fact that quite a few good works on the ethico-religious thought of the Sikhs are already there. Some of the more important ones of these are: *Ethics of the Sikhs*[1]; *Philosophy of Sikhism*[2]; *Philosophy of Sikh Religion*[3]; *Prayer, Its Nature and Technique*[4]; *Nām or Word*[5]; *The Guru in Sikhism*[6]; and *A Critical Study of Ādi Granth*[7]. But, so far as I know, no whole book is available on the three concepts I have chosen as the subject of the present work.

The study I have undertaken is also warranted by the fact that its manner is more or less distinctive; it is no mere generally thoughtful study, but an interpretative attempt in the way of present-day philosophy. Indeed, I have here tried to pay as much attention to the phenomenological approach as to that of linguistic analysis. The essay is phenomenological, first, because it does not rest itself on any prefixed notion of truth and reality, and therefore accords with the phenomenological ideal of presuppositionless philosophizing; and, second, because it seeks to unravel the fabric of the experience of faith, grace and prayer with minimal damage, I hope, to its intricate undividedness. And as for linguistic analysis, I think I have taken pains to keep to it. Close and reverent[8] attention to the literal and suggested meanings of *Gurbāni* has in fact been my guiding principle all along. *The English translations* of the extracts which I had to pick for special attention are all given at the end of this work, not at once where I discuss them; for I did not want to loosen my attention to the original. If, therefore, my study is philosophical in the contemporary sense, it is so essentially because it is all along a search for clarity of meaning, and not because it merely puts, at places, the thought of the *gurus* against the background of present-day religious philosophy.

It should here be easy to see why this work could not avoid being, in part, an essay in hermeneutics regarded not as a mere sub-discipline of literary study, but, first, as that kind of philosophical attempt at understanding which is grounded in traditions of both phenomenology and analytic philosophy; and second, as a working of the 'hermeneutic circle', or as that dynamic process of understanding which is revealed in perceiving how the parts and the whole make each other meaningful.[9]

At this point, however, I would like to make an additional remark. During the course of my work I have found that the transition of interpretative attention from one word to another may well be psychological, and not merely logical. To illustrate, if in the same verse we find the word *Suhāgaṇi* on the one hand, and the following verbal complex: '*vaṇi tṛṇi sabhatu hai*' on the other, we may well be able to see the link between the two by visualizing (not merely thinking) that a *suhāgaṇi* is one who feels protected in, or surrounded by her husband's love; and that the image of 'surrounding' tends to evoke the allied image, 'here, there, everywhere' which, in turn, explains the mind's transition to *vaṇi tṛṇi sabhatu hai*.[10]

But, more importantly, this study is hermeneutical in the sense that it tries to be true to the ideal fixed by Schleirmacher in respect of understanding an author,—that is, the norm of understanding the very spirit 'which initiated and controlled his writing and for whose representation the writing exists'.[11]

The writers, the *gurus,* are all men of the highest stature. On the other hand, and just as undeniably, they are all men of flesh and blood. This at once makes the hermeneutical approach both necessary and possible for us. As Dilthey says: "Interpretation would be impossible if the expressions of life were totally alien . . . (and) it would be unnecessary if there were nothing alien in them."[12] Now, luckily, both sides of the matter are available to us in our present concern. The *gurus,* I repeat, are *great* men admittedly, but they are intensely *human* too. They are eager to help us, by inviting our attention to truths and experiences of surpassing value which we can also attain, if we only follow the way indicated by them.

But though we have to aim at obtaining some insight into the religious experience of the *gurus,* one cannot but begin by attending to individual words of the *text*; and this I have done first by considering the proximate verbal context—that is, the adjacent words within the same verse, and also the immediately preceding and following verses; and, second, by giving some thought to the essential spirit and overall context, that is, to the purpose of the whole work and the general life-style of the *gurus*. It is such a comprehensive way of looking at the sacred texts which has led me, at places, to disagree with the interpretations of the two established commentators, Dr. Gopal Singh[13] and Mr. Manmohan Singh.[14]

Here, however, a question may be put. Is it at all possible to *interpret* the esoteric experiences of religion, as against the familiar ones of everyday life? Now, I see reason to say *yes* readily. The interpretation in question does not have to project (or evoke) any *religious experience* as such; it can simply be an effort to get at the meaning of some *religious language;* and in so far as men of religion, including the Sikh *gurus*, not only record their experiences in language but expect this language to be generally understood, there is no reason to suppose that this record of religious experiences would recalcitrate analytic interpretation.[15] I here feel supported by Von Wright's considered view that even the interpretative efforts of the later *anti*-positivist Wittgensteinians should be regarded as a legitimate exercise in hermeneutics.[16]

Finally, in my hermeneutic endeavour, I am also encouraged by the fact that some eminent scholars believe that the interpretations of the commentators who have so far dominated the field of Sikh religious thought cannot be regarded as 'entirely satisfactory'.[17] Therefore, in my view, interpretation of the religious writings of the *gurus* is both necessary and possible. However, in so far as the life of religion is inseparable from morality, along with the three concepts I have chosen as the subject of this work, I will have to pay a little attention to some moral concepts too, like humility or self-effacement. Incidentally, an apt answer to the question, why the Sikh *gurus* lay so much emphasis on the need to curb egoity (*haumai*), is provided by the following utterances from Kierkegaard and St. Augustine:

> "God in heaven, let me really feel my nothingness, not in order to despair over it, but in order to feel more powerfully the greatness of Thy Goodness."[18]
>
> "Dost thou wish to rise? You plan a tower that shall pierce the clouds? Lay first the foundations of Humility."[19]

As for the plan of this book, it is simple. Besides the Introduction, it comprises three chapters, each devoted to one of the three concepts chosen. The second chapter, devoted to grace, had to be broken up into six sections, mainly because of the richness of material available on this concept. In this chapter, where I struggle to distinguish the various sub-concepts that the Sikh religious view of grace comprises, a measure of overlapping of ideas has been knowingly retained, just to suggest that the subsidiary concepts distinguished alike make for the singleness of the experience of grace. Care has also been taken, in every chapter, to distinguish the generally philosophical perspective of the basic concept (of the chapter) from the Sikh religious view of the same.

Notes

1. Dr. Avtar Singh: *Ethics of the Sikhs,* Punjabi University, Patiala, 1970.
2. Dr. Sher Singh: *Philosophy of Sikhism,* Sterling Publishers, Jullunder, 2nd edition, 1966.
3. Dr. Wazir Singh: *Philosophy of Sikh Religion,* Ess Ess Publications, 1st edition, 1981.
4. Kirpal Singh: *Prayer, Its Nature and Technique,* The Sant Bani Press, America, Tilton, New Hampshire, Fourth Printing, 1974.
5. Kirpal Singh: *Nām or Word,* The Sant Bani press, America, Tilton, New Hampshire, 3rd Printing, 1974.
6. W. Owen Cole: *The Guru in Sikhism,* Darton; Longman & Todd, 1st edition, 1982.
7. Dr. S.S. Kohli: *A Critical Study of Ādi Granth,* Punjabi Writers' Co-operative Industrial Society Ltd., 1961.
8. A measure of reverence here seems warranted by the fact that *śabda,* as words of men of realization, is an acknowledged *pramāṇa* in Indian Philosophy.
9. 'The actual practice of hermeneutics becomes a part-whole-part movement, a constant back and forth or dialectical process . . . . It describes the famous "hermeneutic circle"', Hoy, David Courzens, *The Critical Circle: Literature, History and Philosophical Hermeneutics,* University of California Press, 1978, Cited in *Three Faces of Hermeneutics,* Roy J. Howard, University of California Press Ltd., 1982, p. 10.
10. *Ādi Shri Guru Granth Sahibji,* Standard 1430 pages, Shri Damdami Bir; Bhai Jawahar Singh Kirpal Singh and Co., Amritsar, p. 44.
11. Roy J. Howard, *Three Faces of Hermeneutics,* University of California Press Ltd., 1982, p. 9.
12. Cited in *Knowledge and Human Interests* (Habermas Jurgen), translated by Jeremy J. Shapiro, Boston, Beacon Press, 1971, p. 164.
13. *Sri Guru Granth Sāhib* (English version), translated and annotated by Dr. Gopal Singh, Gurdas Kapoor and Sons, 1960.

14. *Śri Guru Granth Sāhib* (English and Punjabi Translation), Manmohan Singh, Shiromani Gurdwara Prabhandak Committee, Amritsar, 1962, 1st impression.
15. Thus, see: 'In its conception of Philosophy of religion as analysis of language . . . the analytical method is a most appropriate approach in philosophy of religion'. W.F. Zuurdeeg: *An Analytical Philosophy of Religion,* George Allen & Unwin, 1959, p. 17.
16. George Henrick Von Wright: *Explanation and Understanding,* Ithaca, Cornell University Press, 1971, pp. 182-86.
17. W. Owen Cole and Piara Singh Sambhi: *The Sikhs, Their Religious Beliefs and Practices,* Rupa and Co.; 1st edition, 1984, xv.
18. P.D. Lefevre: *The Prayers of Kierkegaard,* University of Chicago Press, 1956, p. 5.
19. St. Augustine: Sermon X on the Words of the Lord.

13. Sri Guru Granth Sahib (English and Punjabi Translation), Manmohan Singh, Shiromani Gurdwara Parbandhak Committee, Amritsar, Ist impression.

14. Hari Ram Gupta, In his [illegible] concept and [illegible] [illegible] [illegible] [illegible] [illegible] [illegible] in the [illegible] of [illegible] [illegible]

[illegible]

[illegible]

[illegible]

[illegible]

1

FAITH

I. THE FABRIC OF CONCEPTS

Faith is the first of the three concepts that make the subject of this work. Here, however, it could at once be contended that the Sikh religion attaches at least as much importance to grace and prayer as to faith; and that, therefore, it has to be explained why I *begin* with faith. My answer to this would be that, of the three concepts I have chosen to discuss, faith alone is freely used also as a word to mean a whole religion, as when we speak of the Christian or the Hindu faith. Further, faith is not only an essential element, but often an important objective of *prayer*; we have not only to pray *in* faith, but often *for* the deepening of faith itself. As for the various expressions of His *grace* in a man's life, they would all be slurred over as mere good turns of luck if the individual in question is not equipped with 'the seeing eye of faith'. To conclude, faith may perhaps be said to cover a larger extent of, and to have richer linkages in, the life of religion than prayer or grace; and so it appears proper to open our discussion with an account of the Sikh view of *faith*.

In Sikh religion, at least seven different words have been used in the context of the life of faith: *oat, tek, bharosā* (or *bharvāsā*), *ādhār, ās, āsarā, sardhā (or śraddhā)*. But for faith itself, as distinguished from what it means to cultivate and hold on to faith in actual life, my feeling, however, is that the right word is *sardhā*, a variant of *śraddhā*. The other concepts may be said to be subsidiary to it, in so far as they represent mere aspects of the content of *sardhā* or faith. Faith is the total fact of being related to God in a multiple way. This way, on the whole and in principle, is one of implicit, undivided, joyous and reverential trust in the Lord. Within the wholeness of this relation, *oat* and *tek* (or *ādhār, āsarā*) may be said to stand for the *objective* side of the relation as experienced, indicating how *God* here appears to us, as a shelter and as an anchor or support, or as the foundational reality; and *bharosā* (or *bharvāsā* or trust) and *ās* (or steadfast hope) may be said to characterize what or how it *feels* to have *faith* in God.

I admit that in the light of popular usage the word *tek* can be taken in two senses: as a point or source of repose to which we turn occasionally between our activities or 'wanderings'[1], and as an *abiding* support. But in the second sense *tek* is indistinguishable from *ādhār*. So we are perhaps justified in taking *tek* and *ādhār* as one. *Bharosā* (or *bharvāsā*) must here be taken as *reverential* trust or in the sense of trust in a Reality as compared to which we appear quite humble in our own eyes. To look on a friend as *ādhār* is simply to feel assured that the trust will not be betrayed. But the *bharosā* which is incidental to *sardhā* (as trust *in the Lord*) is no mere loving trust in a fellow-being, but trust as touched with a measure of reverence (for the Supreme Person). It is all right to speak of having *bharosā* in a subordinate; but we do not ordinarily speak of having *śraddhā* for those who are inferior to us in rank. As for the word *āsrā*, it may be taken to mean either that (Reality or Being) which serves as a support or the (more or less) confident expectation of assistance, tinged with a moving dependence on the source of assistance. Finally, we must remember that God as *ādhār* is the fundamental and *abiding* support; it is no mere *pre*-condition, but an *underrunning* determinant or sustainer of whatever is or happens. Did He merely precede what He creates, God would exclude, and so be limited by what follows the primal instant of creation.

II. PHILOSOPHICAL PERSPECTIVE

The little *argument* I have just now put forth may be taken as an index of the way I propose to proceed. It would help understanding if we look at the Sikh view of faith from the viewpoint of philosophy. This viewpoint requires us (a) to clarify the concepts relating to the life of faith; (b) to discuss the traditional philosophical questions of knowledge, reality and truth in relation to faith as projected in the Sikh scriptures; and (c) to carry out the discussion in the context of the life of religion taken quite generally, so that the philosophical requirement of comprehensiveness or adequacy of concern may also be met. What the philosophical problems of faith as such are can here be indicated only briefly, for our emphasis has to be on *the Sikh view* of faith.

Now, the first of these problems may be said to relate to meaning. What does faith mean? If we go by its dictionary meanings, the word 'faith' may be taken in (at least) three senses: as belief in the truth of revealed religion; as the living reception of religious belief; and as genuine trust and confidence in God. It seems to me that in the Sikh scriptures the last of these meanings dominates.

However, it is hardly enough to say that faith is trust in God or *sardhā* (*śraddhā*); and we must set out to see what the details of the life and experience of faith are. This indeed is what the key philosophical question, what really is faith, requires us to do. Now, by way of answering this question, we may begin by considering the ways in which faith is commonly spoken of by ordinary people, by those who do philosophy, and by saints or sages.

As for *ordinary men*, the more important ways in which they talk about faith may be roughly put as follows:

(a) I do not *have* any faith in God.

(b) I do try to pray, but my faith in God is *still quite weak*.

(c) I do not understand all this talk about faith. How can one have faith in something that is not visible?

(d) Faith in God—how is it at all necessary? Why should we not depend on our own efforts, instead of leaving everything to God?

Now it is easy to see how philosophical reflection is set astir by such ways of speaking about faith. To begin with (*a*) if faith is a kind of *having*, what is this precise kind? Surely, it cannot be the same kind of having as the owning of some property; for whereas such ownership does not usually bring about any qualitative improvement in the life and conduct of the owner, the acquisition of faith is known to have transformed even sinners into saints. The distinction which Marcel draws between *being* and *having*[2] is surely no disjunction, for there *are* some invasive experiences, like prayers of soulful petitioning or confession, which enrich or deepen our being with their very incidence. Faith, too, is a having *and* an exaltation or steadying of being. To *have* faith in God is at once to *be* bound to God in the relation of love. The word 'bound', however, may at once suggest a question. If faith is a kind of binding, does it deprive us of all freedom? Interestingly, the Sikh answer here is that real faith in God can certainly make us *free from* all apprehension (*andeṣā*) and the bondage of the senses,—nay, even from the birth-death cycle. But the *gurus* do not discuss, they do not even pose, the question if a man of faith has freedom to do anything without the aid of, if not in opposition to God. Philosophy is troubled by a different question too. May faith be said to provide for cognitive *freedom*? The common answer here is that one cannot be *compelled* to really believe in God. Thomas Aquinas says:

> "An article of faith is some irreducible truth about God, binding us to belief. Yet belief is voluntary. No one believes except by wanting to."[3]

And, according to St. John,

> "Believing is not only an act of the mind, assenting to revealed truths; it is also an act of man's free will."[4]

Philosophers seem to share this view. Thus, Marcel says:

> "Faith is only possible to a free creature, that is, a creature who has been given the mysterious and awful power of withholding himself."[5]

John Hick believes that faith is a kind of 'seeing as' or 'interpreting' with 'cognitive freedom'. But Vivekananda would point out that where faith is consummate, one neither can, nor desires to break away from the spell of governance by God. To illustrate,

> "When Gandhi is faced with a huge problem and looks humbly to God for help, the response often comes as a call that *enforces* obedience, and allows no freedom to act or to interpret . . . . (His) 'irrevocable' decision to 'fast for removal of untouchability' was taken in instant and unquestioning obedience to a perfectly clear injunction of the inner voice. The whole experience is but the receipt and instant acceptance of a message, quite without probing for any covert meaning."[6]

As for the Sikh *gurus*, they would readily agree with Vivekananda's insistence that consummate faith is acceptance of *apratikūlya*; that a man who is blessed with it is convinced that *everything* that happens, because it is the handiwork of (a benevolent) God, is bound to be somehow good for him . . . (and that) the highest reaches of faith are no mere interpretation.[7]

In respect of (b), some philosophic remarks may be made at once. If faith can be more or less steadfast—as only seems proper to believe, for men of religion are freely seen to pray for a *deepening* of faith—it must be regarded as a kind of vital, personal relation, and not as a merely inert one like contiguity of things in space; and if it is a vital relation, it cannot be said to merely fall *between* the two related terms, but must be taken to affect their inner being too[8], and as standing in need of careful nurture. The Sikh *gurus,* we shall later see, speak of being suffused with, and being dyed in love of God; and the way they are found to look on faith, praying in earnest for its maturation (*sardhā pūrī*), is indistinguishable from Kierkegaard's fervent utterance that faith is a commitment of one's whole life and being, and that there is only a single prospect of victory that keeps one glued to this commitment: the consummation of faith into utter self-effacement.[9]

The question projected in (c) is perhaps the most natural expression of the average man's scepticism about faith. But to this the religious man's ready reply would be that it is precisely because God is not a visible object that faith is necessary. Praying to a God who is directly seen would be a merely human kind of petitioning; and acquiescence in what is given to sense is mere belief, not religious faith. Nor should we suppose that just because God is not visible, faith in His reality is wholly unwarranted. The warrant of faith, as one sets out on the path of religion, is no immediate evidence, but the accumulated testimony of saints of every religion. This is why Gandhi says that 'true faith is appropriation of the reasoned experience of people whom we believe to have lived a life purified by prayer and penance'[10], and this, again, is why the Sikh *gurus* freely recommend a recourse to the *tek* or *oat* of saints. Finally, a *realization* of God is possible; and this realization, though it is supersensuous, can be so comprehensive and immediate that, as in the recorded experience of the Sikh *gurus,* one may find it impossible to shake off the feeling that God is present everywhere.

The question that comes next, (d), doubting the utility of faith as against that of human effort, is relatively easy to answer. Saints, including the Sikh *gurus,* do not underestimate the value of human effort; they only enjoin a measure of change in its direction. Our efforts, they suggest, should be directed not only at the attainment of merely empirical ends, but also at the subjugation of innate evil propensities like anger and lust; and, above all, at the supreme end of curbing self-will and commitment to the Will (or *hukam*) of God. The *gurus* would here like to add that truly to depend on God alone and not on any worldly source of help, is itself the greatest effort we are capable of. The truth indeed is, as one's own experience may bear out, that it is extremely difficult to abstain from dependence on such earthly sources of help as friends and our own financial resources.

Philosophers have spoken of faith as the will to believe (William James) and as a venture (Bultmann), and even as a leap into the unfathomable depths of the unknown (Kierkegaard). Philosophical *thinking*, however, if it cares—as it should—for adequacy of concern, cannot help putting some questions about such views from the viewpoint of religious experience *as a whole*. There is no doubt that religious faith is marked by a certain obduracy and insistence, and that it may therefore be regarded as an express willing to believe. But we must also remember that, insofar as faith is at once a kind of love that grips the heart, as an exercise of the will to believe it must be taken to preclude such feelings of constraint and stress as are seen to go with the dogged pursuit of empirical ends. Again, though faith *is* a leap in the sense that we can never know how exactly the divine mind works and in what precise way He may be expected to provide the relief that we seek, it is also, at the same time, a time-tested—and so wholly dependable—way of dealing with the problems of life, the relevant evidence being provided by the experience of men of faith all over the world. Finally, though it is true that a life of faith is a venture in the sense that it is at once to expose faith itself to the possibility of being tested, the risk of its weakening is here substantially minimized by the fact that we can pray, as the Sikh *gurus* freely do, *for the steadfastness of faith itself.*

Finally, *saints and scriptures* speak of faith quite differently. The Sikh *gurus*, like saints everywhere, proclaim that faith in the Name of the Lord is the surest way to dissipate sinfulness (*kil bikh*), and so to put an end to the sorrow which results from sinful acts. They also hold the view, like Gāndhi in modern India, that faith is essentially a fascination of the heart[11]. Gandhi distinguishes faith from reason by pointing out that when in an extremely difficult situation reason finds itself utterly beaten down, faith may be seen to shine with undimmed vigour. The Bible declares that 'all things are possible to him that believeth', or that the true believer is an irrepressible optimist. If all these views are taken together, it would be clear that faith is a blend of the gentle delight of contentment and assuredness, and of love and undying hope. All these emotions and attitudes, we may note, have a natural tendency to prolong themselves; and, therefore, when we are told that, even in as small a measure as a mustard seed, faith in God is enough to save a man, the meaning simply is that because of the self-quickening character of its three constituents, and also because what is here depended on is, so to say, a living Reality that is never slow to answer—and so to feed—the trust that is reposed in It, faith is automotive, though the effort of prayer is doubtless necessary to actualize the implicit dynamism of faith.

III. THE SIKH VIEW

A. Faith as Sardhā:

To turn, now, to the Sikh view of faith, we may begin with *sardhā. Sardhā,* or the actual having of faith, is not the experience of a simple and isolated state. It is rather an intricate fabric of some attitudes, feelings and relations. On the inside, faith is no simple dependence on God, but is also (a) a kind of incessant, if implicit, thirst for closer approximation to Him. Further (b) it is accompanied by a measure of felt detachment towards what the family and the world in general have to offer by way of help and solace. And, on the outer side, faith (or *sardhā*), is related (c) to the kindness or judicious guidance of the *gurū* and (d) to God-realization as our spiritual destiny though (e) the immediate or proximate cause of attaining to this end is only His grace[12]. To illustrate the individual points we have just listed about *sardhā,* the following extracts from the *Ādi Granth* may be cited:

> *Hari jan ke vadbhāg vaderey jin Hari Hari sardhā Hari piyās. Hari Hari Nāmu miley triptāsahi mili sangati gun pargās.*[13]
>
> *jin sardhā Rām Nāmi lāgi tinh dūjei chitu na lāiyā Rām. je dharti sabh kundanu kari dījai binu nāvai avaru na bhāiyā Rām.*[14]
>
> *Satigurū hoi daiyāl ta sardhā pūriye satigurū hoi daiyāl nā kabhū jhūriye. Satgurū hoi daiyālu ta sachi samāiye.*[15]
>
> *eku arādhi parāchhat gaye. mani tani antari ek Prabhu rātā. Gurprasādi Nanak iku jātā.*[16]
>
> *meri sardhā pūri jagjīvan dāte mili Hari darsani manu bhīje jīo.*[17]
>
> *jo janu suney sardhā bhagati seti kari kirpā Hari nistārey.*[18]

If a question be put as to how faith develops, the Sikh answer would readily be the same as those of other religions: it is, in the main, faith that enkindles faith (*sardhā sardhā upāi milāye*). It is the living example of other men of faith—aided, of course, by the inherent, if dormant impulse of one's own devotion to God, and the teacher's revelation of the mysteries of the life of faith—that enables a man to progress on the path of faith.[19] I say so in the light of the following:

grām grām nagar sabhi phiriā
rid antari Hari jan bhāre.
sardhā sardhā upai milāe
mokau Hari gur guri nistāre.[20]

Mr. Manmohan Singh translates the above lines thus:

> "I wandered from village to village and through all the cities, but through the Lord's slaves I found God in my very mind. Faith and confidence have welled up within me and the Great Gurū God has emancipated and blended me with the Lord."[21]

But I think it would be truer to the text if we interpreted the lines in question as follows:

> "I keep moving, from village to village depending (*bhāre,* having *āsrā* of)[22] in my heart (*rid antar*) only on the example and guidance of those who are themselves devoted to the Lord (*Harijan*). It is indeed this visible demonstration of how the life of faith is to be lived that reveals to me the method (*upāi*) to deepen my faith. The Lord, as revealed or responding to my faith, and the spiritual formulae (*gur*) revealed to me by my teacher (who, we may add, knows the *ātmatattva*[23] and whose life is a paradigm of faith)—it is these that conduce to my own emancipation (*mo kau Hari gur guri nistārey*).

Faith, indeed, is the pre-eminent way to realize the Lord because (in so far as He Himself is Love) the way of faith and devotion has an easy, natural appeal to Him:

a. *Hari sardhā te miliā.*[24]
b. *merey Prabhi sardhā bhagati mani bhāve, jan kī paij savāre.*[25]

But the surpassing importance of faith makes it all the more necessary for us to realize its true nature. It is surely not a state of somnolent or inebriate love; in truth it is consummated in the unwinking sense of His Presence[26]:

chīti āvai tān sardhā pūri.[27]

Chīti, I venture to suggest, is unceasing attestation; and I may here cite, by way of support, the following utterance of Gabriel Marcel:

> "Faith in itself is not a movement of the soul, a transport or ravishment; it is simply unceasing attestation."[28]

Nor is faith or *sardhā* an instantaneously accomplished relation between man and God. We have rather to cultivate it in various ways, say, by singing His glories and listening to their recitation:

> *gāvat sunat sunāvat sardhā Hari rasu pī vadbhāge.*[29]

One has also to invoke His grace in prayer for the cultivation of *sardhā* in His Name:

> *Hari Hari kṛpā karahu jagjīvan main sardhā nāmi lagāvaigo.*[30]

This is necessary because faith is not really our doing, but is only our response to what God initiates:

> *tū āpai sardhā lāihi.*[31]

Yet, though we *have to* cultivate it, faith or *sardhā* is no joyless exercise. It is at once a kind of being held in a spell by (the infinite charms of) the Lord:

> *Hari Hari sardhā sej vichhāi Prabhu*
> *chhodi na sakai bahut mani bhāiā.*[32]

Indeed, to have *sardhā* in the Lord is at once to love Him intensely:

> *main mani tani premu agam thākur kā*
> *khinu khinu sardhā mani bahut uthāiā.*[33]

This is why, we may add, the man of faith is never tempted to find fault with the Lord, however unfortunate be his present wordly lot. Yet, the love of God that is implicit in *sardhā* is no mere luxuriance in feeling, for (I repeat) it embraces a kind of gentle tension, a longing, a quiet praying for its own fulfilment:

> *kari kirpā pārbraham daiyāl . . .*
> *Nank kī prabh sardhā pūri.*[34]

It is because of this positive element that *sardhā* cannot bear alienation from the Lord:

> *sardhā lāgī sangi prītmai iku tilu rahanu nā jāi.*[35]

B. God as the Haven: Oat

God as *prītam* is the loving assurance of absolute protection. Faith is indeed a trust not only in His reality but in His infinite attributes. In the Old Testament, we may note, faith in God:

> "includes the whole relationship that exists between God and man. It has for its object God's Omnipotence, His purpose in choosing His people, His love for them. His constancy and fidelity and the fulfilment of His promise."[36]

Contemplation of, and faith in His *attributes* enables us to steady ourselves in *specific* situations. It can also sustain and give direction to our moral endeavour. Indeed, there is a difference between His attributes as they may be said to hold quite generally and as we consciously avail of them, or, say, between the general protection of God that we all enjoy without asking for—or being aware of—it, and the explicit act of consciously and humbly putting onself under the *oat* of God. We must also remember that the Providence that God is, for one and all, is no dead weight on our individual freedom. His is only to provide the general pre-conditions of life, and what we make of the years granted to us, a life of ascendant nobility, or of deepening hellishness, is left wholly to us. The outer, material bases of life—that is, agriculture and commerce—may be said to proceed essentially under the *oat* of the Name of the Lord. It is true that the human individual has to put in some initial effort, and to follow it up with occasional supervision to make agriculture or business take root and flower. But, in the main, these material conditions of human existence flourish of their own impulse *according to the average man of the world*; and under the *oat* of the Lord, *according to the man of faith.* However, I repeat, this provision of the material basis of life by the Lord is as such no compulsion on us to be good *or* bad. The provision is just a bundle (*poat*) or the possibility (*bīj*) of vice and virture (*pāp puṇṇ*). But, because his being is riddled with the innate defects of desire and anger, what the human individual tends, in general, to choose is a life of utter indifference to the Name, so that when he passes away his state of being is, so to say, freckled with impurity:

> *khetī vaṇaju nāvai kī oat*
> *pāp puṇṇ bīj kī poat.*
> *kām, krodh, jīu mahi choat*
> *Nām visāri chaley mani khoat.*[37]

Here I think it essential to explain why in interpreting these lines (before citing them) I have found it necessary to deviate from Mr. Manmohan Singh's translation which runs thus:

> ". . . *My* cultivation and trade lie in the support of Lord's Name.
> Of the seed of sin and virtue *the mortal* is the bundle . . ."[38]

In the text, I submit, there is nothing to justify the translation of the opening words as '*my* cultivation'. I believe that what is here projected is a quite impersonal or general truth. Further, if we accept the translation just cited (in brief), the first two lines of the text would appear utterly disjoined. What is more, in the second line (of the text) there is no synonym for the words 'the mortal', which the distinguished interpreter has introduced in the translation. I have preferred to interpret the word 'seed' as 'possibility', and to translate the first two lines *connectedly* by suggesting that the material bases of the sustenance of human life (cultivation and commerce) are themselves a bundle of the possibility of both sin and virtue, in so far as one is free to avail of the bases in question in living a life of virtue *or* of vice. The *oat* or shelter of His Name facilitates righteous living.

However, how exactly a particular person can avail of His *oat* cannot be predetermined, for it would depend on the precise degree of his moral refinement, and the specific situation which he finds himself in and which calls for redress, neither of which can be known beforehand. But, philosophically, or in terms of general reflection, it *is* possible to think out *how* the shelter (*oat*) in question can be availed of, and how its actual incurrence feels. However, as we set out to essay this task, it is important to see what it means to speak of *God* as an *oat* or shelter *for man*. The image of a merely human refuge, say, an air raid shelter, is here only helpful, not enough. True, in the way of such material shelters, God as *oat* has to be regarded as one and seamless, not sparse; as unyielding, not wobbly; and duly extensive, to provide ample coverage. But the crises in which man turns to God not only call for protection, relief and material replenishment, but at times for proper guidance. The 'shelter' divine can also be a light that may relieve the gloom of a desperate situation or show us the way out of the dark and burning pit of worldly attachments. See, here, the following:

> "How am I to convey to you the faith that fills me? Whenever the clouds were the thickest, He showed me the way."[39] (Gandhi)

mahā dutaru māiyā, jaise pavan jhulāiyā.
suni hī darāiyā, kararo dharamrāiyā.
grih andh kūpāiyā pāvaku sagrāiyā.
gahī oat sādhāiyā Nanak Hari dhiāiyā.
ab mai pūrā pāiyā.[40]

Turning now to a fuller account of our understanding and experience of God as *oat,* which (we have said) is involved in faith or *sardhā,* we may proceed along the following lines:

1. *God's appearance* as *oat* to a man of faith.
2. The subjective *pre-conditions* of availing of God as our *oat.*
3. *Our experience* of God as *oat.*
4. *The need* to turn to God as our surpassing shelter.

1. Beginning with the first point, I find it reasonable to suggest that a Reality which is to serve as an unfailing shelter (or *oat*) should Itself be changeless or eternal. Further, in so far as the act of giving *effective* shelter is at once to provide the precise kind of relief that the person in distress may *need, that* which may be regarded as an authentic haven must also be rich in the power to provide. This indeed is so, says the devotee, in the light of his experienced relation to God:

asthir kartā tū dhaṇī tisahi kī main oat.[41]

2. This experience, however, is not easily accessible. It can be had only by the man who fulfils some essential pre-conditions.

If he is sincere in seeking the shelter of God he must do so out of deep love for Him, or in utter self-surrender, so that his concern for self is wholly dissipated (*hau muī*). But how can such self-effacing love of the Lord be cultivated? Obviously, not by admiring the visible beauty of God—for, He is non-material and invisible, because quite above change and decay—but only by contemplating His excellences. This indeed is the message of the following lines which come in the wake of *asthir . . . oat:*

guṇ kī mārī hau muī śabadi ratī mani choat.[42]

Here, incidentally, two more points may be made. First, the contemplation of His attributes should not be merely philosophic or aesthetic, but must be done in a spirit of deep devotion; for, in so far as God alone is the source of true love, genuine faith or love of God cannot be had except through an intense desire for a closer approximation to Him:

jah tei upjī tāhi mili sāchi prīti samāhu.[43]

Second, the conquest of egoity needed for a total surrender to God demanded by *sardhā* can be had only through an overwhelming and happily grateful realization of His excellences (*guṇ kī mārī*), and not in any other way such as the whiplash of affliction, for a painful outer curb does not really dissipate, but only suppresses egoity. There is indeed wisdom in the following:

> "What happens to those whose 'I' has been destroyed from outside by affliction? . . . Though they may have lost 'I' it does not mean that they have no more egoism. Quite the reverse . . . the being is reduced to naked vegetative egoism . . ."[44]

Humility cultivated as a reflex of love and service is indeed quite different from the unhappy sense of incapacity generated by intense misery and repeated frustration.

Wilful surrender to God as our *oat* is also helped by a discriminating realization of the ultimate vanity of other sources of help:

avar oat mai sagalī dekhī ik terī oat rahāiye.[45]
. . . sang sakhā sabh taji gaye kou nā nibahiyo sāth.
kahu Nanak is bipat mein tek ek reghunāth.[46]

3. But, whatever be the ways of evoking the self-effacing love demanded by turning to God as our *oat*, once such love is lit up in our hearts it cannot but be returned by Him, forthwith and overflowingly, because outgoing love for His *bhaktas* (it is held) is the very essence of His Being. So, we may say, to try to seek the shelter supreme is at once to secure it. Indeed, the very steadfastness of one's faith—and the felt preservation of one's honour as a devotee: *rākhi līnī Hari merī*—may therefore be regarded, in all humility, as but a reflex of the constancy of God's own solicitude for man. And once the individual in question comes to develop such sensitiveness, he finds it easy to make his contemplation of God steadfast and unremitting, and to thereby get, by His grace, the peace that abides:

tū mero merū parbatu suāmī oat gahi mein terī.
nā tū dolahu nā hum girte rākhi līnī Hari merī.
ab tab jab kab tu hī tu hī hum tua parsād sukhī sad hī.[47]

Therefore, quite unlike the protection provided by a mere building which remains a resolute other to the one who is protected, the experience of God as our *oat* is at once a kind of 'exchange of being' in love, so that the true devotee, or the man of implicit faith, just loses himself in the service of the Lord.

oat gobind gopāl rāi
sevā suāmi lāhu.[48]
Hari kā nām dās kī oat.[49]

This enthralment in love does not in any way make one feel humiliated; for it involves a very willing submission to Him who has saved millions of men and whose Name is the source of ineffable peace, and is no mere abject kneeling to the might of a tyrant:

bhagat janā kī bartani Nāmu.
sant janā kai mani bisrām.
Hari kā nāmu dās kī oat.
Hari kai nāmi udhrei jan koat.[50]

But love as directed to the Lord is necessarily accompanied by non-attachment to other possible sources of help. To step into His shelter (or *oat*) is at once to develop *Vairāgya* in respect of other relations:

tudhu binu avaru na koī karte
main dhar oat tumārī jīo.[51]
Hari charan kī oat satānī
sabh chūkī kāṇi lokāṇi.[52]

Positively, the experience of God as our *oat* is, of course, utter freedom from anxiety:

Prabh jī terī oat gusāin
jo janu bhajanu karey Prabh terā
Tisai andesā nāhi.[53]

It is not only to remember Him continually, but also to feel assured that from now on one's present life and its beyond are both in safe hands:

prātahkāli Hari nāmu uchārī
īt ūt kī oat savārī.

sadā sadā japīye Hari nām.
pūraṇ hovahi man ke kām.[54]

Here, however, the last line calls for a little comment. If we take it along with the preceding line, as we should, it would become clear that the cherished objectives which commitment to the Name is said to help us realize can only be noble, because he who recites *Harinām* with every breath cannot entertain any ignoble desire. And this inner recitation is at once a happy and grateful, if implicit, sense of His glories:

sās sās terey guṇ gāvān.
oat Nanak gur charan jīo.[55]

This unheard singing of His excellences is at once a quiet inner growth. To put oneself under His *oat* is at once to enter a process of ever fuller blooming of the heart in the way of love. He who takes the *oat* of the Lord looks upon Him as the anchor of his life not in the metaphysical sense that He is the ultimate substance, or the First Cause, but as a lover looks upon his lady-love as the very throb of his life. Further, the process of inner quickening (*man bigsārey*) in question is not a progress in *comprehending* the Lord ever better—for He is, the *gurus* insist, *agam* and *agochar*—but the dawn of a growing diminution of egoity in ever undivided love of God (*Nanak simrei din raināre*):

tū prītam tū prān adhāre.
tumahi paikh paikh manu bigsāre.
anik joni bhrami bhrami bhrami hāre.
oat gahī ab sādh sangāre.
agam agochar alakh apāre.
Nanak simrei dinu raināre.[56]

This love is internally rich and diverse. It comprises a feeling of utter and exclusive dependence on the Lord; the sense that one is wholly under His spell, or in constant and loving fellowship with Him; and a feeling of creatureliness, or of being a child of God:

tujh binu avar nāhī mai dūjā
tū merey man māhi.
tū sājanu sangī prabhu merā
kāhe jīu darāhī.

tumrī oat tumārī āsā
ūthat baithat sovat jāgat
bisaru nāhi tū sās girāsā
rākhu rākhu saraṇi prabh
apanī agani sāgar vikrālā.
Nanak ke sukhdāte satgur hum
tumre bāl gupāla.[57]

Here, however, attention to four of the lines just cited (2 to 5) suggests a difficulty. If the devotee regards the Lord as his *sājan* and *sangī*, and if he remembers the Lord incessantly (line 4), why does he yet need to pray to the Lord that he be kindly kept under His protection (line 5)? The answer is provided by the consideration that however unbroken be one's sense of fellowship with God, the blessed relation does not abide automatically; and that one has got to pray to the Lord to grant steadfastness to his faith, which is what the prayer, (*rākhu rākhu saraṇi Prabh apnī*)—really means. A devotee's willed persistence in the *oat* of God, we must remember, is quite different from our effortless dwelling under a man-made shelter. The former is necessarily, if in part, *an effort* to hold on to God as one's only support, because of our innate human weaknesses. This is why the Sikh scriptures repeatedly speak of *seizing* the *oat* of the Lord (*oat gahī*). See, for instance, the following:

oat gahi gopāl daiyāl kṛpānidhe.[58]
prabh ek anik alakh thākur oat
Nanak tisu gahī.[59]
Hari charaṇ saraṇ apār prabh
ke dṛdu gahī Nanak oat.[60]
man sagal siyāṇap rahī
karan karāvanhār suāmī Nanak
oat gahī.[61]

Yet, in spite of the fact that holding on to the *oat* of the Lord is something of an effort, it is by no means a joyless enterprise. Like the act of creating a rich and fascinating work of art, the endeavour to keep oneself continually under the wings of God is at once to revel, so to say, in the inhaled presence of an object of love and beauty. The devotee who puts himself under the *oat* of the Lord focuses on His lotus feet (*charaṇ kamal*), and he feels impelled to sacrifice his all at the sweet fellowship vouchsafed to Him:

charaṇ kamal basiyā rid bhītri sāsi girāsi uchārio.
Nanak oat gahī jagdīṣur punah punah balihārio.[62]

The 'fellowship' is an approximation to a Reality which not only relieves one of fear (*bhai haraṇi*), but gratifies the inner eye which intuits the presence of the Lord, and relieves the devotee of all his pains:

patit pāvanu bhagati vachhalu bhai haraṇ tāran taran.
nain tiptai darasu pekhi jasu tokhi sunat karan.
prāṇ nāth anāth dāte dīn gobind saraṇ.
ās pūran dūkh bināsanu gahī oat Nanak Hari.[63]

Be it noted that we have spoken of the devotee-deity 'intermingling' as a 'sweet fellowship that is *vouchsafed* to (not attained by) the devotee'. Indeed, if cognitive freedom be understood as the individual's own ability to identify God, the Sikh scriptures may be said to deny it to man. Their view is that He comes to be known only by those to whom He graciously decides to reveal Himself:

jisahi janāvahu tinahi tum jāte.[64]

And even the wisdom to see the need to regard Him as our *oat* has to be prayed for:

Mādhve aisī dehi bujhāi.
sevahu sādh gahau oat charnā.[65]

But it is also necessary to see that the awareness of God which a person secures by putting himself under His wings (*oat*) is not analytical. The individual concerned does not come to know *how* exactly He helps, but only *that* He helps and protects the honour of the devotee:

tumrī kṛpā tei tudhu pachhāṇā.
tū merī oat tu hai merā māṇā.[66]

Here, the first line gives me occasion to say a little more on a point which I have already touched. When philosophers of religion discuss the question of cognitive freedom what they have in mind is just the openness *to believe* or not in the existence of God. The line under review, on the other hand, speaks of identifying (*pachhāṇā*) or *becoming directly aware of* the existence of God; and in respect of this direct awareness, we are here told, man is *not* free in so far as it is the gift of God, and not the result of any human effort.

However, the awareness of the truth *that* He helps, once we have truly put ourselves under His *oat,* is said to be very comprehensive. It is the deeply satisfying sense that God helps us so variously that He can both be credited with the unfailing patience and tenderness of a mother and the awesome qualities and disciplinary authority of a father:

tū merā pitā tū hai merā mātā
. . . tū merī oat tū hai merā māṇā.[67]

Finally, an important result of being under His *oat* is also utter freedom from determination by worldly attachments:

dhāri oat gopāl
saraṇi pario pūraṇ parmesur
bigasey sagal janjāl.[68]

This freedom, however, does not directly follow the act of taking His *oat.* What comes between the two, as a vital determinant of ultimate detachment, is a thorough saturation of self with the sense of His glories:

Prabh kī oat gahī tao chhūto.
sādh prasādi Hari Hari Hari gāye.
bikhe biādhi tab hūto.[69]

Hence, the importance of humility, prayer and *Śabadkīrtan.*

4. What we have said just now prepares the way to the final question. Why should we at all think of turning to God as our *oat*? To this a ready and brief answer would be that taking refuge in the name of the Lord conduces, on the one hand, to a refinement of our sense of values, and ultimately to spiritual liberation, on the other:

re man oat lehu Hari nāmā.
jā ke simrani durmati nāse.
pāvahi padu nirbānā.[70]

The ultimate end here referred to is obviously not easy to attain. One has to break through the fetters of *Māyā,* and here too it is of great value to turn to the Lord as our *oat.* According to the Sikh scriptures, indeed, the way to overcome determination by the all-pervading *māyā* is not so much the exercise of philosophic discrimination as an humble recourse to the shelter (or *oat*) of the Lord in the way of devotion. Love of God destroys covetuousness and so serves as a shield against the lure of *Māyā*:

mūlu biādhi biāpasi lobhā.
māiyā biāpat bahu parkārī.
sant jīvahi prabh oat tumārī.[71]

The need of cultivating the love in question, or of resorting to God as our *oat*, is heightened by the fact that the raging fire of worldly passions (*agani sāgar bikrāl*)[72] is matched in its extent only by our utter inability to face the challenge on our own:

main nirguṇ guṇ nāhi koī.
. . . *mūrakh mugadhu agiyānī avichārī.*
. . . *kachhu na jānā mati merī thorī.*
binvanti Nanak oat prabh terī.[73]

For the average man, however, who likes to give way to fleshly passions rather than to overcome them, there are some more obvious and appealing reasons for turning to God. God, say the *gurus*, is not merely the sovereign controller, but also the ever faithful ally of every human being, so that it is plainly absurd to turn to other sources of help, and to refrain from His unfailing assistance:

tākau dhokhā kahān biāpe
jākau oat tumhārī.[74]
sarab jīā hahi jāke hāthi.
kadey na bichhuḍe sabh ke sāthi.
upāo chhodi gahu tisu kī oat.[75]

What is more, the Lord is not only Omnipotent, and the admitted redeemer of numberless people in the past, but also the immanent knower (*antarjāmī*) so that, we may add, He can be expected to see and relieve even such problems as trouble the innermost depths of our being, and so cannot be objectified and put in terms of words:

tū samrathu tū hai merā suāmī.
sabhu kichhu tum te tū antarjāmī.
pārbrahm pūran jan oat.
terī sarṇi udhrahi jan koti.[76]

This is why the Sikh sages insist that the realization of God as one's true support (or *oat or ādhār*) is the only true source of happiness and ultimate victory; and indifference to the Lord, a guarantee of pain and perdition:

jih jan oat gahī prabh terī
se sukhiye prabh sarṇāi.
jih nar visariyā purakh bidhātā.
te dukhiyā mahi gantey.[77]
Nanak dukhiyā sabhu sansār.
manne nāo seī jiṇī jāī.[78]

One is, of course, free to wonder why the Sikh scriptures attach so much importance to the *oat* of the Lord and to the protective association of saints. But the *gurus'* ready answer would here be that whereas the codified ways to God-realization (*panthās*) are many and even mutually discordant, the way of devotion to the Name is one, unambiguous and unfailingly effective; and that one can easily get imbued with the love of the Name in the company of saints because they keep reciting His Name with every breath or morsel of food that they take:

jinā sāsi girās na visārai
Hari nāmā mani santu
dhanu si soi Nanaka
pūraṇ soi sant.[79]

It may be noted that between the two sources of help, the *oat* of the Lord and the association of saints or the *Satgurū*, there is no conflict at all; for, what the *Satgurū* and the saints recommend is only devotion to the Lord, and a cultivation of the sense of the all-pervading presence of God:

nirmal sant sangen oat Nanak Parmesurah.[80]
Satiguri mo kao dīā updesu
jīa pindu sabhu Hari kā desu.
jo kichhu kari su terā tāṇu.
tū meri oat tun hai dībāṇu.[81]

In the end, it may be noted that the concepts of *oat* and *ās* are inter-connected. One naturally expects help or relief (*ās*) from that which is looked upon as one's *oat* or protection. See, here, the following:

jis kī oat tisai kī āsā.[82]
avar oat mai koī na sūjhe ik Hari kī oat mai ās.[83]

C. *God as Anchor:* Tek

The *oat-ās* relation is, however, not the only conceptual linkage to be understood in the context of faith or *sardhā.* We have also to see how *oat* differs from, and is related to, *tek.* Now, at least one difference between the two is clear. Quite unlike *tek,* the word *oat* may well be translated as *ohlā* or *pardā,* though we have not so far used *oat* in this sense. *Tek,* on the other hand, is best translated as that which supports us or keeps us steadfast. Indeed, from the viewpoint of the practice of religion we could fairly say that the Lord is both the *tek* of His devotees in so far as He keeps them steadfast in devotion, and the shield (or shelter) or *tek* of the saints, for they do not depend on any earthly shelter or protection. The following utterance may here be cited:

bhagatān kī tek tū santā kī oat tū.[84]

But, in so far as that which shields or protects us in crises may also be said to provide a kind of support or assistance, whatever we have said about *oat* in the previous section is also relevant to *tek.* By way of illustrating this point, the following may be cited:

ek oat Gobind kī tiāgi un ās.
sabh ūpari samrath prabh pūran gun tās.
jan kā nāmu ādhāru hai prabh saranī pāhi.
Parmesar kā āsrā santan man māhi.[85]
sung sakhā sabh taji gaye koi nā nibhahio sāth.
kahu Nanak ih bipat main tek ek raghunāth.[86]
birthā bharvāsā lok, thākur prabh terī tek.[87]

Putting it generally, quite like *sardhā* in God as our *oat,* implicit faith in Him as our *tek* is said to work for our good in many ways. It puts an end to needless involvement in the world; sustains, as nothing else does, the poor and the suffering; radiates bliss to the godly; enables us, in the end, to transcend the birth-death cycle or *saṁsāra;* relieves us of all fear; and serves as the true source of all honour and strength[88] that may distinguish a man's life.

But it seems to me that there is at least one idea which the *Ādi Granth* projects more freely in the context of God as our *tek* than in that of God as our *oat*. This idea may be put thus. Faith in the Name as our *tek* is at once the conviction that if we only surrender ourselves to Him, He will direct all our steps, exactly as a blind man is enabled to 'see' his way by the stick in his hand:

jia andhule hathi tohaṇī Harināmu hamāre.
Rām nāmu Hari tek hai nisi daut savāre.[89]

One is here reminded of the Biblical utterance: 'Acknowledge Him in all thy ways and He shall direct thy paths.' Perhaps, in Sikh scriptures the ideas embodied in the following too are more relevant to God as our *tek* than to God as our *oat*:

tīne tāp nivāraṇhārā dukh hantā sukh rāsi.
tākao bighanu na kou lāge.
jākī prabh āge ardāsi.
sant prasādi baid nārāyaṇ karaṇ kāraṇ prabh ek.
bal budhi pūran sukh dātā Nanak Hari Hari tek.[90]

In other words, faith in God as our unfailing *tek* is grounded not only in the implicit faith that He *is* there, but in the additional faiths that He alone can redeem us from the three kinds of suffering; that we can turn to Him freely for peace and happiness; and that he who surrenders himself in prayer to God cannot be held back by any obstacle. If it be wondered, here, as to how an average man, who is very far removed from the ideal of perfect purity, can at all establish a genuine relationship with God who is supremely pure, the Sikh answer would readily be that the relation in question is possible not because we *deserve* God, but because we *need* Him; and that the acknowledgment of both our lack of merit *and our need* is enough to bring about the relation in question.

D. The Lord as Ādhār:

It is probably from this point of view that the Sikh *gurus* insist that the name of the Lord is (in principle) the *ādhār* of all men and women:

Hari Hari nāmu jan prāṇ adhāru.[91]

To the man of faith, however, the name of the Lord is important not as merely one of the many bases of life, but as the only true foundation of all that is there, and the redeemer of the whole world:

terā eku nāmu tāre sansār
main ehā ās eho ādhāru.[92]

However, it is not enough merely to speak or think thus. One has to try out, and to *realize* the futility of, the worldly sources of help before one can truly say that the Lord alone is the true *ādhār:*

kinahī kahiā bāh bahu bhāi
koi kahe main dhanahi pasārā.
mohi dīn Hari Hari ādhārā.[93]

The sense of dependence on our ordinary human relations is, however, not easy to shake off. So it can facilitate our looking upon God as our true *ādhār* if we dwell upon the thought that God can take the place of all the other human sources of help:

tum hi pitā tum hī puni māta
tum hi mīt hit bhrātā.
tum parvār tumhī ādhārā
tumhī jīa prāṇdātā.[94]

But, it is important to note, *Nām* does not become the effective *ādhāru* of one's life unless one communes with It repeatedly:

Nām sangi kīno biuhār.
Nāmo hī isu man kā ādhāru.[95]

Such communion is, of course, difficult. But it is by no means an unnatural or impossible effort, for He already dwells within every heart:

ramat Rām ghat ghat ādhāru.[96]

One practical way to commune with the Name is to seek to steady oneself in crises by reflecting that it is He who has created us; and that, therefore, He may be confidently expected to look after us:

tū kāhey dolahi prāṇiyā tudhu rākhegā sirjanhāru.
jini paidāisi tū kīya saī deh ādhāru.[97]

It is important to note that a Reality which can truly be looked upon and used as *ādhāru* must in some sense be determinate, though not necessarily limited. Here, *Nām* is obviously of great help; and this indeed is why in Sikh religious writing we freely come across utterances such as the following:

Hari ke nām ko ādhāru.[98]
sāchā nāmu merā ādhāro.[99]
amrit nāmu manahi ādhāro.[100]

In the Sikh scriptures, we may further note, the *gurū* is also spoken of as the *ādhāru* of the devotee:

gurū merī jivani gurū ādhāru
gurū merī vartani gurū parvāru.[101]

The *gurū* here referred to is, however, no ordinary teacher. He is *satgurū*, a man of realization. It is to such a *gurū* that one has to pray for the ability to make *Nām* as the *ādhār* of one's life:

Satgurū pās bainantiā millai nāmu ādhār.[102]

Finally, one makes the Lord the *ādhār* of one's life not merely in a fit of despair—for, did one do so, commitment to the Lord would disappear along with the termination of the unhappy state—but in a spirit of worshipful humility and recurrent impulsion to sacrifice oneself at the altar of His glory:

Prabh jī tū merey prāṇ adhāre
namaskār dandauti bandan anik bār jau bāre.
. . . jo tum karahu soi bhal hamrey pekhi
Nanak sukh charṇāre.[103]

E. Faith as Reverential Trust (*Bharosā* or *Bharvāsā*)

The first of the lines just cited bespeaks implicit trust in the Lord. So the Sikh scriptures speak of *bharosā* or *bharvāsā* too in the context of faith. As here used, however, these words signify not mere trust, but trust as touched with a measure of reverence. We can trust a man without in any way subordinating ourselves to him; but to trust the Supreme Person that God is, is necessarily to put oneself under His wings:

terī ṣaraṇ terey bharvāse.[104]

Yet, implicit trust (*bharosā*) in the Lord is not merely to put oneself under His shelter, but to do so with the conviction that He is the ocean of mercy, and so can be expected to redeem us:

ab mohi Rām bharosau pāye
jo jo sarani pario karuṇānidhi.
tai tai bhavahi tarāye.[105]

It need hardly be pointed out that to trust (or to have *bharosā* in) the Lord is at once to be freed from all apprehension:

Rām janā kau Rām bharosā.
Nāmu japat sabhu mitiyā andesā.[106]

To look upon the Lord as our only shelter (*oat*) or hope (*ās*), and to *trust* Him as such is no mere exercise of the intellect; here, one's heart is gripped by love of God, so that to have faith in God is not only to regard Him as our only unfailing source of strength, but also to surrender ourselves to His Will, though this surrender is accomplished only through His grace:

tumrī oat tumhārī sarnā.
tumrī ās bharosā tumrā.
tumrā nām ridey lai dharnā.
tumro balu tum sangi suheley.
jo jo karahu soi soi karṇā.[107]
jā tisu bhāve tā hukamu manāve.[108]

This, indeed, is why one has to pray to Him for steadfastness in faith:

rākhu suāmī āp bharose.[109]

At the same time one's *bharosā* or trust in the unfailing protectiveness of the Lord is also helped by a recollection of the cases of those who have been redeemed in the past by the power of the Name:

Hari ko nāmu sadā sukhdāyī. jā kau
simari Ajāmalu udhrio gankā hu gati pāyi.
Pānchāli kau raj sabhā mein Rām nām sudhi āyi.
tā kā dukhu hario karuṇāmei apnī paij badhāyī.
jih nar jasu karuṇānidhi gāiyō tā kao bhaiyo sahāī.
kahu Nanak mai uhī bharose gahī ān ṣarṇāī.[110]

Notes

1. Through different births, as the Sikh scriptures would say.
2. Gabriel Marcel: *Being and Having,* translated by Katharine Farrer, The University Press, Glasgow, 1949.
3. Summa Theologica, 2a, 2ae, 1, 2, p. 29.
4. *New Catholic Encyclopaedia,* McGraw Hill Book Company, 1967, Vol. V, p. 796.
5. Marcel: *Being and Having,* p. 212.
6. S.K. Saxena: *Ever Unto God: Essays on Gandhi and Religion,* Indian Council of Philosophical Research, New Delhi, 1988, p. 131. Emphasis added.
7. Ibid., p. 126.
8. G. Marcel: *Faith and Reality,* (part II of *The Mystery of Being*), Gateway Edition, 1960, p. 68.
   Also see: ". . . Faith, when it is most real and most like itself . . . is most sure to issue from the whole being of a man and to involve him."
   Marcel: *Being and Having,* p. 210.
9. Soren Kierkegaard: *Edifying Discourses,* A Selection, edited by Paul L. Holmer, Harper Torch Books, New York, 1958, pp. 19, 25, 27.
10. *The Collected Works of Mahatma Gandhi,* The Publication Division, Ministry of Information and Broadcasting, Govt. of India, Vol. 33, pp. 231-32.
11. M.K. Gandhi: *In Search of the Supreme,* compiled and edited by V.B. Kher, Navajivan Publishing House, 1961, Vol. I, pp. 112, 208.
12. Cf. "With the intellect of a Plato, with the iron self-control of a Stoic, with all the goodwill of which man is capable, he can do nothing to prepare himself for faith without the help of God's grace." Canon George D. Smith, ed., *The Teaching of the Catholic Church,* Macmillan, New York, 1949, I.17. Cited by Brand Blanshard in his *Reason and Belief,* George Allen & Unwin, 1974, p. 31.
13. *Ādi Granth,* M.4, p. 492.
14. Ibid., M.4, p. 444.
15. Ibid., M.4, p. 149.
16. Ibid., M.5, p. 289.
17. Ibid., M.4, p. 95.
18. Ibid., M.4, p. 493.
19. Cf. "Religion is like a rose. It throws out the scent which attracts like a magnet and we are drawn to it involuntarily. The scent of religious contact has a greater pungency than the scent of the rose."
    Collected Works of Mahatma Gandhi, Vol.XLVIII, pp. 121-22.
20. *Ādi Granth,* M.4, p. 983.
21. *Ādi Granth,* tr. by Shri Manmohan Singh, Vol.VI, p. 3221.
22. *Shri Guru Granth Kosh,* Bhai Sahib Dr. Veer Singh ji,

Khalsa Tract Society, Amritsar, p. 691.
23. Ibid., p. 284.
24. *Ādi Granth,* M.4, p. 982.
25. Ibid., M.4, p. 1201.
26. Here, the reference is to *Simran* which, along with *bhajan* and *dhyāna*, forms the threefold discipline emphasized by Sikhism as a part of *Nām Yoga* or *Sahaja Yoga.* It enjoins the cultivation of the unremitting sense of the presence of God.
Harbans Singh: *The Message of Sikhism,* Sikh Gurudwara Management Committee, Delhi, 1978, p. xix.
27. Ibid., M.5, p.1141. Cf. "... Faith is nothing but a living wide-awake consciousness of God within." *The Mind of Mahatma Gandhi* compiled and edited by R. K. Prabhu and U. R. Rao, Navajivan Publishing House, Ahmedabad, 1967, p. 63.
28. G. Marcel: *Being and Having,* p. 215.
29. *Ādi Granth,* M.5, p. 1206.
30. Ibid., M.4, p. 1310.
31. Ibid., M.5, p. 749.
32. Ibid., M.4, p. 836.
33. Ibid., M.4, p. 836.
34. Ibid., M.5, p. 893.
35. Ibid., p. 928.
36. *New Catholic Encyclopaedia,* McGraw Hill Book Co., 1967, Vol.V, p. 793.
37. *Ādi Granth,* M.1, p. 152.
38. *Ādi Granth,* tran. by Mr. Manmohan Singh, Vol.II, p. 508.
39. Pyarelal: *The Last Phase,* Navajivan Press, Ahmedabad, 1958, p. 215.
40. *Ādi Granth,* M.5, p. 746.
41. Ibid., M.1, p. 936. Emphasis added.
42. Ibid., M.1, p. 936.
43. Ibid., M.5, p. 135.
44. Simone Weil: *Gravity and Grace,* Routledge and Kegan Paul, 1972, p. 23.
45. *Ādi Granth,* M.5, p. 625.
46. Ibid., M.9, p. 1429.
47. Ibid., Kabirji, p. 969.
48. Ibid., M.5, p. 135.
49. Ibid., M.5, p. 264.
50. Ibid., M.5, p. 264.
51. Ibid., M.5, p. 107.
52. Ibid., M.5, p. 622.
53. Ibid., M.5, p. 630.
54. Ibid., M.5, p. 743.
55. Ibid., M.5, p. 100.
56. Ibid., M.5, p. 740.
57. Ibid., M.5, p. 378.
58. Ibid., M.5, p. 456.
59. Ibid., M.5, p. 458.
60. Ibid., M.5, p. 502.
61. Ibid., M.5, p. 529.
62. Ibid., M.5, p. 534.
63. Ibid., M.5, p. 1306.
64. Ibid., M.5, p. 563.
65. Ibid., M.5, p. 609.
66. Ibid., M.5, p. 103.
67. Ibid., M.5, p. 103.
68. Ibid., M.5, p. 676.
69. Ibid., M.5, p. 673.
70. Ibid., M.9, p. 901.
71. Ibid., M.5, p. 182.
72. Ibid., M.5, p. 378.
73. Ibid., M.5, p. 388.
74. Ibid., M.5, p. 712.
75. Ibid., M.5, p. 177.
76. Ibid., M.5, p. 193.
77. Ibid., M.5, p. 613.
78. Ibid., M.1, p. 954

79. Bhai Sāhib Dr. Veer Singh: *Shri Guru Granth Kosh,* Khalsa Tract Society, Amritsar, 1960, p. 120.
80. *Ādi Granth,* M.5, p. 709.
81. Ibid., M.5, p. 371.
82. Ibid., M.5, p. 1145.
83. Ibid., M.5, p. 1304.
84. Ibid., M.5, p. 746.
85. Ibid., M.5, p. 812.
86. Ibid., M.9, p. 1429.
87. Ibid., M.5, p. 896.
88. Ibid., M.5, p. 1147.
89. Ibid., M.1, p. 422.
90. Ibid., M.5, p. 714.
91. Ibid., M.5, p. 183.
92. Ibid., M.5, p. 24.
93. Ibid., M.5, p. 913.
94. Ibid., M.5, p. 1215.
95. Ibid., M.5, p. 863.
96. Ibid., M.5, p. 897.
97. Ibid., M.5, p. 724.
98. Ibid., M.5, p. 1121.
99. Ibid., M.3, p. 917.
100. Ibid., M.5, p. 1215.
101. Ibid., M.5, p. 1270.
102. Ibid., M.5, p. 746.
103. Ibid., M.5, p. 820.
104. Ibid., M.5, p. 750.
105. Ibid., M.5, p. 1204.
106. Ibid., M.5, p. 194.
107. Ibid., M.5, p. 1299.
108. Ibid., M.9, p. 337.
109. Ibid., M.5, p. 829.
110. Ibid., M.5, p. 1008.

2

GRACE

I. SOME GENERAL REFLECTIONS

1. The Terminology

We may begin by giving a little attention to the more important terms which have been freely used for grace in Indian religious literature, say, the following: *anukampā, anugraha, prasāda, dayā* and *kṛpā*. So far as I know, the first one of these does not occur noticeably in the writings of the Sikh *gurus*. On the other hand, the *Ādi Granth* avails of some other concepts which are not to be found in Indian religious literature taken generally. These are: *nadar, karam, mihar* and *bakhsīs*. It seems to me that all these concepts signify but different aspects or details of our experience and understanding of what is called 'grace' in English. But, then, we must make it clear how these concepts may be distinguished,[1] and how they yet seem to make for the meaning of 'grace', just as naturally as *oat, tek* and *ādhār* are covered by 'faith' or *sardhā*.

Now, to begin with *anugraha* and *anukampā*, both words are freely used to mean *kṛpā* and *dayā*. But they have some distinctive meanings too. *Anugraha*, for instance, means dissipation of misfortune (*aniṣṭa nivāraṇa*), and *Anukampā* may be translated, quite faithfully, as 'vibrating in sympathy with', or sensitiveness to the sufferings of others. *Dayā*, which is an admitted meaning of both *anugraha* and *anukampā*, may itself be credited with a meaning of its own: say, that sweetly painful impulsion of the mind which moves us to relieve the suffering of others. But in so far as it is dubitable if the being of God or the working of His Mind can be said to include an element of *pain*, in the general context of our talk about God *dayā* may be taken in its simpler meanings, that is, as mercy (or *karuṇā, raham*). *Kṛpā*, too, signifies mercy and forgiveness; but it can also be fairly taken to mean the tendency or desire to do good to others *without any thought of return*. As for the word, *prasāda*, one meaning of it which cannot be ascribed to any of the other terms we have interpreted is: that which is given by a great man (or by the Lord) to his dependents (or devotees) for the sheer pleasure of helping them, and not because of any rightful claim of theirs. But, it must be added, the word is also freely used in the sense of *kṛpā* and *anugraha.*[2]

Of the terms that dominate Sikh writings on grace,[3] *Mihar* may be taken to mean, *kṛpā*; *bakhsīs,* or that which is given free, or as a gift; *karam, bakhsīs;* and *nadar,* the look of mercy (or *kṛpādṛṣṭi*). Most of these Hindi and Punjabi terms have some common meanings, and so as we set out to discuss them in the context of Sikh religion, a measure of overlapping and repetition will be unavoidable; but this element may, in a measure, be balanced with some separate attention to the *distinctive* meanings of the terms given, as follows, alongside every one of them.

(a) *Anugraha:* Removal of misfortune.
(b) *Anukaṃpā:* Sensitiveness to others' suffering.
(c) *Bakhsīs, Karam:* Gift.
(d) *Dayā:* The impulse to relieve others' suffering.
(e) *Kṛpā/Mihar:* Selfless help or service.
(f) *Nadar:* Look of mercy.
(g) *Prasāda:* Unforced and utterly selfless relief to others, sustained only by the sheer joy of giving.

We may now indicate, with the help of a simple example, how all these concepts may be covered by a single experience of grace. Suppose that a man of faith and prayer finds himself in a very tough situation; further, that he is unable to deal with it on his own, or with the help of the resources at his disposal; and that in a moment of anguished helplessness he turns to God in prayer for help and relief. Now, when he does so, he will naturally think of God as the Supreme Person who is ever so *sensitive* to the needs of his devotees (*anukaṃpā*), and may therefore be expected to *look* sympathetically at the devotee (*nadar*), and to *feel moved* to give him (*dayā*) the precise help that he needs, *quite without any thought of return,* because He does not need anything (*bakhsīs/karam; kṛpā, mihar*), and only because He revels in helping His devotees (*prasāda*).

2. The Christian Tradition

It seems to us, however, that none of these concepts, perhaps not even their aggregate, quite captures the multifaceted way in which grace has been regarded in the Christian tradition; and therefore—

partly because a philosophical essay has to aim at comprehensiveness, and partly because the need to acknowledge the validity of plurality in the language of grace is today widely recognized—we may give some attention to the Christian view of grace as well.

Here we find that the word 'Grace' is derived from the Greek *charis*, which is freely used in the Bible, specially in the New Testament. Our concern, however, is with the meaning of the word, not with the way it has come to be what it is; and the meaning, or meanings, of the word may be listed as follows: charm or beauty; love or generosity as shown by the giver, or the feeling of favour or gratitude on the part of the recipient; and finally, the gift itself, the concrete testimony of the giver's goodness.

St. Paul, however, interprets the word in question in a yet quite different sense, say, as 'the favour of God to undeserving men.'[4] But a question may here be readily put. Does His grace come only to those men who *do not* deserve it, and not to those who may be said to *deserve* it, say, by virtue of their moral merit? One can hardly say, yes. But, then, how are we to resolve the difficulty? By resorting to the thought, I suggest, that the word, *undeserving*, is here used not to *oppose* the deserving to those men who are not so, but to imply that *all* men, however exalted they be, are more or less undeserving as compared to 'the surpassing value of *the gift of the love of God*', which is, we are further told, 'spontaneous, beautiful, unearned, and *at work* in *Jesus Christ* for the salvation of sinful men.'[5]

Words such as these, it is obvious, are likely to impress us; for they talk of God, Christ and salvation. But it is important to see that they are meaningful too. In fact, there is a logic in the very way the adjectives are here put. Grace is spoken of as a kind of *love* which, as we know, is a vital outgoing impulse. This may be said to be true of both human and divine love. But, whereas human beings have often to struggle to love, and to keep in peace with one another, God loves us all and ceaselessly. We may indeed imagine God's love as a kind of rivulet flowing of its own impulse (or spontaneously) towards all men; and the moment we do so, we are struck by the aptness of the second adjective, 'beautiful'; for a movement which is rhythmic and seemingly effortless is freely said to be marked by grace which is a lighter form of beauty, the beauty of grace. God's creatures, on the other hand, are on the receiving end; and they get grace, without any *matching* merit of their own. His grace is, in principle, open to all; and a clear expression of it is the advent of Christ, of God Himself as a person, to share life with us and to blazon the path of love and sacrifice.

The Hindu and Sikh conceptions of grace do not look on any particular individual as the pre-eminent vehicle or locus of His grace. There are some other differences too between the Christian and Indian conceptions of grace. Yet it seems possible to discover a measure of agreement as well between the two traditions, and to frame thereon a fairly acceptable, if not quite exhaustive, conception of grace.

3. The Concept of Grace

It would, however, be wrong to assume that we talk of grace only in the context of religion. The concept can also be considered from the moral and aesthetic points of view. Aesthetically, 'grace' is used in respect of an object that owes its charm to rhythmic, effortless movement, may be actual or merely suggested (or virtual), say, because of some given or created lines and curves. Morally, or in everyday life, that person is said to be gracious who gives liberally —that is, without caring too much for the merits of the needy—and without exhibiting any sense of self-importance or expectation of returns. In its religious sense, grace is the reflex of God's essential benevolence, which is, in turn, related to His nature as Providence, or as Love, rather than to His metaphysical attributes like omniscience and omnipotence; and which is, what is more, not exacted by any merit of ours, but is only made manifestly available to the man of faith in various ways.

It would make for better understanding if we here bring out the different ideas implicit in what we have just said about grace in the religious sense. To begin with, those who in fact feel favoured with the descent of His grace in an emergency never think that they really *deserve* it. This is indeed why whenever they consciously acknowledge the receipt of grace, they do so in a spirit of humility. The moment is one of gratefulness, and not of any feeling of achievement or heightened self-esteem. Here, incidentally, we see something that distinguishes the grace of theistic *religion* from gracious conduct which we value in *moral life*; for the life of morality is essentially a matter of self-effort, and is, as a rule, marked by the sense of agency.

4. The Experience of Grace

From the mere concept, we may now turn to the *experience* of grace. The first question, here, is obvious. When, or on meeting what preconditions, do we come to experience grace? The answer may be put as follows:

Generally, one is blessed with the experience of grace only when one's faith in God is very intense and when it tends to be exclusive (*ananyabhakti*), that is, when we depend on God alone as the *basic and unfailing* source of relief. Such is, indeed, the assurance of the Lord Himself in the *Gītā*:

> 'Abandoning all *dharmas*', (of the body, mind, and intellect), take refuge in Me alone; I will liberate thee from all sins; grieve not.'[6]

Be it noted, however, that the faith here recommended can work only when one turns to God *after* having tried (in vain) to meet an emergency with the help of all the human resources at one's command.[7] Further, the very act of refusing to depend on merely worldly aids—and to rely solely on His Providence—involves a courageous exercise of the will. So, the descent of grace does not make human effort unnecessary, though, of course, no such effort can be said to *compel* the descent in question. In other words, human effort as growing religiousness is an essential pre-condition, but not the necessitating cause, of the experience of grace.

As thus regarded, however, grace is only episodic. Indeed, so far we have not said anything about the other view of grace put forth by men of consummate faith like Shri Rāmakrishna Paramhansa,—the view that grace is a ceaseless or ever-operative blessing of God.

This view, however, is not wholly different from the first one. For both admit the value of implicit faith as an essential pre-condition of the *experience* of grace; and faith can in no case be developed without the intense self-effort of prayer and prayerful living.

If, however, the word 'when' in the question, *when do we experience grace*, is taken as a demand for the *occasions* on which we experience grace, as distinguished from the *pre-conditions* of such experience, the answer may be put as follows. We may become aware of grace *in prayer*, as a felt assurance from God and as a steadying of the self; *in crises*, as a quite unexpected and favourable turn of events which may defy comprehension; and, as a sudden and heightened sense of steadfastness in a moment of intense temptation which one struggles, but is not able, to overcome on one's own. Above all, according to the *Gauḍīya* school of Śrī Chaitanya, *prasāda* (or the descent of grace) appears just before the emergence of *uttam* or *nirguṇa bhakti*,[8] and *after prapatti* or absolute surrender which must come before, but cannot yet be said to coerce, the advent of grace.

This takes us to another question. *How* do we experience grace? Or what is the *character* of our experience of grace? Here, we may answer thus: the experience of grace comes as a very humble, joyous and grateful acknowledgment of the gift (or help, whatever it be) with the implicit urge to return the kindness somehow, say, by being truer to Him, or by worshipping Him through the service of His creatures. Where life itself is acknowledged as a gift of God, the experience of grace makes for contentment with one's present material possessions in case they are reasonably adequate, and a resolution to make the most of one's capacities in the way of service. This brings about refinement of conduct and character, which means that grace is by no means unrelated to morality. Further, in the setting of the good life taken generally, grace is experienced not as an insurance against the possibility of committing sin in future but only as an assurance of being ever acceptable to God, in case one is able to repent genuinely.[9] Finally, our repentance itself may be regarded as His grace at work.

But how do we identify, or what are the marks of, the descent of grace? In Indian religious literature, due thought has been given to this question. Thus, in his commentary on the *Gītā*, entitled *Bhāvārtha Dīpikā*, Sant Gyāneswar emphasizes the following distinctive marks of the working of grace: the dawn of renunciation in the heart, and interest in listening to scriptural recitations out of a genuine yearning to know the real (*tattvajijñāsā*). Rāmānuja regards the ability to discriminate between true knowledge and ignorance as a sure sign of grace at work. A more elaborate account of the matter is to be found in *Bhāgavad Viṣaya* by Sant Satkop. According to him, it is the following that betoken attainment of grace: interest in *Satsang*, not for the sake of any empirical end, but for one's own spiritual regeneration; and emergence of the true *Vaiṣṇava* spirit which comprises compassion, forgiveness, inner and outer purity, spontaneous sharing of the joys and sorrows of others, and liberality and freedom from jealousy, besides other virtues.

5. As a God-Man Relation

Excellences such as these, it is obvious, are of a very rare quality. Yet, it would be wrong to suppose that they are for ever inaccessible to us. For, we are told, grace is a quality of God's very nature. He loves us, and is ever anxious to redeem us. It is in this original relation of God's love for man that grace is grounded. Grace is nothing but this relation at work. God loves His creatures so much that He is always ready to make Himself available to us in any loving relation that we may choose to get closer to Him. He wants everyone to be saved, and in order to help us achieve this end He occasionally even descends into our world in a visible form.

This descent, however, in the form of an *avatāra,* is not only visible, but can even touch the heart, and be grasped by the mind. For, as Rāmānuja points out, God's descent among men reveals not only His transcendent attributes,[10] but also His immanent ones, say, the gracious qualities like compassion (*kāruṇya*), kind condescension (*sauśīlya*), *maternal* solicitude (*vātsalya*), generosity (*audārya*), goodwill (*sauhārda*) and tender affection (*anurāga*).

But, be it noted, God's descent into this phenomenal world does not in any way affect His essential nature. Rāmānuja's own words may here be cited:

> 'In order to fit Himself to be a refuge for gods and men etc., the Supreme Person, without however putting aside His true nature, associates Himself with the shape, make, qualities and words of the different classes of beings and thus is born in many ways.'[11]

6. Grace and Incarnation

An important purpose of the grace of incarnation, according to the *Gītā* (4:7), is to rid the world of evil-doers and to re-establish the rule of eternal righteousness (*dharma*). Still another valuable aim of such grace may be put thus. An incarnation teems with personal charms. Therefore, He readily captivates our hearts. Almost without notice, we are persuaded to surrender ourselves to His lotus feet. As a result, our faith and prayer gain in steadiness, and we get duly disposed to receive the grace of the Lord and to progress on the way to salvation. God does not straightaway reveal the transcendental glory of His Super-Personal Being (or *virāṭrūpa*), for such surpassing splendour may be unbearable to us.

In any case, if we look on incarnation as a mere *līlā* or sport of the Lord, we are sure to miss the essence of the matter. The real purpose of an incarnation is not merely to invite, but to deepen our commitment to God and His attributes. Because of His personal charms, we have said, our attention to an *avatāra* is ready and abiding; but, on the other hand, though His own infinite *rūpa* is not at once vouchsafed to us, His miraculous achievements, and the supernatural qualities they reveal, generate wonder and reverence,[12] and so prevent us from getting tied down to the merely personal and sensuous. It is here necessary to remember that the supernatural attributes of God are transcendent, not only in the sense of being out of the world, but also in that of being surpassing. Rāmānuja takes pains to point out that even the compassion of God is infinitely greater than our human concern for one another,[13] though it is of course a quality which at once serves as a vital bond between God and His creatures. Above all, it is, according to Rāmānuja, a clear mark of His grace that He is the indwelling spirit (*antaryāmin*) in every human being, and so very close to us, in spite of His transcendent qualities.

The concept of grace as a primal God-Man relation is, however, not confined to Indian religions. It is easy to cite parallels from the Christian tradition. Let us consider, for instance, the following:

> 'The Grace of God which we are to consider here is a ray of divine beauty, infused by God into the soul of man. There it sheds such a bright and beautiful light that the soul delights the eye of God and is most tenderly loved by Him: it is adopted as His child and spouse and is elevated from earth to heaven above all the confines of nature.'[14]

In the passage quoted above, grace is considered as a permanent equipment of the being of man. It is, we are told, not merely episodic, but a feature of the abiding man-God relation. Further, grace is here acknowledged as a ray not of light, but of beauty. This is significant; for, whereas light may occasionally dazzle one's vision and so cause discomfort, beauty is always a source of joy. Awareness of grace is a moment of gladness and a felt inward expansion. This is also true of our experience of a benefactor's grace in the context of purely secular, human relations.

It is because of grace,—or rather because of the presence in it of the ray of divine beauty—that the human soul has to be regarded as a part of God, and not of nature. That this relation is original is argued by the fact that the soul is readily accepted by God when it turns once again to Him after a spell of sinfulness.

The moment a man becomes conscious of divine grace—that is, of the original relation of his soul to God—he not only ceases to be dependent on nature, but comes (in a way) to partake of the glory and beauty of God. In other words, awareness of grace is not merely a release from the tyrannical hold of the world, but a positive participation in God's free and blissful nature. Freedom from enslavement to the world is at once an experience of spiritual plenitude.

We may now consider some more Christian utterances on grace to see how they are similar to the Indian ideas, already discussed.

(a) 'Grace is altogether a supernatural gift, that is, it is a gift which no created nature can possess by itself or claim as rightfully due to itself.'[15]

Grace is here spoken of not as an intrinsic property of man, but as a *supernatural gift*. It is a *gift* because we do not quite deserve it by virtue of any merit or endeavour of ours; and it is a *supernatural* gift because it is bestowed on us by God. It is supernatural also in the sense that, as opposed to natural gifts which are temporary and therefore liable to perish, this gift is eternal like the nature of God Himself.

(b) 'Neither man nor any other creature bears in his nature even the least germ of grace; further, . . . nature has the same relationship to grace as inanimate matter has to the principle of life. Lifeless matter cannot give itself life; it must receive life from a living Being. Similarly, the rational creature has no grace of itself; and cannot even acquire it by its own labour or merit. God alone can, out of pure love, give this grace by opening the abyss of His Omnipotence, and by pouring out upon nature His divine power. How great must that good be which so eminently surpasses the nature, power and merit of even the highest angels.'[16]

This passage may be explained as follows:

Grace is as far removed from human nature (as such) as life is from matter. Just as matter is made living not by itself but by life, so man comes to have grace, not because of anything in himself, but because of the Supreme Spirit or God.

Indeed, as already said, grace is traceable to God's own nature or attributes. This can be brought out in a simple way. We commonly identify grace as the unexpected, and yet quite appropriate, help which comes somehow, but strictly in accordance with the specific need of the individual. In other words, grace is a sign of the inexhaustible ability of God to give any one whatever help he or she may need. This is a clue to the relation of grace to God's metaphysical attributes. He is present everywhere and in every situation (omnipresence). He knows even our unspeakable agonies (omniscience); and He *can* provide any kind of help that we may need (omnipotence). But these metaphysical attributes of God only make it *possible* for Him to help us. That which makes for the effective descent of God's help is His overflowing love for us. It is love which provides the impulse for the exercise of the metaphysical attributes.

> (c) 'For although we do not produce grace in ourselves, we can, with divine assistance, prepare ourselves for grace and make ourselves worthy of it.'[17]

Here, three distinct ideas may be distinguished. First, *we* do not produce grace in ourselves; *God* does it. Second, we can yet seek to *prepare* ourselves for grace with divine assistance. Thirdly, again with the help of God, we *can* make ourselves worthy of receiving grace properly.

The first of these ideas has already been developed at fair length. So we may turn straight to the second. Here, at once, we are faced with a difficulty. We were told earlier that the *getting* of grace is not the result of any effort on our part. Why, then, are we here required to *prepare ourselves*? Is not self-preparation a kind of effort? It seems that we are here faced with a contradiction. But the seeming contradiction disappears at the touch of closer attention. What was earlier said to be independent of human effort was only the *getting* or achievement, not the acknowledgment of grace. If we make some effort to prepare ourselves for the mere receipt of grace, it would be no effort to *secure or force* the descent of grace. Even in daily life the right way to acknowledge a gift is to take it happily and gratefully. So, preparing ourselves to receive the gift of God's grace is no exercise in self-assertion; on the other hand, it is only an effort to make and keep ourselves humble in relation to God. However, quite unlike our everyday gifts, grace that we here speak of is a gift from God who is obviously not a visible person. Hence, the preparation in question requires that we come to develop a faith in the invisible power that God is. *Without* such a faith, any unexpected help that we come to get in life is likely to be taken as a mere matter of luck, not as a gift *from God.* Faith is necessarily a dependence on God, a growth in humility in relation to Him. This at once gives us a hint for meeting the difficulty suggested by the third idea. Making ourselves *worthy* of grace only means that we become duly humble to receive it, and develop the seeing eye of faith to identify the issue of unexpected help in crises as the working of *His* Grace. The *getting* of grace is not the result of any effort or merit on our part. But the proper *receipt* of it necessarily demands the effort of cultivating faith and humility, of course with God's assistance, say, by praying to Him for faith and humility.

The way is now paved to consider an important philosophical question. How is grace related to human effort? The question may be answered in the light of the following:

> 'In the ordinary created thing God is present only as its maker and conserver. Without His presence in this way things could not exist. But in the soul having grace He is present as sanctifier, giving Himself to the creature and sharing with him the holiness of His own being.'[18]

Men of religion commonly believe that God is the creator, indwelling spirit and preserver of all that is. As such, His grace may be said to be everywhere. However, He is said to have a special relation with the *human soul*, in so far as it alone is capable of *acknowledging* the relation instead of being merely *in* it. This seems to be the meaning where the passage in question speaks of soul's having grace. The point has, however, to be brought out a little more clearly, say, as follows:

In such a soul, we are further told, God is present as the sanctifier. But how exactly is the soul, here, sanctified or made pure? Our answer may open by suggesting that one who is sincerely and consciously aware of being intimately related to, and dependent on God, feels humble and grateful. This gives us a clue, it appears, to *understand* what the passage only *affirms*—that is, God's working as a sanctifier. But let me explain:

The man who feels humble because of his dependence on God, at once becomes self-critical. His very contemplation of the infinite goodness of God heightens by contrast his own many weaknesses. This heightened sense of imperfection in his own being, which comes as a reflex of his love of God, works in two ways. On the one hand, in so far as he is now acutely conscious of his *own* defects, he becomes patient with similar defects in his *fellow-beings*. On the other hand, he seeks to invoke God's help in overcoming his own so far unsuspected weaknesses which now engage his attention. But two points may here be emphasized, for we are likely to ignore them.

First, the two directions of effort we have listed as coming one after the other—that is, being patient with others and taking God's help in removing one's own weaknesses—do not exclude each other in practice. In fact, in the very act of trying to be patient with an evil person, one may have to invoke God's help. Conversely, as one sets out to pray for freedom from self-concern, praying for the good of others may seem to be the only way. But, because the before-after order cannot be avoided in the discursive use of language, it is difficult to be true in writing to the almost simultaneous direction of a good man's attention to both God and fellow human beings.

Second, though a man's felt humility in relation to God certainly impels and enables him to become ever better, this process can never be completed. God's goodness is infinite. As compared to it, the devotee's own improving goodness will always appear very slight, and the individual will be impelled to go on trying unceasingly. I have thought it essential to emphasize this point because the passage in question only speaks of God's being '*present* as sanctifier' in the soul having grace. The thought that God is (merely present as) sanctifier is not quite adequate to the truth that in the being of a man who acknowledges the receipt of grace God *continues to work* for ever as a sanctifier.

This does not, however, mean that even the conscious experience of grace can be had as a readymade gift; and we have indeed to discuss the question as to how such experience is related to human effort.

7. *Karma and Grace*

The word *karma* may be taken in two senses: as human action in general, and as the metaphysical principle which determines the relation of our actions to their consequences in accordance with the moral quality of our conduct. Descriptions of the experience of grace often tempt us, and we may well be impelled to ask as to what we should *seek to do* to get grace. In other words, how is grace related to human effort? This question becomes more difficult in view of the common insistence, already noted, that human merit can never equal the value of grace. For if the emphasis is true, are we to suppose that human effort is quite unnecessary for the getting of grace? This cannot be so; for the saints, who were blessed with the receipt of grace, have all been men of incessant moral endeavour. So, some kind of effort must be said to be necessary for the attainment of grace. But of what kind? And how far can it help us?

Now, a good deal of ethico-religious effort *is* necessary, as a pre-condition for having a conscious experience of grace. This is commonly acknowledged. It is indeed natural to suppose that one has to prepare oneself to register and acknowledge such a great gift as that of His grace. However, what all our effort is directly able to bring about is not the descent of grace as such, but the requisite state of utter purity as humility or egolessness in which this gift is to be taken. Our effort is said to consummate in *prapatti* or absolute surrender to God. The *Gītā*, we may note, regards *amānitvam* as the highest kind of knowledge. But, we may note, *prapatti* is only the immediate pre-condition, not the direct cause of the descent, of grace. This may be understood with the help of an example. Just as the proper integration of *sthāyibhāva, vibhāva* and *anubhāva* only facilitates, but does not guarantee, the emergence of *rasa*, in the same way human effort, in the form of moral improvement, only paves the way to, but does not necessitate, the descent of grace; and, again, just as *tādātmya* on the part of *rasikas* is essential before they can come to experience *rasa*, in the same way, *prapatti* or absolute surrender to God is necessary before we can really experience the descent of grace.

II. THE LOOK BENIGN

Nadar: Its Marks and Effects

Now, we may turn to the Sikh view of grace. Some distinctions have to be drawn—and some meanings, made definite—before we can make a real beginning. An essential, if incomplete, meaning of *nadar* is 'look'. But if the way the Sikh *gurus* generally speak of *nadar* is duly taken into account, the word 'look' *as used in relation to His grace* cannot be taken to signify a mere, momentary act of looking; it has to be taken as (what Ryle would call) a *heed* concept; and in so far as *God's* caring for His creatures has never been regarded as a staccato affair, 'nadar' must be taken to signify His unremitting *looking after* us. 'Looking-*after*', however, is not a mere 'looking *at*' for long and ceaselessly. Even in art contemplation the admitted meaning of *Nazar* or *Nigāh* is discriminating awareness or percipience; and where the look in question is one of His *grace* (*kṛpādṛiṣṭi*), it must be regarded as attention to an individual regarded not merely as numerically single, but as a specific person with his own unique needs of which even he himself may not be quite conscious. I here feel tempted to cite the following from Kierkegaard's *Prayers*:

'Thou hearest the cry of all men *without confusing their mixed voices* . . . Thou hearest not only the voice of one who is responsible for many others and so prays to Thee in their name; as if his high function could bring him nearer to Thee; Thou hearest not only the voice of one who prays for dear ones, as if he could thereby attract Thine attention, he who is privileged in having the dear ones; no, Thou hearest also the most miserable, the most abandoned, *and most solitary man*—in the desert, in the multitude.'[19]

Further, though as indicated earlier, distinctions may well be drawn between the various Sikh equivalents of 'grace'—and also, we may add, between the nature, marks and pre-conditions of grace—in so far as no such distinctions appear full-blown in the living unity of religious experience which the texts in question embody, the right way to proceed would be to follow the *lead of the text* in its own intense or non-analytic, yet insightful form, and to draw the necessary distinctions, where possible, only incidentally.

In *Gurbāni*, indeed, the question, what is grace, is not a philosophical one. The *gurus* do not keep debating as to whether grace is an attribute (of God) or a relation (of love) between God and Man. They are no mere philosophers of religion, but men of practical religiousness; and grace is for them no mere concept, but a vital, helpful force which, they believe, is actually at work in their psycho-physical being, a fact which they gratefully acknowledge:

'*man tan antari tudhu nadari nihālī.*'[20]

But some questions may be readily put here. Does the utterance just cited merely express the devotee's love, as may seem to be suggested by a casual look at its context, or is it expressive of some solid truth as well? To me it appears reasonable to say 'yes' to the second question, provided the truth desired be taken to mean such truth as is revealed only to the eye of faith; and I say so on the basis of what the verse itself may be taken to mean in the light of a closer look at the lines which precede it. The context, it appears, requires the verse to be interpreted as follows:

(a) A man of practical religion is not too keen about a mere enumeration or abstract understanding of the various excellences of God ('*kiā guṇ terey ākhi samāli*'). What he really cares for is the actual awareness of the working of divine grace in his mental and bodily life. A devotee does not seek so much to distinguish God's numberless excellences as to avail of them, and to see them work in his own life and experience.

(b) If it be wondered as to what it could possibly be to feel, and so acknowledge, the working of His grace 'in' one's body and mind (*man tan antari*) our answer will have to be divided. We will have to say that whereas seeing His grace *in* the body is to 'see' it in the making of our person '*Māt garabh mahi tum hī pālā*'[21], and so to take our physical frame as itself a gift of His grace, the sense of being blessed with His grace *within* the *heart* may be interpreted quite differently, say, as the perception that the love of God which suffuses one's heart is such that it spills of itself into an effortless singing of His glories '*Rang ratey guṇ gāvaṇiā.*'[22]

It is only when a man feels overwhelmed with delight and gratitude at the feel of His grace all around that he is impelled to sing the glories of God; and (in his view) only then does speech attain to its true function '*sachi vāṇi Hari guṇ gāvey nadrī nadar nihāl.*'[23] Further, grace or rather the awareness of it, may also be said to enable one to ensconce the Name in the heart, and to thereby feel refreshed and rekindled in spirit '*Nām japat mani tani hariāvalu prabh Nanak nadri nihāre jio.*'[24] Recitation of the Name, we are here told, is no mere exercise of the vocal chords; it is, instead, at once *a quickening of one's entire being* (*mani tani hariāvalu*). The ability to pray with such involvement and fresh-blown delight, we may note, does not come to us easily. One may have to pray in humility for its acquisition, as Kierkegaard does:

> 'Father in Heaven! When the thought of Thee wakes in our hearts let it not awaken like a frightful bird that flies about in dismay, but like a child waking from its sleep with a heavenly smile.'[25]

Of course, by virtue of His grace, once the Name gets settled in the heart—that is, when one gets totally committed to God—quite a few other marks of the working of grace appear forthwith. All oscillation now vanishes in respect of the choice between right and wrong, or between good and bad; for, one clear criterion—that is, progress in deepening the vassalage supreme (*bandagi*)—becomes the sole determinant of doing and suffering. Further, all impurity disappears not only from the body, but from thought and speech. Indeed, how can a man who is committed to the Name, or to a God of love and purity, and who looks on Him as the source of whatever measure of these excellences is there in his own being, fall a prey to transgressions of sense, impurity in thought, and anger in speech?

nadri karey ṣabadu ghati mahi vassey.
vichahu bharamu gavāye
tan man nirmal nirmal
vāṇī nāmo mani vasāye.[26]

The point here is that it is His grace which makes one pure all over and steadfast in righteousness. The sense of oneness with God is now quite secure, and so is the eventual realization of truth:

nadari karey prabhu āpaṇi guṇ ank samāvai
Nanak mailu na chūkai lāhā sachu pāvai.[27]

In other words, only that man comes to know the right way to live on whom God has already bestowed His grace:

jisno nadari karey soi bidhi jāṇey.[28]

But there are still greater gifts which accrue to those who are rightly oriented towards God, who acknowledge His grace, and who get inwardly committed to His feet. They attain to *the blessed* state of equipoise (*sahaj samādhi*), and so to eternal life:

oi sadā sadā jan jīvatey jo Hari charaṇī chitu lāhi.
Nanak nadri mani vassey gurmukhi sahaji samāhi.[29]

However, the bestowal or withholdment of His grace determine not only the inner quickening or rotting of spirit, but inequalities in respect of empirical fortune:

ik nihālī pei savanhi ik ūpari rahani khadey.
tinā savārey Nanaka jin kau nadari karey.[30]

In this context, *nadar* appears more as a look of power than as one of mere love. We may here wonder if this uneven distribution of fortune—so that one man becomes a king, and another remains a mere watchman—is just a whimsical expression of unchallengeable might, or the result of adherence to some superior, hidden principle. That higher principle, if there be any, can only be love. Indeed, this alone can be the view of a man of devotion like Guru Nanak. However, even upon this view, the difficulty would persist. For, if the (seeming) *misfortune* of a watchman is in truth an expression of God's love, how is this 'truth' to be ascertained and verified? How could any promise of good be really implicit in a manifest lack of life's basic comforts? The *gurus* would here say that the answer can be had not by any act of thinking or imagination on *our* part, but only by the person in question himself; and that he can get the answer only through the effort of prayer and prayerful living. God's purposes can never be made public. They reveal themselves to the devotee in the active exercise of faith. From the outside, all that we can truly say is that penury is by no means an unmixed evil, and that it *can* even be congenial to one's efforts for God-realization which is admittedly the highest end of man.

But, of course, this is very far removed from a glib apotheosis of poverty in general, as also from a specific explanation as to how exactly the lack of basic material comforts *is* an expression of God's love for the poor man.

We may now turn to consider the consequences of the bestowal of His grace. These too, we may at once add, are discerned within the ambit of faith.

To put it quite generally, the deeper and the more steadfast a man's faith, the greater is likely to be the number of things and happenings that he may be impelled to attribute to His grace. But, whatever be the quality of a man's faith, that which he sincerely attributes to the *grace* of God must always appear a bit too good for him, that is, unmistakably superior in value to *what he (in his own view) may be said to deserve* in virtue of his overall quality as a person. The latter—that is, one's rightful claim—would depend on how a man estimates himself. Saints, like the Sikh *gurus,* who have shed away all egotism in their consuming love of God, look on themselves as mere non-entities; and therefore they do not believe they *deserve* anything, and so are prone to regard *everything* as a gift of His grace. On the other hand, ordinary mortals, just because they find it impossible to renounce the sense of self-importance, regard only those few spectacular things as the gifts of God which very clearly seem to exceed what they think they deserve. Now, in so far as the Sikh scriptures are not only meant for us, the common people, but also reveal the sublime experiences and the states of being of the *gurus* themselves, quite often even the simplest things of life are here said to bespeak the grace of God.

The verses of *Gurbāni*, we repeat, nowhere draw a sharp distinction between the marks and consequences of grace. But for the sake of our understanding, a distinction may perhaps be made. A mark is a noticeable detail which serves as the sign of something else. So the *marks* of grace may be said to be such desirable changes in the behavioural attitudes of its recipient as are, as a rule, observable from the outside. Two of these marks are: a serene bearing in the midst of a calamity, and abstention from angry, retaliatory behaviour even when one is unduly provoked or insulted. These marks are noticeable—and, more or less, interpretable—from the outside as indices of some inner transformation. The *general consequences* of grace, on the other hand, may be taken to mean all those desirable changes in the inner states and outer life of the individual which he alone regards as traceable to grace because of his 'seeing eye of faith'. Some of these changes which appear to be the consequences of grace *to the man of faith* are: acquisition of such inner states of being as tranquillity and freedom from the very craving for material possessions or sense-indulgence; and the seemingly lucky finding of a *satgurū*. However, in so far as the 'marks' are as much a sequel to the getting of grace as the 'general consequences' we have just listed, the former may be regarded as but a sub-class of the latter. If all these expressions, public and relatively private, are taken into account, grace is bound to appear as related to the totality of a man's being, behaviour and experience.

But, one may wonder, how can anything be regarded as the effect or consequence of grace in case 'effect' is taken, as it commonly is, to be *due to* or *because of* the cause? Has not Hume so clearly shown that the effect only regularly *follows*, and that it cannot be said to be *necessarily related to*, or to be because of, the cause? To questions such as these our answer could readily be that, if in spite of such a theoretical refutation of causation as a *necessary* relation, we continue to believe, and to regulate our daily living by the belief, that an effect is due to and is actively produced by its cause, why should it not be taken to be proper to live by the faith that unexpected relief in crises, or the heightened ability to withstand them, is the result of His grace, specially when such faith actually conduces to added courage, and makes life bearable, and not only practically liveable? Surely, the ability to bear 'the slings and arrows of misfortune' is no less important than the everyday wisdom implicit in such causal beliefs as the thought that dark, gathering clouds mean imminent rain, and that one would, therefore, do well to either stay indoors *or* to carry an umbrella in such weather.

Now, speaking quite generally, all the major riches of a devout life, as distinguished from mere peace of mind which can perhaps also be produced by sheer (moral) self-discipline, may be said to be the consequences of His grace. But in so far as the very initiation into, and progress on the path of devotion depend on the help of a *gurū* of the right kind, we may begin by considering what the *gurubāni* has to say about grace in this context. Now, here we are at once rewarded with utterances such as the following:

Satgurū bhete so sukhu pāye.
Hari kā nām manni vasāye.
Nanak nadari karey so pāye.
ās andhese te nihkeval haume ṣabadi jalāye.[31]

It is by His grace, this *ṣabad* says, that one is able to find a *satgurū*, that is, a teacher who is himself a man of realization; and it is then, through the grace of the *satgurū*, that we are able to imbue our hearts with faith in the name of the Lord which ultimately frees us from egoity and worldly expectations and anxieties. This is the clear literal meaning of the verse in question. But two points, here, deserve a closer look. First, the sequence of *haume* upon *ās* and *andesā* is not merely incidental; it rather signifies a necessary connection in the fabric of the good life. The truth here suggested is that the duality of hope and anxiety in relation to the things of the world is there because of persistent egoity, and that the attitudes in question disappear the moment we are able to surrender our own ego at the feet of the Lord. (See: *Hari kā nām manni vasāye*). Second, the *sukh* that is said to accrue from access to a *satgurū* is no ordinary pleasure, but that bliss which follows the freedom from determination by dualities such as hope and anxiety, on the one hand; and from a heartfelt commitment to His Name, on the other.

Indeed, it is because of the surpassing excellence of the gains that accrue from a *satgurū's* tutelage that one's access to him may be regarded as a gift of God's grace. The 'realized' teacher does not simply set an example of righteous conduct, but gives us understanding which, however, is not merely abstract, but relates to the actual cultivation of proper values in real life; and this, in turn, brings about freedom from the heat of passions, besides generating the ability to revel in the very Name of the Lord:

pūre guri samjhāiyā mati ūtam hoī.
antari sītalu sānti hoi nāme sukhu hoi.
pūrā satgurū tā miley jā nadari kareī.[32]

However, none of these gains can be had unless one is able to get at the real significance of the *satgurū's* words through the grace of God:

gur ke sabadi pachhaṇiye jā āpe nadari kareī.[33]

This verse, it appears, can be properly interpreted only if we take it along with the earlier utterance:

ihu manu dhāvatu tā rahe jā āpe nadari kareī.[34]

Taking the two together, we may determine the meaning thus. Only that man is able to identify the distinctive significance of the *Satgurū's* words who has been blessed with the grace of God; for, as has been said earlier, it is only His grace which prevents the mind from running after material pursuits and enables it to focus on the truths of the spirit. (It is hardly necessary to add that the import of the words of the real *gurū* is deeply spiritual.) Again, it is under the guidance and protection of such a teacher that a man is able to free himself from the fear of death. One attains to this freedom not really because of self-effort, but because God reveals Himself in the heart of the man who is doubly blessed with the grace of God and the guidance of a truly spiritual teacher:

nadari karey pūrā gurū bhete
jam-jandaru na māre phete
jio jali antari kamal bigāsī
āpe bigasu dhiāidā.[35]

However, it is not any man, but only those who are steadfast in keeping godward (*gurmati sūrā*) that the *gurū's* guidance is able to help in becoming one with the Name:

jis kau nadari karey gurū pūrā.
sabadi milāe gurmati sūrā.[36]

Here, however, we must explain why we interpret the words, *gurmati sūrā*, as 'steadfast in keeping godward', rather than as the *chivalrous gurū*.[37] There is admittedly some warrant for translating the word *sūrā* as 'chivalrous'. For, does not the great gurū Gobind Singh declare: '*sūrā so pahchāniye jo larey dīn ke hetu?*' And, I add, may not this famous utterance be aptly translated thus: 'the truest mark of a *sūrā* is to fight for the sake of the poor and the defenceless (*dīn*)? One who engages himself in such a fight must surely be said to be chivalrous. But, I suggest, it would clearly be fairer to interpret the verse in question in the light of its own preceding context than on the analogy of a quite disconnected utterance, however significant that utterance be. And the verse which precedes the one being debated is a clear exhortation to turn away from worldly attachments and *to turn towards God* as the only real *gurū*:

> *moh pasār nahī saṅgi belī*
> *bin Hari gur kini sukh pāiā.*[38]

Those who are turned or oriented towards God are (*gurmati*); and *gurmati sūrā* may therefore be taken to be those who are *steadfast in being (and remaining) oriented towards God.* We may add that even the definition of *sūrā* we have cited may be quite properly translated to suit our purpose, say as follows: 'He alone is a *sūrā* who fights for the sake of his religion (*dīn*), *or for his own chosen way to God.*'

Anyway, it is to these *gurmati sūrās*—that is, to those who are godward and committed to the Name in a settled way—that the *gurū* unravels, by degrees, the subtleties of the life of religion. But this calls for some explanation. Ordinarily, immanence and transcendence, both alike aspects of God—and equally essential for the life of faith and prayer—are generally so regarded that they appear to be quite unrelated to each other. But the *gurū* makes his disciples see the immanence of the transcendent itself. And he repeatedly exhorts them to realize that it is a sheer waste of life if one fails to see the *infinite* plenitude of truth and charity that is present *within* us all:

> *eko hai dātār sachā āp dhaṇi*
> *so sachu terey nāli hai gurmukh nadari nihāl.*
> *. . . so sahi sachā*
> *vīsarey dhṛg jīvan sansār.*
> *nadari karey nā vīsarey gurmati vīchār.*[39]

It is as a consequence of guidance from such a *gurū*, secured through the grace of God, that one is ultimately able to emancipate himself from the cycle of births and deaths:

nadari karey tā satgurū miley.
praṇvati Nanak bhavjalū tarey.[40]

The supreme consequence of the grace of God is, however, only a consummation of the many subsidiary gains that accrue from it, two of them being indicated in the following:

pūrā sāch piyāla sahje tisahi piyāe jā kau nadari karey.
amrit kā vāpāṛī hovai kiā madi chhūchhe bhāu dharey.[41]

It is important to see what the drinking of the cup of whole (or perfect) truth (*pūrā sāch piyālā*) here means. It cannot be the pleasure of a mere moment. If what is drunk, or what one becomes imbued with, is the blissful feeling of the *whole* truth or of God's reality, satisfaction must abide and relate to every basic demand of our being. Such perfect quenching of our 'wonted fires' is not provided by any worldly pursuit. This, indeed, is the evidence of everyday experience. Therefore, the man who is blessed with the grace of God soon comes to realize the utter futility of clinging to worldly pleasures (*kiyā madi chhūchhe bhāv dharey*). In other words, he comes to develop detachment as a reflex of his realization that God alone is the true source of perfect happiness, or the highest value. Moral acquisitions like detachment, though they are only means to attainment of *mokṣa*, are yet of very great value. *Vairāgya* and *viveka* are indispensable pre-conditions of spiritual liberation.

Here it would be relevant to note that the Sikh scriptures give us a strict warning to eschew the false, though very tempting 'drinks' that the world freely offers us:

jhūthā madi mūli na pīchai jekā pār vasāi.
Nanak nadari sachu madu pāiye Satgurū miley jis āyī.[42]
jit pīte mali dūri hoi baral pavae vichi āi.
apanā parāiyā na pacchhānai khasmahu dhakke khāhi.[43]

These verses may be interpreted thus: 'Do not partake of the false wine, for this wine serves only to blight judgment and discrimination, whereupon one becomes incapable of distinguishing friend from foe (and neglects one's *true* husband). Take only the true wine, or imbue yourself with love of God; for it is this which can induce a healthy kind of self-forgetfulness (or conquest of egoity), and thereby lead to union with God (*Satgurū*). The true-false distinction is, however, accessible only to him who comes to be blessed with His grace:

nadari karey ta bharamu chukāye hukmai būjhe ta sāchā pāye.[44]

This godward orientation, be it noted, is not merely cognitive. It is active commitment to a life which aims at realizing the highest value; and, therefore, it is at once a moral exaltation or purification of the devotee:

> *sach sadā hai nirmalā bhāi nirmal sāche soi.*
> *nadari karey jisu āpani bhai tisu parāpati hoi.*[45]

In other words, God-realization is not a capricious gift of grace; it comes only to those who first become purified—and so, in a way, eligible—by means of commitment to His Name:

> *Nanak rātā sāchi nāmi bhāi.*
> *suṇi manu tanu nirmal hoi.*[46]

But, whatever be the way in which His grace is secured, once it descends on a devotee it takes the sting out of the trials and tribulations of his life:

> *khed na dukhu na danu tih ja kau nadari karei.*[47]

This mitigation of suffering, which is an important consequence of *nadar,* is partly traceable to the fact that the man who is committed to God feels contented with the minimum of material comforts, their littleness being more than set off by his overwhelming sense of the plenitude of grace divine, both within and outside his being:

> *Hari rūkhi roti khāe samāle.*
> *Hari antari bāhari nadari nihāle.*[48]

It need hardly be said that this blessed awareness is at once a sense of gratitude to, and a growing dependence on the Lord; and so it easily makes for a heartfelt recitation of His Name and charitableness in relation to His creatures:

> *Nanak nadari bāharey rāchahi dāni na nāi.*[49]

What is more, the pervasive (*antari bāhari*) and, we may add, unremitting awareness of His grace makes every moment of the devotee's life appear favourable; and he does not have to waste his energy in determining which particular hour of the day is propitious:

> *māh divas mūrat bhaley jin kau nadari karey.*[50]

Here, however, the words, *'jin kau nadari karey'* need a little clarification. Do they mean; 'those select few on whom He showers His grace'? We can hardly say, yes; for if we say so, we would be implying that God is partial to the select few. Such a suggestion must be dismissed as improper, for it is a commonplace of religious belief that we all alike dwell under the wings of His grace. How, then, are the words in question to be interpreted? It seems to me that a helpful hint is here provided by a close look at their context in the text. The lines which precede them are as follows:

kūd gaye dubidhā nasī pūran sāch bharey
Pārbraham prabhu sevadey mani antari ek dharey.[51]

Now, one reputed commentator interprets the second of these lines as a reference to those who 'place *the unique one* in their heart.'[52] But I see reason to differ. I suggest that if, as would only be proper, the second line is taken along with the words—*'pūran sāch bharey'*, in the first line, the words, '*mani antari ek dharey*', would appear to mean: 'those who worship the one transcendent Lord, their heart is *occupied with but one* reality, that is, God'. So, the answer to the problem emerges thus: 'those who have but one commitment—that is, those who love nothing but the Lord Himself, *and so acknowledge His grace* —for them every time is auspicious.' God's grace is, to be sure, *available to* all. But not everyone is *aware of* this truth. For those who *acknowledge* His grace every moment is auspicious. *Their* attitude is exceptional; *God* does not make exceptions. *He* is not partial; only the devoted few distinguish themselves from others by virtue of their intense devotion; and if *they* thereby come to acquire the exceptional ability to look on every moment of time as propitious, how is *God* to be blamed?

Here, incidentally, we think it necessary to bring out a distinction. That a particular moment of time is *accepted* as auspicious by us, ordinary men—say, because an astrologer says so—is one thing; that a great devotee *feels* blessed every moment because of his intense and uninterrupted love or awareness of the grace of God, is quite another. The one is a matter of belief; the other is a finding, a growing evermore into the fulness of Truth (*pūraṇ sāch bharey*). It may here be added that just as the awareness that one is being used as *a mere instrument* of *His* Will is at once an experience of edification and humility, so the sense of being blessed with His grace is necessarily a state of deeply felt gratitude; and that this feeling is such utter contentment with what is presently given to one that no discontent or anxiety, *and so no thought of the inauspicious*, can here arise. Contentment that is a reflex of being nourished in spirit by Truth alone is, indeed, an important consequence of grace:

ihu manu sāchi santokhiyā nadari karey tis māhi.[53]

At this point too, however, a little reflection is called for. Is it here suggested that a man who is favoured with His grace becomes quite satisfied *with himself, and so morally inert?* The devotee's answer would probably run thus. What is recommended in the verse being discussed is satisfaction not with the *moral* quality of one's being, but only with one's present *material* possessions. To adopt the distinction that Marcel draws between being and having, we should be contented with what we *have* for a reasonably comfortable living, but not with the present moral quality of our *being*. Such a divided contentment cannot make for inactivity. He who acknowledges His unremitting grace and is therefore possessed of a deep love of God is at once committed to goodness, for God is goodness supreme; and if such a man accepts his own individual worldly lot with faith in a *good and loving* God, he cannot but keep trying ceaselessly to serve his fellow-beings, though he may well be relatively indifferent to his *own* material needs. The devotee would here like to add that the kind of faith that is here spoken of is itself the highest improvement that a man's worldly existence admits of, and that the question of *its* substitution with anything higher does not arise.

It may also be said, in this context, that the contentment we have spoken of does not come at once. A man has to learn to discriminate the abiding values of spiritual life from the ephemeral charms of the world before he can develop an attitude of contentment with minimum material comfort. Such discrimination alone is true knowledge (*giyān*); and abidance in Truth and contemplation of the spiritual is alone the right kind of *dhiyānu.*

satu santokh giyān dhiyānu piāre jisno nadari karey.[54]

A man who is thus equipped with the priceless gift of grace acquires perfect control over his mind, which has a natural tendency to stray from the path of righteousness:

ihu manu dhāvatu tā rahey jā āpe nadari karey.[55]

God Himself, we are told, takes charge of the life of the man whom He blesseth with grace:

nadari karahi je āpaṇi tā āpe laye savāri.[56]

The meaning, here, cannot be that the individual's own effort henceforth become unnecessary; it cán only be that such a man will receive the Lord's active help in meeting challenges and in abstaining from transgressions (*savāri*). Be it noted, further, that this caring of the devotee by God as an exercise of His grace is not an *ad hoc* affair. Grace manifests itself as detailed assistance which a man receives *all along* in dealing with the various steps to his spiritual destiny. Man's crowning attainment is to become one with the will or commands of God. But this, in turn, requires that we first come to know what the Will Supreme requires us to do. Such knowledge (of His Will) cannot come to us unless we first rid ourselves of self-will. But this riddance demands that we saturate ourselves with the love of God and so become indifferent, in this very life, to the pursuit of purely mundane interests. However, such a cultivated indifference itself depends upon His grace:

nadarī satgurū seviye nadarī sevā hoi.
nadarī ihu manu vasi āve nadarī manu nirmal hoi.[57]

It is as a result of His grace that one comes to be blessed with the following superlative gifts: settlement of the Name in the heart; the privilege of loving access to His feet, or the bliss of devotion; and imperviousness to the corrupting influences of the world:

kājar koth mahi bhayī na kārī
nirmal baranu baniyo ri
mahā mantra gur hirday vasio.
achraj nām suniyo rī.
kari kirpā prabh nadari avlokan.
apuney charaṇi lagāi
prem bhagati Nanak sukhu pāiyā
sādhū saṇgi samāī.[58]

It may here be noted, in passing, that such affirmations of the practising men of religion are a direct challenge to the philosophic thesis that no necessary relations are to be found in the region of fact. Increasing devotion to God is *necessarily* a growing freedom from enslavement to the world; and *vairāgya*, we may add, is as much a directly felt *fact* to the man of devotion as his growing closeness to God. Renunciation is simply a reflex of genuine *bhakti*. But what is vital here is the inner fact of feeling free from the bondage of things and worldly relations. It does not matter much where one abides, or what company one keeps. It is immaterial whether one stays in a family or all by himself in a graveyard; for attachment to the riches of the world may persist even in the latter case. It disappears, and one becomes liberated from worldly bonds only when the name of the Lord comes to abide in one's heart. The individual then lives in a state of blessed attunement; he is not really alone; and even when he happens to dwell in the company of saints, his detachment does not dwindle, so that he does not feel any pain of estrangement as he leaves one group of saints to join another:

hoi avadhūt baithey lāi tārī, jogī jati pandit vīcharī.
gahī madi masāṇī ban mahi basatey
ūthi tinā ke lāgī pāliya, kātey
bandhani thākur jā ke, Hari Hari
nām basio jia tāke. sādh sangi
bhaye jan mukte, gati pāyi Nanak nadari nihāliā.[59]

At the same time, it is not enough to be merely *with* the godly. To elicit the requisite guidance *from* them one has to serve them in the humblest of ways and in a spirit of utter self-effacement. But this itself requires us to pray for the look of His grace, because our innate egoity makes it difficult for us to serve others ceaselessly, and without at all caring for our own comforts and needs:

pakkhā pāṇī pīsi bigasā pair dhoi.
āpahu kachhu na hoi prabhu nadari nihāliye.[60]

In case the author of this verse is required to explain the relation between God's grace and self-effacing service a little more clearly, he would probably reason the matter thus:

> It is the inward acknowledgement of the grace (or *unmerited kindness*) of God that makes and keeps one utterly humble; and it is this religious humility, and not any training in good manners, that enables one to serve others in a spirit of absolute humility. It may be added, incidentally, that an important hint is here provided to meet a difficulty which is likely to be faced by one who is committed to the good life. As Gandhi clearly saw, no vow seems to be properly observable without humility. Yet if one makes an active attempt to be humble, the very sense of agency is likely to

generate conceit. How, then, can one *become* truly humble? The Sikh *gurus*' answer would readily be: by acknowledging the grace of God in the tiniest details of life.

We also here get a clue to understand what it means to serve the sick and the suffering in the Name of God. The true man of religion who takes to such service works in a spirit of gratitude to God. The logic here implicit is that in so far as God has graciously given so much to him, the individual devotee should also do his best for his fellow-beings, for they are all alike children of his own benefactor: God. Service is here but a conscious exercise in gratitude. However, an overwhelming sense of gratitude to God for His grace not only makes one serve His creatures selflessly, but also helps one in renouncing the sense of agency even in respect of his *own* praying:

nadari tudhu ardās merī jini āpi upāiyā.
tāmey kahiyā kahanu jā tudh kahāiyā.[61]

'My praying', the *gurū* here says, 'is nothing but a working of His grace. It is He who creates favourable conditions for my prayers; and I pray in whatever words He puts into my mouth'. It is importantly as a result of praying in this spirit, or with a conscious sense of being able to pray by virtue of His grace, that one comes to feel protected in the true sense:

so sahiyā sohāgaṇi jin kau nadari kareyi.[62]

Here the word 'offers' (*kareyī*) calls for some comment. Generally, everybody can be said to be the recipient of His grace in so far as the basic kind of protection—such as nourishment by water, air and the sun—is provided by Him to us all. But the person on whom the grace of God appears to descend visibly, say, in terms of an unexpected favourable turn of events—and who is duly conscious, we may add, of the receipt of this grace—is alone blessed with the feeling of being protected *in every way*. The risk of interpreting the word '*sohāgaṇī*' in essentially *human* terms is here easily avoided if we take care to reflect that the writer, himself a man of consummate devotion, feels perfectly settled in the grace *of God*. Even generally, however, the awareness of God's grace is no mere incident, but often an influence over a man's whole life, attitudes, and value-sense. A person who is so blessedly aware is likely to become uncommonly conscious of his own weaknesses, and so genuinely humble. At the same time, he may also feel a little elevated, because the very dissatisfying awareness of evil in one's own being is an implicit step in the direction of goodness; and also steadied by the reassuring thought that, in spite of all his weaknesses, he is being looked after by God:

ikanha andari khoti nit khotu kamāvahi
oh jehā bīje tehā phal khāye.
jā satgurū sarāf nadari kari dekhe.
suāvgir sabhi ughad āye.[63]

Grace, however, reveals to us not merely the truth of our own imperfect being, but also that of God's absoluteness. The sense that God alone is the ultimate certainty and the substantial reality of which the scriptures speak, is the immediate result of a felt descent of His grace. To put it differently, it is only when He condescends to reveal Himself that we come to see His distinct reality and truth:

nadari karahi tā sāchu pachhāṇā.
sācho pachhāṇa tāmi terā jāmi āpi bujhāvahe.[64]

The key word here is *pachhāṇā* which means: 'to identify' or 'to recognize', and not merely to find or to see. To identify is to at once become assured of the distinct character of the given. In the case in question, the given is no mere fact, but the highest value.

It is indeed He alone who, in His grace, enables us to realize, in terms of our own experience, that there is no more precious gem than the Name of the Lord, and that the heart in which It gets settled itself becomes a priceless pearl:

hīrā nām javāhar lāl. man moti hai tis kā mālu.
Nanak parkhey nadari nihālu.[65]

The devotee (who is aware of His grace) abides in the bliss of the recitation of His Name and feels sheltered by His grace. He says to himself: 'My family is His grace; it indeed *enwraps me in* love. But what I *feel supported by*, is His Name alone.'

ghar mandari khuṣī nām kī nadari teri parvāru.[66]

Here even a little attention to the opening words, like *ghari mandari khuṣī nām kī* makes it clear that the *gurū* is careful to emphasize the blissful aspect of the life of the spirit.

Here, incidentally, a general remark may also be made. Grace is the very generous and intimately solicitous love of God towards those who are committed to His service. It works and affirms itself without being deterred by any thought of the lowly status of those who serve Him. This is obviously quite unlike the behaviour of the human master who is often seen to tyrannize over his servants:

dās rākhey kanthi lāyi nadari nihālion.[67]

The Lord's gracious love is, however, no mere emotion; it is at once a redemptive influence. It is indeed this which enables His devotee to cross the painful and frightful cycle of births and deaths (*saṃsāra*); and it is because of this vital assistance towards the consummation of his whole life that the devotee comes to look on His grace not as a momentary or superficial help, but as permeating his life and being through and through:

anchali lāi tarāiā bhāī bhavjalu dukhu sansāru.
kari kirpā nadari nihāliā bhāī kītānu aṅgu apāru.[68]

Such 'seeing', however, is no easy or isolated act; it rather consummates a whole life of devotion. This is why even the saints are exhorted to *try* to cultivate the sense of His gracious immediacy:

Hari santahu dekhahu nadari kari nikati vasahi bharpūri.[69]

The importance of this verse is, in my view, twofold. First, the way in which it has been translated by Manmohan Singh—that is, as follows: 'Ye saints, see with the searching glance that God abides close by and is fully pervading everywhere'[70]—does not appear to be correct, for it interprets 'nadar' as *searching glance*, a sense in which the word *nadar* has not been used anywhere else in the work. Second, the alternative meaning that I propose to put on this verse gives us an additional idea about grace: say, the thought that the very metaphysical attributes of immanence and omnipotence are subordinate to God's moral attributes. To put it clearly, I interpret the verse in question thus: 'O saints, make no mistake about it, it is out of His own grace that God is close to (or immanent in) us in a surpassing degree (*bharpūri*). I get this meaning by re-arranging the text of the verse as follows:

santahu dekhahu Hari nadari kari nikati vasahi bharpūri.[71]

When the devotee feels overwhelmed with the bliss of His look of grace (*Nanak nadarī nadar nihālu*) he attains to spontaneous, self-sustaining happiness (*sahaj sukh*) and dances in sheer delight:

seyi nāchahi jo tudhu bhāvahi, ji gurmukh sabad vīchārī.
kahu Nanak se sahaj sukhu pāvahi jin kau nadari tumārī.[72]

This joy may also express itself in *harikīrtan* or the singing of His glories. However, such expression is not really the devotee's own doing. The vital impulse to so express oneself comes from (or as) His grace. It is again because of this divine assistance that one comes to feel settled and secure in Truth.

nadari karey tā Harigunṇ gāve nadarī sachi samāvaṇiā.[73]

Singing His glory and prayerful recitation of His Name are alike grounded in the faith that the God of grace takes care of one's present and future lot. In other words, the consciousness of grace is also a felt assurance of absolute security. The state, here, is one of *humility without unsteadiness:*

Gurcharaṇ lāge sadā jāge man vajīyān vādhāiyān.
karī nadari sūāmī sukhah gāmī.
halat palatu savāriyā binvanti Nanak nit nāmu
japiye jīo piṇḍu jini dhāriā.[74]

However, the working of grace is to be seen not only in the final attainment of the legitimate goals that we seek, but also, and more importantly, in the radical transformation of the worst of men:

kyā hansu kyā bagulā jā kau nadari karey.
je tisu bhāve Nankā kāgahu hans karey.[75]

Here, the emphasis is that God is the redeemer of the lowly, and that it is only His grace which can bring about a qualitative lift in the state of a depraved person:

jithe nīch samāliyan tithe nadari terī bakhsīs.[76]

The supreme gift of grace is, however, the attainment of the highest end, that is, liberation:

karmī āve **kapaḍā** *nadarī mokh duāru.*[77]

To speak thus is to highlight the surpassing potency of grace by means of a contrast. Whatever be its quality, human action leads only to a fresh embodiment, better or worse; it is grace alone which can deliver us from the cycle of *saṃsāra*.

The truth that such *deliverance* is by no means easy becomes manifest when we reflect that it is our common lot to get intensely attached to the insubstantial charms that surround us in daily life. Ignorance of the highest value that is implicit in such attachment can be dispelled only by a conscious surrender to the highest truth or God. He alone is both kindly and powerful enough to release us, by means of His grace, from the bondage of temporal attachments which have no real value:

kūḍī karaṇi vadaiyā, kūḍe sio lagā nehu.
Nanak sachā āp hai āpe nadari kareyi.[78]

His grace, we are told, is so powerful that even a single look of it can give us freedom from the cycle of births and deaths. It may seem fantastic to say so. But the seeming oddity would disappear, or at least be mitigated, if it be borne in mind that the 'look' in question is no ordinary one, but that of God; and that, as regards the getting of freedom from *saṃsāra*, what is here said is not that under the impact of His grace the freedom in question can be had *at once*, but only that *a single look* of His is enough to make us realize (sooner or later) the freedom Supreme. If, as evidenced in our own day by some of Gandhi's fasts, even a quiet invitation to turn to the path of sanity, extended by someone whom we deeply love—and who, we may be sure, himself loves us deeply—can suffice to wean us from evil ways, why can't an 'intimation' from God, received in an attitude of faith and humility, be credited with the power to put us on the path of righteousness that leads ultimately to the goal of liberation? The moral disciplines, which may thenceforth be demanded, can become quite easy to practise by virtue of His grace:

āpu vīchāre su parakhey hīrā.
ek dṛṣṭī tāre gur pūrā.
aisī sāhu sarāfi karey.
sāchi nadari ek liv tarey.[79]

Be that as it may, we must have the faith that He, who has been the *real agent* (*kartā*) of all that happens throughout the ages, will alone be the source of the issue of grace by which we may come to be united with Him:

> *āpey kartā jugi jugi soī.*
> *nadari karey melāvā hoī.*[80]

But, we may wonder, whither are we to look for divine grace? God is said to be formless; so *where* can we find Him? Now, here it is the *gurū* alone who can be of effective help to us. It is he who gives us the assurance that grace can be secured only by modelling our lives on the spiritual utterances of the holy men who have themselves been blessed with the grace of God. But here another difficulty arises. How can we locate and identify such men? To meet this difficulty, luckily, the *gurus*, themselves all recipients of His grace, provide a helpful clue. They assure us that, in so far as total commitment to the Name is impossible without His grace, any one who shows such commitment may be taken to be a truly holy man. I get at *this* thought by considering together the first and the last lines of the following extract:

> *chhutte tāke boli sāhib nadari jisu.*
> *ghalle āṇe āpi jisu nāhi dūjā koī.*
> *dhāhi usāre sāji jāṇe sabh koī.*
> *Nau Nanak bakhsīs nadarī karamu hoi.*[81]

But however earnest and successful be our effort to model our lives on the example of godly men, it is only by praying directly to God Himself for grace that we can find God who is the essence of life and who dwells in the mansion of Truth; and can thereby secure our liberation:

> *sur nari nāth beyant ajoni sāche mahali apārā.*
> *Nanak sahaji miley jagjīvan nadari karahu nistārā.*[82]

A part of the meaning here clearly is that God who dwells in Truth can be realized through commitment to Truth; but the second line also presents a difficulty. However large and splendid it be, a *mahal* is necessarily a bounded building, and *apāra* means 'beyond limit' or limitless. How, then, can the two be put together? How is it possible for the same thing to be both *unlimited* and a *definite place* of abidance? The answer, I suggest, is provided by the immediately preceding word *sāche* in the same line. *Sāche* means 'true' or 'of truth'. So the net meaning of the first two lines, in my view, is that God is to be found *in an abiding state of truthfulness.* In other words, if a man practises truth in all walks of life he will become generally truthful. His state of being will be one of abiding purity, for purity is nothing but freedom from untruth; and it is in this state of purity that God can be found, though never exhaustively, because Truth, which is His abode, is limitless (*apārā*). If it be wondered, because of the difficulty they cause for interpretation, as to why these three words: *sāche mahal apārā,* have been juxtaposed, the answer could be that the saintly author *had* to say something rather positive as to where God is to be found, after causing a little uncertainty in the mind of the devotees by speaking of God in purely negative terms, or as *beant, ajonī.* However, an objection could also be made in respect of the disposition of the whole extract cited. In the first two lines, the *gurū* praises the Lord; and in the 3rd and 4th lines he wishes to get something from God. Does it not seem a bit too similar to the familiar human trick of tickling the ego of a superior with the intent of securing some favour from him? In other words, is the *gurū* here praising the Lord as a matter of policy? Our answer here would be readily negative, and this because of the following reasons:

First, when the *gurū,* himself a man of devotion, openly says that God is to be found in the temple of *truth,* how can he (be said to) make a *pretence* of praising God?

Second, what the *gurū* prays or pines for in the second line is liberation from the trammels of worldly attachment and vices (*nistārā*) which cannot be secured by means of merely human effort. He feels imprisoned in the *dwandas* of the world, and prays for liberation from a *desperate* situation. *In such a situation* the act of praising God or of praying to Him cannot but be sincere.

Pre-conditions of Nadar

The grace of God, we are told, is a tender and continually solicitous love actively working for the devotee's welfare, and not merely as a kind of supervisory look:

jeo jananī sutu jaṇi pālatī rākhe nadari majhār.
antari bāhari mukh de girāsu. khin khin pochār.
teo satgurū guru sikh rākhdā Hari prīti piyāri.[83]

Now, one good thing about such a conception of grace is that, if it is truly believed in, it is likely to produce in us the love (and not the mere fear) of God which is so vital for true commitment to the life of religion. The verse just cited declares that His *look* (of grace) is not merely tender and caring like that of a mother, but also watchful in a comprehensive manner (*pratipāli*) so that He is able to look after our everyday needs in the way of a human father:

ham bārik Hari pitā pratipāli.[84]

The image of a human father here conveys an additional idea. Just as the earthly parent generally looks after all his children more or less equally, but yet feels more concerned for, and pays extra attention to, a sick or otherwise specially needy child, so God too offers special help to a devotee who turns to Him for relief in an emergency after having tried—desperately, may be, but in vain—to deal with the intractable situation on his own, and with the faith that it is He alone who may be expected to provide the much needed help:

tū samrathu sarani jogu tū rākhahi apanī kali dhāri.
jāp tāp nem suchi sanjam nāhī in bidhi chhutkār.
garat ghor andh te kādahu prabh Nanak nadari nihāri.[85]

We are, therefore, advised to consciously look upon God's grace (*or nadari*) as the only true source of happiness. Once a man comes to develop this faith, his daily living will automatically tend to become *God-centred.* This, in turn, will save him from being excessively *preoccupied with self,* which would in itself be a great gain, because it is the attitude of being *manmukh* (or self-willed) that makes a man wretched beyond redemption:

nadari terī sukh pāiyā Nanak sabadu vīchāri.
manmukh bhūle pachi muye ubre gur bīchāri.
ji purakhu nadari na āvayi tisu kā kiyā kari kahiyā jāyī.[86]

It may be added that the emphasis here is on developing faith in the power of *nadari* to give us every kind of *bliss.* This is noteworthy, for men of religion often tend to commit the mistake of over-emphasizing the value of *rigorous* self-restraint for God-realization, and do not duly project the *joy-giving* aspect of the discipline of faith.

Whether we know it or not, we all depend on God's grace for relief of our daily difficulties. But the *kind* of help we *expect* from His grace reveals what kind of persons we are. An exalted soul as he is, Guru

Nanak depends on God, and prays for His *nadar* not for any empirical end, but for His self-revelation to him:

Nanak māṅge sachu gurmukhi ghāliye.
mai tudhu binu avaru na koi nadari nīhāliye.[87]

There is a logic in the content of such prayers. If one has really come to develop *ananyabhakti* or exclusive and loving dependence on God; and if, what is more, in accordance with the essential impulse of *bhakti* greater emphasis is put on His solicitude for us than on His metaphysical attributes, it would be natural for a devotee to rely on God's grace alone for revelation of the final Truth and concomitant liberation. Indeed, it seems to me that, according to the Sikh *gurus*, such a consummate faith is a faith more importantly in the *nadar* than in the merely superhuman qualities of God:

antari gurgiyānu Hari ratanu hai mukati karāvanhārā.
Nanak jisno nadari karey so pāye so hovai dari sachiārā.[88]

We are here clearly told that it is only by virtue of His grace that we can gain access to the right kind of *gurū* who alone can make the love of the holy Name settle in our hearts; and that it is only as a result of this settlement that, on the one hand, we get closer to God's criterion of righteousness, and, on the other hand, become eligible for *mukti*. In other words, our moral progress and spiritual emancipation both alike depend on His grace.

Here, however, a question may be put. If *faith in the value of grace*, as against our own independent moral struggles, is so important, surely we must be told as to how we can develop this faith. Are we to follow some specific discipline to attain this faith, or merely to have faith in such utterances of the *gurus* as emphasize the value of the faith in question? Now, the answer which *Gurbāni* here offers is clear: one must (also) try to transform one's own personality into the pure gold of righteousness by conquering the evil emotions of lust and anger:

kām krodh kāiyā kau gāle.
jeo kanchan sohāgā dhāle.
kasi kasvatti sahe su tau.
nadari sarāf vaṇīs chaḍao.[89]

Such a purified person alone becomes acceptable in the eyes of God, the supreme jeweller or assessor of worth. Yet, on the whole, His *look* is one of grace as abiding solicitude (or *nadari*), not of mere critical inspection; and he who seeks to become eligible to receive a little more of His love—say, by acquiring purity and egolessness, and so the serenity which is both the locus and effect of deepening faith—is naturally better looked after by Him, so that there is, henceforward, no possibility of such a man's tarnishing his hands again with the wilful doing of evil deeds:

kīchaḍ hāthu na būdayī ekā nadari nihāli.[90]

A person so fortified against evil comes to secure perfect control over his mind and becomes dead, so to say, in this very life, to interests that are merely mundane:

mani māre jīvat mari jāni Nanak nadarī nadari pachhāṇ.[91]

The *gurū* further advises us to hold on to the right and the good (*kharā*) ceaselessly (*nit nit*) because, we are warned, the path of falsehood can never make us eligible for grace. The best thing, therefore, is to burn up all our evil passions and desires:

nit nit kharā samāliye sachu saudā pāiye.
khote nadari na āvanī lai agani jalāiye.[92]

If not explicitly, we are also here made to see how moral discipline, the grace of God, and human happiness are all disposed in relation to one another in Sikh philosophy of the good life. It is suggested that we should first saturate ourselves with the faith that His grace alone is the true source of all blessings, including settlement of the Name in the heart and access to a *satgurū*; and that then, as a result of faith in—and love of—the Lord, our happiness will be automatically ensured, and so would be the requisite control over our 'wonted fires':

nadari karey sabadu ghat mahi vassey.[93]
vichahu bharamu gavāye.
nadari karey tān satgurū meley
ta nij ghari vāsā ihu manu pāye.[94]
kām. krodh, bikhu, agani nivāre
Nanak nadarī nadari piyāre.[95]

But, of course, no one can *command* the conscious experience of God's grace. All that one can do is to develop some pervasive attitudes, such as unceasing love of God, and the incidental surrender of egoity; and then to humbly wait for a glance of His grace:

medā man ratā āpaṇe pir nāli.
hau gholi ghumayi khaniye kīti.
hik bhori nadari nihāli.[96]

It may here be added that the bliss of experiencing a descent of His grace would fade away fast if there is no pre-existent love of God to relish it. That is why it is emphasized that faith in God is the essential pre-condition of a definite experience of grace, and of a consequent refinement of value-sense.

The refinement in question is inevitable. Every conscious experience of grace makes one a little humbler. The *gurū* (-author) speaks of his own life as one of commitment to the service of the lowly:

nadari karahi tū tārahi tariye.
sachu devahu dīn dayālā.
praṇvati Nanak dāsani dāsā tū
sarab jiyā pratipālā.[97]

What is here important to note is that in so regarding himself the *gurū* at once appears to be imbued with a divine attribute. This becomes clear when we attend to the simile which is here suggested, and which may be brought out thus: just as God looks after every living being without being deterred by our individual demerits, so the *gurū* regards himself as the servant of even those whom the world dismisses as being very lowly.

Such a self-effacing concern for His creatures is facilitated by the faith that God Himself dwells in them and that by working for them a devotee can come closer to his Lord, his service of the poor and the weak being a mere expression of his love of God. Humility, along with the purity it produces by freeing one from egoity, is the only title to grace; and, it appears, it is just this truth of the good life that the Sikh *gurus* emphasize in talking repeatedly of the need to develop a faith in the efficacy of grace (or *nadari*):

bhī sālāhih sāchā soyī jā kī nadari sadā sukhu hoyī.[98]

Here, incidentally, we are given a clue to see a basic difference between our *human* loves and our love *for God.* There is no single empirical objective by labouring for which—or by loving or pursuing which—an individual could satisfy *every* basic demand of his being;

and so one has to keep trying to meet diverse needs, one after the other. Realization of God alone puts an end to such ceaseless hankering. But is this end accessible to all? Can everyone avail of the grace of God? Yes, says the following verse. Grace is nobody's monopoly, and the gains it bestows are various and adapted to individual needs:

ek nadari kari vekhe sabh ūpari.
jehā bhau tehā phalu pāiye.[99]

Here, the opening words of the second line: *Jehā bhau* call for careful attention. Their literal meaning is: *however you love Him.* But I may venture to give these words a richer meaning, say, the following: '*with whatever degree of intensity or for whatever (legitimate) purpose you love Him*'. In other words, our love of God is always, more or less, rewarding; and there is no desirable purpose for which His help cannot be enlisted. That is why the feeling of having been favoured with grace serves as a warrant of faith, and renews our humility and gratitude in relation to God. This suffusion with gratitude, though admittedly a happy feeling, is very far removed from the state of being elated with a self-conscious sense of worldly achievement. It rather inclines the devotee to offer a very humble prayer for ends that are utterly spiritual. 'May He, the immanent Lord, heed and answer my heartfelt need for the supreme gift of His grace, that is, such absolute commitment to the Name that its recitation may become the very breath of my life':

antarjāmī prabh daiyāl.
apaṇe dās kau nadar nihālī.
kari kirpā mohi dehu dānu.
japi jīve Nanaku tero nāmu.[100]

Progress on the path of prayer, of course, calls for earnest self-effort, but its consummation or absolute commitment to the Name comes only as a gift of His grace.

binu karme nāu na pāiye pūrey karami pāiya jāi.
Nanak nadari karey je āpaṇī tā gurmati meli milāyi.[101]

Here, I would like to interpret the words *'pūrey karami pāiyā jāi'* differently from the way they have been taken by Manmohan Singh and Dr. Gopal Singh.[102] They translate the words in question as 'perfection of one's destiny'. If this interpretation is accepted, destiny *too* will have to be regarded as the source of the bliss of devotion. But this cannot be allowed, because the very opening words say it clearly that the bliss in question cannot be had without His grace. Hence, I suggest, the words: *pūrey karami*, may be taken to mean the continuous bestowal of grace as a result of constant effort (by way of growing self-surrender to God) on the part of the devotee.

Such effort, however, is not quite self-evolved. It arises only as a sequel to rigorous training in self-effacement involved in serving the exemplar of spiritual values that a *Satgurū* is. It is indeed such service which makes one really keen to deepen one's religious orientation. But here too grace is essential; for it alone can provide the courage and intensity of commitment demanded by a life of wholly selfless service:

gur Pīrān kī chākari mahā karaḍi sukh sāru.
nadari karey jisu āpaṇī tisu lāye het piyār.[103]

If it be wondered as to how exactly it is difficult to serve the *gurū*, an answer may be readily given by pointing out that what the service in question requires is no mere physical closeness to the teacher, but active accordance with his austere *way of living*, and absolute indifference to one's own personal comforts.

III. DIVINE LIBERALITY

(KIRPĀ AND MIHAR)

1. *What is Kirpā?*

We may now turn to consider *kṛpā* or *kirpā* which is very close to, though not identical with *nadar*, in meaning; and which occurs freely in *gurbāni*. Here I am struck by the fullness of the way in which the Lord's *kṛpā* is acclaimed. We are told that It not only lends firmness to the devotion of the *bhaktas*, but is congenial to liberation of the entire mass of humanity; and that, what is more, it looks after the whole creation, besides caring for the spiritual uplift of those that inhabit it, simply because of its own inherent quality as kindliness, and not because of determination by any external force:

kṛpā kṛpā kari bhagati dṛdāye.
jan pīchhe jag nistāre āpan āp āpi Prabhu āpe srisati savāre.
jan Nanak āpe āpi sabhu varatey.
kari kirpā āpi nistāre.[104]

It is easy to see that in its ability to accomplish this stupendous task *kṛpā* draws upon those moral and metaphysical attributes which are commonly ascribed to God. But what it needs some definite effort to mark here is that, *from the devotee's point of view,* every attribute of God can be taken as a mode of His *kṛpā.* Indeed, a true *bhakta* contemplates the omnipotence of God not as the invicible might *against which nothing can be done,* but as a boundless and unfailing power *with the help of which* the highest end can be achieved:

> *merā prabhu ati ūcho ūchā kari kirpā āpi milāvaṇiyā.*[105]

And when a genuine *bhakta* thinks of the divine attributes of omnipresence and omniscience, he is not troubled by the uneasy thought that, however much one may try, nothing can be kept hidden from God's all-seeing eye, but only feels steadied by the faith that, in so far as everything is open to His view, one can be assured of His watchful and protective care at all times and in every situation. To a true devotee the all-seeing eye of God is not a malevolent agency that pries into our private affairs, but the sovereignty of a wholly beneficial Power which registers every turn in an individual's fortunes, and so *can* provide appropriate help, if only it is rightly appealed to. In any case, the *kṛpā* of the Lord must be regarded as a pervasive—or, as the philosopher, G.E. Moore, would like to put it, a toti-resultant—attribute of God.

Incidentally, a little close attention to the extract from the *Ādi Granth* that I cited (on the previous page) can be quite rewarding. The first two lines, I find, deliver the idea that, if only by slow degrees, the great God so deepens and illumines His devotee's *bhakti* that he gets initiated into a whole discipline of devotion which *can* be availed of by, and can serve to redeem the entire world. Further, the *kṛpā* of the Lord is here spoken of in such a way that, strange though it may seem, it at once appears also as a mark of His humility,—the humility of greatness, as opposed to the humility of literal lowliness. Is it not a sign of His condescension that, in spite of His transcendent greatness and all-controlling power, He is so concerned about our *true* welfare, even though we ourselves may be said to be generally indifferent to it?

Here, incidentally, a point may be made to bring out the inadequacy of a merely theoretical conception of God. Logically, the infinite seems to be merely opposed to the finite. But, as an object of the religious attitude, the *infinite* is so—that is, infinite—also in respect of Its concern for the finite. This is no mere talk, for the evidence of the life of religion truly is that the moment we admit our weakness and inability in sincere prayerfulness, His readiness to care for the lowliest of us—or His humility—is at once brought into play, and we are duly granted the relief or shelter that we seek. God's omniscience, too, is not merely an all-encompassing vision, but at once a *pervasive* love and concern; and it is indeed with the intent of following the way of God that the Sikh *gurus*, like saints of other religions, are never tired of praying that they be granted the opportunity to serve the lowliest of the lowly. To be sure, the infinite *as such* defies understanding; but, the infinity of *His love*, may well be availed of, *and so practically realized*, by the devotee through a prayerful confession of his own weaknesses, even after the most serious transgressions. *Kṛpā* is the reflex of a quite uncalculating love which surpasses justice regarded as the getting or bestowal of what is truly deserved—on merit. This is implicit in the *gurū's* assurance that though we must always appear very deficient from the viewpoint of His exacting standards, liberation can yet be granted to us provided we enter His court with due humility:

ohu ādi jugādī Rām sanehī.
dargah mukati karey kirpā bakhasey avaguṇ kīna hai.[106]

It would, however, be wrong to suppose that the *kṛpā* of the Lord leaves our weaknesses untouched. They all alike come under Its influence, if indirectly; and it is easy to see why it should be so. The life of a devotee is lit up with experiences of divine help received in unforeseen ways. This naturally deepens his love and gratitude for God, which, in turn, impels him to draw closer to Him, to take His moral attributes as ideals to live by, and to temper by degrees his own human weaknesses, whereupon he finds himself rewarded with an ever more intimate feeling of oneness with God (*Kanth lāi*):

kṛpā katākhya avalokan kīno
dās kā dūkhu bidāriyo.
Hari jan rākhe gur gobind.
kanthi lāyi avaguṇ sabhi metey
daiyāl purukh bakhsand.[107]

Indeed, the working of His grace is not merely gratuitous but perfectly autonomous. It is under the stress of His own *kṛpā*, and not because of any outer compulsion, that the Lord reveals His resplendent presence in the devotee's heart as a distinct content of consciousness:

ugviyā asrūpa dikhāvai kari kirpā apuṇe ghari āvai.[108]

This unforced and manifestative descent of God can occur in two ways. Out of sheer compassion for His devotees He may either appear in a human form (*avtaran*), *or* enshrine Himself manifestly in the heart of a devotee (*bhakta*). The second kind of 'descent' may be spoken of as follows:

kari kirpā ghari āiyā, āpe miliyā āi.[109]

Such a loving condescension of God is commonly believed to be gentle and gradual, quite unlike revelation which comes as a sudden and spectacular event. What is more, it comes through the mediative help of the *gurū*; but this help too, we may note, is traceable to His *kṛpā*:

kṛpā kṛpā kari gurū milāye ham pāhan sabadi gur tārey.[110]

Here, the idea of the *gradualness* of the way in which His *kṛpā* comes to us is suggested by the very opening *repetition* of the word. To put it more clearly, it is by graciously regulating our life-situations and attitudes by slow degrees that God ultimately opens our minds to the truth of His reality. And once we are blessed suchwise, we begin to see richer meaning in, and so to benefit better from, the *gurū's* words of spiritual wisdom, by the patient and discriminating study of which over a course of time we become quickened spiritually, in spite of our inertia (*pāhan*) and original insensitiveness to matters of the spirit; and are ultimately enabled to attain the goal of liberation.[111]

Indeed, the *kṛpā* of the Lord is no mere hypothesis. The saints see it at work in redeeming those who cannot shake off their depravity on their own; and they also experience it positively as beatitude:

Hari kṛpā nidhi patit udhāran.
koti janam dūkh kari pāio.
sukhi Nanak guri nām dṛdāio.[112]

The Lord is here addressed (by the fifth *gurū*, Arjan Dev ji) as an ocean of mercy, not merely formally, but sincerely, because in the last line the writer attributes his own present beatitude to the deepening of his commitment to the Name which, we have seen, is repeatedly said to be a mark of His *kṛpā.* In the same breath, the Lord is here referred to as the redeemer of the lowly. Putting the two ideas together, we get the thought that in realizing the infinite *kṛpā* of the Lord as the saviour of the fallen, the *gurū* is not leaving out his own case. Like anyone else, he too has been saved and put at peace with himself by His *kṛpā* received in the way of a deepening of faith in the Name. This at once gives us a hint as to how, unlike the discipline of philosophic discrimination or *jñānayoga,* the way of devotion or *bhaktiyoga* never alienates a man from his fellow-beings. On this path, indeed, one's progress in devotion or love of God is at once a growing and deepening sense of fellowship with His creatures.

The domain of the operation of *Harikṛpā* is immeasurable. It is said to protect our body and material possessions, nay, the very entirety of our mundane existence:

> *jīa prāṇ tanu dhanu rākhey*
> *Hari kirpā rākhi jindu.*
> *Nanak sagaley dokh utāriyanu.*
> *Prabhu pārbraham bakhsindu.*[113]

The Lord is here spoken of as *Pārabhrahma* or the supremely transcendent reality. Yet He is said to look after everything that belongs to us, and to redeem us from our defects, because He is ever forgiving. In other words, the surpassing quality of the Lord is to be understood not as a mere matter of height or altitude, but in terms of the boundless measure and sensitiveness with which He cares for us.

Our life itself is a gift of His *kṛpā.* Therefore, it must be properly lived, that is, in a spirit of devotion and gratitude to God:

> *jīo piṇḍu jini sājiyā kari kirpā ditīnu jiṇḍu.*[114]

The faith of the devotee in the Lord and in His *kṛpā* is so firm that it remains quite unruffled even when contradictory or conflicting attributes are used with reference to God. See, for instance, the following verse:

> *bhramto bhramto hāriyā anik bidhi kari torey.*
> *kahu Nanak kirpā bhaī sādh sangati nidhi morey.*
> *chintāmṇi karuṇāmaye dīndayāl pārbraham.*

jā ke simran sukhu bhaye.
akāl purakh agādhbodh.
sunat jaso koti agh khaye.
kirpānidhi prabh mayādhār.
Nanak Hari Hari nām laye.[115]

Here, a close look at the adjectives used in relation to God may suggest two questions to the reader:

(a) On the one hand, the *gurū* calls Him *agādhbodh,* that is, beyond comprehension; and, on the other hand, He is also said to be (or, we may add, He is *known to be*) *karuṇāmaye* etc. Does it not look a little inconsistent to say that God is *unknowable* and yet to suggest that we *know* Him to be '*karuṇāmaye*'? Let us see:

Consider *agādhbodh,* first. It only means *unfathomable by* human knowledge, but not wholly *unrelated to* our knowledge. We can never know Him *fully,* but we do know *something* about Him. The whole life of devotion would become impossible if the devotee is *not* somehow *convinced* that God is merciful.

Here, in passing, another point may be made. The truth that the *gurus* do know something definite about God is indicated not merely by the fact that they use specific adjectives in relation to Him, but by the very soulful quality of their entreaties to God. For how can a petition or request be sincere in address unless one has some definite idea of the nature of the person addressed?

To conclude, *agādhbodh* only means 'not *totally* knowable', not '*entirely unknowable*'. Therefore no contradiction is involved in ascribing the two attributes to Him.

(b) Again, the *gurū* speaks of God as *pārabrahma,* on the one hand, and as *kirpānidhi* on the other. Here, again, the two sides seem to clash. How can the Deity which is transcendent of all limits, and *so above characterization,* yet admit of description in terms of words like *kirpānidhi*? Here, too, however, we can find a way out if we only bear in mind the evidence of religious experience. As a *word, kirpānidhi* may well appear to be limited, for its meaning is definite; it certainly excludes, and so is limited by, its opposite, 'cruel' or '*tyrannical*'. But, the *fact* or the *truth* which the word *kirpānidhi* stands for is exhaustless. The genuine *bhaktas* declare that whenever they

> have prayed for His help sincerely, It has always come; and, as men of faith, they feel assured that it will ever keep coming. To sum up, *kirpānidhi,* as a word, is limited in meaning; but as a vital Reality, or as an experienced and never-failing source of *kṛpā,* '*kirpānidhi*' is unlimited (and so *pārabrahma*). Thus, in the verse being discussed, God is not said to be limited and unlimited from the same point of view; and so no contradiction is involved.

The Lord is the boundless plenitude of *Kṛpā.* This is a recurring refrain in *gurbāni.* To be assured of His protection the devotee has only to surrender himself to His care with the implicit faith that He is bound to extend the required help. It is this unruffled reliance on the exhaustless and ever sensitive *kṛpā* of the Lord that enables the devotee to shed all self-concern, and to let His Will sway his daily life in a spirit of joyous subservience:

āpu gaiyā ta āpahi bhaye.
kirpānidhān kī sarṇi paye.[116]

Considered in relation to God, the word *kṛpā-nidhān* signifies not merely a very *big* source of *kṛpā,* but a Reality with an infinite capacity for forgiveness and tolerance. The emphasis is qualitative. It is only under the wings of such a Lord that the devotee can put himself with absolute assurance.

Manmohan Singh's rendering, on the other hand, appears to involve a clear contradiction. He translates the verse in question thus: "When the ego is gone, then (the man becomes the Lord Himself), (and seeks the shelter of the treasure of mercy)". But, I venture to ask, once a man has become the Lord Himself, would it make sense to say that he (or now *He*) seeks the shelter of Divine mercy? Be that as it may, once a man becomes assured of His total protection, he begins to look on God as his only true friend, and as the kindly custodian of both his present and his future. Further, as a gift of His *kṛpā,* he gets devoted to the Name with such self-abandonment that his egoity is dissipated, and he comes to experience such a seamless oneness with God as may be seen in the merging of two kindred streams:

Satgurū bājhu na beli koi.
aithey othey rākhā prabhu soi.
Rām nāmu devey kari kirpā.
hau salaley salal milātā hai.[117]

2. Its pre-conditions

Such a benediction, however, is not a random happening. Though it cannot of course be *coerced* by any factor, *kṛpā* descends manifestly only when the Lord is *pleased* with the individual's eagerness to come closer to Him by way of faith, prayer and righteous living in general. The effort to pray for His grace may itself be regarded as a sign of *kṛpā*. Thus, see the following:

kṛpā karahu dīn ke dāte.
merā guṇ avguṇ na vichārahu koī.
māti kā kyā dhopae suāmī mānas kī gati ehī.[118]

The key words in this verse are the opening ones: '*kirpā karo dīn ke dāte*'; for if these words are not given the attention they deserve one would be tempted to think that the devotee is here invoking the *kṛpā* of the Lord simply on the basis of the *argument* that in so far as man, being merely a product of clay, can never be quite pure, his moral defects should not be allowed to stand in the way of being blessed with His *kṛpā*. Such an interpretation would be quite impersonal, which is generally not the character of a devotee's prayers. If, on the other hand, we pay due attention to the words in question, the full meaning would be that in so far as, as a clear illustration of the general truth that human clay can never be quite free from foibles, he (the devotee) too remains an incorrigible sinner—and in that sense '*dīn*'—there is no way open to him other than that of appealing to His *kṛpā*, with emphasis on the faith that He alone is the redeemer of the lowly. In other words, the key requirement here are the *devotee's personal realization of his own unworthiness and his faith in the abundant and non-calculative kṛpā of the Lord.*

This is why the devotee is seen to pine for His *kṛpā* in the manner of the bird *sārang*. As this bird can never be satisfied with anything other than the raindrops, in the same manner the writer-*gurū's* anguished need (for spiritual upliftment) can only be fulfilled by God's grace which is of surpassing value:

kṛpā jal dehi Nanak sāring kau hoyi jāte terey nāi vāsā.[119]

It is here implicit that only such a man is eligible to receive His grace as is desperately and consciously in need of it. The cry for grace is no mere asking. It is, so to say, an upwelling of one's entire being; and when it is answered by the descent of grace, one simply comes to abide in the name of God, in peace and utter tranquillity.

The pre-eminence of *kṛpā* is further heightened by marking the loftiness of the supreme purpose for which it may be invoked, that is, for the sake of being admitted, discernibly, to the shelter of His wings, or for '*śaraṇāgati*':

> *kari kirpā prabh rākhi lehu horu nāhi karan karen.*
> *Hari tudhu viṇu khāku rulnā kahiye kitthe vain.*[120]

Here the *gurū* seems to express the conviction that nothing else will serve the crowning purpose. Why should he direct his attention and petition, he asks himself, to any other possible source of help when he sees it clearly that being under His wings is the only thing that really matters, and that everything else is in truth worthless? The human resources of memory and understanding, on which we so often rely, do not always help:

> *surati mati nāhi chaturāi.*
> *kari kirpā prabhu lāvahu pāi.*[121]

In other words, that which makes for surrender to God is not merely the observance of any formal discipline, but the living realization in everyday life that one's own powers are not really enough to meet every challenge. This is, however, not to suggest that our embodied existence is quite without value. In fact, if the *gurū* (-writer) has faith in the possibility of realizing God in this very life, it is partly, but importantly, because the body itself is said to be helpful for attainment of the goal supreme:

> *kṛpā kṛpā kari piyāre gurṣabadi Harirasu pīje*
> *kāiyā nagaru hai nīko vichi saudū Hari rasu kīje.*[122]

The devotee is, however, grateful to God for His *Kṛpā* not only as implicit in the gift of the human body, but also as It works to make due provision for its maintenance:

> *sabhu kichhu bahuto bahutu upāiyā.*
> *kari kirpā prabhi āp rajāiyā.*[123]

Here, the devotee recognizes not merely the truth of His *kṛpā* as an operative force, but its *bounty*. Further, as in the verse to be cited presently, he also seems to be mindful of the fact *that we all depend on this bounty*. This, indeed, is why he prays to the Giver Supreme that this munificence which has so far been a relief to all those who have turned to Him, may continue to be available, so that all living creatures may be assured of the possibility of securing perfect contentment:

dāti karahu merey dātārā jīa junt sabhi dhrāpe jīo.[124]

As a conscious human experience, however, the *kṛpā* of the Lord can be invoked only when in an extremely difficult situation a man finds himself utterly ineffective on his own, and sees it clearly that He alone can relieve the present distress. Such a religious sense of humility, however, need not be merely episodic. It may even become a settled disposition because of unceasing love and admiration for those who are better dedicated to a life of God; and, as in the following, its expression may sometimes take the form of a *delicate self-withholding:*

kṛpā kṛpā kari dīn prabh saraṇī.
Hari jan meli piyāre.
Nanak dāsu kahatu hai hum
dāsan ke paṇihāre.[125]

The *gurū*, in this verse, begins with the prayer that he be straightway taken under the shelter of His wings. But the moment he does so, he (so to say) corrects himself by reflecting that it is perhaps a little too ambitious a request, and that it smacks of a little arrogance. So he quickly withdraws (or attenuates) his initial request and expresses satisfaction with the awareness that he is the servant of those who are devoted to God, and that he is thus able to cherish his love for, and dependence on God, say, from a distance, and therefore with due reverence. It can hardly be over-emphasized that religious truths are to be verified not in the neutral and merely inquisitive way of a philosopher, but in terms of personal experience. In the case of the former, the preparation that is required is only the assumption of a watchful, neutral attitude; but in the case of the latter, the necessary orientation consists in the cultivation of a deep yearning for God-realization:

amrit nām sunīje terā kirpā karahi tā
pīvā ās piāsi pir ke tāi jeo
chātriku bunderey.
kahu Nanak jīaḍā balihārī.
dehu darasu prabhu merey.[126]

The translocation of truth from the region of mere understanding to that of personal (or religious) realization becomes possible only by cultivating an intense desire for greater closeness to God. In this context a significant point to be noted is the nature of religious language as used by the practising men of religion. Such language is not merely meaningful but true; and it is *true* not merely in the sense that it corresponds with an objective reality, but in the subtle sense that, because of faith in God as the indwelling Reality (*antaryāmin*) whose eye misses nothing, whatever words a person uses should reflect his actual inner state at the moment. See, for instance, the following verse:

kari kirpā gobind prabh
prītam dīnānāth sunahu ardāsi.
kaṙu gahi lehu Nanak ke suāmī.
jīo piṇḍu sabhu tumari rāsi.[127]

Here, as the *gurū* addresses the Lord as *dīnānāth,* he actually looks upon himself as *dīn* or as a poor and lowly person, and on the Lord as really the Lord of the lowly. Bearing this in mind, the verse in question, may be interpreted thus:

> 'O Lord, my master, my beloved, be a little kind to listen to my humble prayer of entreaty (*dīnānāth sunahu ardās*). Hold me by Thy hand, my Lord; I want to entrust myself, body and soul, wholly to Thy care.'

Here, we may note, it is implicit faith that links the two parts of the situation projected in the verse: one, that He may kindly listen to the prayer being offered; and the other, that the devotee happily surrenders everything that is his to the care of the Lord. It is here important to mark that the *bhakta* does not wait for any gesture of acceptance on the part of the Lord before making his absolute surrender. The reason for this beautiful impatience is that the devotee is so convinced of the sensitive and responsive nature of God that the moment he is able to pray fervently he is assured of the fact that His prayer has been heard sympathetically; and it is on the strength of this assurance that he is able to make the supreme surrender. However, prayer and surrender to God are by no means easy. They call for *purity*; and our success in respect of the ability to acquire this excellence can be determined only by Him as an act of grace:

1. *kari kirpā prabhi āpanī.*
   Hari āp parakkhe.
2. *Nanak chalat na jāpanī*
   ko sakke na lakkhe.[128]

We have to spend a little time over this verse: first, because it seems to deliver some important points about *kṛpā*; and second, because we have to explain why we have thought it necessary to interpret it differently from the way it has been understood by the eminent translator, Manmohan Singh. This is how *he* puts it:

> 'Lord God Himself tests and assays those, unto whom He extends His mercy. Nanak, Lord's plays are not known; no one can understand them.'[129]

Such a rendering, it appears to me, does not really follow the text. In case the *order* of the words it comprises is given due attention, the first line of the *bāni* in question printed in two halves would appear to mean the following: 'as an act (or exercise) of His *kṛpā*, the Lord Himself assesses and determines the truth (or value) of . . .', *not*: 'the Lord Himself tests those whom He beslows His *kṛpā* on . . .' Further, the words '*chalat na jāpnī*' really mean 'No appearance (here) serves or works' (*chalat*). To translate these as: 'Lord's plays are not known' is clearly a loose attempt; it just misses the distinctive meaning of *chalat* which is 'serves' or 'works'. Finally, to translate the whole second line (also printed in two halves) as: 'Lord's plays are not *known*; no one can understand them' is simply to ignore the distinction between *chalat* and *lakkhe*, the one (I repeat) means 'serves'; and the other 'directly or truly see'. Now, because this has been the essential way of my interpreting the sacred texts all along, let us look at the verse in question *in its proper context*:

> *soī ubarai jaggey vichi je sachche rakkhe*
> *muhi ditthe tin ke jīviye Hari amrit chakkhe.*
> *kām, krodh, lobhu, mohi saṅgi sādha bhakkhe.*
> *kari kirpā prabhi āpaṇi Hari āp parakkhe.*
> *Nanak chalat na jāpanī ko sakey na lakkhe.*
> *Nanak soi dinaru suhāvaḍā jitu prabhu āvae chiti.*
> *jitu dini visarey Pārbrahamu phit bhaleri ruti.*

Thus viewed in relation to what precedes and follows them, the lines being discussed may be interpreted as follows:

They alone are able to rise above the trammels of the world who are sustained by the grace of the true Lord. And it is by orienting one's way of living on the model of such great men's lives that one is ultimately able to taste nectar (of spiritual realization or eternal life). Such an orientation of life means that we try to overcome lust, anger, greed and attachment by cultivating the company of saints. But, however hard we try in this matter, no mere impression (*jāpnī*)[130] of *ours* in respect of success will serve; and it *cannot* serve, for no human impression is able to hit the truth (*na lakkhe*). *The truth of our control over passions can be known only to God.* He alone can assess and confirm our success in achieving self-control, whereupon He may kindly grant us the freedom that we seek. (If it is thus the Lord Himself who helps us secure not only the *supreme* end of spiritual freedom but also the means thereto, it is only proper that we remember Him every moment of our lives). Nanak for one is steeped in the faith that only that moment is blessed when our mind dwells on Him, and that any number of days passed in forgetfulness of God is but accursed season.

This is, however, not to deny that human beings, on their part, *can* try their best to come up to Lord's exacting standards and to somehow become acceptable to Him. But what is just as important is the realization that the various moral and spiritual disciplines are, in themselves, quite incapable of taking us to God-realization; and that only by His *kṛpā* does He reveal Himself to us. The various disciplines serve only to make and keep us humble, and so eligible to receive and ready to acknowledge His grace:

jatan jatan anik upāv re tao miliye jau kirpāyī.
Prabhū daiyār kṛpār kṛpānidhi jan Nanak sant renāī.[131]

This humility, be it noted, does not merely come *after* the practice of the disciplines, as a separate event. It rather takes shape during their very practice, in so far as no real progress in this sphere is possible without humble reliance on His help, which is exactly why Nanak feels committed to the saints whose lives are models of faith in, and dependence on God:

kirpā kījai sā mati dījai āth pahari tudhu dhiāyi.
garab na kīje reṇu hovije tā gati jīare teri.
sabh ūpari Nanak kā thākuru mai teri ghaṇ cheri Rām.[132]

However, prayer for the conquest of egoity and for absolute surrender to Him bears fruit only when the devotee comes to acquire the ability to serve people in general, and not merely his own *gurū* or the saints of his choice. But this acquisition of humility too cannot be had by mere self-effort; it stands in need of His *kirpā*. And the explanation is here easy. The more actively a person tries on his own to overcome egoity, the greater will be the rise in his sense of self-importance as the agent of the effort. So the only way open to him is to invoke His *kṛpā,* in prayer, for the attainment of the following attitudes which necessarily conduce to humility: self-identification with the lowliest of the lowly (*jan dhuḍi saṅgi samāo*); happy acceptance of whatever worldly lot is granted to one by Him; utter dependence on the Lord for such daily needs as food and clothing (*jeo tū rākhahi teo rahā terā dittā painā khao*); and commitment to only that self-effort which consists in singing the glory of His Name in the company of saints:

kari kirpa prabhu āpaṇī
jan dhūḍī sang samāu
jeo tū rākhahi teu rahā.
terā dittā painā khāo.
udamu soi karai
Prabh mili sādhū guṇ gāo.[133]

Humility, upon this view, cannot be the direct target of any human effort; it arises only as the necessary reflex of faith, surrender and service.[134]

It is noteworthy that the *kṛpā* of the Lord, though it is said to be the source of the riches of the spirit like devotion, abiding blessedness, fearlessness and cessation of doubt (in respect of the true and the real), is not regarded as the source of *ordinary* personal excellences. The reason perhaps is that such excellences can be acquired by just following the example of the everyday living of one's own individual teacher. The *Gurbāni,* however, attaches due importance also to the *kṛpā* of the *gurū* and the saints, and not only to that of God:

gun pūjā giān dhiyān Nanak sagal ghāl
jisu kari kirpā satguru miley daiyāl.[135]
sant kṛpā te mitte moh bharam.
sādhren majan sabhi dharam.
sādh kṛpāl dayāl gobindu.
sādhā mahi ih hamrī jindu.

kirpā nidhi kirpāl dhiāvau
sādh sangi tā baithan pāvau.[136]

True, infinite *kṛpā* is an essential attribute of God; and, what is more, it is only as a result of the devout contemplation of His grace (*kṛpā*) that one is able to gain access to the company of saints. But it is no less true, we are here told, that self-purification attained through the self-effacing service of saints is also a key pre-requisite for obtaining God's *kṛpā*.

What is, however, here noteworthy is the implicit reason because of which the company of saints is given such importance. We cannot directly invoke His grace and secure release from attachment and doubt. The saints must help us by virtue of the example of their everyday living. The vanity of attachment, for instance, cannot become a living realization to us through the force of mere argument. What we need is the living example of someone who is free from attachment; and is, in addition, happy and serene because of this very freedom. God cannot be expected to set such an example, visibly; He is formless. The saints, on the other hand, are embodied beings. Their nearness to us is also an observable fact, and so is the quickening sight of unruffled repose in their being and behaviour because of the very non-attached and steadfast quality of their way of life. In any case, the *kṛpā* of the teacher is here spoken of as the source of all excellences,—that is, of qualities that relate not only to knowing and action, but to being and attitudes.

As for the *kṛpā* of the Lord, we cannot understand how it becomes available to us unless we resort to a devout contemplation of His nature. On the one hand, the Lord is unfathomable; His greatness is surpassing. Yet the devotee *knows* it for certain—because, we may add, as a matter of personal experience—that He is the ocean of mercy (and so possessed of a definite attribute too in an infinite measure), and is also the source to which we can turn for the cultivation of all excellences:

tū athāh ati bado suāmī kṛpā sindhu pūraṇ ratnāmī.
Nanak jāchaku Hari Hari nāmu māṇge.
mastaku āni dhario prabh pāgī.[137]

Here, however, a question seems natural. How exactly does the devotee know what, we have said, he does? The answer may be put thus. The devotee has been repeatedly saved (in crises) by the *kṛpā* of the Lord; and, what is more, it is his personal experience that through devotion to the Lord one is able to acquire all the moral excellences of character and the riches of the spirit. There is another bit of knowledge which seems to be directly implicit in the insistent and humble way in which the writer here prays for the gift of devotion in ever fuller measure. This is the knowledge, or the personal realization, that God is a Reality in being devoted to which one feels far more deeply satisfied than in the pursuit of other ends. Why otherwise should he pray for devotion with such self-effacing intensity?[138]

Another reason for which the saintly author invokes the *kṛpā* of the Lord is his intense desire to keep reciting the name uninterruptedly. This may be brought out as follows. As in the case of doing any other work single-mindedly, so for *kīrtan*, what is absolutely necessary is such a regulation of one's circumstances and resources that one may be able to free oneself from undue distractions. In the case of everyday work, the help of one's parents and friends may be needed and available. But, for the devotee, the Lord is the only dependable source of help. Therefore, in invoking the *kṛpā* of the Lord, the devotee is really seeking to provide for all the conditions that are required for uninterrupted devotion:

tū merā pitā tū hai merā mātā.
tū merey jīa prāṇ sukhdātā.
tū merā thākur hau dāsu terā.
tujh binu avaru nahin ko merā.
kari kirpā karahu prabh dāti.
tumri ustati karahu din rāti.[139]

The *bhakta* is fully aware of the fact that to become eligible for the conscious receipt of His *kṛpā*, recitation of the glories of the Lord, ceaseless contemplation of His name, and service of the saints, are all alike necessary; and that none of them can be secured without His grace:

Nanak ihu sanjamu prabhu kirpā pāiye.[140]

3. Marks/Consequences of Kirpā

In order to deserve the bounties of God's grace, the devotee has not only to seek the guidance of the right kind of *gurū*, but also to follow the life-style of the saints. All this, however, is itself made possible only by the *kṛpā* of God:

jin kau kṛpa karī sukhdāte tin sādhū charan lai ridey parāte.[141]
Harijī kṛpā karey jau apnī tau gur kai sabadi samāvahinge.[142]

What is emphasized in the above is not merely the grace (or *kṛpā*) of God but even that of the teacher. It is the latter, the grace of the *guṛū*, which is here said to facilitate devotion to God. The full truth is that whereas, on the one hand, the *kṛpā* of God is invoked for the sake of securing a true *gurū*, the latter's *kṛpā* is found to be just as necessary for the sake of deepening one's devotion to God:

ei jī rākhahu paij nām apune kī.
tujh hī sio bani āyī.
kari kirpā gur darasu dikhāvahu haumae sabadi jalāi.[143]
bhāi re gur kirpā te bhagati thākur kī.[144]

It may here be added that in so far as the true teacher is a God-intoxicated soul, there is no essential difference between the grace of God and that of the teacher, and that God's own *kṛpā* may be said to flow through the *gurū's* gracious life and personality. Another way in which His *kṛpā* may be said to be transmissible is as follows:

It is by virtue of the Lord's *kṛpā* that men become devotees; and then it is by gaining access to the company and guidance of these men of God that people in general benefit—from the Lord's *kṛpa*, if indirectly:

Hari kirpā te hoā Hari bhagati
Hari bhagat janā ke muhi ditthe.
jagat tāriyā sabhu lōḍiye.[145]

Indeed, on his initiation into a life of devotion, the *bhakta* too, as distinguished from his teacher, comes to realize the infinite potency of the redemptive power of Lord's *kṛpā*. On the one hand, His *kṛpā* frees the mind from its inherited attachment to objects of sense-indulgence, enabling the blessed individual to assume a death-like indifference to the sensuous in his everyday life; and, on the other hand, by providing him with the purifying company of saints, it ultimately makes him so righteous that he becomes acceptable to God:

manu bikhey hī mahi loojhi hai.
jā kau re kirpā karey jīvat
soyi mar sādh sangi māiyā tarey
Nanak so jan dari Hari sijjhi hai.[146]

An important idea here is that the *kṛpā* of the Lord is powerful enough to destroy the most deeply entrenched evil habits. *It not only descends from the heavens, but can also penetrate and purify the deepest recesses of the nether world of evil.* This is important; for, purity is essential. Longing for the vision of God arises only in a purified heart:

pathik piyās chit sarovar ātam jalu lain.
Hari daras prem jan Nanak kari kirpā prabh dain.[147]

This longing, it is said, is the thirst of a spiritual wayfarer which can be quenched only in the depths of self-realization. So, no trips to holy places in the outer world or pilgrimages are really necessary.

Kṛpā is said to be capable of cancelling our estrangement from God in spite of the inhibiting power of our misdeeds:

kirat karam ke bīchhuḍe kari kirpā melahu Rām.
chār kunt dah dis bhramey thak āīye prabh kī sām.[148]

It is also said to be the source of the truly transcendental bliss, that is, a happiness which is in no way affected by the dualities of the world, such as pain and pleasure, profit and loss, honour and dishonour:

kirpā te sukhu pāiyā sāche parthāi.
gur binu kinne na pāiyā ketī kahe kahāyee.[149]

It is a mark of the *kṛpā* of the Lord that one is able to establish oneself in, and also to radiate Truth:

pāi parah satgurū kae jini bharamu bidāriyā.
kari kirpā prabhu āpaṇī sachu sāji savāriyā.[150]

Again, the conscious acknowledgement of *kṛpā*—or of the Lord's protectiveness—at once makes a man so fearless that he remains undaunted even in the face of death:

sāchā sāhib kirpā karey so sevaku jam tae kaisā darey.[151]

It is hardly necessary to add that a man who is so fearless is not affected by the pains and sufferings of the world. A feeling of undividedness with Him is another possible consequence of the *kṛpā* of the Lord:

kirpā karke āpaṇī, āpe laye samae jīo.[152]

The devotee now feels saturated with an intense sense of His presence. This may bring about a total subdual of his egoity and a participation in the infinite glories of God even in this very embodied life:

kari kirpā gharu mahalu dikhāiyā.
Nanak haumai māri milāiyā.[153]

The point is further brought out with the help of a simile:

Hari jīo hau piru rāvai nāri.
tudhu bhāvani sohāgaṇī apṇī kirpā lehi savāri.[156]

The parallel here drawn is obvious. Just as, according to the Indian tradition, true womanhood is thought to be attained only when a lady comes under the protection of her husband, so the conscious sense of being sustained by the grace of God is considered as the highest gain that man can ever attain to. The feeling, we may note, is not merely one of utter security, but of the attainment of one's highest aspirations.

An indirect gift of Lord's *kṛpā* is refinement of one's speech. Further, the individual who is so blessed gains access to the company of saints, which creates and gradually develops in him sensitiveness to intimations from the Lord which may not take the form of human speech:

kari kirpā jo apunā kīno tā kī ūtam bāni.
sādh saṇgi Nanak nistariye jo rāte prabh nirvāṇī.[155]

The exalted quality of the *bāni* which is here said to be *uttam* is manifest most clearly in recitation of His Name. Be it noted, however, that persistence in such recitation depends not only on the *kṛpā* of the *gurū* and the Lord, but also on the fact that the true God, or God as really experienced and not as a mere concept, is ever new:

sachu Parmesaru nit navā.
gurkirpā te nit chavā.
prabh rakhvāle māyi bāp.
jāke simran nahi santāp.[156]

The meaning, here, simply is that as we persist in the life of faith and prayer we come to perceive ever newer truths about His nature, and also about His evermore various ways of helping us in different situations. This, in turn, enables us to contemplate God as a Being of infinite richness, and so to avoid the sickening of interest that may issue from focusing attention on a Reality of barren selfsameness.

This also partly explains why the ways of worshipping God are so many and various.[157] But, we are also told, the mystery of God's nature, or the highest expression of His *kṛpā*, becomes accessible only to him who, by regulating his life in the way of faith, prayer and righteous conduct, becomes aware of the command of God, and so at once feels impelled to live a life of growing purity.

A little more attention may here be given to the thought of identifying the will of God. Saints, in general, tell us that the will of God is revealed only to those who are steeped in genuine goodness, and that the moment the command of God is truly heard and identified, one cannot but set out on the righteous course of action implicit in the command in question. In other words, true knowledge of the mysterious essence of the (*kṛpā* of) Lord comes not at once from an isolated effort of the human will, but through general, voluntary and happy subservience to His Will as seen in the requirement for righteous living. God's *kṛpā* permits us to worship Him in diverse ways. But the highest form of His *kṛpā* is to invite, and hold us on to the single path of righteousness. Anyway, the essence of His *kṛpā* is known only to those who just give themselves up to the Will and protection of God:

tau main āiyā ṣaraṇi āiyā. bharose āiyā.
kirpā āiyā jeo bhāvey teo rākhahu
māragu gurahi paṭhāiyā.[158]

The development of faith in His Name as the mainstay of one's life is the supreme sign of having received His *kṛpā*:

satgurū miliye kirpā kīni amrit nāmu adhārā.[159]

Truly to realize His mercy (*kṛpā*), instead of merely talking about it, is at once to put oneself under His wings; and this, in turn, immediately cancels one's dependence on all other things:

Nanak saraṇi kṛpā nidhi sāgar binsio ān nihor.[160]

The devotee gets convinced that the Lord alone is the True Reality:

kari kirpā merā chitu lāiyā.
satgurū mo kao ek bujhāiya.[161]

This radical change in our sense of values enables us to free ourselves from wrong attachments. It is, however, not brought about by the Lord directly. Rather, because of His *kṛpā*, He just puts us in the company of saints; and it is this which makes for the change in question. Therefore, we may say, there is a certain humility or self-effacement about the way in which God bestows His *kṛpā* on us:

kari kirpā pārbraham suāmi ih bandhan chhutkārī.
būdat andh Nanak prabh kādhat sādh jan sangāri.[162]

This is commonly acknowledged that the *kṛpā* of the Lord will be available to us only if we are humble in our relation to Him. But *this* truth is not generally seen that humility itself is really a gift of the *kṛpā* of the Lord:

kari kirpā jis ke hirdey garībī vasāye.
Nanak ihā mukatu āge sukh pāve.[163]

In other words, we cannot acquire humility as the result of our own efforts; we can only receive it as a gift of His *kṛpā*, may be *by praying* for humility, and by concentrating on the deepening of our faith in Him.

Even the ability to carry out His orders and to serve Him is said to be the result of the *kṛpā* of the Lord Himself, and not of any effort on the part of man:

sāhibu hoi daiyālu kirpā karey tā sāyī kār karāisy.
so sevak sevā karey jisno hukamu manāisi.[164]

Here, however, a doubt arises. Are we not often commanded by men of religion themselves to actively obey the laws of God? If yes, how can we say, as is here done, that it is only the grace of God which enables us to serve Him? An answer to this question may perhaps be developed as follows:

At the purely moral level—that is, so long as we do not come to develop the insightful faith that it is He who regulates everything—it is certainly *we* who have to try to abide by the laws of God. But when, after years of religious living, we come to develop the vital faith that nothing happens except by His Will, we come to realize that even the ability to serve Him is a boon of His *kṛpā*. We may here visualize the author of the verse under review as putting a meaningful question to us. If, as is the common view of those who believe in Him, God alone is the regulator of *all* that happens, how can one's ability to serve Him be taken to fall beyond the scope of His governance?

However, according to the Sikh *gurus*, the greatest expression of His *kṛpā* is the gift of devotion to His Name. God's being is as such unfathomable. His Name is a kind of a foothold, so to say, which He Himself provides us for contemplation of His infinite Being. What is more, it is only by virtue of His *kṛpā* that we do not merely take His Name, but become devoted to its recitation in utter freedom from dependence on everything else. The Name is the only proper means for establishing a relationship with God. We can never *understand* Him, but we can certainly call out His Name even in moments of acute distress which, it is obvious, do not permit a leisurely, philosophic reflection on His nature:

gur gur karat sadā sukhu pāiyā.
deen daiyāl bhaye kirpālā apnā nāmu āpi japāiyā.[165]

Those who are thus able to make the merciful Lord their beloved gradually come to be blessed with an abiding and intense love of the Name of God:

jā kau bhaiyo kṛpāl bīthulā.
tini Hari Hari ajar jaran.[166]

Not only improvement in the quality of one's devotion, but the very excitation of a yearning for His *darśana* is a gift of His *kṛpā*.

kari kirpā līno kari apnī upji daras piyās.[167]

It is perhaps this yearning which has been spoken of as *jaran*. In any case, it is because of a keenly felt need for Him that God comes to nestle, as an 'object' of conscious experience, in the devotee's heart, making his devotion steadfast in the manner of an unflickering candle:

kirpā karahi gāvā prabhu soī.
Nām ratanu sabhu jag mahi loi.
gurmukhi vāni meethi lāgī.
antaru bigsai andinu liv lāgi.[168]

Quite a few fruits automatically result as a consequence of such steadfast devotion. Worldly affluence and prosperity are merely the outer marks of the dawn of His *kṛpā*:

jeo kirpā gobind bhai.
sukhu sampati Harināmi
phal pāye satguru milayi.[169]

The more important 'fruit' is self-effacement or conquest of egoity, which is indeed a significant achievement *where it occurs in the midst of outer affluence:*

teri sarṇi pūran sukh sāgar
kari kirpā devahu dān.
simari simari Nanak prabh jīvae
binasi jāi abhimān.[170]

What is more, the welfare of the devotee, both in this life and in the next, is henceforth ensured:

bhaiyo kṛpāl ṭhākur sevak kao savarae halat palāta.[171]

This, however, is not the complete meaning here. If we only take care to consider, as we should, the preceding verse:

sahaju anandu rakhiyo grih bhītari ūthi uāhū kao daureo,

as also the words that follow the ones being discussed, the full meaning which emerges is that God has ensured the devotee's welfare in the present and future lives by graciously granting him the gift of single-minded devotion or *ananyabhakti*. Such a man is not only a man of devotion, but also a man of widsom:

kahu Nanak kirpā bhayi bhagat giyānī soī.[172]

This, however, seems to be immediately open to two questions: First, does the Lord extend His *kṛpā* only to some, and not to all? Second, how can the single act of the descent of His *kṛpā* at once give one access to wisdom?

Luckily, questions such as these are not too difficult to answer. The first one may be answered by reflecting on what is meant by asking whether His *kṛpā extends* only to some people. If 'extends' is here taken to mean 'covers' or 'is available to', we must say: "No, His *Kṛpā* is (in principle) available to all; and it surely 'covers' everyone in the sense that God is solicitous about everybody's welfare." If, on the other hand, the word in question—that is, 'extends'—is taken in the sense, 'is consciously experienced', we will have to say: "yes, as such—that is, as a conscious experience—grace is available only to those who are men of faith, prayer and righteous conduct". And the moment we have said this, it becomes possible to answer the second question too. Here, we may visualize the *gurū* himself as providing the answer in terms of the following:

> 'I know in the light of my personal experience that *the moment* I experience His *kṛpā and consciously acknowledge it as such,* I feel humble and grateful to God; my devotion is deepened; and I come to 'see' it clearly that for everything indeed we depend on Him. The realization is at once the highest wisdom (or *jñāna*) because it comes as the consummation of spiritual enlightenment.'

In brief, the moment of a person's heartfelt acknowledgement of His grace is at once the moment also of a sudden deepening of *bhakti* in his heart, and the dawn in his mind of the truth that He alone is the ground of all that is or happens.

In the end, the supreme mark of the *kṛpā* of the Lord, which may also be called the central theme of the *Gurbani,* is its relation to human activity:

> *kari kirpā bhagati pragtaiyā.*
> *sant saṅgi mili Hari Hari japiyā.*
> *binasey ālas rogā jīo.*[173]

The meaning of these lines may be put thus:

> 'It is His *kṛpā* which has given *bhakti* a firm grip over my heart; and it is because of my being possessed by devotion that I am now able to recite His Name in the company of saints; and, finally, it is because of this association with the holy that my indolence has been cancelled. In other words, His grace is the real, if indirect, source of my ceaseless activity in the cause of righteousness.'

However, because the above interpretation of the verse cited differs from the meaning that is put on it by Mr. Manmohan Singh and Dr. Gopal Singh, it is necessary to *explain* why I interpret this verse in the way I have done. Both the commentators interpret *pragtāiyā* as 'acclaimed' or 'renowned'. But the natural meaning of the word is 'made manifest' or 'made to dawn'. My interpretation, however, admits of a further refinement. The second line of the verse speaks of *ālas rog.* Now, if *ālas* or indolence is a disease, it must be regarded as a state which persists or continues for a while. Further, hardly any other indolence, it appears, is so persistent as our recurring indifference in respect of a heartfelt recitation of His Name. So, the crux of the meaning of the whole verse could well be that it is the Lord's own *kṛpā,* manifest as a quickening of devotion in one's heart, which, through the reformative influence of the company of the holy, destroys the devotee's recurring indifference in respect of *Nāmasmaraṇa.*

Here, it, would perhaps be relevant to invite attention to the very formal or sonant character of the word, *pragtāiyā.* There is a suddenness in the very sound of the letter *pra.* So the word may be taken to suggest, instead of merely meaning, that the dawn of devotion in the *gurū's* (or the author's) heart is a sudden emergence because of the *kṛpā* of the Lord, rather than the end-product of any sustained effort on his own part. It may be added, by way of reinforcing the point I seek to make, that the Sikh *gurus* were not merely religious teachers, but sensitive musicians as well; and that, therefore, they could not have been indifferent to the very sound of the words that they picked for poetic treatment.

The common assumption is that God's vision is granted to the devotee only after *his heart* has become imbued with the love of the Lord. But here we are told that, as a sign of His *kṛpā, the Lord* may reveal Himself, so as to intensify devotion in the heart of the devotee:

kirpā pāye sahjāye darsāye ab
rātiyā gobind seo. sant sevi
prīti nāth rang lālan lāye.[174]

God's *kirpā,* however, is (I repeat) by no means confined to His devotees: it extends to all. This will become clear presently as we turn to a synonym of '*Kirpā*', namely, *Mihar.*[175]

4. *A synonym of Kirpā: Mihar*

As an attribute of God, *Mihar* is regarded as the life-giving elixir for all creatures:

miharvānu, miharvānu, sāhib merā miharvānu.
jīa sagal kau deyi dānu.[176]

However, a distinction is also suggested in *Gurbāni* between the operational range *and* the availability of His *mihar.* No doubt His *mihar* is all-pervasive; the very creation of the universe, we are told, is nothing but an expression of His *mihar*. But the way to actively avail of this source of every kind of happiness (*sabhi raṅgi māṇiyā*) lies only through the ceaseless recital of His Name:

simar Simar dātār sabhi raṅg māṇiyā.
pargatu bhaiyā sansāri mihar chhāvāṇiyā.[177]

The *mihar* or the grace of the Lord can redeem us in spite of our being riddled with numberless weaknesses. What is more, the passions which keep our hearts aflame and the conflicting desires which keep our minds divided can all be overcome, and the peace and unity of being restored, if we come to see the Will of God. We lose our peace and happiness only because, instead of following the Will of God (or the law of righteousness), we live by our own self-will which is controlled and driven by our instinctive impulses. But the ability to identify the Will of God is itself a result of His grace:

jetā samundu sāgaru nīri bhariyā tete auguṇ hamāre.
daiyā karahu kichhu mihar upāvahu dubde pathar tāre.
jīadā agani barābar tappe bhītar vagge kāti.
praṇvati Nanaku hukamu pachhāṇe sukh hovae din rātī.[178]

True enlistment in the service of God is also possible only as a result of His *mihar*:

jisno teri mihar su teri bandagi.[179]

The same may be said of the ceaseless remembrance of the Lord:

mihar karey je āpaṇī chasā na visre soi.[180]

A genuine devotee, of course, prays fervently for being allowed ever greater closeness to Him, but this prayer for his own (spiritual) interest is preceded by the clearly altruistic prayer that His grace or *mihar* may work for universal welfare, and that everybody's basic needs—for food and water, relief from pain and suffering, and for ultimate liberation—may all be met by the Lord Himself:

sabhe jīa samāli apanī mihar karu.
ann pāṇī muchu upae dukh dāladu bhanni taru.
ardāsi suṇī dātāri hoi sisati tharu.
levahu kanthi lagāi apdā sabh haru.
Nanak Nāmu dhiyāyi prabh kā safalu gharu.[181]

IV. AS COMPASSION AND REDRESS (DAYĀ, ANUGRAHA, PRASĀDA)

DAYĀ

1. Dayā in its two senses

Yet another synonym of grace, which is seen to punctuate the entire extent of *gurbāni*, is *dayā*. Ordinarily, *dayā* is regarded as the impulsion to relieve a person's distress, a melting of the heart, so to say, accompanied by the sweet pain of compassion. But in the extracts from *Gurbāni* that we propose to examine in this chapter, the term has been used in a broader sense too, that is, as *dayā* at work in the overt act of providing assistance or relief in various ways. See, for instance, the following:

āppai satgurū āpi Hari āppai meli milāi.
āpi daiyā kari melasī guru satgurū
pichhe pāi. sabh jagjīvan jagi
āp hai Nanak jalu jalahi samāī.[182]

Here, *dayā* is regarded as that quality of God which not only sustains the entire world, but is as much the benevolent impulse that enables a person to gain access to the right kind of teacher; facilitates not only his emancipation from suffering and impurity, but the deepening of his godward orientation; and also takes care of the everyday happenings in the world. In other words, man's realization of God is not an accidental coming together of two utterly diverse sides, but a re-union, so to say, of two spiritual realities which are originally akin, and the present separateness between which is but a passing estrangement. This alienation disappears when we somehow become actively and truly aware of His *dayā* as a force which sustains and permeates whatever is there, the awareness being at once a part realization of our destiny:

gurmukhiyā sohāgaṇī tin daiyā payī mani āyi
Satgurū vachanu ratanu hai jo manney su Hariras khāyi.
se vadbhāgī vad jāṇīahi jin Harirasi khādhā gurbhāī.
ihu Harirasi vaṇi triṇi sabhatu hai bhāghīn nahī khāyī.[183]

Here a phenomenological link of not a little beauty can perhaps be traced between the ideas envisaged in *vaṇitriṇi sabhatu hai* and

Sohāgaṇī. For an Indian lady, the living experience of being *sohāgaṇī* is at once a feeling of being constantly protected and enfolded by the husband's love. This idea of a kindly influence *encompassing* the position where a person is, is very likely to evoke the image of 'everywhere' (*vaṇitrini sabhatu hai*). But, it is clear, the awareness that God's love is omnipresent is not easy to attain. We have first to grow truly godward; and it is here that the words of the *satgurū* (or the *gurū* as a man of realization) are of infinite value. It is he, the 'realized' teacher, who awakens in us such an intense faith in God's love that we begin to feel nourished and sustained by it. This love, it is emphasized, is present everywhere; and those who do not consciously relish (*khāī*) this love are extremely unfortunate. What indeed can be a greater misfortune than the failure to realize that wherever we be, and whatever we may be doing, we are always under the wings of a benevolent Power!

Here, however, a powerful protest (made by Antony Flew)[184] must be taken note of. He visualizes the case of a child suffering from inoperable cancer of the throat; and says that though the (human) father and the doctor on duty may well appear to be visibly worried, the heavenly Father does not seem to show any signs of concern. How, then, is it proper to insist on *God's abiding love?* What more should happen to convince the man of faith, logically and rightly, that there *is nothing* like a loving and all-controlling heavenly Father? Now, it is true that it is not possible to explain, quite satisfactorily, why there is so much of obvious evil and suffering in the world if it is really ruled by an all-powerful and kindly God. But, on the other hand, there are numberless cases of people in distress whose prayers have been answered almost visibly, and their distress relieved. If it be protested that we never *see* any link between a prayer's being offered and its being granted, our answer would be that the link in question is provided by the man of prayer's faith, and that faith too may be regarded as a kind of discernment in so far as it enables a man to see how to hold on to the path of righteousness in the ups and downs of life. As for the case cited by Flew, though (we repeat) it is impossible to quite reconcile the occurrence of *any* suffering with God's alleged benevolence, could it not be fairly said that the unruffled efficiency with which the doctor is able to work in this trying situation, and the little peace that the parent can manage to get by growing a little prayerful, are themselves clear signs of some help from a God of Love who often chooses to work through human agents?

The distinctive meaning of *dayā*—that is, as an impulsion to relieve pain and suffering—is indeed quite manifest in the way God is conceived in *Gurbāni*. *He* is, it is held, supremely compassionate (*daiyāl*) because He is the giver not merely of our individual blessings such as good health or beauty, but of the very basic conditions of existence:

tū daiyāl dayāpati dātā kiyā ehi jant vīchāre.
mukat bandh sabhi tujhte hoe aisā ākh vakhāṇe.
gurmukhi hovai so mukati kahiye manmukh bandh vīchāre.
so jan mukatu jisu ek liv lāgī.
sadā rahae Hari nāle.[185]

Our actual state of life can, of course, be one of undiscriminating bondage *or* one of a watchful struggle for emancipation. But neither bondage nor emancipation is *inflicted* on us by him. Did He compel us, against our will, to turn to Him, it would not only relieve our devotion of sincerity, but, in a way, detract from His own limitless *liberality*. If he is the Giver (*dātā*) Supreme, it is (partly) because He gives us the freedom to remain bound, as much as the freedom to turn to Him.

Incidentally, I disagree with the interpretation of *kiā ehi jant vīchāre* as: 'what can these creatures be before or against Thee'[186], because such an interpretation would be quite out of tune with the words that follow. It is indeed commonly believed, says the writer, that bondage and liberation, which are the only two ways in which we can exist (hence the word *sabhi*), are alike impossible except in relation to (and without the consent of) God. *Daiyāl* as He is, He lets us enjoy a double freedom. If we choose to be *manmukh*, we are free to please ourselves; but then we shall remain bound. Alternatively, if we choose to become *gurmukh* and incessantly and exclusively devoted to God, we are equally free to do so. In neither respect are we coerced by Him into submission. But, whatever we are, free or bound, our mode of existence is possible only in relation to Him. Being directed to Him is liberation; being averse *to Him* is to be bound. The latter relation too is possible only because He permits it; therefore, it is only being away from Him, so to say, *not against* Him.

God as such, say the *gurus*, is infinite *dayā* or compassion:

tū sāhabu agam daiyāl hai vad dātā daṇā.
tudhu jevadu mai horu ko disi na āvayi
tū hai sughaḍu merey man bhāṇā.[187]

A close look at this verse encourages me to reflect as follows:

> The Lord is said to be the very embodiment of *dayā* (*daiyāl*) and the Greatest Giver (*vad dātā*), His surpassing greatness being manifest in the very quality of His *dayā* which is infinite, and not merely inscrutable (*agam*). Yet, the excellence in question is tempered with wisdom, because of which He is said to be *dāṇā* as well, and not *dātā* alone. But, it may be at once asked, if the *dayā* of the Lord is *tempered with* wisdom, how can it be said to be infinite? The infinite means that which is not limited by anything; and if His *dayā* is regulated—and so restricted—by wisdom, how can it be said to be infinite?

To objections of this kind, the *devotee's* answer could well be as follows:

> 'To check if one attribute of God is logically consistent with another is not my concern. That is the task of the *philosopher.* I go simply by the evidence of my experience; and my experience, as a devotee, warrants the faith—and, with the eye of faith, I see it clearly—that God is possessed of all these attributes, and that His Being, the plenum of all these attributes, *appears* quite shapely and attractive (*sughāḍu*) to me.'

In passing, it may here be pointed out that the way a devotee looks at the various attributes in the Being of God is that of aesthetic accord rather than that of logical consistency. How these two kinds of agreement differ is easy to see. Logically, or in respect of meaning, 'silence' and 'sound' are opposed to each other. But in the region of *music* silence is essential to the art, both as an encompassing lack of noise which facilitates proper listening, and as pauses between the various *svaras* (notes) which permit the mind of the listener, and not merely his ear, to get attuned with the ongoing form of music. The man of religion may like to take an example from everyday life. It is quite possible for a grown up son to see, after a little reflection, that in the very act of *denying* what he (the son) asks for, his father is acting *both* wisely and benevolently because if the liberty asked for were granted, it could perhaps be ultimately ruinous to his youthful years.

Be that as it may, the *gurus* are convinced that whatever glory his saints come to acquire in the world is traceable to the simple fact that He imbues their hearts with a little of (His own) *dayā*:

jai jaikār kīno sabh jag mahi daiyā jīan mahi pāiyo
kanthi lāi apuno dās rākhiyo tāti vāu na lāiyo.[188]

The Lord, it is added, keeps His slave close to His heart, so that he may remain untouched by passion (*tāti vāu na lāiyo*) and also ready to serve his fellow-beings, because of utter freedom from the heat of anger and jealousy. As for the way in which the Lord bestows His *dayā* on His devotees, it may be said to be quite humble. He, the compassionate (*daiyāl*), Himself condescends, or becomes *dīn* in a way, and makes Himself available to us:

Rām nāmu hai joti sabāi gurmukhi āpey alakh lakhāiyā.
Nanak deen dayāl bhaye hain bhagati bhāi Hari nām samaiyā.[189]

What this verse truly means may be put thus: 'The glory of the Name of the Lord permeates everything. But it is invisible to the naked eye (*alakh*). However, those who become truly directed towards God (*gurmukh*) are able to see this glory automatically (*āpey*). The moment the devotee gratefully realizes that it is God Himself who has condescended to grant him the love of the Name, he feels deeply touched by the feeling of devotion (*bhagat bhāi*) and loses himself in the Name of God'.

The Name is a priceless jewel, and the devotee is convinced that it is out of sheer compassion that the Lord has condescended to imbed His own Name in his heart, so that he does not have to depend on any alien source of help:

merey mani gupati hīru Hari rākhā.
dīn daiyāl milāiyo gurū sādhū
Gur miliye hīr parākhā.[190]

It seems to us that the key to the essential meaning of this verse is provided by the opening word *merey* which obviously signifies a personal or individual mode of utterance. This word could well have been replaced with others like *sabke* or *mānas.* If this has not yet been done, there must surely be a special reason for sticking to the word *merey.* This reason may be brought out by interpreting the verse as follows:

'God is not merely the overlord. He is also compassionate towards the lowly. Not only does He imbed His own Name in *my* heart, but, because of His intrinsic compassion, He also puts me in touch with *my* saintly *gurū,* who, in turn, in accordance with *my* individual aptitudes and limitations, has shown me the way to God in a special way, and has enabled me to realize the priceless worth of the jewel *in my own individual manner.*'

Looking at the matter from the side of God, it may be said that it is a *pre-eminent* mark of His *dayā* that He reveals His nature to a devotee by putting him in touch with a teacher who all along keeps an eye on the devotee's individual capacity, and finally reveals Himself to the devotee in such a way that the manner of self-revelation is quite in harmony with the limitations and character of the devotee in question.

In sum, we may say that it is the *dayā* of the Lord Himself which puts a man in touch with a true *gurū* and thereby enables him to relish the name of the Lord which makes for the life eternal:

Hari kā nāmu amrit Hari Hari Harey
so pāye jisu Rām piyāsī
Hari āpi daiyālu daiyā kari meley
jisu satgurū so janu Hari
Hari amrit nāmu chakhāsī.[191]

Within this overall working of the *dayā* of the Lord, however, a distinction is to be made between what the devotee owes to the teacher *and* what is traceable solely to the *dayā* of God. The teacher gives the devotee the first taste of the Name. His *dayā* is ever active (*sadā hoi*), and it is its intrinsic nature to extend to one and all *andarahu nirvairu.* This is so because he, the *gurū* 'sees' the presence of the same Brahman in one and all:

Satgurū dātā daiyāl hai jis no daiyā sadā hoi.
Satgurū andarahu nirvair hai sabhu dekhe iku soi.[192]

However, it is God alone who, by virtue of His *dayā,* enables the devotee to drink deep at the nectar of the Name. An allied expression of the Lord's *dayā* is His self-revelation in the form of the blissful relish of *Harikīrtan*:

Hari Hari Hari rasu āpu hai, āpey Harirasu hoi
āpi daiyā kari dekhsī gurmukhi amrit choi.[193]

This truth, however, is *seen* only by that person to whom—again because of His *dayā,* we are told—the nectar of the Love of God (or faith) has been already provided through the mouth of the teacher.

In other words, the original impulse to godward orientation, as well as its consummation as the relish ethereal, are both alike His own doings. However, not merely the joys of the spirit, but every kind of happiness is said to be due to His *dayā*:

tudhu bhāvai tā gāvān bāṇī.
tudhu bhāvai tā sachu samāṇī.
tudhu bhāvai tā satgur maiyā.
sarab sukhā prabh teri daiyā.
jo tudhu bhāvai so nirmal karmā.
jo tudhu bhāvai so sachu dharmā.
sarab nidhān guṇ tum hī pāsi.
tū sahibu sevak ardās.[194]

These lines may be translated as follows:

'I can sing the *bāni* or speak the truth only with Thy consent and help. Similarly, I can win the favour of my teacher only if it be Thy Will. Your *dayā* is indeed the source of all that is pleasing to the spirit (*sarabu sukh*). On the other hand, no action is good, and no way of living righteous, unless it meets Your approval. You are indeed the source and measure of all that is good. It is with this faith that I appeal to you for spiritual uplift, exactly as a servant depends on his master for his everyday living.'

2. Its marks/consequences

It is indeed for the exaltation of his spirit that the *bhakta* appeals to the *dayā* of the Lord. He knows that single-minded and self-effacing faith is not by itself enough for God-realization. However intense and exclusive be one's yearning for God, it will not bear fruit without the descent of His grace. Faith cannot bear fruit—that is, God cannot be realized—without His *dayā* which alone is the immediate cause of the vision of the Lord:

thākur charan suhāve Hari santan gāve.
āpu gavāiya sev kamāiyā guṇ rasi rasi gāve.
Ekahi āsā daras piyāsā ān na bhāve.
daiyā tumārī kiā junt vīchārī Nanak bali bali jāve.[195]

We may here remind ourselves that a man's realization of God is not the coming together of two quite separate entities. It is rather the mere undoing of a long estrangement of the human soul from God to whom it is originally related: (*miley chir vichhunniyā*); and this undoing is the surpassing gain which follows man's conquest of egoity (*Harilābh*):

Hari lābh pāiyā āpu mitāiyā miley
chiri vichhunniā
gahi bhujā līney daiyā kīney
prabhu ek agam apāro.
binvanti Nanak sadā nirmal
sachu sabadu ruṇjhunkāro.[196]

It hardly needs to be said that once a man's egoity is transcended, he cannot but look upon his own redemption as *God's* active doing. The writer's final submission (*binvanti*) is that those who keep themselves immersed in the music of the recitation of the word of the Lord ever remain pure, that is, free from egoity; and so, we may add, keep united with God.

Union with God is undoubtedly the consummation of man's destiny which, we are told, is made possible only by Lord's grace. But it is also equally true that the whole process, nay, every single step leading unto it—right from man's initiation into the good life—is made possible by nothing but His *dayā.* A very apt expression of this idea is to be found in the following verse:

dhādī karey pukār prabhū sunāisy.
andari dhīraki hoi pūrā pāisy.
jo dhuri likhiyā lekh se karam kamāisy.
jā hovai khasamu daiyāl ta mahalu gharu pāisy.
so prabhu merā ati vadā gurmukhi melāisy.[197]

The literal meaning here is, on the whole, clear; but it would look coherent only when a little phenomenological construction is done on the basis of what the words obviously mean. I propose to do this as follows, taking care to put the superadded meaning within brackets:

The minstrel addresses the Lord and the latter listens. (The fact that the minstrel utters a cry is, of course, observable; but the 'fact' that the Lord listens is just an insistence of the devotee's faith that He is present here and now). In other words, so far as the minstrel is concerned, the Lord alone is the audience; or his attention is focused on God alone. At the same time, he cannot help using words, specially those that serve as attributes of God. As words, these attributes of course have a *general* meaning. Yet their use in the present case does not distract the attention of the devotee from his own individual relation to God, because every attribute that he here ascribes to God strikes, if subduedly, a sympathetic chord in the region of his own past experience. In fact and in substance, the *pukār* in question is no isolated cry, but the soulful utterance of a person whose whole life has been an essay in devotion. It is this truth of faith, felt afresh, which accounts for the fact that in the very act of addressing the Lord the minstrel feels perfectly at peace with himself (or completed in the fulness of faith) and is thus able to realize his appointed destiny as a human being i.e., a living faith in His presence.

I have so far confined my attention to the first three lines of the present verse. But it is also important to see how these are related to the remaining two lines. The third line ends with the word *kamāisy* which may convey the (wrong) suggestion that the fulness and peace of faith we have spoken of are an achievement of the man who addresses the Lord. It is precisely this suggestion which the fourth line serves to cancel. It says: anyone on whom the Master takes pity will find his house transformed into a palace—because of the realized immanence of God. In other words, if we take the first four lines together, we get the idea that, though intense yearning for God is a necessary pre-condition for receiving a response from the (ever sensitive) Lord, it is by no means a *sufficient* condition or necessitating determinant of the descent of His Grace. What ultimately counts is the *dayā* of the Lord Himself. This is indeed what explains the fact that the writer finds himself in the company of those who are oriented towards God (*Gurmukh*).

An important expression of the *dayā* of the Lord, we have said, is the gift of the relish of devotion that He gives to the devotee. It is supremely important as a pathway to life eternal (*amrit Hari rasi*):

Hari Hari āp daiyā kari devey.
tā amrit Hari rasu chakhiye.[198]

However, the relish in question is not merely an isolated feeling attached to the act of uttering His Name, but is the dawn of the abiding sense that one is all along protected and sustained by the Name. The relish is at once a breath of abiding sustenance. To take His Name truly is at once to feel that one is secure under His wings:

Hari nāmu daiyā kari pāiya merey
Gobindā jan Nanaku saraṇi tumārī jio.[199]

The Gurbāni happily (*vāhu vāhu*) assures us that we have simply to turn our lives godward to receive the gift supreme, i.e., love of the Name. If our godward attitude abides, He will give us the gift in question because of His own *karam* or *dayā*. We have, of course, to prepare ourselves to receive the gift in question by becoming godward; but the gift is only received, not secured by us as a result of any effort on our part:

> *vāhu vāhu karmī pāiye āpi daiyā kari daiyī.*
> *Nanak vāhu vāhu gurmukhi pāiye andinu Nāmu layayī.*[200]

The word *pāiye* here means a grateful receipt and acknowledgement, not an achievement or acquisition. And once we have been able to get the gift, we have only to hold on to it in terms of, or by means of ceaseless recitation; and, then, all would be well with us.

In the eyes of a devotee the Lord is not only merciful, as He is commonly said to be, but has done him a special favour. God has not only blessed him with the love of *Hari kīrtan* but has impressed his heart with faith, and has given his bodily behaviour a clear godward turn:

> *Hari daiyāli dayā prabhi kīnī.*
> *merey mani tani mukh Hari boli.*
> *gurmukhi rangu bhaiyā ati gūḍā.*
> *Hari rung bhīni merī choli.*[201]

In other words, it is due to the *dayā* of the Lord that the whole being of the devotee is suffused with devotion to Him. This devotion, however, is not merely total; it is also immeasurably intense (*ati gūḍā*); and intimately personal. It would perhaps be proper if the words *bhīnī merī choli* are allowed to suggest that, because of his humility, the devotee blushes in the act of admitting his love for God, for though He is of course very close to his heart, God is a Reality of *surpassing* exaltation.

3. Pre-conditions of Dayā

Though it is (in principle) open to all alike, the *dayā* of the Lord involves, in its operation, a dynamic inter-relation between human effort and the *gurū's* teachings and his love for the pupil. From the human side, we could put the matter thus. Man has to begin with a comprehensive effort to purify himself; it includes purification of the body (through bathing etc.) and of the mind by letting it dwell on the Lord; by listening to *gurbāni*; and finally, by saturating himself with faith through repeated prayers of gratitude to God for granting him the gift of life:

Gur Satgur kā jo sikh akhāye
su bhalke uthi Harinām dhiāvai
udamu karey bhalke parbhāti Isnān karey
amritsar nāvey. updesi gurū Hari Hari japu jāpe.
sabhi kilbikh pāp dokhi lahi jāvey.
phiri chaḍey divasu gurbāni gāvey.
bahdiyā, uthadiyā Harinām dhiyāvey.
jo sāsi girāsi dhiyāye merā Hari Hari
so gurmukhi gurū mani bhāvey.
jis no daiyālu hovey mera suami.
tisu gursikhi guru updesu sunāvey.
jan Nanak dhūḍi maṅgey tisu
gursikh kī jo āp japey avrahu
Nāmu upāvey.[202]

It is only after thus becoming pure that a Sikh (disciple) is first able to win the affection of a teacher; and, then, through the *dayā* of the Lord as it operates through the teacher, to receive, and to profit from, the teacher's sermons that elevate the soul and take one closer to God.

However, it is no mere self-effort (*manhathi*) on the part of man, but utter self-surrender to the feet of the Lord which quickens His *dayā* for him and enables him to attain the cherished goal. Apart from external and internal purificatory actions, the devotee has also *to cultivate absolute trust in the protective power of God:*

hau gur sarnāi dhahi pavā kari daiyā meley prabhu soi.
manhathi kinai na pāiyā kari upāv thakei sabhu koi
sahaj siyāṇap kari rahey korey ruṅg na hoi
kūdi kapati kinai na pāiyo jo bījai khāvai soi.[203]

It must, however, be added that the cultivation in question is at once to become wedded to the good life, and an utter abdication of evil ways. Putting oneself under the wings of the Lord is at once a self-commitment to the life of righteousness, and this commitment is also a growing awareness of God:

guṇ main guṇī samāiyā

These words may also be taken to mean that in order to realize God, 'guṇī' *par excellence*, we do not have to go beyond the region of morality to some other utterly different region; and that God is to be realized only in (or as) the perfection of righteousness itself. Religious realization is no mere abdication, but only a consummation, of the life of morality. Perhaps a more intelligible way to interpret this line would be as follows:

> The end is God-realization. Its immediate cause is the quickening of the *dayā* of the Lord. This quickening can be brought about not by any merely human effort which is always liable to go astray, but by means of utter self-surrender to the protective power of the Lord. Such surrender, we may note, is no mere abdication of activity, but is itself the highest kind of effort, in so far as it implies ceaseless and ever-improving cultivation of righteousness in the course of daily living. Alternatively, adherence to the evil ways of the world can only make us ever more satanic, and can never lead us to God who is the goodness supreme.

Of righteous living, a quite important mark is the development of a balanced way of looking at the dualities of life—say, of pain and pleasure, success and failure—which torment us all. With the help of a *gurū* one comes to develop the faith that the Lord is the author of both life and death. This indeed is why one can easily see the truth that no bodily pain or suffering will remain for ever:

> *tujh hi kīyā jamṇā marṇā Gur te samajh paḍi kiyā darṇā.*
> *tū daiyāl daiyā kari dekhahi dukh daradu sarīrahu jāi hāi.*[204]

A protest, of course, may here be easily made. If the *dayā* of the Lord brings every suffering to an end, why should it not also cancel the sting of the pain so long as it lasts? To this our answer could be that the required attenuation can also be secured, provided the faith of the suffering person in God's love and protectiveness is absolute and utterly self-effacing.

As a result of such faith, *God reveals Himself* in the form of some very rare qualities or attitudes as they appear in the life and experience of the devotee or the man of deepening faith. Otherwise, however devoted he be, *a man as such* cannot arrive at God after, so to say, probing the mystery of God's excellences which are numberless and exhaustless. An example may be taken to illustrate the point I am seeking to make. If in a specially difficult situation one is somehow able to steady himself as a result of intense prayerfulness, that heightened fortitude may well appear to him, or rather to his eye of faith, *as God Himself*, and not merely as an influx of courage provided by Him.[205]

In purely human relations it *is* possible for a man to have faith in a fellow-being and yet not to *depend* on him, or to depend on him but minimally. In the case of man-God relation, however, to have faith in God is at once to depend on Him unreservedly. Indeed the ideal here is to depend on Him in all that one does, though, of course, not to the extent of abjuring self-effort. One has to depend on God, not as the visible initiator of an activity, but as the invisible impulse behind all righteous effort, and as the source of sustenance in difficult moments:

tu agam daiyāl daiyāpati dāta.
sabh daiyā dhāri rakhi lījey.
sarab jīā jagjīvan eko Nanak pratipāl karījey.[206]

In the above verse the *dayā* of the Lord is said to be immeasurable (*agam*) or infinite. This is, however, done not by way of a merely objective description of the nature of God, but with a view to steadying one's faith. Devout contemplation of the fathomless *dayā* of the Lord is at once a moment of felt steadiness in faith. The devotee feels assured by the faith that if the Lord can sustain the entire world and its creatures, why can't He be requested and expected to take him as well under His wing?

To *speak* of the Lord as *daiyāl* is one thing; to *acknowledge* Him as such on the basis of one's personal experience of His varying help in different situations, is quite another. It is the latter which makes God lovable:

merā prabhu rāṅg ghaṇey ati rūḍo
dīn daiyāl prītam manmohanu ati ras lāl saguḍo.[207]

Perhaps the beauty of the Lord is nothing but a reflex of the faith of the devotee; and this faith is freely nourished by his conviction that the Lord is the very embodiment of *dayā* towards the needy (*dīn daiyāl*). For such a devotee it is natural to come to attach surpassing importance to *dayā*; and to himself acquire pre-eminence (as a *bhakta*):

daiyā devatā khimā japmāli te maṇas pardhān.[208]

Here, it is suggested that he alone may be regarded as a man of superlative quality who (among other things) looks upon compassion as his deity. Now, if it be wondered as to how this could be taken to make sense, the answer would be that a *devatā* is one who gives, and that therefore *dayā*, because it is the very source of all heartfelt giving, may (as compassion) be also taken to be the source or giver of all excellences of the religious life. It is not for nothing that Tulsidas sang:

dayā dharma ko mūl hai pāp mūl abhimān.
Tulsī dayā na chhoḍiye, jab lagi ghat mein prāṇ.

It is not, however, easy to rightly avail of *dayā*. One has to use it in everyday life without expecting any return. Thus alone can a person get established in truth, self-control and devotion:

duādasi daiyā dānu kari jāṇe.
bāhari jāto bhitari āṇe.
baratī barat rahey nihkām.
ajapā jāpu japey mukhi Nām.
tīni bhavan mahi eko jāṇe.
sabhi suchi sanjam sāchu pachhāṇe.[209]

These lines from the *Ādi Granth* are not quite easy to follow, and I find it necessary to explain them:

> Love of the Name or faith in God may be regarded as the highest skill that is open to man. It is superior to all other worldly skills, first, because whereas every human skill is relative to but one field of activity, faith is an attitude with the help of which man can go ahead in all walks of life; and, secondly, because, whereas no human skill can be sure of accomplishing all that it seeks to do, faith is necessarily an attitude of infinite optimism. Situations, needs and problems in human life are infinitely diverse. But, quite independently of their individual character, they can all be successfully dealt with in the spirit of faith:

chhodi siyāṇap bahu chaturāyi
mun binu Hari nāvey jāi na kāyī.
dayādhārī Gobind gusāyi.
Hari Hari Nanak tek tikāī.[210]

That is why the Lord is earnestly requested to take pity on us, and to give us refuge under His wings in extremely difficult, even desperate situations which we cannot manage on our own, that is, as merely human beings:

main mūrakh mugadhu ūpari karahu daiyā.
tau sarṇāgati rahau paiyā.
kahatu Nanak sansār ke nihphal kāmā.
Gurprasādi ko pāvai nirmal nāmā.[211]

What the above verse visualizes may be put as follows:

> Our everyday actions are motivated by the need to gratify specific desires. We try to get things which meet our needs; but they do so only for a while, whereafter dissatisfaction arises anew. This endless cycle of gratification and recurring discontent cannot be broken by a man through his merely human efforts. There is nothing in the world the attainment of which could be said to provide abiding satisfaction to all the basic demands of our being. Perfect satisfaction can be had only by acquiring love of the Name through the grace of the teacher. The *gurū's* grace blesses the pupil with the relish of devotion. This relish, we may emphasize, is not a mere isolated feeling attached to the act of uttering His Name, but is the dawn of the abiding awareness that one is all along protected and sustained by the Name:
>
> *Harijanu daiyā kari pāiyā merey Gobindā*
> *jan Nanak saraṇi tumārī jīo.*[212]

This is why—of course, mainly as a result of the stimulus and help provided by the teacher—Nanak invokes the mercy of the Lord and wishes to be taken under His protection, if also for the purpose of a direct vision of the Lord:

rātey sāchi Harināmi nihālā.
daiyā karahu prabhu dīn daiyālā
tis binu avaru nahī mein koī.
jeo bhāvey teo rākhey soī.
Gur gopāl merey mun bhāye.
rahi na sakau darsan dekhey binu.
sahaji milau gurū meli milāye.[213]

And this, again, is why he invokes the *dayā* of the Lord with the same intensity of feeling as is seen to mark a lady's agonizing wait for her beloved husband whose arrival may be overdue:

āvahu daiyā karey jīo prītam ati piyārey.
kāmani binao karey jīo sachi sabadi sīgārey.[214]

However, perhaps the most soulful invocation of the *dayā* of the Lord takes place when it is needed to enable one to rise above such intractable weaknesses and attachments as are found to be formidable obstacles to one's progress in spiritual life:

vaisākh bhalā sākhā ves karey.
dhan dekhey Hari duari āvahu daiyā karey.
ghar āo duārey dutar tārey tudhu binu adhu na molo.[215]

It is generally believed that to pray is necessarily to pray for some empirical end. But, in *Gurbāni* prayer is not always so presented. Here, the devotee is often seen to pray only for the *dayā* of the Lord as required for ceaseless meditation on Him:

tumh karahu daiyā merey sānyī.
aisī mati dījai merey thākur
sadā sadā tudhu dhiyāyī.[215]

The Lord's *dayā* refines a man's sense of values infinitely, so that, like the swan, he finds it easy to pick only what is of value, ignoring things that are trivial:

baguley te phuni hansulā hovai je tu karahi daiyālā
praṇvati Nanaku dāsanidāsā daiyā karahu daiyālā.[217]

This verse also projects the idea that one who wishes to pray well for the *dayā* of the merciful Lord must be a man of utmost humility (*dāsanidāsā*). The devotee even goes to the extent of regarding himself as a mere insect, obviously in the spirit of intense humility, with a view to invoking the *dayā* of the Lord:

Hari ke jan satgur sat purakhā.
binau karau gur pāsi.
hum kīrey kiram satgur sarṇāyī.
kari daiyā nānu pargāsi.
merey mīt gurdev mokao Ram nām pargās.[218]

Here, however, a question may be put. Does not the attitude we have just emphasized bespeak extreme self-deprecation, as distinguished from healthy self-criticism? If yes, how can we approve of it? Here, our answer could be that the devotee belittles himself not in the benumbing isolation of bleak despair, but as a reflex of his clear awareness of, and pining for, the Name which illumines being (*Nām pargās*); and that what he here experiences as he utters the words of seeming self-deprecation is at once also, if in part, a feeling of elevation, for his mind remains focused on the glory of the Lord *as contrasted with which alone he, as merely human, appears to be a worm* in his own eyes. The total experience, I suggest, is a kind of tension between one's own realized littleness and the prospect of being uplifted into an intense love or vision of God, of course as a result of His *dayā*. The overall feel of the experience is, in fact, one of sublimity rather than of dark pessimism. One is here reminded of Hegel's view that the 'genuine' sublimity of Psalms in the Old Testament is rooted in two factors: a clear recognition of the nullity of objective fact, and a corresponding 'exaltation and extolment' of God.

Indeed, if we keep reminding ourselves of God's infinite value for us, our attitude towards God will at once be one of wonder, love, joy and hope. In other words, we shall be able to develop towards Him an ever better attitude of reverence which is so necessary for approaching a parent or teacher:

amul guṇ amul vāpār.
amul vāpāriye amul bhandār.
amul āvahi amul lai jāhi.
amul bhāe amul samāhi.
amul dharamu amul dīvanu.
amul tulu amul parvāṇu.
amul bakhsīs amul nīsanu.
amul karamu amul phurmaṇu.
amulo amul ākhiyā na jāi.
ākhi ākhi rahey livlāyī.[219]

It seems to me that the significance of this extract can be duly brought out by considering it in the light of two distinct questions. First, when there are so many other impressive and positive attributes of God, why has '*amulu*' or 'invaluable' been chosen here for special emphasis? Second, why is this word so often repeated? Both these questions may be answered by explaining that we are, in general, so deeply attached to the world that unless we *repeatedly* remind ourselves of His *surpassing* value (or invaluable quality) we cannot hope to replace our intense attachment for the world with love of God.

But one cannot even think of treading the path of devotion without the guidance of a realized *gurū*. However, recognition of the right kind of *gurū* is itself impossible without the *dayā* of the Lord:

tum daiyāl saraṇi pratipālak
mokau dījey dānu Hari hum jāchey.[220]

When an appropriate *gurū* has been found, one is required to develop, with his help, absolute dependence on recitation of His Name for salvation. Such dependence, however, cannot be cultivated without explicit praying for His *dayā*:

sālgrām bip pūji manāvahu.
sukṛt tulasī mālā.
Rām Nāmu japi bedā bāndhahu
daiyā karahu daiyālā.[221]

At the same time, one has also to give substance to this orientation towards God by means of righteous conduct; to look upon the service of the holy as worship of *sālgrām*; and to regard good actions themselves as *tulsīmālā*. Yet, be it remembered, every single action has to be performed in a spirit of utter humility, which is itself a precious gift of the Lord. In *gurbāni*, we may note, this gift is sought in the form of a prayer for the dust of the feet of those who have gained access to a *Satgurū*:

Hari daiyā dhāri prabhi benati Hari Hari chetāiyā.
jan Nanak munge dhūḍi tin jin Satgurū pāiyā.[222]

However, the ultimate purpose of such prayers is nothing but a direct realization of the glory of God (*darasu dikhāvahu*):

daiyā karahu Hari darasu dikhāvahu
merey mani tani loch ghaṇerī.[223]

Here, a point of some value can perhaps be made about what the word *tani* here contributes to the total meaning. Why did not the august writer, one may wonder, use the word *vichei* in place of *tani*? The substitution would not have damaged the rhythm of the line. The reason we are seeking perhaps is that the *loch* or yearning in question is not merely an intense desire, but a felt discomfort, the discomfort of a relative estrangement from some one who is deeply loved; and is therefore a discomfort which expresses itself in a visible restlessness of the body, such as (we may say) the quick changing of sides. In other words, *tani* has been used to convey the idea that the *loch* here spoken of is not merely a keen desire, but an anguish of the whole being.[224] The anguish, we may note, is by no means unwarranted. It arises as a reflex of the devotee's awareness that one has no one else to depend upon. This is why he turns to the Lord in a spirit of utmost surrender, and invokes His *dayā*, not merely generally, but for the express purpose of finding a way out of the deep darkness of ignorance or *māyā*:

daiyā māiyā kari prāṇpati merey
mohi anāth ṣaraṇi prabh tori.
andhkūp mahi hāth de rākhahu
kachhu siyāṇap ukati na mori.[225]

What is required of the devotee is undivided and unremitting devotion to God, which again is possible only when, in the varying circumstances of life His different forms or attributes are contemplated in accordance with the demands of the individual situation:

chit chitvahu Nārāyaṇ ek.
ek rūp jā ke raṅg anek.
Gopāl Dāmodar dīn daiyāl.
dukh bhanjan pūran kirpāl.
simari simari nāmu bārambār.
Nanak jea kā ihae ādhār.[226]

A very helpful conception of God is provided by the thought that He is perfect and gracious (*pūraṇ kirpāl*); and that He can fulfil all our needs and relieve us of all our suffering by means of the bounty of His grace. It is with this faith that the *gurbāni* emphasizes His Name repeatedly. When the devotee ultimately succeeds in realizing the Lord, he also comes to see it clearly that the 'realization' is not the mere perception or finding of an outer object, but is also utter self-surrender in love to a Reality acknowledged by the heart:

milu milu sakhi Hari kathā sunāiyā.
Satgurū daiyā karey prabhu meley.
mai tisu āge siru kati kati paiyā.[227]

Here, the words: *tisu āge siru kati kati pāiyā* are of course not to be taken literally, for an offering of one's own head may also be made in a moment of religious frenzy which can seldom, if ever, be justified. The real meaning is that the devotee has come to develop an indescribably intense and intimate love of God. Our suggestion is borne out by the words that follow the verse being discussed:

romi romi mani tani ik bedan
mai prabhu dekhe binu nīnd na paiyā.[228]

What is more, even in the verse in question itself (*milu milu sakhī*) there is an idea which seems to support our interpretation. The writer (-devotee) imagines himself as a lady and invites 'her' *sakhis* to participate in the recitation of the glories of the Lord. Now, the image of the gathering of *sakhis* at once conveys the idea of sharing intimate secrets of love, in relative isolation from the world at large. Indeed, to develop love of God is at once to be initiated into the mysterious inner world of spiritual life.

ANUGRAHA

The word *anugraha* may be translated as *kṛpā,* and also as *aniṣṭa nivāraṇa* (dissipation of ill luck). However, the *kṛpā* of the Lord, as also the cancellation of pain and suffering, alike manifest themselves in many ways. Therefore, the expressions of His *anugraha* too are said to be richly various. See, for instance, the following:

(a) [*dhāri anugraho apnā kari līno Rām.*]

(b) [*bhujā gahi kādhi līo.*]

(c) [*sādhū saṅg dīnā Rām.*]

(d) [*Hari arādhey sagal kalmal dukh jale.*]

(e) [*rasnā arādhey eku suāmi.*
Hari Nām mani tanu bhīnā.]

(f) [*Nanak jisno Hari milāye*
so sarab guṇ parbīnā.[229]]

Here, it is obvious, (a) and (e) speak of intense and single-minded devotion to the Lord as a mark of His *anugraha;* and (b) looks similarly upon the disentanglement from worldly attachments that results, in the main, from divine help. Access to the society of saints and collective adoration of God in their company (c) is yet another mark of His *anugraha;* and so is the destruction of evil and suffering (d). To conclude, it may be briefly said (f) that he who is made His own by the Lord (as a mark of His *anugraha*) comes to be blessed with every desirable quality, such as surpassing humility, absolute fearlessness and freedom from the basic human defects like desire, anger and wrong beliefs:

Nanak āpi anugraha kīā hum dāsani dāsā.[230]
karahu anugraha suāmī merey mun te kabahu na dāriyo.
sādhu dhūri lāyī mukhi mastaki kām krodh bikhu jārio.
sabh te nīch ātam kari mānao mun mahi ihu sukh dhārao.[231]
dhāri anugraha Pārbrahami rākhe bhrum ke khule kapāt.[232]

PARSĀD

Though *parsād* (or *prasāda*) is quite an important synonym of grace, the *gurbāni* does not freely relate it to God. It rather talks eloquently of the *parsād* of the teacher, or *gurparsād*, without taking care to specify whether the *gurū* meant is human or divine. Luckily, however, I have been able to find one or two direct references to *parsād of the Lord*. See the following, for instance:

jihu prasādi chhatīs amrit khāhi.
tisu thākur kau rakhu mun māhi.
jih prasādi sugandhat tani lāvahi . . . kamal bigāsu.[233]

Here, it is obvious, *parsād* is generally acknowledged as His help in restoring the devotee's tranquillity. According to this verse cited from the *gurbāni*, the suggestion is that the numerous worldly pleasures that we enjoy everyday are good only in so far as they remind us of the *parsād* of the benevolent God, from whom the various blessings flow. In other words, what makes these everyday comforts good for us *as spiritual beings* is the awareness that they are all alike expressions of the *parsād* of the Lord.

What is more, it is in virtue of His *parsād* that the devotee has come to be blessed with the nine forms of spiritual enrichments or devotion (*navdhā bhakti*). How, then, can he ever forget such a benevolent God?

jisu parsādi navai nidhi pāyi.
so prabhu mun te bisrat nāhi.[234]

This verse explains a signal way in which an awareness of the *parsād* of the Lord impresses the heart of the devotee indelibly with the image of the Lord. But here I make bold to disagree with the two recognized commentators in respect of one detail, Both of them interpret the words *navai nidhi* in the material sense. But I venture to disagree on the basis of the following argument:

In the text, words that immediately precede the ones in question are as follows:

jini kītā besurat te suratā.[235]

That is to say, God is the one who has transformed me from a quite undiscriminating creature to a *spiritually sensitive being.* This seems to support my interpretation; for, the *gurus* whose lives have been all along spiritual could not have attached great value to material riches as such.

V. THE GRACE OF GIVING (BAKHSĪS AND KARAM)

BAKHSĪS

1. What is Bakhsīs?

As used in relation *to God,* the word *bakhsīs* conveys three distinct ideas: first, the tangible quality of the relief given or obtained; second, its being in excess of what the receiver may be said to deserve by virtue of his merit; and, thirdly, the idea that he (the recipient) acknowledges the superior status of the giver *without any feeling of humiliation* as distinguished from humility.

The *gurbāni* seems to support what I have said. See, for instance, the following:

gung banārasi sifati tumārī nāvain ātamrāo.
Sachā nāvanu tā thīye jā ahinisi lāge bhāo.
ik lokī horu chhamichhari Brāhmaṇ vati pindu khāi.
Nanak pind bakhsīs kā kabahu nikhutasi nāhi.[236]

Quite unlike the generosity and alms-giving of man, the grace or *bakhsīs* of God is inexhaustible. Throughout this extract the merely human or the empirical is opposed to the spiritual or the divine. Our human pilgrimage consists in visiting holy rivers and places (*gung banāras*). But the pilgrimage of the soul consists in revelling in the contemplation of the glories of the Lord; and the true kind of bathing, it is suggested, is nothing but a ceaseless contemplation of the Lord, and the concomitant purification of the self. It is here essential to add that this heightening of the contrast between our everyday ways and the life of true religiousness serves a practical purpose. It enables us to avoid many ways of behaviour which are quite unnecessary, and thus to economize not only time and energy, but our other human resources.

Again, in so far as God is a truly sovereign or infinite power, His *bakhsīs* or bounty is illimitable. In a moment He can raise a lowly man to the status of a king; and, with equal suddenness, He can make a blind man see things clearly. What is more, so essential is giving (*bakhsīs*) to the Lord's nature that He does not keep an account of what He bestows on us. Nor should His ability to work miracles surprise us; for, He is the master, the creator of all that is there—of body, soul and consciousness:

khin mahi nīch kīt kau rāj.
pārbraham garīb nivāj.
jā kī dṛsti kachhu na āvai.
tisu talkāl dahdisi pragtāvae.
jā kau apnī karey bakhsīs.
tā kā lekhā na gaṇey jagdīs.
ghati ghati pūraṇ Braham pragās.
apnī baṇat āpi bāṇāyī.
Nanak jīvae dekhi badāyī.[237]

For *Gurbāni*—that is, from the generally religious point of view—the wondrous sense of the bounty and sovereignty of God is no source of discomfort; for here, as opposed to the region of philosophy, the purpose is not to *understand* the surpassing excellence of the Lord, but simply to revel in, and to feel nourished by, His inexhaustible power and glory.

Everyone is subject to the Will of God. It is this Will that decides as to who shall be granted release, and who is to be kept confined to the cycle of births and deaths. But when this truth comes to be 'seen' as a matter of personal realization (*bujhāi*), the very possibility of anyone's saying, *I am,* disappears. The moment of listening to the command of God is at once a total disappearance of self-assertiveness,[238] and so is an instantaneous setting out to obey the command in question. This is what makes the *hukamu* of the Lord so very different from that of a human master. A human command *can* be easily ignored. The *hukamu* or the command of God is either not heard; or if it is heard, it is necessarily obeyed:

iknā hukamī bakhsīs ik hukmī sadā bhavāiahi.
hukmai andar sabhu ko bāhari hukamu na koī.
Nanak hukmai je bujhae ta haumai kahae na koyi.[239]

The recognition of the supremacy of His Will is, however, not the only content of a devotee's consciousness. He also feels convinced that whoever receives any help or lift in life receives it really from Him alone. *Bakhsīs* or giving is, in fact, His essential nature; and, though very few are able to 'see' this truth, He keeps helping us all of His own free impulse:

sabhnā kā dātā eku hai āpe bakhas kareyī.
kahaṇā kichhu na jāvai jis bhāvae tisu deyi.
Nanak gurmukhi pāiye āpe jāṇe soyī.[240]

Yet we, ordinary humans, cannot say anything about the details of the way he regulates His giving. Nor can we say that He is *compelled* to give by some specific reason or circumstance. In the exercise of His *bakhsīs* He is indeed His own master; He helps those whom He wishes to help. But the genuineness of all these 'truths' cannot be realized on one's own, nor even with the assistance of a mere scholar. To get such knowledge we have to go to those who are genuinely godward (*Gurmukh*); for they have realized these truths themselves. In other words, the mystery of the *bakhas* of the Lord cannot be understood by any effort from the outside; it only *reveals itself* to those who have established a personal relationship with the Lord. It is, in the main, an individual realization.

2. *Pre-conditions, Marks/Consequences*

God, we are told, is (in principle) readily accessible. But He grants immediate relief only to those who consciously depend on Him *alone*:

ghalai āṇey āpi jisu nāhī dūjā mattey koi.
dhāhi usārey sāji jāṇey sabh soi.
Nāu Nanak Bakhsīs nadari karamu hoi.[241]

The devotee who seeks relief must feel convinced that it is He who creates, embellishes and destroys all that is there. Such a faith alone entitles him to the gift or *Bakhsīs* of the (love of the) Name. But such undivided faith is itself impossible of attainment without His *bakhsīs.* What is more, if He does not condescend to reveal Himself, no one can know Him; and if one becomes fond of reciting His Name, that attitude too is to be taken as a gift of the Lord Himself:

> *tū jāṇāihi tā koyī jāṇe.*
> *terā dīyā Nām vakhāṇe.*
> *tū achraju kudrati teri bismā.*
> *tudhu āpe kāranu āpe karnā.*
> *hukmai jamaṇu hukmai maraṇā.*
> *Nām terā mun tan ādhārī.*
> *Nanak dāsu bakhsīs tumārī.*[242]

It is obvious, however, that the thinker may here like to put a question. God's *bakhsīs* (we have seen) is first said to follow undivided faith; but this faith itself (in the above extract; see the second and the last two lines) is said to follow His *bakhsīs.* Is this not a clear case of arguing in a circle? On behalf of the *bhakta,* however, the following may be visualized as a rough answer:

> '*Argument* as such is not my business. What I treasure most is my devotion, my love of God; and my overriding concern is to keep my faith in Him steadfast. On the whole, I "see" it clearly that behind every good that I am capable of, it is really His grace which is at work. But this "seeing" is not yet perfected. There are occasions—as, for instance, the moment of thinking that the faith which *I* am required, or *have come,* to develop is the pre-condition of His *bakhsīs*—when I tend to stray from the norm of tracing *everything* good to His grace and assume a measure of (spurious) independence from Him; but, because of humility, I see the lapse at once, and so remind myself that faith which precedes *His grace* is itself one of *Its* many results. To conclude, what appears to be arguing in a circle is, in truth, but a moment of self-correction on the part of the humble devotee that I am. Should the questioning persist, and I be asked as to which of the two comes first, my humility which enables me to see the lapse *or* His grace, my unhesitating answer would be that this humility itself is,—for me, in my present state of being—a *Bakhsīs* of His; that I am not concerned with the question of a First Cause in the sense of that which *comes before* everything else in point of time; and that

presently, in so far as it alone is of help to me, I regard my faith in His *Bakhsīs* as the only thing of value.'

As a natural reflex of such faith, the devotee wishes to serve the lowliest of the lowly. He sees no good in trying to keep pace with those who are thought to be great by worldly standards. This is so not merely because he simply loves the lowly—may be, because no one else cares for them—but because he sees the working of His *Bakhsīs* (or the grace of providing for our needs) most clearly where the lowliest of the lowly are somehow able to manage to keep alive:

nīchā andarī nīchi jāti nīchī hun ati nīchu.
Nanak tin kae saṅgi sāthi vadiyān sio kiyā rīs.
jithai nīch samāliyani tithae nadari terī bakhsīs.[243]

This is, we may add, no mere imagining. It is a fact that he who works selflessly for the relief of the utterly destitute finds it easy to secure for them—though His grace, as the man of service is often seen to insist—financial and other kinds of assistance for them from the most unsuspected sources. The success of Mother Teresa's charitable institutions is a living illustration of the point.

The supreme gift or *Bakhsīs* of the Lord is nothing but the love of the Name. But though this love is unrivalled, and so singular in its value, in the economy of the good life it is not isolated, but is related to specific pre-conditions and after-effects:

dībānu hamāro tuhi ek.
sevā thārī gurahi tek.
anik jugati nahi pāiyā.
gur chākar lai lāiyā.
mārey punch bikhādhiyā.
gur kirpā te dal sādhiyā.
bakhsīs vajahu mili ek nām.
sūkh sahaj ānand visrām.[244]

The pre-conditions may be listed as follows: the faith that He alone is our true master; service of God under the guidance of a *satgurū*; the realization, which deepens faith, that our merely human devices are unavailing so far as the getting of the gift of the Name is concerned; and the conquest of the five principal impediments to spiritual progress, again with the help of the *gurū*. The necessary and immediate consequences of the gift of the Name are prosperity, restfulness, and a joy that is quite independent of the flux of individual circumstance.

KARAM

1. What is Karam?

Karam is another synonym of grace which is used in the *gurbāni*, sparingly no doubt, but always with the due measure of reverence. It is used to signify, I suggest, not the blind inexorableness of fate, but grace which may even be regarded as our common destiny.[245] Above all, it is spoken of as that attribute of God in virtue of which one is able to churn out and taste the nectar of His Name from within this very life of baneful sense-attachments:

sachchā saudā lābhu sadā khatiā nām apāru.
bikhi vichi amritu pragtiā karami piāvanhāru.
Nanak sachu salāhiye dhanu savāraṇhār.[246]

Here, I may add, the wondrous quality of the *karam* of the Lord is suggested not only by the meaning, but by the very sound of the word *pragatiyā.* The word does not mean a mere appearance, but the appearance of something *out of the ordinary*, or emergence; and the audile character of the opening *'pra'* also suggests a measure of suddenness or abruptness. Religious experience is indeed not merely opposed to, but gains its value from its contrast with, our everyday experience.

2. Consequences and Marks

The Love of the Name, in turn, enables us to overcome enslavement to the five senses. And it is then that we come to enjoy that unstruck, hence undivided, music (*anhad nād*), which is perhaps the melody of self-discipline:

dhuri karami pāiyā tudhu jin kau si nāmi Hari ke lāge.
kahey Nanaku tah sukhu hoā titu ghari anhad vāje.[247]

The ultimate result is man's deepening orientation towards God because of His *karam* manifested as the gift of the Name:

karami pavai nīsānu na challe chalāiyā.[248]

This godward orientation, however, does not make the devotee indifferent to his daily activities. He only comes to see it clearly that Truth is of pre-eminent value, and that everything else is but a secondary matter. However, what is still higher from the human point of view, is *conduct* based upon a perception of the basic truth: the truth that we are all mere different utensils, so to say, created by the one God, and that the same light shines in us all. The moment this truth is inwardly accepted, one ceases to oppose some men as intrinsically superior to others:

sachu orey sabhu ko ūpari sachu āchār.
sabhu ko ūchā ākhiye nīchu na dissey koi
ikne bhānde sājiye iku chānaṇu tih loi.
karami miley sachu pāiye dhur bakhasi na mittey koi.[249]

However, this perception of the primal truth cannot be had except through His grace. And conversely, the moment His grace descends on us we just cannot fail to perceive the truth in question. The perception of this truth is indeed the necessary and primal gift (*dhuri bakhas*) of His grace.

3. Pre.-conditions of Karam

Is the Lord's *karam* meant for one and all, or is it the privilege of a select few? Do we need to develop certain specific qualities for being eligible to receive it? Questions such as these have often been asked. Let us see what the *gurbāni* has to say in this regard:

Hari kī kīmati kin bidhi hoi.
Hari aparampār agam agocharu.
gur key sabadi miley janu koi.
gurmukhi kīmati jāṇey koi.
virley karam parāpati hoi.
ūchi bānī ūchā hoi.
gurmukhi Sabadi vakhāṇey koi.[250]

In the present verse, I suggest, the following line is to be interpreted with special care: *virley karami parāpāti hoi.* It cannot mean that His 'karam' is *meant* only for a few of us, for He is always solicitous about the good of one and all. The meaning can only be: 'rare indeed are those who are able to *acknowledge* His grace as such'. This has to be so, because only they can identify the receipt of His grace who are spiritually sensitive; and such sensitivity is admittedly a rare quality, because the moment a man acknowledges His grace in the truly godward (*gurmukh*) attitude, he becomes exalted above others (*ūchī vāṇi ūchā hoi*). The way I have here interpreted the line containing the word *karami* is also supported by the real meaning of the last line which runs thus: *gurmukhi sabadi vakhāṇe koi.* This line cannot be taken to mean that the *Gurbāni* is recited by, or is meant for only a few, because in fact there are numberless people who do it. The meaning can only be that very few people can recite *gurbāni* in the right spirit.

The *karami* of the Lord is considered as the *chintāmaṇi*, that is, the deliverer of the highest good that is relevant to man. This supreme end cannot be attained except through commitment to Truth or God. It is only as a sequel to this commitment that we can get His grace. But this commitment itself involves our entire personality. It requires that by controlling the mind (*mun*) we direct the five bodily senses to dráw sustenance from the same source, that is, Truth or God. In other words, we have first to control our senses as incidental to a deepening commitment to God. It is only then that we acquire the spiritual sensitiveness needed to identify His grace or *karam*:

> *binu sāche kiu chhūtiye Hari gun karami maṇī.*
> *āpi chhadāye chhūtiye vaddā āp dhaṇi.*
> *gurparsādī chhūtiye kirpā āpi kareyi.*
> *apṇe hathi vadāiyā jai bhāve tai deyi.*[251]

Another way, suggested by the *gurbāni*, to become eligible for the fulness of His grace (*pūrey karami kamāvā*) is selfless service (*sevā*) of the devotees of the Lord:

> *sevak jan kī sevā māṅgey.*
> *pūrey karami kamāvā.*
> *Nanak ki benanti suāmī*
> *terey jan dekhaṇu pāvā.*[252]

Why this alone is the way to the end in question will become clear as I proceed to translate the verse as follows:

> 'I worship the Name of the Lord. I sing Its glories. Indeed my heart is imbued with the love of the Name. But in so far as this devotion to the Lord *in thought and speech alone* is not enough, I must express and test my love of God in terms of action as well.

So, as a devotee or *sevak* of His, I pray for the privilege of serving the living devotees of God. My faith or love of God will be verified only when I am able to serve *His* devotees cheerfully, without keeping a count of the troubles that I may have to undergo in the process. Faith or love is verified only in enduring suffering for the sake of those whom we profess to love. Therefore, O my Lord, I pray that I may be enabled to meet some of your genuine devotees, so as to get a chance to serve them, and to thereby test my faith and to become eligible for the fulness of Thy grace.' (*pūrey karami kamāvā*). True contemplation, we are further told, is possible only *in* the fulness of His grace. His grace is *the matrix, and not merely a pre-condition* of the gift of God-contemplation:

sabhnā jīā kā sukhdātā pūrey karami dhiāiyā.[253]

Here, in interpreting *pūrey karami* I differ from Mr. Manmohan Singh and Dr. Gopal Singh. Both translate the words *pūrey karami* as 'perfect destiny'. On the other hand, I choose to interpret the words in question as 'in the fulness of Thy grace'. My argument is that my interpretation is warranted by the demand of the context. The two immediately preceding lines clearly say that all that a devotee can do is to serve the Lord and to keep praying to Him, and that the gift of proximity to Him can be granted by God alone:

sevak sevahi karahi ardāsi.
tū āpe meli bahālahi pāsi.[254]

However, though the devotee cannot claim His grace as a matter of right, he can certainly steady himself with the reassuring thought that, after all, it is He who can give peace and happiness *to all living creatures.* It is this image of *totality* evoked by the word *Sabnā* which demands self-completion in the thought that it is only in *the fulness of His grace* (*pūrey karami*) that God can be properly contemplated.

In order to be eligible for this fulness, and to secure a vision of God, one has to cultivate implicit faith in Him alone. We win His grace in proportion as we come to depend truly on the Lord:

jā kai Rām ko balu hoi.
sagal manorath pūran tāhū ke.
dūkh na biāpai koi.
jo janu bhagatu dāsu niju
prabh kā suṇi jīvān tisu soi.

udamu karau darsanu pekhan ko.
karami parāpati hoi.[255]

The desires of a man who depends on God, more than on anything else, all get duly fulfilled. (This is so, I may add, because one who really depends on God, who is the ultimate Good, cannot cherish any ignoble desire; and because the very having of a righteous desire is at once a coming closer to God as the Goodness Supreme.) Precisely for the same reason, such a person will not be subjected to any felt unhappiness. Unfortunate *happenings* will not of course disappear from his life; but in so far as he is devoted to God—and committed to the faith that whatever happens is but an expression of His Will—even the seemingly unhappy happenings will not ruffle his *inner* beatitude. The writer-devotee attaches so much importance to a man's dependence on God that he can manage to live even by the accounts of the goodness of those who are devoted to God.

4. *Karam as the destiny of Grace*

For the man of implicit faith, we may finally note, a subtle way is open to interpret *karam*—a way which not only provides for the two meanings of the word, that is, 'destiny' and 'grace'—but makes the doctrine of destiny look relatively inoffensive. A true devotee, indeed, tends to believe that grace is an essential attribute or attitude of God in relation to men; that it is, so to say, inherent and cannot be withdrawn; and that *his destiny is nothing but governance by his grace alone.* This is obviously a very different conception of destiny from the one which looks upon it as a mere imposition on man by an alien and almighty power; but, I believe it is very much there in the Sikh scriptures.

VI. AS SATGURŪ'S BENEVOLENCE

1. *Gurparsād*

In *gurbāni* the importance of *gurparsād* (or *gurū's* grace) is obvious. For, in the *mūl mantra* itself with which the *Ādi Granth* opens, it is clearly said that God is known with the help of *prasād* of the teacher. Throughout this great work, indeed, the *prasād* of the teacher is regarded as an important pre-requisite for obtaining a vision of God. It is this, we are told, which sets the individual on the road to the consummation of his destiny as union with God.

Let us now try to trace the various steps of the process, each of which is alike said to depend on the *prasād* of the *gurū*. The very first step on the way to God—that is, control of the craving for sense-indulgence—needs the *prasād* of the teacher:

gurparsādi bikhiā par harey mun kī vāsanā mun te tarey.[256]

In case I am interpreting these lines correctly, the view here expressed may well be said to be different from the *Gītā* view that *rasa* or craving for sense-objects disappears only when one comes to 'see' God.

The immediate gain, however, which issues from the *prasād* of the teacher is intense devotion. It is because of the overpowering spell of this gift that things of the world lose their charm in the pupil's eyes. He relinquishes all desire for them, and so rises above quite a few occasions that prompt one into anger and boastfulness. Anger generally arises when there is a delay in the getting of things we desire; and conceit is the self-conscious feeling of possessing those things in abundance which are objects of our desire, and which we therefore value:

gurparsādi Hari rung māṇu.
binsae kām, krodh ahankār.
Nanak gurmukhi utrahi pāri.[257]

Again, it is as a result of the *gurū's prasād*, we are told, that one is able to transcend the (illusory) spectacle of plurality, and to incur the vision which sees nothing but God all around:

gurparsādi durmati khoi.
jah dekhā tah eko soī.[256]

However, it becomes easier to avail of the *gurū's* assistance, and to cross the sea of *saṃsāra*, if one is already a little non-attached to the world. This is borne out by Kabir's utterance that (only) his body dwells in the world, and that therefore he has been easily able to secure liberation with the help of the grace of the teacher:

ih basatī tā basat sarīrā.
gurparsādi sahaji tarey kabīrā.[259]

However, renunciation—and the discrimination that it involves and demands—can be fully secured only by means of the *gurū's prasādi.*

The very words of the *gurū* bespeak his concern for us. For instance, he emphasizes the truth that commitment to the one Lord is the surest way to genuine renunciation; and that those, on the other hand, who go on performing actions without caring for this truth—that is, without dedicating all their actions to God—are doomed to dwell in darkness forever:

gurparsādi būjhi ley tau hoi niberā.
ghari ghari nāmu niranjanā so thākur merā.
binu gur ṣabad na chhūtiye dekhahu bīchārā.
jo lakh karam kamāvahi binu gur andhiārā.[260]

However, the value of the devotee's own effort is not to be underestimated. The truth indeed is that direct realization of the whole truth can be had only with the *prasād* of the teacher as coupled with incessent striving on the part of the devotee:

sodhat sodhat sodhat sījhiā gurparsādi tatu sabhu būjhiā.[261]

Once a devotee has been blessed with *gurparsād*, he becomes ceaselessly watchful in respect of avoiding falsehood and impurity. The vigilance, however, is no strain on him, for it is only the natural concomitant of the abidance of the purificatory Name of the Lord in his heart:

kūdu kusatu tinā mailu na lāge.
gurparsādi andinu jāge.
nirmal nāmu vasai ghat bhītari
jotī joti milāvaṇiā.[262]

The grace of the teacher also serves to hasten surrender to the Lord by inducing humility and purity in the devotee:

gurparsādi se nar ubrey ji Hari sarṇāgati bhaji paiyā.[263]

As a result of these helpful attitudes, and also because of the unremitting *prasād* of the teacher, one abides constantly in God-consciousness, and thereby attains both illumination and peace:

gurparsādi sahaji gharu pāiyā mitiyā andherā chandu chadiyā.[264]

The peace that results from *gurparsād* is no mere passing suspension of turbulence; it is an abiding peace which sustains one in both life and death:

sansār sāgaru jini upāio ṣarani prabh kī gahī.
gurparsādi prabhu arādhey jamkankaru kichhu na kahī.[265]

This becomes quite clear when we attend to the details of the text, specially to the thought that the Lord is the creator of the world-ocean. The God who is adored by a man who has been blessed with the *prasād* of the teacher is here spoken of in a particular way: that is, as the creator, I repeat, of the world-ocean. The devotee who turns to such a God will naturally seek shelter, quite hopefully, from the tumult and infinite complexity of life. And, as a result of his godward orientation, what he secures is not merely peace in the midst of the troubles of life, but even the unsought ability to remain unaffected by the fear and mystery of death.

It is in two main ways that *gurparsād* conduces to abiding peace and happiness. On the one hand, it encourages righteous conduct; and on the other, exclusive commitment to Truth or God:

gurparsādi sadā sukhu pāiye.
sachu karani sachī liv lāye.
Satgurū sevaki se vadbhāgī
haume māri sāchi liv lāgī.[266]

Righteous conduct purifies the mind. Purity of mind is at once tranquillity of spirit. It is because of this that *gurparsād* may be said to make for (the essential component of) every kind of happiness:

gurparsādi bhaiyo manu nirmalu.
sarab sukhā sukh pāiau.[267]

A man who is made pure, and so sensitive to the truths of the spirit, by the training of the *gurū*, attains to spiritual tranquillity also because it is the nature of the Lord Himself (as *sukhdātā*) to shower spiritual bliss on those who are ready to receive it. It is the considered view of *gurbāni* that the *prasād* of the teacher can facilitate the *self-advent* of the beloved Lord in the heart of the devotee; and that it is this which finally quenches the fire of man's chronically incomplete satisfaction with all that is there in the world:

sabh mahi jīa jīu hai soī.
ghati ghati rahiyā samāi
apnā kāju savārahu āpe sukhdāte gosāin.
gurparsādi ghar hī piru pāiyā.
tau Nanak tapati bujhāī.[268]

The humble awareness that it is the impulse of His own Love for us which really produces devotion in us is itself a reflex of the spiritual refinement that we gain as a result of the *prasād* of the teacher:

tinhā piyārā Rāmu jo prabh bhāṇiyā.
gurparsādi akathu Nanak vakhāṇiyā.[269]

A man who is so steeped in tranquillity, goodness and devotion to God is naturally not at all disturbed by pain and suffering. What is more, in so far as his heart is now the exclusive locus of love of God, all his desires that seek fulfilment relate to enrichment of the spirit, and not to any worldly object. This is why whatever he (now) intends or expects is turned into reality, because his ceaseless meditation on God cannot but lead to growing attainment of riches of the spirit:

jo chāhau soi soi pāvau āsā mansā pūrau japi prabh kau.
gurparsādi Nanak mani vasiā.
dūkh na kabahu jhūrau bujhi prabh kau.[270]

The *gurū's* grace makes for detachment in respect of the world. Indeed, nothing is as surely conducive to discriminating renunciation as the *prasād* of the teacher. It is this, more than anything else, that enables one to see through the falsity of the irresistible charms of the world which are so rich and various:

jag mohini hum tiāgi gavāyi nirgunu milio vajī vādhāyi.
aisee sundari mun kau mohe vāti ghāti gṛhi ban ban johai.
tun mun lāgai hoi kai mīthi gurparsādi main khoti dīthi.[271]

Such a person is a true *sanyāsi. Sanyās* is the desertion not of one's place of residence, but of one's worldly attachments, in favour of an undivided love of the Lord. It is this attitude of consummate faith which is made possible by the *prasād* of the teacher:

aihu jogu na hovai jogi
ji kutumb chhodi parbhavanu karahi.
gṛh sarīr mahi Hari Hari nāmu
gur parsādī apṇā Hari prabhu lahahi.[272]

A man who has renounced the world in this sense daily grows spiritually richer by keeping his mind fixed on the Lord. On the other hand, one who is not so directed towards the teacher and the Lord, keeps shuttling through the cycle of births and deaths without acquiring any abiding spiritual value:

> *gurparsādī mun jiṇai Hari seṭi liv lāyi.*
> *Nanak gurmukhi sachu kamāvai.*
> *munmukh āvai jāī.*[273]

One who is blessed with *gurparsād* may be said to be spiritually reborn. He is nouṛished not so much by the common eatables as by spiritual experiences which quicken and exalt his entire being:

> *gurparsadī . . . acharu charey vivek budhi pāye.*[274]

The highest spiritual state (*parampad*) is very far removed from the condition of the man who is riddled with common moral weaknesses. On the other hand, if a man somehow arrives at the state in question, he therewith incurs as radical a change in his personality as the sudden greening of a piece of dead wood. But the miracle cannot happen except through the *prasād* of the teacher:

> *merey mādhau jī sat saṅgati miley si tariā.*
> *gurparsādi param padu pāiya sūke kāsat hariyā.*[275]

An obvious and direct gift of *gurparsād* is, we have seen, devotion to His Name. One who happens to receive this gift secures such a foothold in the contemplation of God that he turns to Him alone for all his needs. On the other hand, those who remain attached to bodily appetites (*udar bharan*) cannot help assuming various roles in respect of *different sources of help* for the satisfaction of their needs of different kinds. To illustrate, the average man may have to turn to a lady to satisfy his need for love; and to a doctor for relief from sickness. In the former case he becomes a lover; and in the latter, a patient. But one who has been blessed with the love of the Name has to live only as a devotee of his Lord, and every kind of relief that he may seek would be secured by this singleness of *bhakti*:

> *gurparsādi Hari prabh jāche aisee Nām vadāī.*
> *ayijī bahute bhekh karahi bhikhiyā kau kete udaru bharan ke tāi.*[276]

But though it is certainly a source of surpassing bliss, there is nothing unnatural about attunement with the Name. It is, in a way, just as necessary and natural as the act of waking after a spell of sleep. Commitment to the Name which the *gurū's* grace brings about is not only not opposed, but may well be regarded as a natural sequel, to the spiritual torpor of many births:

gurparsādi nāmi mun lāgā.
janam janam kā soiyā jāgā.[277]

When the Name becomes the guiding principle of life, the devotee begins not only to relish it evermore, but, partly because of the *gurū's* insistence on self-examination, also lets it serve as a revealer of his own failings. As a result, he is emptied of conceit and egoity, and so surrenders himself more fully to the Name which comes to settle in his heart overpoweringly. Henceforth, he begins to live by It, and discovers the riches It embraces. This is why he begins to sing the glories of the Name. Why should he squander his life, he asks himself, in dealing with the many doctrines which merely oppose each other and take him nowhere?

gurparsādi lāge nām suādi.
kāhe janamu gavāvahu vairi vādi.[278]

Once the devotee tastes this nectar, he merges into Truth and dwells lovingly (*rātī*) in the contemplation of the relish of His Name:

rasanā Harirasu chākhiā sahaji subhāe.
gurkirpā te sāch samāe.
sāche rātī gurṣabadu vīchār.
amrit pīvai nirmal dhār.[279]

It is important to see what the word *chākhiā* means as used in the above verse. Tasting can be of two kinds. It may either be just a momentary pecking at what is tasted (which is called *chakhnā* in everyday discourse), or a luxuriance in the taste of what is tasted, which is called *svād lenā* in everyday talk. The second kind of tasting is an act of getting imbued with, or of at least opening oneself to, the relish of the object. *This* is, I venture to suggest, the meaning which is intended here, and I say so because of quite a few other images in this verse. It speaks, for instance, of: merging oneself into Truth, which is surely not a momentary act, instantaneously accomplished; *dwelling lovingly* in the contemplation of the relish of the Name of the Lord; and, finally, *drinking deeply* at the pure and limpid flow of nectar, not of merely tasting just a drop of it.

Indeed, the truth of a man's love of the Name is borne out only when he is able to use recitation of His Name as his primary tool for dealing with the varying situations of life. It is only then—that is to say, only when his love of God has become so undivided that he gives no thought to his own self at all—that even the minimal sense of being apart from God is transcended, and he becomes one with God:

gurparsādi sadā manu rātā.
simari simari jīvahi jan terey.
ekankāri samāyī hai.[280]

This identification is such a glorious vision of the form of the Lord, and such a compelling realization of Him as the source of all values, that unless they are all somehow related to the Name of the Lord, the riches and charms of the world appear to be airy and insubstantial:

aisī pekhī netra mahi pūre gurparsādi.
rāj milakh dhan jobanā nāmai binu bādi.[281]

Here, however, a point of detail must be clarified. Why have we found it necessary to supplement the idea of the vision of the Form of God with the other idea that He is the source of all values? The ready answer is that the immediate experience of God is not the seeing of a mere *object,* but an experience which perfectly satisfies our demand for—and climaxes our pursuit of—Truth, Beauty and Goodness; and the vision sublime or His *darśana* naturally impels one into a joyous singing of His glories:

gurparsādi kinai vakhiānī.
sachu sachu sachu sachu kīnā.
koti madhe kinai virlai chīnā
bhalā bhalā bhalā terā rūp.
ati sunder apār anūp.[282]

But such a vision, we are reminded, comes only to those rare persons who are somehow able to win the *prasād* of the true teacher. God as such is beyond the loftiest human *conception* of truth and beauty. This is precisely why the *gurbāni* is compelled to resort to a plurality of terms like *sat, sachu* and *bhalā.* Yet, we are told, such is the singular power of the teacher's grace that one is thereby enabled to relish and acclaim, though not to comprehend, the reality and greatness of

God; and, in any case, one can surely contemplate the wonderful experience of devotion and closeness to the Lord by simply singing His glories in the company of saints:

> *pragatey Gupāl Gobind lālan.*
> *sādhi suṅgi vakhāṇiyā.*
> *ācharaju dīthā amio vūthā.*
> *gurparsādī jāṇiyā.*[283]

However, an inwardly affirmed recitation of His glories in song is made possible by the *prasād* of the teacher, which alone can purge the devotee's inner being and his overt utterance of all evil and discord:

> *gurparsādi param pad pāiyā.*
> *antar nirmalu nirmalu bāṇī*
> *Hariguṇ sahajae gāvaṇiyā.*[284]

The *bhakta* now comes to feel that a great good has happened to him:

> *gurparsādi parampadu pāiyā vadī*
> *vadiyāyi hoi, andinu gun gāve*
> *nit sāche. sāchi samāvai soi.*[285]

Here, however, I propose to interpret the words, *vadī vadiyāyī hoi* as 'a very great good has come to happen to me', and not as 'great has become *my* glory', as is done by Mr. Manmohan Singh. For, he who eulogizes the highest spiritual state (*param pad*) and also the habit of ceaselessly singing the glory *of the Lord* (*andinu gun gāve*) cannot, in the same breath, attach great value to *his own* acquisition of glory. But, of course, the sincere singing of His glories has its own rewards. The Lord is pleased, and by virtue of His grace, the *prasād* of the *gurū* for the pupil is further ensured:

> *gun Gobind kīrtan janu gāvai.*
> *gurparsādi Nanak phal pāvai.*[286]

At this point a question may suggest itself readily. If one sings His glories *in*sincerely, nobody, not even the teacher, can bring about good results; and if the *kīrtan* is sincere, one should be able to get the reward, whatever it be, directly from the Lord Himself. How, then, does the teacher here enter into the picture? A possible answer, I suggest, is that though the benefit of soulful *kīrtan* issues from God

Himself, in so far as the gains here are mainly spiritual, and so not visible, the guidance of the teacher, or the religious faith he might already have evoked in us, is necessary for identifying the benefit truly. *Kīrtan* only deepens our faith and humility; and the guidance of the *gurū* or rather the spiritual sensitiveness that this guidance produces in us, is required to make us relate the gain of deeper spirituality *to the kīrtan* we have done.

As for *kīrtan* as such, the need for it is clearly felt also because God is unfathomable, defying all description; and because He is not open to everyday perception. We can only feel His presence in our hearts. This inner realization, however, is not given to one and all. Very rare, indeed, is the man who comes to be blessed with it, of course, mainly, because of the *prasād* of the teacher. It is from the teacher that spiritual wisdom or knowledge of eternal values wells up spontaneously, and only he is able to drink deep at this wisdom to whom it is gifted by the grace of the teacher:

agam rūp kā mani mahi thānā.
gurparsādi kinai virlai jānā.
sahaj kathā ke amrit kuntā
jisahi parāpāti tisu lai bhunchā.[287]

A person who is blessed with such experience becomes established in the knowledge that there is but one God:

mani tani antari ek prabhu rātā.
gurparādi Nanak eku jātā.[288]

What the 'knowledge' in question means is, however, to be determined with care. It certainly does not mean a merely intellectual acceptance of the reality of the one God. A clue to what is positively meant is provided by the first line which says: 'My mind and my body are alike inwardly committed to the one Lord'. The reference, here, is clearly to the godward orientation of one's entire life and being; and it is the *prasād* of the teacher which is said to facilitate such a total commitment. It is this—that is, *gurparsād*—that makes for the miracle (*achraj*) of a revelation of the *all-pervasive* and priceless (*amolak*) Lord *in the heart* of the devotee:

ek achraju jan dekhahu bhāi.
dubidhā māri Hari mani vasāi.
Nām amolak na pāiyā jāi.

gurparsāḍi vasai mani āi.
sabhi mahi vasai prabhu eko soī.
gurmatī ghati pargati hoī.[289]

It is indeed only the infinite potency of *gurparsād* which can establish a relation between two seemingly opposite sides of God's nature, that is, His Universal presence as *impersonal truth*, on the one hand; and Its *personal* realization by a devotee, on the other. The evidence of religious experience also enables us to meet some difficulties of the way we talk about God. In religious discourse we generally use diverse attributes of God almost simultaneously, which is bound to look odd to a common man. But the oddity may be removed on a little closer look. Consider, for instance, the following:

pārbrahama prabhu dṛṣṭiāiyā pūran agam vismād.
Nanak Rām nām dhanu kītā pūre gurparsādi.[290]

Here, the individual meanings of the words: *pūran, agam, vismād,* are clear; they are, respectively, complete, fathomless, wondrous. But if they are considered in relation to one another, some new thoughts may be seen to arise. All the three adjectives are applied to the *same* Lord who is said to be transcendent; so their individual meanings should not clash with each other. Thus, the word 'complete' (*pūran*) cannot be taken on the image of an all-inclusive circle; for, however big and inclusive it be, a circle is always a limited form; and so it cannot go with the word *agam* which means fathomless or immeasurable. But if from the region of mere meaning we turn to that of experience, we may see the possibility that an object (here God Himself) can excite such a wondrous feeling (*vismād*) that it may not only seem to fill our being with joy and wonder, but also strain our apprehending powers, so that, along with appearing to be wholly satisfying to the heart, it may also seen to be quite beyond the grasp of the intellect. Here, the soul-filling quality of Reality as experienced will demand the word *pūran* and the surpassing, incomprehensible quality of what is experienced will justify the word *agam.* These reflections enable me to interpret the verse in question (*pārbrahama . . . gurparsādi*) finally as follows:

> The devotee says: 'The *prasād* of the teacher has so filled my being (*kītā pūrey*) to overflowing with the riches of His Name that, in terms of a perfectly fulfilling—yet overwhelming—realization, I have been able to take a very satisfying, if not, comprehensive

look, at the transcendent Lord (*pārbrahama prabhu*). It may here be noted, in passing, that whereas the two distinguished commentators, Manmohan Singh and Gopal Singh, take the word *pūrey* along with the one that follows it—that is, *gurparsād*—I prefer to club it with the ones that precede it: *Nanak . . . kītā.* If we accept *their* interpretation, that it is with the grace of the perfect (*pūrey*) *gurū* that Nanak has come to regard the Name (*pūran, agam*) true wealth, no clue would be provided to solve the difficulty I have posed,—that is, the question as to how the same Lord can be both complete and yet fathomless (*pūran, agam*). On the other hand, as already indicated, the difficulty in question *is* answered if we take the words, *pūran* and *pūrey* to refer to the completeness of the devotee's (or Nanak's) own satisfaction, though, of course, *what* he experiences, as distinguished from *how* he experiences it, is not—nor can ever be—the whole Reality, which is *agam.*

The devotee who has been able to saturate himself with the love of the Lord, essentially in virtue of the *prasād* of the teacher, is (we have seen) necessarily a man of surpassing faith and humility. Both these attitudes make him feel convinced that the devotion to God which he has come to be blessed with, is not really his own acquisition—because it so excels in value his own imperfect moral being—but is only the descent of a gift which his kind Lord had already decided to bless him with. The ego-sense of this man is so utterly undone in faith and humility that he cannot help attributing all that is good to His grace:

gurparsādī Hari mani vasiyā pūrab likhiyā pāiyā
kahe Nanak ehu sarīru parvānu hoā jini
satigur sio chit lāiyā.[291]

The pre-ordination (*pūrab likhiyā*) here referred to is not the laying down of a rigid and restrictive plan by an impersonal destiny but, so to say, the loving pre-planning by a benevolent Father for the good of His children. Here, we may note, it would be curious to suggest that when a son realizes that provision for his present needs had already been made in the past, he feels it as a kind of restriction on his liberty to act. To feel obliged to one's parents for the provision they made long ago for what one enjoys in the present is only to feel happy and grateful; and this feeling is quite removed from the rebellious impulse to somehow break through an unfeeling and inexorable plan which has been imposed upon one by an alien and not necessarily friendly power. We freely pre-plan for those whom we love; and when they see and acknowledge such thoughtfulness, they only feel happy at the pre-planning. Faith often renews itself in the form of a happy and grateful acknowledgement of such pre-determination.

But, one may ask, will not such a man who believes that his consummate devotion is but a pre-fixed gift from God become inactive and inert? The answer would obviously depend on what it really is to attribute one's successes or achievements to God. God is commonly regarded as the highest spirit and as a Reality of surpassing goodness. Now, a man who is really committed to *such* a God can only be untiring in his pursuit of goodness. It is impossible for him to be inactive or to knowingly stray from the path of virtue.

The gracious guidance of the teacher enables the devotee to pursue the path of virtuous living. The former does so by completely destroying the pupil's liability to fear, doubt, and other moral weaknesses. As a result, the devotee becomes committed to the service of the teacher, body and soul. Further, because of the guidance of the *gurū* he comes to develop implicit faith in God. And so long as his earthly sojourn continues, he lives by the faith that God is benevolent, or that He not only controls all that happens *to* him (alone), but is also the kindly indwelling spirit *within* us all. Such a devotee comes to be blessed with two helpful attributes. On the one hand, he neither feels too elated at any lucky happening—for he now looks upon them all as *His* gifts, and not as his own achievements; and, on the other hand, he does not get depressed at the onset of unlucky events. Because of his faith in the benevolent sovereignty of God, he regards the unfortunate happenings too as His gifts, so not without some hidden, benevolent purpose; and as therefore to be accepted with equanimity. As a result, he also ceases to be partial to some men and indifferent to others; for he is now imbued with the faith that God dwells within every heart, making everyone equally important, as a child of God:

gurparsādi sukh dukh sam jāṇey.
ghati ghati Rām hiāliye.[292]

The love of God which now grips the devotee's heart, as a result of the *prasād* of the teacher, is steadfast and knows no waning:

gurparsādi untari liv lāgai itu saṅgati nā hī marṇā.[293]

This, however, is a significant verse, and I think it necessary to explain why *I* interpret it differently from the way it has been translated by Mr. Manmohan Singh[294], and Dr. Gopal Singh.[295] They put it thus:

> 'The devotee, in whom the love in question has been awakened, is no longer subject to the sting of death.'

But I prefer to say that it is the link of love itself—and not the devotee who is but one term in the link—that is here regarded as being above death; and I do so by attending to the lines that precede the ones under review.[296]

Three lines earlier, it is said that only that person turns towards God to whom He takes a special fancy, or that the impulse to religious devotion is provided by the Lord Himself; that once the love of God is thus awakened in man, all doubt and illusory beliefs disappear; and that when these inhibiting factors have ceased to operate, one's love of God abides in a quite effortless (*sahaj*) way. It is this preceding inter-relation of human and divine love which the *prasād* of the *gurū* serves to re-activate and cement; and this is why the steadfast love of God which has now been awakened in the heart of the devotee abides.

The tangible marks of such an abiding faith are equally important and beneficial. *Gurparsād,* we need hardly add, is strictly spiritual in character, and it makes for a man's deliverance from such problems as cannot be overcome by ordinary human endeavour. Further, it enables one to meditate on the Lord; and this, in turn, dispels his doubt or lack of faith, his suffering, ignorance and fear; and, above all, the restrictive influence of his moral misdeeds:

> *gurparsādi prabhu dhiāyiā gai saṅkā tūti.*
> *dukh anerā bhai vināsey pāp gaye nikhuti.*[297]

The *gurū* not only teaches and argues for the surpassing reality of God, but models his own life on this faith. Thus, through both precept and example, the grace of the teacher (or *gurparsād*) enables us to see the illusory nature of our belief in the ultimate reality and value of worldly things, and to develop faith in the one true Lord:

> *gurparsādi bharam kā nāsu.*
> *Nanak tin mahi ek bisāsu.*[298]

Here, incidentally, I have thought it proper to interpret the word *Bharam* as 'illusory belief'—in respect of the value of worldly things—and not as 'doubt'; as is done by Mr. Manmohan Singh and Dr. Gopal Singh. And so I move on to say, along with a verse to be cited presently, that once the devotee is able to see through the illusory beliefs, *gurparsād* helps him identify the Will of the Lord. Be it noted, however, that the identification in question is not an act of cool cognition. It is at once a total self-commitment of the devotee to the Lord and consequent abstention from pursuit of interests that may be merely mundane:

gurparsādī hukamu pachhāṇe.
dhāvat rākhe ikatu ghari āṇe.
Nāme rātā sadā bairāgī Nāmu
ratanu mani tāhā hai.
sabh jag mahi vartai iko soi.
gurparsādī pargatu hoī.
sabadu sālāhahi se jan nirmal.
nij ghari vāsā tāhā hai.[299]

The result is that the devotee comes to develop an introverted, self-critical attitude, quite opposed to the outgoing concerns of the average man. This also makes for a belief in, and contemplation of, the Lord as the *antaryāmin:*

gurparsādi āpu pachhāṇe kamal bigsai budhi tāhā hai.[300]

This is the stage where one comes to realize the supreme value of the Word of the Lord. God's Will, as expressed in *ṣabad,* is indeed of surpassing value. It is here, in His Will, that the secret of immortality resides; indeed, there is no way to eternal life except through a growing surrender to His Will:

gurparsādī sabadi sālāhī.
terey bhāṇe vichi amrit vassai.
tu bhāṇey amritu pīāvaṇiyā.[301]

Of course, a person who has been able to identify, and to attune himself with, the Will of God appears to be serene and contented even from the outside. But his contentment, we may note, is no mere lack of ambition which is so apparent in the life of the lazy. It is rather the detachment which emerges as the mere reflex of the acquisition of that state of being and experience than which there is nothing higher, and which is perfectly satisfying, —that is, unremitting devotion to the Name of the Lord:

Hari rasahi aghāṇe sahaj samāṇe
mukh te nāhī jāt baran
gurparsādi Nanak santokhe
nāmu prabhu japi japi udharani.[302]

It is such a disposition which leads one to deliverance, and which is found to distinguish gods like *Indra* and *Brahmā*, and ascetics like *Sanak* and *Sanandan.* It is the highest state of spiritual exaltation, and it can be attained only with the assistance of the *prasād* of the teacher:

gur ke sabadi tarey muni ketey Indrādik Brahmādi tarey.
Sanak Sanandan tapsī ketey gurparsādi pāri parey.[303]

2. *Gurkirpā*

Some of the most lucid verses of *gurbāni*, it seems, are devoted to the praise of *gurkirpā.* Let us now consider some of these:

gurkirpā te hukam pachhāṇe jugah jugantar kī bidhi jāṇey.[304]

What is here said is clear. It is by means of the *kirpā* of the teacher, and not because of any effort of one's own, that one comes to know the Will of God, which knowing is at once a realization of the eternal way of *dharma* or righteousness.

The *kirpā* of the *gurū* can exalt even the lowliest of us. It is indeed the *gurū* who makes it possible for us to enter the palace of Truth and to see It in its purity. The veil (of duality) is now wholly lifted; the devotee sees it clearly that he belongs to God, and that, instead of being far away, He is enshrined in his heart:

gurkirpā te nīchu nivājiā.
kholi kivādā mahali bulāiyā.
jaisā sā taisā dikhlāiyā.
kahu Nanak sabhu paradā tūtā.
hau terā tū mai mani vūthā.[305]

This realization of Truth is, however, no struggling attainment by discursive understanding. It is rather a serene ingress into Truth;

and, in respect of present ease and directness, it is comparable to one's inhalation of, and suffusion by, the fragrance of a flower. An example of such self-approximation to Truth is provided by the life and personality of the *gurū* himself:

gurkirpā te jāṇiyā jithai tudhu āpu bujhāiyā.
sahaje hi sāchi samāiyā.[306]

As indicated in the following verse, it is a special mark of the *kirpā* of the *gurū* that he enables us to develop an intimate relation of love with God:

mītu hamārā veparvāh.
gurkirpā te mohiasnāhā.
mītu hamārā antarjāmī.
samrath purakhu pārbraham suāmī.
hum dāsai tum thākur merey
mān mahatu Nanak prabhu terey.[307]

A close look at the above reveals that a subtle matter of detail is here suggested in respect of the relation in question. The very first line deserves attention. It says that God, now a friend (or *mītu*) of the devotee, is *veparvāh.* What could this word possibly mean? Surely, in so far as He is commonly regarded as Providence, God cannot be said to be *veparvāh* in the literal sense of being careless or indifferent to our needs. The appropriate meaning of the word emerges only when we pay due attention to the second line as well, specially to the word (*asnāhā*). Thereupon we get the significant meaning that whereas God Himself *does not mind* whether we love Him or not, and is in this sense *veparvāh*—for, whatever be our attitude, He continues to take care of us—the devotee, to be sure, is greatly benefitted when he comes to develop, by means of *gurkirpā,* a uniquely intimate and personal love for God. It is precisely this feeling of intimacy which is emphasized in the *third* line. This line does not make the impersonal statement that God is the indwelling spirit in us all; it says instead: '*my friend* dwells within my heart', which suggests that the devotee cherishes the love in question in the intimate recesses of his heart. Taken as one, the first three lines suggest a kind of contrast between God and man. *He* does not worry whether we love Him or not, but *we* stand to gain immeasurably if we come to love Him. The contrast reaches its climax in the next three lines. Here, the devotee speaks of the Lord as the all-sufficient and transcendent master, and of himself as a mere servant of His, declaring that all that is worthy and respectable is to be attributed to the Lord alone. To conclude, the highest spiritual wisdom that man, on his own, is a mere nothingness, and that God is the all-controlling Overlord, is made accessible to the devotee by the *kirpā* of the *gurū*.

God never ceases to work as our protective parent. But within this sweet and essential changelessness, or rather because of it, He is ever new in the sense that He helps us differently in times of need of evermore various kinds. A realization of this truth too is to be had with the help of *gurkirpā*. It is the *gurū* who, in his grace, makes us see the truth that the single discipline of reciting His Name soulfully can make for the cancellation of every kind of pain and suffering:

sachu parmesaru nit navā.
gurkirpā te nit chavā.
prabh rakhvāle mai bāp.
jā ke simraṇi nahi santāp [308]

Again, it is only as a result of the *kṛpā* of the teacher that one can acquire the ability to sing the glories of the Lord with such depth that one is at once freed from ignorance, and gets lit up with true knowledge:

gurkirpā te guṇ gāi apār.
mun bhītari hovai pargāsu.
giān anjanu agiānu bināsu.
miti nāhi jā kā bisthāru.
sobhā tā kī apar apār.
anik ruṅg jā ke gaṇey na jāhi.[309]

How is the glory of God *apar* and *apār*? In this sense, we may say, that though every attribute of His has of course a determinate meaning, and may in this sense be said to be limited, the ways in which a divine attribute can be seen to manifest itself or be made use of, are unlimited.

However, from the human point of view, the basic way in which we come closer to God, who is supremely pure, is by trying to rid our own selves of impurity. Such riddance is, of course, possible only with God's help, and not through our own unaided effort. This is why growth in purity is at once a growth in humility. Indeed, we cannot really come closer to God by just enlarging the extent of our knowledge or power. What alone is here of help is the attempt to get imbued with some godlike qualities, by cultivating purity with the help of the teacher:

gurkirpā te manu tanu nirmalu
nirmalu nāmu dhiyāvaṇiā.
jīvanu maranu sabhu tudhai tāi.
jisu bakhsai tisu de vadiāi.[310]

Purity of heart is no mere singleness of the will (as Kierkegaard thought), but at once a growing likeness to God in respect of quality. My suggestion that purity is a possible bridge between man and God is perhaps warranted by the precise *positioning* of the two *nirmals,* one of them qualifying the human body and mind, and the other, the Name of the Lord. The thought may not be dismissed as odd; for the authors of these texts are not mere saints and philosophers, but musicians and poets too; and so they may well be expected to be alive to the significance of the very placement of words, and to the formal effects it can produce. The second *nirmal,* we may note, could well be replaced with words like '*Hari kā*' without any loss of metrical length or of overall meaning. From the purely poetical and aesthetical point of view, the reason of putting the two *nirmals* so immediately together, the one serving as terminus of one idea, and the other forthwith initiating another, could only be that the author wants to convey the idea that gradual elimination of impurity is *at once* a movement towards God, the perfectly pure.

Those who come to so realize—as a result of the *kṛpā* of the *gurū*—the surpassing value of the Name, become tranquil and self-possessed as the heaven itself. They indeed come to abide in the innermost depths of serenity. Beatitude becomes their natural mode of existence; and they alone are able to sing the glories of the Name as they have themselves identified It (*pachhāṇiyā*):

gurkirpā te Nām pachhāṇiyā
gagan gambhir gagnantari vāsu.
gun gāvai sukh sahaji nivāsu.[311]

It is because of the *kṛpā* of the *gurū*—that is, as a sequel to the religious instruction provided by him—that one's entire psycho-physical being becomes suffused with the love of God; it is only then that one attains to the supreme bliss of God-realization. All this is borne out by the following verse:

gurkirpā te mun tanu bhīje.
rasnā Nāmu dhiyāye ras bhīje.
ras hi te rasu pāidā.[312]

The settlement of the Name in the devotee's heart which the *kṛpā* of the *gurū* brings about, first makes for steadfastness of mind; then, enables the devotee to see through the vanity of worldly riches; and finally, enables him to secure release from *saṃsāra.* In other words, the Name, as properly recited, is not a mere word, but a sure and powerful impulse towards the attainment of our spiritual destiny:

gurkirpā te hirdai vasey.
bhavjalu pāri parlā.
Nāmu nidhanu mun atal.
tā chhūtahi māiyā ke patal.[313]

However, a question may here be readily put. How can one verify the wondrous power that is often attributed to the *kṛpā* of the *gurū*? The mere assertion that one sings the glories of the Name because of the grace of the teacher hardly seems convincing. For whereas people can easily hear the Name being talked about (*vakhāṇu*), they do not—and they cannot—readily see the *kṛpā* in question which is said to be the source of one's effusive love of God. The real witness to the whole truth, that one can sing the glories of the Name sincerely only by virtue of the *kṛpā* of the teacher, is provided only by those men of realization who have actually become imbued with the love of the Name:

gurkirpā te Nāmu vakhāṇu.
kahu Nanak so janu parvāṇu.
jā kai ridài vasey bhagvānu.[314]

The verification is, in the main, subjective. A clear clue to this interpretation, we may note, is provided by the way in which the *gurbāni* here opposes *Nāmu vakhāṇu* to *ridai vasai.*

In case my interpretation is true, as it appears to be, the order of the details of the life of devotion may be put thus. The *kṛpā* of the *gurū* makes for the settlement of the Name in the pupil's heart; and then, because whatever affects the heart presses for expression, the Name, so say, spills over into the singing of His glories. This at once gives us some new meanings of at least two concepts or images projected in this verse. *Vakhāṇu* now ceases to mean mere projection in terms of speech; it is rather seen to signify an inwardly affirmed expression of one's love of God. And the settlement of the Name in the heart (*hṛday vase*) is no mere deposition, as it were, of an inert object in an unfeeling chamber, but the buoyant quickening of one's entire being with the love of God, so that the outer singing is but a musical welling up of heartfelt devotion. In saying so I am here guided by the thought that phenomenological analysis is not the mere fragmentation of a whole into its constituent parts, but an attempt to see the character and impulse of every element of experience *in* the setting of the dynamic inter-relatedness of the whole.

Again, it is the *Kṛpā* of the teacher which enables the devotee to realize or experience the beloved Lord as the infinite ocean of nectar, and to so merge himself in the experience of His sweetness that he may lose the sense of his being a distinct individual, and become a mere channel, so to say, for the Lord's own speaking and seeing:

gurkirpā te pāiye piārā amrit agam athāh.
āpi suṇi sabh vekhadā piārā mukhi boley āpi muhāṇi.[315]

The possibility that a man *can* so become a mere channel of the power that God is, is borne out by the fact that, saturated as they are with the love and overpowering sense of the reality of God, the Sikh *gurus* themselves speak a language which is not really theirs, regarded as merely human, but that of God Himself, that is, language of universal love, humility and purity. The *gurus* indeed seem to see all men as God does, that is, as equal; and the language that they speak is also one of concern for all.

The *gurbāni* assures us that, as one who has himself realized the highest truths of the spirit, the *gurū* alone can enable us to secure freedom from attachment to the world of sense, or control over the mind, for he is virtually the Lord Himself, and may well be taken as such for purposes of guidance and sustenance.

gurkirpā te mugadhu manu māniā.
gurū kartā gurū karṇai jogu.
gurū Parmesarū hai bhi hogu.
kahu Nanak prabhu ihai janāī
binu gur mukati na pāiye jāyi.[316]

It is, of course, very difficult to be favoured by the teacher with a direct relish of the sweetness of God's word, and with recognition of It as the quintessence of all knowledge and contemplation. But such a realization *is* accessible (that is, in principle) to those who tread the path of devotion. *Karam-kānda*, on the other hand, enjoins a multitude of actions which only add fuel to the fire of ego-sense, and confirm one's entanglement in *saṃsāra* because they are not performed in the spirit of inner dependence on the Name, that is, with the humble feeling that He is the real agent of whatever little good we are able to do:

giyān dhyān gursabadu hai mīthā.
gurkirpā te kinney virlei chakhi dīthā.
karam kāṇḍ bahu karahi achār.
bin Navai dhrigu dhrigu ahaṅkār.
bandhan bāndhio māiyā phās.
jan Nanak chhūtlei Gur pargās.[317]

The *gurū* imparts the sense of discrimination, and so makes it easier for one to tread the path of devotion without faltering. Faith in the teaching of the *gurū* makes for humility and simplicity, whereas the path of egoity leads to needless involvements and bondage.

It may be noted that I have here interpreted the words, *dhrigu dhrigu* in a sense that is akin to 'fiercely burning', unlike the leading commentators who take the word to mean *dhikkār.* My argument is that in everyday usage the word *dhikkār* is never repeated. It is surely not common to say: *dhikkār hai, dhikkār hai.* On the other hand, with reference to a raging fire we freely use the iterative *dhag dhag.*

Again, if we interpret *bin nāvai dhrigu dhrigu, ahaṅkār* as 'ego-sense without the Name, is to be condemned', then it would be implied that ego-sense, *together with* the Name, is *not* to be condemned. This implication cannot be accepted because of two reasons. First, the *gurus* are *categorically* opposed to *haumai.* Second, when actions are performed in the spirit of inner dependence on the Name, ego-sense automatically begins to wane, generating humility, so that the two, ego-sense and true love of the Name, cannot co-exist for long.

Ordinarily, every conscious effort heightens the sense of agency and self-esteem. This, in turn, raises a kind of barrier between self and God. Complete self-identification with God is possible only through utter self-effacement. Such a complete negation of egoity is possible only through love and selfless service; and *gurkirpā* is, in this context, of very great help:

gurkirpā jihi nar kau kīnī.
tin ih jugati pachhāṇī.
Nanak līn bhaio Gobind seo.
jeo pānī saṅgi pānī.[318]

Gurkirpā, we are told, invests a man's speech with eternal significance. The blessed individual comes to gain such insight into spiritual values that he can truthfully declare:

gurkirpā tai amrit meri vāṇī.[319]

With the help of but a single gift issuing from the *kirpā* of the *gurū*—that is, love of the Name—the devotee is able to control the whole army of evil in his own being. This at once makes for the bliss of self-control, which is a happy state of resting on one's own self. The individual now realizes that there is no better way to live than that of willing servitude to the Lord. All this, however, is a matter of inner realization, and is therefore dubitable to ordinary men who can observe only the outer behaviour of the man of religion. *They* need some external, visible proof of the inner humility and bliss. Luckily, even such a mark is available. The very faces of those who are able to secure self-control, through love of the Name, radiate the light of purity:

gurkirpā te dalu sādhiā.
bakhsīs vajahu mili eku Nāmu.
sūkh sahaj ānand bisrām.
prabh kai chākar sai bhalai
Nanak tin mukh ūjalai.[320]

So far we have been discussing what *gurkirpā* does to the devotee or a man of faith. But we must also consider how God appears, or is conceived, in the relation of devotion. Now, in the actual religious relation, both God and Man may be said to share a feature. This common excellence, we repeat, is humility. But whereas the humility of God is the reflex of His surpassing greatness and concern for His creatures, our humility is the obvious demand of our literal finitude. This is suggested, if but indirectly, by the following verse:

bhagati vachhalu Hari vasai mani āi.
gurkirpā te sahaji subhāi.
bhagati karai vichahu Apu khoi.
tadahī sāchi milāvā hoi.
bhagat sohahi sadā Hari prabh duāri.
gur kai heti sāchai premi piāri.[321]

What is here said may be roughly put thus. It is not because of any effort on the part of the devotee, but because God Himself is the *bhakta's* lover that He has come to dwell within the latter's (devotee's) heart, out of the spontaneity of His own loving nature.

What is more, His wondrous humility manifests itself in the fact that, to avoid *exhibiting* the fact, so to say, that He is the real source of the good, God works through the *kṛpā* of the teacher. That is why, because of growing godliness, the devotee too loses all thought of self—that is, all egoity and all worry about self—in his devotion to the Lord. This indeed is the essential pre-condition of approximation to the Truth supreme. But this approximation is no isolated act, instantaneously accomplished; it has to be *kept* so. What is more, the realization, though of infinite value, is but an approximation. The devotee can never claim equal status with the Deity. The best that he can hope for is to keep ever standing at the door of His court. But such a reverent disposition of the self in relation to Truth can be secured only through the instrumentality of the teacher.

A fine example of the devotee-deity relation is provided by the following verse:

merā Prabhu nirmalā sabh te rahiā samāi.
Gurkirpā te miley milāī.
Hari dāsan ke dās sukh pāye.
Merā Hari Prabh in bidhi pāiya jāye.
Hari kirpā te Rāmgun gāye.[322]

The writer-devotee is here speaking of God not as such, but as his own (*merā Prabhu*) and the same air of intimacy is seen to sweeten the verse all along. It may further be noted that this verse reveals a kind of tension between two attitudes which gives us a clue to an essential feature of the life of devotion. On the one hand, the writer speaks of God as his own; and, on the other hand, he does not hesitate to emphasize the immanence of God *in every heart*, or to suggest, *to one and all*, a sweet and simple way to realize God. *This ability to establish a deeply personal relationship with God, yet without any jealous feeling that no one else may gain access to Him, emerges only when the devotee has been able to efface his egoity in the love of God.* The fact indeed is that it is only a truly humble man—that is, one who does not wish to place himself above others in any way—who feels impelled to share his most precious experience or realization with others, instead of keeping it confined to himself.

Further, if only in a measure, this humility must precede, and not merely issue from, one's experience of God. In the present verse the clearest mark of personal humility is, of course, seen to occur only in the last line where the saintly author says that it is only as a *kṛpā* of the Lord that he is able to sing His glory. But this detail of order is due only to an unavoidable limitation of language which just cannot say everything at once, and so must follow the before-after order. In point of fact, on the other hand, humility is present even as the writer sets out to speak; and we may truly imagine that the first three words: *merā Prabhu nirmalā* are uttered in a spirit of sweet, inner bowing; for otherwise the immanence of God *in every heart* could not be emphasized so readily *and so happily* in the second half of the first line itself.

I may now put the meaning of the verse thus:

> 'My God, I know, is not averse to anyone. *He* abides in every heart, as He does in my own, in spite of all its impurities. This very humility—that is, His being present in *our lowly being* in spite of His *surpassing excellences,* may be taken to suggest that the right way to serve God is to serve the very servants of those who are devoted to God. But the details of the way to God are, of course, graciously revealed to us by the *gurū.*'

God blesses us with His grace without, so to say, announcing that He is doing so. He does it through the *kṛpā* of the teacher. The efforts on the part of the devotee and his moral merits do nothing to justify this consummation of his destiny. It is God Himself who brings it about, and to Him it is but a play to bless man with this gift. Life and death are alike His gifts. Once the devotee comes to develop this faith, no room is left for doubt as to the hidden goodness of whatever happens to him, nor even for the thought that he himself is the real initiator of what he is (seemingly) able to do or accomplish:

kari prasādu ik khel dikhāiyā.
gurkirpā te parampadu pāiyā.

kahat Nanaku māri jīvālai soī.
aisā būjhahu bharamu na bhūlahu koī.[323]

To sum up, three ideas are here suggested. First, the self-effacing quality of the way in which God showers His grace on us; second, faith in His benevolence as the ground of equanimity; and, thirdly, faith also in His supreme power as the most effective antidote to egoity.

Finally, a note may be added by way of bringing out, a little better, the importance of the *gurū* in the practice of religion. We cannot point to God Himself in the way we can indicate the presence of a thing. Nor can we illustrate Him in the way we exemplify the concept of triangle by drawing an actual triangle. But merely because of such inability the reality of God may not be denied. For whereas our human truths and beliefs are all alike grounded in evidence provided by things and happenings in the world, the world as a whole is said to be grounded in God; and of a God so regarded, the right kind of verification should be sought not in any particular region of life and experience, but in His availability for use, so to say, as the anchor *of the whole course of our life and experience.* Now, according to the Sikh scriptures, it is in the life of a *satgurū* that God is seen to function in this basic and all-regulating way. The *gurū* really looks on God as the real agent of whatever (good) he is able to do. He does it all with the conviction that it is God's Will that is working Itself through him. What is more, whatever happens to him, he endures it with the courage and equanimity provided by the sense of his rootedness in God. This indeed is why the Sikh scriptures attach the highest importance to the *gurū*. The *gurū*, in his daily life, projects the power and reality of God, if but incompletely.

Conclusion

These, then, are the basic ideas which may be said to form the Sikh view of grace. Yet, my account of the matter is by no means complete; and it would serve to relieve this incompleteness, provide a fuller illustration of my hermeneutical approach, and also contribute a fitting conclusion to this Section, if, through some detailed interpretation of a few select passages from the Sikh scriptures, an attempt is made to bring out how grace is related to such essentials of the life of religion as fear of God, non-attachment towards the world, faith, patience or fortitude, and personal, discriminating realization of the truth that He is the true source of all blessings, be they mundane or spiritual.

To begin, now, with the fear of God (or *bhau*), the following verse may be picked for attention:

bhau muchu bhārā vadā tolu.
manmati haulī boley bolu.
siri dhari chaliye sahiye bhāru.
nadrī karmī gur bīchāru.[324]

The literal meaning of *the first two* lines may be put thus: the fear of God is very heavy and massive in weight; on the other hand, the utterances (or dictates) of self-will (or *manmati*) are relatively feeble.

But in order to get at the real meaning of these (first two) lines we have also to consider the ones that follow. And as I do so I come to see that the fear in question cannot be merely negative, like the fear of a dangerous animal or reptile which only impels us to move *away* from the source of danger, because the third line requires us *to live positively* in accordance with what is demanded by the ideal of a god-fearing life. The (third) line, however, calls for a little more pointed attention. Here, if the words *siri dhari chaliye* are taken quite literally—that is, as signifying, 'carry (a load) on your head'—they would only seem to anticipate, instead of *adding* something significant to, the meaning of *sahiye bhārū.* Therefore, they should rather be taken to mean: 'respectfully acknowledge as a guiding principle of life'; and if they are so understood the whole line will appear to deliver the following beautiful meaning:

> 'Acknowledge, with due deference, the value of the norm of a god-fearing life; and with your head bowed, as if in reverence, live in accordance with the exacting demands of this ideal.'

This requirement, however, cannot be easily met, for living in the fear of God, *who is pure goodness and all-seeing*, cannot but demand the avoidance of evil in all that we think or feel, speak or do. To put it positively, the demand is for an unremitting conformity with the law of righteousness. This, in turn, calls for an infinite measure of vigilance, courage and wisdom. Luckily, for the cultivation of such rare attitudes, three powerful sources of help are (in principle) available to us: His grace (*nadarī*), self-effort (*karmī*) and the guidance of the teacher (*gurū*). The exactions of a god-fearing life can indeed be easily met if we bear in mind the general availability of these three sources of help.

Of all these, however, *nadari* or His grace may be said to be pre-eminent, which is perhaps the reason why it is put as the opening word of the line: *nadrī karmī gur bīchārū.* To conclude, it is faith in His grace which can help us carry the cross of a god-fearing life steadfastly.

How grace is related to some other essentials of the good life may be brought out by reflecting on the following:

Farida dilu rāttā isu dunī siū.
dunī na kitte kammi.
misal fakīrā gākhaḍī su pāiye karammi.
pahilai paharai phulaḍā phalu bhi pacchha rāti.
jo jāganhi lahani sei sāī kanno dāti.
dātī sahib sandiā kiyā chalei tisu nāli.
ik jagandey nā lahanhi iknhā sutiyān deyi uthāli.
dhūndediyān suhāg kū tau tani kāyi kor.
jinhā Nāu suhāgaṇī tinha jhāk na hor.
sabar manjh kamān e sabrū kā nītāno.
sabar sandā bāṇu khālak khata na karī.
sabari andari sābarī tanu aive jālenhi.
hoṇ najīki khudai dei bhetu na kissai deni.
sabaru eh suāu je tu bandā diḍu karahi.
badhi thīvahi dariāo tuti na thīvahi vāhaḍa.
Farīdā darvesī gākhaḍī chopaḍī parīti.
ikanni kinnei chīliye darvesāvī rīti.[325]

Let me first translate[326] this text before subjecting it to analysis:

Addressing Sheikh Farid, the *gurū* says: it is natural for man to be attached to this world. But the world is of no real value (for, *we* may add, it is neither the source of the greatest blessings that are attainable by man, nor, *as we shall see a little later,* helpful in making us hold on to the truth that righteousness is the essential pre-condition of getting Lord's blessings). On the other hand, it is not easy to shake off our worldly attachments. It is indeed quite a task to tread the path of renunciation (*misali fakīrā gākhḍi*). But this need not discourage us, for His grace is of great help here. And once this truth of the efficacy of His grace is allowed to grip the heart, and the journey of life undertaken with grace as one's anchor, the emergence of (the flower of) devotion is bound to be followed by the fruit of renunciation (*pahiley pahirai phulaḍā phalu bhī pacchā rāti*). Those who thus become alive (*jāgani*) to the power of His grace become eligible to receive His blessings (*jo jāgaṇhi lahani se sāi kanno dāti*). Yet, be it noted, one can never be sure of *getting* them as a matter of right, so to say. Their actual dispensation is entirely His concern (*dāti sāhib sandiā*), and its rationale, beyond our understanding. In the effort to understand how grace works, a look at the world around us is of no help at all. What is worse, the looking around may even unsettle our faith in His sense of justice; for, in the world it may well be seen that whereas those who are spiritually asleep are suddenly surprised with windfalls of every kind, those who are spiritually awake, or mindful of true values, have to live even without the minimal blessings of God (*ik jāgande na lahani iknhā sutiyān deyi uthāli*). The wise course of action, therefore, for those who seek a consummation of their worldly existence is to stop looking outside (*jinā nāu suhāgaṇī tinna jhāk na hor*); to focus on (and eradicate) the evil (*tanu evai jālenhi*) embedded in their own bodily frame (*tanu kāī kor*); and, above all, to cultivate the faith, in unwearying patience, that the Lord never makes a mistake (*khālak khatā na karei*) and that we are bound to get, sooner or later, what *in His eyes* we truly deserve. Patience that is an essential ingredient of faith is indeed of surpassing value here. It is patience which can serve as a true means (or *kamāṇu*) to hit the target or the supreme objective of life, and we should therefore practice patience as a discipline and a commitment (*sabrū kā nīhāṇu*). It is in the practice of patience (implicit in faith) that one can burn out the bodily passions (*sabaru andaru sābarī tanu aivai jālenhi*). Indeed, patience alone can make a devotee perfectly steadfast in his *godward endeavour*, (*sabaru eh suāu jei tū bandā didu karahi*) making such striving a powerful torrent, and preventing it from dissipation in other directions (*badhi thīvahi dariyau tuti na thīvahi vāhḍā*). Progress on the path of renunciation may well be difficult; indeed it *is* (*darvsī gākhḍī*), which is exactly why very few are seen to tread this path (*ikani kinne chīliye darvesāvī rīti*); but the rigour is softened—nay, even made likeable—by the balmy leaven of devotion (*chopaḍi parīti*) which explains why those who have attained to eventual proximity with God do not think it necessary to talk (to others) about what they had to undergo, as if in purgatory, on their way to God:

(*sabari andari sābari tanu aivai jālenhi*
honi najīki khudai de bhetu na kissai deni).

All this, however, important though it is, does not exhaust the Sikh view of grace; and the following may be said to provide a necessary supplement:

> *jatu pāhārā dhīraju suniāru.*
> *ahirani mati vedu hathiāru.*
> *bhau khalā agani taptāu.*
> *bhāṇḍā bhāu amrit titu dhāli.*
> *ghaḍiye sabadu sachi taksāl.*
> *jin kau nadari karam tin kār.*
> *Nanak nadarī nadar nihāl.*[327]

How exactly this verse may be said *to add to* the meaning of the previous one will become clear if we begin by reflecting that whereas the earlier verse listed some quite important pre-conditions of eligibility for the grace of God, emphasizing patience (*sabaru*) as the pre-eminent one, in the present verse, on the other hand, these pre-conditions themselves are said to be the mark of, and so to depend on, His Grace. Here, in the verse just cited above, we are told that a life equipped with patience, continence, discrimination, scriptural knowledge, fear (of God), self-discipline and a loving heart is distinctive of those *who are already blessed with the grace of God.* This means that the attitude listed earlier as the pre-conditions of grace are themselves *grounded in* grace.

What is more, a close look at the verse under review delivers the idea that it is grace which consummates the worldly life of the devotee. We attain to this idea by means of a simple argument. *Nadarī nadar* (or His look of grace) is said to make for perfect blessedness (*nihāl*). Bliss or attainment of perfect happiness may be said to be man's highest goal, for we all strive for it, though often in wrong-headed ways. So, the experience of grace is also the fulfilment of our destiny. In short, it is His grace which initiates a man into righteous living, enables him to hold on to this path steadfastly, and also consummates the endeavour.

Nor is there anything odd, we may add, in such talk about grace, that is, about the suggestion that grace precedes, underruns and consummates the good life. For, such a way of talking is a feature of our daily life as well. Do we not freely say that some energy is needed for physical exercise, that it sustains the discipline, and that (in its developed form) it is also the goal and fruition of physical exercise? If it yet be contended that such a total way of talking about grace does not satisfy reason, and that we must be told as to which of the two comes first, grace *or* its pre-conditions, the *gurus*' answer would be that the question is unanswerable, and that the entire matter is wrapped in, or is itself, a mystery. And they would hasten to add that the mysterious nature of grace is only of a piece with the finally incomprehensible nature of God and His ways. Thus in Japji (M.1, p.5) we are told that just as we cannot praise Him really enough (*antu na siftī kahaṇi na anti*), nor arrive at an *exhaustive* understanding of His workings (*antu na karṇey*) or of His creation.[328] (*antu na jāpey kītā ākāru*), in the same way the operation of His grace—that is, of how and why it bestows the favours that it does—and of the number of bounties in which it expresses itself, cannot be finally known. We can only say, as a reverent confession of humility, that grace comes to us only because of His own gracious nature, and that its bounties are innumerable:

Nanak nadarī karmī dāti.
bahutā karamu likhiyā na jāī.[329]

We must, however, take care not to exaggerate the *unknowability* of grace. Nor may this character of grace be allowed to evoke any feeling of fear or uncertainty in us, as the region of the unknown is often seen to do. For, as the *gurus* insist, something *is* known about the grace of God; and, what is more, this little knowledge is at once a message of hope for us. For instance, it *is* known (to the *gurus*), that grace is as much a gift of His Will as enslavement to the birth-death cycle is an infliction from Him (*iknā hukmī baksīs iki hukmī sadā bhavāiahi*)[330]; and that His grace is as surely a source of liberation as our deeds are the cause of embodiment (*karmī āvai kapadā nadarī mokhu duārī*).[331] Yet, be it noted, though the working of His grace is inscrutable, it may not be said to affect us merely negatively, as is often done (we repeat) by the unknown. For grace is not only said to be unfathomable, but is also regarded as the source of infinite bounties. Therefore, the devotee's natural attitude to the mystery of grace is only one of joyous wonder. This is borne out by the following exclamatory utterance of Guru Amar Das:

O my True Master
What is there that cannot
be had in Thy house of
Grace?

God's house has everything:

> *. . . Sayeth Nanak,*
> *my True Master, What is not there*
> *in Thy house of Grace?*[332]

But if grace is such an infinite source of blessings it becomes necessary to reflect as to how we could get it. How is it related to human effort? The answer has to be thought out with care. On the one hand, it is obvious that we cannot idly expect grace to descend on us as a mere matter of chance. As Guru Nanak declares, human effort is required for attainment of every end:

> *In this Universe that*
> *I behold,*
> *What can a man get without*
> *exertion.*[333]

If this is so, if even ordinary ends cannot be realized without some exertion, the effort required for attainment of life's highest blessing cannot but be considerable. Nor can grace be said to come to us as a matter of chance. The Sikh *gurus* do not accept the Paurāṇic view that even a chance or casual recitation of His Name can get us His grace.[334] They insist that the observance of ethical disciplines is necessary.

But, on the other hand, no effort on our part (it is added) can *directly* lead us to the actual *attainment* of grace. All that we can do is to make ourselves fit to *register* the advent of grace whenever it arrives. In addition to this, we can only beg or pray for grace. *Haṭh yoga* has been criticized by the *gurus* precisely because it directly aims at the actual attainment of grace.[335]

What is more, the *gurus* appear to believe that even in respect of sensitiveness to grace we are not really our own masters; for, however able we might become to *register* the grace of God, *the effective operation* of this ability, or the actual awareness of His grace as such, or its dispensation by God to men, itself depends on His own benign grace. I make this suggestion on the basis of the well-known emphases of the *gurus* that (the gift of) grace is a matter of His Will (*hukam*), and that the identification of His *hukam* as such is also a gift of His grace. Consider, here, the following in relation to each other:

a. Grace is a matter of His *hukam.*[336]

b. Yea, they alone submit to the Will, on whom is the Lord's grace.[337]

Hukam is registered by, and is acceptable to only those persons who are blessed with His grace.

In fine, our effort in relation to the grace of God consists only in the cultivation of an attitude of what has been called a wise passivity. Faith and the ethical disciplines sure give us the requisite ability to identify the occasional (or special) manifestations of His grace. But having acquired this ability, we can only wait for the descent of grace, albeit in hope and humility. The actual experience of grace is in every case His gift. Here, however, it is important to remember that the *special* manifestations of grace on specific occasions in the lives of some people are not everything about grace. Basically, grace is His general concern for one and all, and is grounded in His very nature as Love:

All work in His Grace,
No one is outside its pale.[338]

However, *Karma* does not mean action or effort alone; it is also freely used to mean *the law of Karma.* How is *this* related to grace? Here the *gurus* are clearly of the view that the grace of God can override the operation of the law of *Karma.* This is borne out, for instance, by the following unmistakable words of Guru Arjan Dev:

As one soweth, so one reapeth.[339]
yea, from him, on whom is the
Lord's grace,
No account is asked by the
master of the Universe.[340]

Finally, some attention may be paid to the Sikh view that grace comes to us through (the grace of) the *gurū.* Here, it is naturally essential to see what the word *gurū* means, and how the grace of God is related to the *gurū.* Now, to speak quite generally, the word *gurū* means a teacher. But in the context of the life of religion the word bears a special meaning; it means a teacher who is himself a man of realization, and can therefore show us the way to the supreme end of life. In Sikh religion, however, the word *gurū* means, first God

Himself; second, the ten *gurus* who may all be fairly regarded as true teachers or men of enlightenment; and thirdly, the *Gurū Granth Sāhib.* All these senses are borne out by the following:

a. The *gurū* and the God are one,
He is the Divine Master,
Pervadeth all and is everywhere.[341]

b. To love the Word of the *true*
gurū is to serve God.[342]

c. The Word of the true *gurū*
Is the *gurū* Himself.[343]

d. The Word is the *gurū,*
And the *gurū* is the Word.
The *gurū's* Word is the elixir,
Whosoever shall obey, what the
Word commands,
Verily, he shall get salvation.[344]

To turn now to the relation of the grace of God to (the grace of) the *gurū,* the first point that may be safely made is that the (grace of the) *gurū* serves as the vehicle of God. In other words, he does not merely receive the grace of God, but imparts it to the devotee. Thus we are told:

> Nanak, he whom *the guru blesseth with His grace,* to him everything belongs.[345]

> Through the Guru's grace, is the Lord enshrined in the mind.[346]

If these two utterances are taken together, some important ideas would seem to emerge. The experience of grace is inseparable from the conception of God as the God of love. This is why when one experiences grace God is no mere object of contemplation, but a Reality that appears adorable and so at once grips the heart. This is the grain of truth in words such as the following:

> '*enshrined* in the mind' and

> 'whoever wins His grace *merges* in the Nām'.[347]

To sum up, the concept of grace is inseparable from the idea of God as the Supreme Person (*param purakh*). Grace may indeed be defined as the giving/caring aspect of God as love which operates not only as the general maintenance of His entire creation—including, of course, His creatures too—but acts as occasional succour in our moments of need. Being an essential attribute of a personal God it is only proper that grace should operate through the medium of personality, say, that of the teacher; and is consciously acknowledgeable only by persons. In no case, however, does it merely confine itself to the being of a mere individual, however holy he may be. Love is essentially an outgoing power, and so is grace. It is therefore natural for the grace of God to, so to say, spill over into the hearts of God-intoxicated souls (like the *gurus*); and it is just as natural for a human *gurū*, partly because of the very joyous—and so irrepressible—character of the experience of grace, to impart it to those who are willing and eligible to receive it. If it be wondered, by men of philosophy, as to whether grace is a quality *or* a relation, the Sikh answer would readily be that in relation to the personality of God grace is a quality or excellence; and that in relation to God *as the creator of all that is there,* it is also relation—of love, caring, redress and redemption. Such a view of grace is clearly adequate to our needs and to religious experience. But I find it difficult to say if it is distinctive. For, whatever is distinctive is different; and the question, whether the Sikh view of grace is different from other religions' conception of grace or not, can be decided only on the basis of a comprehensive knowledge of all the great religions which I cannot claim to have.

Notes

1. We cannot obviously be sure that the *gurus* themselves distinguished *nadar, karam, bakhsīs* in the way we have done in the following pages of this chaper, for their personal corroboration is no longer available to us. But, on the other hand, it does not seem feasible to suggest that the *gurus* used these terms indiscriminately. All that we can do, and have done, is to make our distinguishing appear reasonable.
2. In interpreting all these Hindi words I have followed: *Sanchhipt Hindi Sabd-Sāgar* edited by Ramchandra Varma, Nagri Pracharini Sabha, Kashi, 8th edition, 1981.
3. Here, I go by *Sri Guru Granth Kosh.*
4. A.M. Hunter, *The Gospel according to St. Paul,* Lodon, 1966, p.13, cited in *Divine Grace and*

Human Response, edited by C.M. Vadakkekara, O.S.B., Asirvanam Benedictive Monastery, Bangalore, 1981, p.256.

5. Ibid.
6. *The Holy Geeta*: Commentary by Swami Chinmayananda, Central Chinmaya Mission Trust, Sandeepany, Sadhanalaya, Bombay, XVIII, p.66.
7. *Apbal, tapbal aur bāhubal,*
   Chautho hai bal dām.
   Sur kishore kṛpā te sab bal hāre ko bal Rām. —*Sūrdās*
8. Uttam or *nirguna Bhakti* is neither *Āropasiddha* (devotion because of the fruits) nor *Sanghasiddha* (devotion because of the constituent elements); this is why it is different from *Sāttviki Bhakti*.
9. Thus, see the following:
   'It is not in immunities that grace "abounds" but in the inexhaustible possibilities of reconciliation; it does not eliminate sin but reclaims the sinner; and that is its *work par excellence*', H.D. Lewis: *Our experience of God*, George Allen and Unwin Ltd., London, 2nd impression, 1962, p.273.
10. The transcendent attributes are said to be the following six (*ṣadguna*): knowledge (*jnāna*), untiring strength, power of endurance (*bala*), sovereignty (*aiśvarya*), strength (*vīrya*), creative power (*śakti*) and splendour (*tejas*).
11. *The Gītābhāṣya of Ramanuja*, translated into English by M.R. Sampat Kumaran, M.A., Vidya Press, Madras, First edition, June, 1969, p.297.
12. 'Having done such divine acts as ravished the minds and eyes of all men; having killed many demons or evil men; and having refreshed the entire universe with the nectar of His looks and words, pregnant with boundless compassion, friendliness and love . . . (an *avtār*, both amazes and bewitches us because of His), surpassing beauty, affability and such other qualities.' Ibid., p.3.
13. 'No other is equal to you by virtue of even any (single) quality like compassion . . . . You are . . . greater than all . . . by virtue of qualities like compassion.' Ibid., p.330.
14. 'The Nature of Grace' from *The Glories of Divine Grace*, Matthias, J. Scheeben, translated by Patrick Shanghnessy, O.S.B., S.T.D., A Grail Publication, Third Printing, 1948, Part-I, p.1.
15. Ibid., p.3.
16. Ibid., p.1.
17. Ibid., Chapter Three, p.14.
18. Ibid., 'Union with God', Part-II, p.6.
19. Perry D. Lefevre: *The Prayers of Kierkegaard*.
20. *Ādi Granth*, M.5, p.132.
21. Ibid.
22. Ibid.
23. Ibid., M.3, p.600.
24. Ibid., M.5, p.105.
25. *The Prayers of Kierkegaard*, p.38
26. *Ādi Granth*, M.1, p.944.
27. Ibid., pp.228-29.
28. Ibid., M.1., p.1330.

29. Ibid., M.3, p.308.
30. Ibid., M.1, p.475.
31. Ibid., M.1, pp.467-68.
32. Ibid., M.3, p.424.
33. Ibid., M.3, p.37. Also see: *āpey nadari karey bhāo lāye gurṣabadī bīchāri.* Ibid., M.3, p.65.
34. Ibid., M.3, p.30.
35. Ibid., M.1, p.1036.
36. Ibid., M.1, p.1043.
37. See translations by Dr. Gopal Singh, p.993, Vol. IV and Mr. Manmohan Singh, p.3424, Vol.6.
38. *Ādi Granth,* M.I, p.1043.
39. Ibid., M.3, p.755.
40. Ibid., M.1, p.354.
41. Ibid., M.1, p.360.
42. Ibid., M.3, p.554.
43. Ibid.
44. Ibid., M.3, p.1169.
45. Ibid., M.5, p.609. Parāpati: finding, not attainment cf. With Bhakti Sutras, in respect of this distinction.
46. Ibid.
47. Ibid., M.5, p.253.
48. Ibid., M.5, p.105.
49. Ibid., M.1, p.15.
50. Ibid., M.5, p.136
51. Ibid.
52. Mr. Manmohan Singh: *Translation of Sri Guru Granth Sahib,* Vol.I, p.451. Also see Dr. Gopal Singh's interpretation of the second line: 'Thus, they remember the Lord, the God, knowing no other but one God.' Vol.I, p.127.
53. *Ādi Granth,* M.1, p.19, also see: *jiu bhāve tiu rākhi rākhanhāriyā tudhu binu avar na koi nadari nihāriyā.* M.3, p.398.
54. Ibid., M.5, p.641.
55. Ibid., M.1, p.30.
56. Ibid., M.3, p.1420.
57. Ibid., M.3, p.558.
58. Ibid., M.5, p.384.
59. Ibid., M.5, p.1004.
60. Ibid., M.5, p.518.
61. Ibid., M.1, p.566.
62. Ibid., M.3, p.38.
63. Ibid., M.4, p.303.
64. Ibid., M.1, p.567.
65. Ibid., M.1, p.414.
66. Ibid., M.1, p.16.
67. Ibid., M.1, p.653.
68. Ibid., M.5, p.640.
69. Ibid., M.3, p.27.
70. Tr. by Shri Manmohan Singh, p.93, Vol.I.
71. *Ādi Granth,* Ibid., M.1, p.8.
72. Ibid., M.3, p.506.
73. Ibid., M.3, p.119, also see pp.1014, 733.
74. Ibid., M.5, p.782.
75. Ibid., M.5, p.1384.
76. Ibid., M.1, p.15.
77. Ibid., M.1, p.2.
78. Ibid., M.4, p.311.
79. Ibid., M.1, p.413.
80. Ibid., M.3, p.664.
81. Ibid., M.1, p.729.
82. Ibid., M.1, p.489.
83. Ibid., M.4, p.168.
84. Ibid., M.4, p.1134.
85. Ibid., M.5, p.1301.
86. Ibid., M.1, p.937.
87. Ibid., M.1, p.420.
88. Ibid., M.3, p.593.
89. Ibid., M.1, p.932. It is here interesting to note that Socrates too speaks of moral excellences as a kind of gold. Thus, see his following prayer:

   "O beloved Pan! Give me the inward beauty of the soul. May I reckon the wise to be the wealthy, and may I carry such a quantity of gold as only a temperate man can bear . . . . May the inner and the outer man be at one."

I must add that this is not a verbatim record of the prayer. However, the way I have put it is quite in accord with the spirit of the original prayer.

90. Ibid., M.1, p.1411.
91. Ibid., M.1, p.1343.
92. Ibid., M.1, p.421.
93. Ibid., M.1, p.944.
94. Ibid., M.1, p.945.
95. Ibid., M.1, p.943.
96. Ibid., M.1, p.1014.
97. Ibid., M.1, p.1112.
98. Ibid., M.1, p.595.
99. Ibid., M.3, p.602.
100. Ibid., M.5, p.1183.
101. Ibid., M.3, p.648.
102. See translation by Mr. Manmohan Singh, p.2127, Vol.IV, and translation by Dr. Gopal Singh, p.624, Vol.II.
103. *Ādi Granth,* M.4, p.1422.
104. Ibid., M.5, p.982.
105. Ibid., M.3, p.112.
106. Ibid., M.1, pp.1027-28.
107. Ibid., M.5, p.681.
108. Ibid., M.1, p.930.
109. Ibid., M.3, p.32.
110. Ibid., M.4, p.981.
111. Also see: *jis tū rākhahī kirpā dhāri būdat pāhan tārahi tāri.* M.1, p.352.
112. Ibid., M.5, p.1301.
113. Ibid., M.5, p.46.
114. Ibid., M.5, p.137, also see: *anik jatan bahu jonī bhramiyā bahuri bahuri dukhu pāiyā. tumri kirpā te mānukh deh pāi hai dehu darasu Hari raiyā.* M.5, p.207, also see, *kirpā karahu prabhu karne hāre teri bakhash nirālī. jīa jant sabh terey kīte ghati ghati tuhi dhiyāyiye. teri gati miti tu hi jānahi kudrati kīn na pāiye.* M.5, p.748.
115. Ibid., M.5, p.212.
116. Ibid., M.5, p.202.
117. Ibid., M.1, p.1031–32.
118. Ibid., M.5, p.882.
119. Ibid., M.1, p.13.
120. Ibid., M.5, p.136.
121. Ibid., M.1, p.750.
122. Ibid., M.4, p.1323.
123. Ibid., M.5, p.104.
124. Ibid.
125. Ibid., M.4, p.981.
126. Ibid., M.1, p.1117.
127. Ibid., M.5, p.204.
128. Ibid., M.5, p.318.
129. Tr. by Mr. Manmohan Singh, p.1062, V.2.
130. I interpret *japni* as appearance or impression, in accordance with the dictionary meaning of the word, *Shri Guru Granth Kosh,* p.358.
131. *Ādi Granth,* M.5, p.1307.
132. Ibid., p.779.
133. Ibid., M.5, p.137.
134. Gandhi: *In Search of the Supreme,* Vol.II, pp.126-27.

    'Humility cannot be an observance by itself. For it does not lend itself to being deliberately practised . . . . It has never come to any one by practice.'
135. *Ādi Granth,* M.5, p.187.
136. Ibid., p.183.
137. Ibid., M.5, p.1301.
138. *Bhramto bhramto hāriyo anik bidhi kar toreye.*

    kahu Nanak kirpā bhai sādh

sangati nidhi morey . . . nām laye. Ibid., M.5, p.212.
also see: *tumri kirpā te japiye nāu, tumrī kirpā te dargah thau. tujh binu Pārbhaham nahi koī. tumri kirpā te sadā sukh hoi. tum mani vasse tau dūkh na lāge. tumri kirpā te bhram bhau bhāge.* Ibid., M.5, p.192.

139. Ibid., M.5, p.114. Also see:
    a. *kahu Nanak prabh kirpā kari sās giras japahu Hari Hari.* Ibid., p.1148.
    b. *Nanak kau prabhu kirpā dhārī.*
    sāsi sāsi Hari dehu chitārī. Ibid., p.1150.
140. Ibid., p.299.
141. Ibid., M.5, p.1083.
142. Ibid., Kabirji, pp.1103-4.
143. *Ādi Granth,* M.1, p.504.
144. Ibid., p.505.
145. Ibid., M.3, p.550.
146. Ibid., M.5, p.213.
147. Ibid., M.5, p.1273.
148. Ibid., p.133.
149. Ibid., M.1, p.420.
150. Ibid., M.5, p.399.
151. Ibid., M.1, p.661; also see: *janam maran kā bhau gaiyā jīvan padvi pāī. Nanak ihu martabā tisno deyi jisno kirpā karey rajāyi.* Ibid., M.5, p.556.
152. Ibid., M.1, p.73.
153. Ibid., M.1, p.153.
154. Ibid., M.1, p.54.
155. Ibid., M.5, p.1220. Also see; Ibid., pp.1221–22, 1270.
156. Ibid., p.1183.
157. We have here in mind the well-known poetic passage which opens as follows:
    koi bole Rām Rām koi khudāyi. Ibid., M.5, p.885.
158. Ibid., M.5, p.746.
159. Ibid., M.1, p.635.
160. Ibid., M.5, p.1228.
161. Ibid., M.5, p.223.
162. Ibid., M.5, p.681. Also see: *kirpā kirpā kari jagat pit suāmī hum dāsani dās kīje panihāri. tin mati ūtam tin pati ūtam jin hirdaye vasiyā banvārī. tin kī sevā lāyi Hari suāmī tin simrat gati hoi hamārī.* Ibid., p.1135.
163. Ibid., M.5, p.278.
164. Ibid., M.1, p.471.
165. Ibid., M.5, p.1341.
166. Ibid., p.1206.
167. Ibid., p.1228.
168. Ibid., M.3, p.232.
169. Ibid., M.5, p.402.
170. Ibid., M.5, p.1221.
171. Ibid., M.5, p.1000.
172. Ibid., M.5, p.251.
173. Ibid., M.5, p.108.
174. Ibid., M.5, p.408.
175. *Guru Granth Kosh,* p.716.
176. *Ādi Granth,* M.5, p.724.
177. Ibid., M.1, p.1291.
178. Ibid., M.1, p.156.
179. Ibid., M.1, p.961.
180. Ibid., M.1, p.49.
181. Ibid., M.5, p.1251.
182. Ibid., M.4, p.41.
183. Ibid.
184. 'Theology and Falsification', in *The Philosophy of Religion,* edited by Basil Mitchell, Oxford Readings in Philosophy (O.U.P. 1977 Reprint), p.15.
185. *Ādit Granth,* M.3, p.796.
186. Translation by Mr. Manmohan Singh, p.2594, vol.5.
187. *Ādi Granth,* M.4, p.305.
188. Ibid., M.5, p.1270.
189. Ibid., M.4, p.833.
190. Ibid., M.4, p.696.

191. Ibid., M.4, p.1202. Also see: *ham achit achet na jānahi gati miti guri kīye suchit chiten. prabhi dīn daiyāli kīo angīkṛt mani Hạri Hari Nām japen.* Ibid., M.4, p.129–30.
192. Ibid., M.5, p.302.
193. Ibid., M.4, p.41.
194. Ibid., M.5, p.180.
195. Ibid., M.5, p.407.
196. Ibid., M.5, p.545.
197. Ibid., M.3, p.510
198. Ibid., M.4, p.170.
199. Ibid., p.174.
200. Ibid., M.5, pp.515-16.
201. Ibid., M.4, p.168.
202. Ibid., M.4, pp.305-6.
203. Ibid., M.4, pp.39-40.
204. Ibid., M.1, p.1022.
205. Cf. 'He is formless. But we experience Him when, imperfect beings all, we are able to . . . tread the strait and narrow path unfalteringly . . . That strength is from Him. It is Him.'
Pyarelal, *The Last Phase*, Navajivan, Ahmedabad, 1958, p.191.
206. *Ādi Granth,* M.4, p.1326.
207. Ibid., M.1, p.1331.
208. Ibid., M.1, p.1245.
209. Ibid., M.1, p.840.
210. Ibid., M.5, p.891.
211. Ibid., M.3, p.1170.
212. Ibid., M.4, p.174.
213. Ibid., M.3, p.1172.
214. Ibid., M.3, p.245.
215. Ibid., M.3, p.1108.
216. Ibid., M.5, p.673.
217. Ibid., M.1, p.1171.
218. Ibid., M.4, p.492.
Also see:
santan kī sarnāyi paḍiyā.
jīa prān dhanu āgey dhariyā.
sevā surati na janā kāī.
tum karo dayā kirmāṇiyā.
Ibid., M.5, p.1078.
219. Ibid., M.1, p.5.
220. Ibid., M.4, p.169.
Also see:
Madhusūdan Hari mādho prānā. merey mani tani amrit mīth lagānā. Hari Hari daiyā karahu gur melahu purakh niranjan soi Rām.
Ibid., M.4, p.698.
and
āpey daiyā karey prabhu dātā
satgurū purakhu milāye.
janam janam ke bichhude jan
meley Nanak sahaj subhāye.
Ibid., M.4, p.773.
221. Ibid., M.1, p.1171.
222. Ibid., M.3, p.163.
223. Ibid., M.5, p.170.
224. Cf. It is an unbroken torture to me that I am still far from Him, who . . . governs every breath of my life, and whose offspring I am.
M.K. Gandhi: *An autobiography or The Story of My Experiments with Truth*, Navajivan Publishing House, Ahmedabad, 1958 reprint, Introduction, p.xvi.
225. *Ādi Granth,* M.5, p.208.
226. Ibid., M.5, p.295.
227. Ibid., M.4, p.836.
228. Ibid., M.3, p.836.
229. Ibid., M.4, p.548. Here the brackets have been put by me, to facilitate subsequent attention to individual points.
230. Ibid., M.4, p.443.
231. Ibid., M.5, p.531-32.
232. Ibid., M.5, p.1269.
233. Ibid., M.5, pp.269–70.
234. Ibid., M.5, p.177.

235. Ibid.
236. Ibid., M.3, p.358.
237. Ibid., M.5, p.277.
238. 'When we are with "Sat" our ego is reduced to zero.' *The Collected Works of Mahatma Gandhi*, the Publication Division, Ministry of Information and Broadcasting, Govt. of India, Vol. LIII, 1972, p.483.
239. *Ādi Granth,* M.1, p.1.
240. Ibid., M.5, p.30, Also see: *āpe āpi daiyāl hai piārā jan Nanak bakhasi milāhu.*
241. Ibid., M.1, p.729.
242. Ibid., M.5, pp.563-64.
243. Ibid., M.1, p.15.
244. Ibid., M.5, p.210.
245. This point will be brought out later, as the 4th point of this Section.
246. *Ādi Granth,* M.3, p.646.
247. Ibid., M.3, p.917.
248. Ibid., M.2, p.150.
249. Ibid., M.1, p.62.
250. Ibid., M.3, p.361.
251. Ibid., M.1, p.934.
252. Ibid., M.5, p.802.
253. Ibid., M.3, p.1067.
254. Ibid.
255. Ibid., M.5, p.1223.
256. Ibid., M.5, p.274.
257. Ibid., M.5, p.1339.
258. Ibid., M.5, p.357.
259. Ibid., Kabirji, pp.480-81.
260. Ibid., M.1, p.229.
261. Ibid., M.5, p.281.
262. Ibid., M.3, p.128.
263. Ibid., M.1, p.433.
264. Ibid., M.5, p.393.
265. Ibid., M.5, p.1017.
266. Ibid., M.3, p.841.
267. Ibid., M.5, p.496.
268. Ibid., M.1, p.1273.
269. Ibid., M.5, p.397.
270. Ibid., M.5, p.700.
271. Ibid., M.5, p.392.
272. Ibid., M.3, p.909.
273. Ibid., M.3, p.87.
274. Ibid., M.3, p.1276.
275. Ibid., M.5, p.495.
276. Ibid., M.1, p.504.
277. Ibid., M.5, p.184.
278. Ibid., M.3, p. 1176.
279. Ibid., M.5, p.158.
280. Ibid., M.5, p.1072.
281. Ibid., M.5, p.810.
282. Ibid., M.5, p.279.
283. Ibid., M.5, p.460.
284. Ibid., M.5, p.114.
285. Ibid., M.3, p.1258.
286. Ibid., M.5, p.285.
287. Ibid., M.5, p.186, also see: *gurparsādī akathau kathiye kahau kahāvai soi. Nanak dīn dayāl hamārai avaru na jāniyā koī.*
288. Ibid., M.5, p.289.
289. Ibid., M.1, pp.663-64.
290. Ibid., M.5, pp.320-21.
291. Ibid., M.3, p.922.
292. Ibid., M.5, p.1019. Also see: *gurparsādī so Hari Hari pai jīo. sabh kichhu prabh kā prabh kīya jāi jeo.* Ibid., M.5, p.217.
293. Ibid., Kabirji, p.92
294. Translation by Mr. Manmohan Singh, p.302, Vol.I.
295. Translation by Dr. Gopal Singh, p.83, Vol.I.
296. *jā tisu bhāve ta lāge bhau. bharam bhulāvā vichahu jāi. upjai sahaju giān mati jāge.* Ibid.
297. Ibid., M.5, p.502.
298. Ibid., M.5, p.294.
299. Ibid., M.3, p.1054.
300. Ibid., M.3, p.1056.

301. Ibid., M.3, p.119.
302. Ibid., M.5, p.1206.
303. Ibid., M.1, p.1125.
304. Ibid., M.1, p.1027.
305. Ibid., M.5, p.887,
Also see:
gur kirpā te ih mati āvai.
jan Nanak Hari ke anki samāvai.
Ibid., M.5, p.379.
306. Ibid., M.1, p.469.
307. Ibid., M.5, pp.187-88.
308. Ibid., M.5, pp.1183.
309. Ibid., p.1235.
310. Ibid., M.1, p.110.
311. Ibid., M.3, p.932.
312. Ibid., p.1064.
313. Ibid., M.1, p.891.
314. Ibid., M.5, p.189.
315. Ibid., M.4, p.604.
316. Ibid., M.5, p.864.
317. Ibid., M.3, p.162.
318. Ibid., M.9, p.634.
319. Ibid., M.5, p.239.
320. Ibid., M.5, p.210.
321. Ibid., M.3, p.1173.
322. Ibid., p.233.
323. Ibid., p.1128.
324. Ibid., p.151.
325. M.5, p.1384, also M.1, p.83.
326. In the translation that follows bracketed words have been added to make for fulness of meaning.
327. M.1, p.8
328. Trans. by Manmohan Singh, Vol.1, pp.15–16.
329. *Ādi Granth,* M.1, p.5.
330. Ibid., M.1, p.1.
331. Ibid., M.1, p.2.
332. Ibid., M.3, p.917.
333. Ibid., M.1, p.2.
334. It may here be noted that Draupadi's cry to Krishna for help is not only one of deep, inner anguish, but is preceded by a general devotional attitude towards Kṛṣṇa; and is, therefore, no mere casual utterance.
335. *Ādi Granth,* M.4, p.1297.
336. Ibid., M.3, p.1234, *jisno nadari karai soi jan būjhei.*
337. Ibid., M.3, p.510, *hukamu bhī tinā manāisī jini kau nadari kareī.*
338. Ibid., M.3, p.66.
339. Ibid., M.3, p.134.
340. Ibid., M.5, p.277.
341. Ibid., M.5, p.53.
342. Ibid., M.3, p.512.
343. Ibid., M.4, p.1310.
344. Ibid., M.4, p.980.
345. Ibid., M.3, p.44.
346. Ibid., M.3, p.123.
347. Ibid., M.3, p.27.

3

PRAYER

From grace to prayer, the transition is obviously in order; for the practice of prayer is an important way to invoke His grace. Prayer, therefore, occupies a very important place in Sikh religion. But those who look upon God as the *surpassing* Reality and *seek His grace for the dissipation of their very egoity* cannot obviously be expected to try to probe the working of the Divine Mind. The Sikh *gurus*, therefore, do not pose and discuss many such questions as are freely put by the non-believer. If He is all-knowing, as He is sure believed to be, why does He not meet our needs without our having to pray for them? If He wishes us well, as again He is taken to do, why does He at all allow us to lapse into evil ways? Above all, how can we pray to God trustingly when there is so much of evil and suffering in the world which He is supposed to govern unchallengeably? Questions such as these do not disturb the Sikh *gurus*. They do not indeed *discuss* the philosophical problems of prayer. Yet, *I* believe, what they say on prayer *can* help the philosopher of religion. So I think it proper to open this chapter with a brief account of the problems that are generally discussed in a philosophical treatment of prayer.

1. SOME PHILOSOPHICAL PROBLEMS

If, as many today believe, a philosophical question is a question about meaning as incidental to cogent thinking and understanding, the basic problem of prayer should be obvious. What does 'prayer' mean? The question is warranted not only because not everyone knows that prayer is, but also because the real meaning of prayer as an act is often quite different from the *obvious textual meaning* of the word.

Consider, for instance, the following from the Lord's prayer:

"Our Father who art in heaven, hallowed be Thy name.

Thy kingdom come. Thy will be done on earth, As it is in heaven . . ."

Here, if in respect of the words: 'Thy Will be done on earth' we adopt a merely linguistic and cognitive approach, the obvious meaning would be roughly as follows: 'We wish that somehow He may be able to accomplish His Will in the world.' But this would imply that at present His Will is not able to assert Itself. Such a suggestion, it is obvious, will not be acceptable to those who are truly religious. Their firm faith indeed is that He is, has been, and ever will be the regulative power behind everything that is or happens in the universe. What could, then, be the real meaning of the words in question? The answer may be had by looking at the facts of religious life itself; and when I do so, I feel encouraged to reflect thus:

A man of religion is watchful distinctively. An average man is, in general, attentive only to those things and happenings which interest him in the *outer* world. A religious person, on the other hand, is just as mindful in respect of *his own inner defects* as well. Of course, like everyone else, he also wants to be happy; and like them, again, he has often to endure what appears to be failure and suffering. But when, in uncongenial situations, he resorts to self-examination, he finds that he is subject to two basic defects. First, he often commits the mistake of supposing that he can control even the consequences of his actions. Second, his actions and attitudes often tend to arise from impure motives, With a view to avoiding these mistakes, he makes in his prayerful moments a double resolve. He decides to leave the results of his efforts to the Will of God, *and* to act, so far as possible, not merely on his own judgement, which often leads him astray, but on his understanding of the way of righteousness, or in accordance with the Will of the Lord. However, in so far as it is not easy to know what exactly the Divine Will requires us to do, all that a man of prayer can immediately do is to act out of the purest of motives, assuming that the Will of God, who is goodness supreme, cannot after all be inconsistent with what is morally proper. So, the prayer 'Thy Will be done' is not really the expression of the mere wish that somehow His Will may begin to work, but *the praying man's decision to surrender his own life to Him*, to act according to His (supremely good) Will, instead of on his own; or as the Sikh *gurus* would say, to be *gurmukh* rather than *manmukh*.

However, the problem of meaning, though admittedly important, is but a recent emphasis in philosophy. The traditional problems of philosophy relate to reality, truth and knowledge. Keeping this in mind, and of course without abjuring our concern with the question of meaning, I may now briefly list the main philosophical problems of prayer as they are discussed today.

a. To begin with, is it *true* that, in soulful prayer Man surrenders himself unreservedly to the Will of God? If yes, how is prayer (as a kind of *surrender*) consistent with human dignity which is inseparable from *self-effort*?

Now, the answer may here be that the alleged inconsistency is only apparent, because authentic prayer is itself *a singular effort*. It is by no means easy to accept the reality of, and to put one's implicit faith in, that which is not accessible to the senses. Indeed, as Kierkegaard and Tillich tell us, faith is a leap and a venture. This, however, is not the leap of despair. It is a sequel to the discriminating realization of the eventual futility of worldly resources; and this realization is itself the product of long years of watchful and self-critical living. Such living is indeed no mere abidance in time. It is rather the observance of some disciplines; and an ever better regulation of one's inner attitudes. Indeed, before we can hope to take refuge in an invisible reality like God, we have to become convinced of the superior *value of attitudes* like purity, self-control, and equanimity, as opposed to the obvious *reality of things and happenings.*

b. Again, is it *true* that when a devotee prays earnestly for relief in a distressful situation, his prayer may be granted *miraculously*? If we say 'no', we oppose the testimony of men of true religiousness. If, on the other hand, we say, yes, fresh difficulties arise. For if the prayer and its fruition are both confined to the situation of *emergency*, it would mean that there was no provision for them in God's general plan for running this world; and that would imply that God's plan is not all-inclusive, which, however, cannot be; for the design of God is by hypothesis perfect. On the other hand, if both the prayer and its granting were already provided for in God's scheme of things, why does He allow the praying person to harbour the illusory belief that it is really *his present effort* of prayer which has brought about the desired result? In other words, how can we reconcile the requisite perfectness of God's scheme with the insistence of the human mind that it is the effort of *present* praying (in emergency), and an *episodic* act of grace on God's part, which really help us in times of difficulty, rather than the generally benevolent character of the plan according to which God may be said to run the universe?

I may here point out, as part anticipation of the Sikh view, that the difficulty just posed is not as insuperable as it may seem to be; and that it seems possible to temper it as follows:

God and man may well be distinct from, but they are by no means exclusive of, each other. God is generally thought of as ever outgoing love for His creatures, including men. Man, on the other hand, is different from other animals, because, quite unlike them, he can essay to realize God. Of course, not everyone is conscious of a desire to turn towards Him. But there is no doubt that, if only in a half-conscious way, we all strive for perfect happiness; and that, according to the greatest men of religion, such happiness is to be had only on attaining a direct experience of God. In any case, human and divine natures cannot be said to exclude each other.

Bearing this in mind, let us now consider what the difficulty in question says with regard to God's plan. True, in so far as He is perfection, God's plan too must be perfect. But how exactly are we to take the *perfection* of the plan of the Supreme Spirit who is also said to be perfect love, and so ever sensitive to our deepest needs, specially those for relief and protection? Surely, *not in the way of a closed circle, but as infinity of provision for the notice and relief of our difficulties.* Indeed, why can't the perfectness of God's plan be taken to mean that it includes this provision in an infinite measure?

Further, would it be improper to suggest that, various though the ways be in which God redresses our *ever-changing* difficulties, what is thereby indicated is only the *unchangeableness* of His love for us?

c. Prayer is said to involve not merely talking to God but also *listening* to Him. But, then, if He at all speaks to the praying man, does God use his (or our common human) language?

Here, our answer may run roughly thus:

First, God may not be said to use our language as freely and casually as is done by our fellow-beings. But, whatever be the precise way in which He speaks to us, this is borne out by the experience of some of the truest men of prayer that what He says is somehow intelligible to us. The saints freely report that in critical moments God has in some way spoken to them. Whether some words are here in fact heard, or what is felt is only a powerful inner impulsion, may be debatable. But we have quite a few utterances which point to the *fact* of talking and listening to God. See, for instance, the following from St. Augustine's *Confessions*:

> 'How long, how long, this "tomorrow and tomorrow"? Why not now? Why not finish this very hour with my uncleanness? . . .
>
> Suddenly a voice reaches my ears . . . "Take it and read it" . . . I snatched up the book, opened it, and read in silence the passage upon which my eyes first fell: *Not in rioting and drunkenness, not in chambering and wantonness, not in strife and envying: but put ye on the Lord Jesus Christ, and make not provision for the flesh in concupiscence.*'[1]

Apart from such exceptional cases, the thought of speaking and listening to God may only be taken to mean that in truthful prayer we *can* open ourselves up to God in a spirit of absolute trust and hope, and can receive helpful guidance from Him.

Second, whereas the needs of everyday talking call for lucidity, the 'talking' to God that *prayer* is requires faith and earnestness much more than correct, intelligible phrasing. Prayer is certainly not ruined by a slip of the tongue.[2] Here, the point at which language falters may in fact be the moment when the heart is suffused with intense and inexpressible love of God.

Finally, what God speaks to the devotee in prayer is inseparable from what He is. What my friend says to me could well be said by another man, but the peremptory and unfailingly helpful 'talking' that God occasionally does with the devout is possible to Him alone:

> 'What God utters is never in any way known and true in abstraction from God Himself. It is known and true for no other reason than that He Himself says it.'[3]

In any case, we may be unsure as to the precise way in which God speaks to His devotees in prayer. But *this* is definite that listening to God is not the same thing as listening to a human speaker. The former requires the long prior practice of moral disciplines, and is at once felt as an imperative to do what one cannot and does not like to reject.

d. Sincerity and inwardness are commonly regarded as the essence of prayer. Does it mean that the truth of prayer is merely subjective and personal? If yes, how can prayer claim to have *objective* value?

Here, I rejoin, a mere look at the actual experience of prayer is enough to provide an answer. Such experience is not merely subjective. Where it is petitionary, as it commonly is, prayer is a sincere longing to get out of a real *and often* clearly objective difficulty with the help of God who is also believed, however feebly, to be *really there.* Faith in a God who is truly (or objectively) there is as necessary a part of prayer as genuine inner longing. This faith is, in fact, what *distinguishes* prayer; for, as may be said to be natural to anyone who finds himself 'hemmed in', one *can* frantically long to get out of a difficult situation even *without* any faith in God.

Faith is hitching oneself to an objective reality also in the subtler sense that it impels the man of prayer to subordinate the whole tenor of his life to his commitment to God, and to even sacrifice his life for the sake of this commitment. The supreme concern of such a person is increasing conformity to God's law, the law of righteousness. His everyday conduct becomes transmuted in quality; and it is this ennoblement of his daily behaviour and attitudes that inclines his fellow-beings to believe that he has somehow come to secure the support of a very substantial, if invisible, Reality; and provides some verification to his emphasis on the value of faith and prayer.

e. Praying, we are told, is to be done with full faith in His goodness. But, one may wonder, when there is so much of evil and suffering in the world of which *He* is said to be the creator and overall controller, how can we pray to God with untroubled faith in His goodness? To put it briefly, faith in the goodness of God which prayer necessarily demands is clearly inconsistent with the *fact* of evil and suffering in the world.

Now, it is clear, the believer too could not be unaware of this fact. Otherwise, he would not try so hard, as he is often seen to do, not only to eradicate the *evil* in his own being, but to alleviate the *suffering* of his brethren, not infrequently with the help of strength derived from prayer. He is also, we may note, expected to have—and is often truly possessed of—an implicit faith in the reality and goodness of God. Such faith is in fact the necessary starting-point for the man of prayer, just as the thinker begins by agreeing to go by the laws of logic. But, and this is what here deserves notice, the former (that is, *the man of prayer*) does not attempt any theoretical reconciliation of the two sides of the matter. He does not give way to the wonder: *why* should, or *how* can, so much of evil and suffering be there in the world if it is ruled by a good and all-powerful God? Or, how can God be really good if He permits so much of suffering in the world? The reason for his abstention from such (merely theoretical) wonder is that the man of faith is essentially practical. He tries to actively reduce or relieve evil and suffering *with* the help of courage and steadfastness derived from prayer; and in this direction his efforts bear fruit. People like Gandhi and Mother Teresa *who in fact practise religion*, instead of merely talking about it, experience God as a living reality; and they are also closer to the reality of suffering than the average philosopher of religion who may look upon it as a merely theoretical irritant. Yet *they* never think of questioning the existence of God because of the undeniable fact of suffering. What is more, if only in a measure, even the average man can see the possibility of 'reconciling', in his everyday life, the fact of suffering with His goodness. For, in moments of intense personal suffering, is there any greater source of relief than a prayer offered in resignation to His Will and protection?

f. God is said to transcend understanding. But, as Ayer once contended, 'to say that something transcends human understanding is to say that it is unintelligible. How, then, can we at all pray to a God so regarded'?[4] The question, here, is if it is possible and useful to pray to a God whom we do not and cannot understand.

To this, the following may be offered as a rough answer:

No man of prayer has ever said that God is *quite* beyond understanding. He would rather insist that though he does not understand *how* God helps, he knows it as a matter of personal realization *that* He helps us if we turn to Him in the way of soulful prayer. Further, we should not ignore the fact that, instead of making prayer unnecessary or impossible, the thought that God is beyond understanding can also evoke the attitude of humility and reverence on the part of the devotee, and so *facilitate* prayer.

g. Long years of prayer are said to make for a state of utter egolessness. Prayers of petition and thanksgiving, on the other hand, call for a measure of egoity. No one can possibly ask for anything unless he remembers that it is *he* who has to get it. Similarly, when a man thanks another person sincerely he feels happy and relieved as a distinct centre of experience, so that egoity must here be said to persist. What, then, is the way to secure the egolessness demanded by the highest kind of prayer?

Questions such as these may be answered by pointing out that the different kinds of prayer make a dialectic; that, ordinarily, one begins with petitionary prayers; that when some such prayers are seen to bear fruit, one is moved to offer prayers of thanksgiving, and is deepened in one's love of God; and that, in so far as true love is increasingly *other*-regarding, the man who persists in offering prayer, naturally comes to be blessed with growing egolessness. Prayer is consummate where it is offered without any concern for self. It may indeed be said that

> 'in ideal prayer, our thought should be empty, waiting, not seeking anything, but ready to receive in its naked truth, the object which is to penetrate it . . . . We do not obtain the most precious gifts by going in search of them, but by waiting for them.'[5]

h. We are required to pray to God with the conviction that he is omnipotent, omnipresent and omniscient, and also possessed of moral attributes like love and benevolence. But the logical positivists contend that statements about God are all unverifiable and that there is no conceivable way to determine their truth. This is so because God is by definition a transcendent or supernatural Being, and so cannot be found anywhere in the observable universe. It is true that incarnations of God are said to have taken place. But it is equally true that the divine attributes of an incarnation are said to be revealed only to the 'eye of faith', and are thus not *verifiable* in the accepted sense of the word.

Now, what may be said to meet *this* difficulty is briefly the following:

> The verification of the truths of religion is personal and subjective; and so, if he is serious about getting an answer to his problem, let the objector take to the path of prayer himself. He must enter into the inside of devotion, so to say, by establishing a personal relation with God (*Sambandh sthāpana*), which is, however, not easy: for, as Newman points out, most 'men of the world know no exercise of the affections beyond what is merely human.'[6]

i. But, one may protest, a paradox seems to infect the essential logic of prayer, and it may be put quite simply. We are required to pray *with the faith* that a good and omnipotent God is there and that He loves us. But if we have faith, we are religious already. In other words, it appears that we cannot try to *become* religious unless we *are* religious already. But it does not seem sensible to think or speak thus.

The difficulty, however, disappears the moment we reflect that the faith or religiousness that is needed at the outset is quite elementary, and that the faith or devoutness that one may grow up into, as a result of habitual praying, is far superior in respect of depth and abidance, so that we are not required to merely *become,* but to *improve* immeasurably upon, what we presently are. (The *Gurbāni,* we may note, abounds in prayers for the deepening of faith.)

Often, when a person finds himself in an extremely difficult and seemingly insurmountable situation, all that prayer requires him to do is to think of God with the mere hope that, in case He is there, he may be somehow relieved (by Him) of his distress, exactly as a man who is threatened with drowning in a flooded river may shout earnestly for help simply with the insistent expectation that someone may be there around. The saints assure us that this *subjective earnestness* coupled, on the one hand, with the awareness that no human help is available—and, on the other hand, with the hope that God is probably listening to one's prayer—is enough to make the needed help arrive, and to thereby bear out the value of prayer. Point to this assurance is lent by a faith that men of religion share, the faith that God Himself is, so to say, anxious to help us. The following utterances may here be cited with advantage:

'We love Him, because He first loved us.' (St. John)

'Thou could not seek me unless
Thou hadst already found me.' (Pascal)

In other words, it is God who really impels us to turn to Him. A parallel from life may here be taken to illustrate the point. We, of course, discern objects by sight and hearing. But we could not do so unless we were open to the impact of light rays and sound waves. The God of religion is, so to say, always expecting us to enter into a personal relationship with Him: 'behold I stand at the door and knock'. The God of the philosophers, on the other hand, is not a Thou, but only an It, or the Absolute.

j. The relation of prayer to faith may also be said to raise some problems. For instance, if faith, on which prayer is (in principle) based, is itself groundless—that is, not supported by objective evidence in the sense that God cannot be seen—how is it at all reasonable to pray?

Questions such as these may be answered by pointing out that all evidence or 'grounds' need not be objective, and that religious faith is grounded not in any merely objective evidence as commonly understood, but in a personal realization of His redeeming power. To accept a proposition or theory on the basis of external evidence is one thing. To have faith in God, to live life in accordance with this faith, and to be thereby enabled to deal with the challenges of life more effectively and with equanimity, is quite another. Further, the value of faith as a determinant of human life, experience and attitudes is indicated by the extent to which the individual concerned comes to acquire what have been called the riches of the spirit, that is, love, joy, peace, long-suffering kindness, goodness, faithfulness, meekness, temperance and self-control.

Actually, there seems to be a basic irrelevance in the protest that faith is groundless. It assumes that faith ought to be grounded in something *more basic.* The fact, on the other hand, is that faith itself is (in principle) the ground of the good man's entire life. The man who has been able to develop true faith acts, and suffers whatever he has to, in the spirit of faith. Faith is no inert dependence on a Reality that merely is there; it is rather the upsurge of moral endeavour and ontological hope. Growing equanimity and fearlessness are more pervasive features of the way in which men of faith deal with their problems than of the lives of those who are dedicated to merely secular pursuits, admirable though they all be.

II. GOD IN PRAYER

The problems of prayer we have discussed so far are, in the main, theoretical. They are not as such, I repeat, the explicit concern of the Sikh *gurus.* Yet it would be wrong to suppose that their attitude to prayer is quite unsupportable theoretically, or that what they say about the details of authentic prayer does not contain any argument. This will be borne out presently as I turn to the Sikh view of God to whom prayers of most kinds relate. Consider, for instance, the following prayer of Guru Arjan which distinguishes quite a few attributes of God:

sukhdātā bhaibhanjano tisu āgai kari ardāsi.
mihar karey jisu miharvānu tā kāraju āvai rāsi.[7]

re man merey tū tā kau āhi
jā ke ūṇā kachhahu nāhi.
Hari sā pritamu kari man mīt
prān adharu rākhahu sad chīt.
re man merey tu ta kau sevi
ādi purakh aprampar dev.
tisu ūpari man kar tū āsā.
ādi jugādi jā kā bharvāsā.
jā kī prīti sadā sukh hoi.
Nanak gāvai gur mili soi.[8]

Here, it is explicitly said that prayer is to be addressed only to God, the One without a parallel, and not to gods and goddesses who are many ('worship the one and none beside'). But, it may be asked, *why* should we pray to the One at all? The answer provided in the above prayer is: because He is *sukhdātā bhaibhanjano.* This is by no means a new idea, but the Sikh scriptures repeatedly emphasize it. Thus see, again, the following from Guru Arjan:

tīney tāp nivāraṇhārā dukh hunta sukh rāsi.
tākau bighanu na koū lāge jākī prabh āgai ardāsi.[9]

The noteworthy point here is that prayer is expressly related to a basic practical interest of Man. For, who is not subject to ills and evils of some kind or the other? And who has not occasionally pined for quick and complete relief from them? The need for peace of mind, and for relief from evil and suffering, is indeed basic. He who prays for the redress of this dual need, therefore, offers a prayer which is *relevant to all.* What is more, such praying cannot but be sincere. Indeed, it is impossible to be insincere when one prays for the relief of one's own present suffering; and the corresponding conception of God is bound to be that of a God who can and does take mercy on us in times of need. In other words, the easy way to pray truly is to think of God as the God of *mercy* which we all need at some time or the other. And if God is so regarded, and so related to our need for freedom from suffering, our right attitude in prayer can only be one of love and trust. This is why the prayer in question says: 'Be saturated, body and mind, in His love'. It is only when we love God 'and keep Him ensconced in our heart' that we can sing His praises and chant His holy Name sincerely. The metaphysical attributes of

God, which speak of Him as 'complete in Himself, all-pervasive and permeating' are important, as this prayer suggests, only in so far as they serve to steady us in the faith that He can relieve everybody's distress in every situation; they do not themselves directly make for sincerity in prayer.

III. THE VALUE OF NĀM

If it here be asked as to how exactly we are to so relate ourselves to Him that our praying may be true at once, the answer would obviously be that the relation in question has to be of an intimately personal kind: hence the great importance attached to *Nām* in the Sikh philosophy of religion. Guru Nanak, the founder of Sikhism, regards It as his only refuge and source of sustenance:

ek oat eko ādhār.
Nanak māṅge Nām prabh sāru.[10]

Why does the great *gurū* pine so soulfully for commitment to the Name? The answer is: because It is not only the highest Reality, and so our unfailing anchor, but also the true source of affluence, and gratifier of all desires. I say so on the basis of the following:

a. *Nām tul kachhu avar na hoī*[11]

b. *binu Nāvāi sabhu koi nirdhan*
satgurū būjh bujhāī.[12]

c. *pārjāt ihu Hari ko Nām.*
kāmdhenu Hari Hari guṇ gān.[13]

The last couplet cited may, however, suggest a question. If the Name is *Kāmadhenu,* does it mean that a recitation of It makes for the fulfilment of *every* desire, fair or foul? Here, it is clear, we cannot say *yes.* Ignoble desires cannot be said to elicit the assistance, or even the approval, of *Nām.* It is only when It is availed of in singing the glories *of* the Lord (*Hari guṇ gān*)—or as an accent of utterly selfless prayer—that the Name serves to meet our (legitimate) desires. The point will become clearer when we turn to reflect on what *Nām* really is. The whole question of *Nām* (as related to prayer) has in fact to be discussed piecemeal, say, under the following sub-headings:

What *Nām* is: the rational and mystical/metaphysical views

The kind of orientation it demands: levels in *Nāmjapa*

What *Nām* does: marks or verification of Its value.

The *Nām* that we are presently dealing with is the Name *of the Lord.* Recitation of It is said to be the highest religion, for it conduces to the attainment of *mokṣa*:

> *sarab dharam mahi sreṣt dharam.*
> *Hari ko nāmu japi nirmal karamu.*[14]
> *Nanak jinkai hirdai vasiyā.*
> *mokh mukati tinī pāiyā.*[15]

In the light of all this, it is obviously unthinkable that *Nām* may also conduce to the fulfilment of *unworthy* desires. All ignoble desire is rooted in the *manmukh* attitude, as opposed to the *gurmukh* orientation of our lives; and in so far as Its very inherent potency is such that It tends to annihilate egoity[16], *Nām* just cannot be said to cater to base desires.

Names of the Lord are, however, infinite in number. Different religions eulogize different names. The Hindus, generally, glorify '*Om*' and '*Rāmanāma*'. The Muslims prefer *Allāh*; and the Sikhs, *Vāhe Guru.* Every religious order has adopted a specific *Nām* as its typical way of, say, addressing the Lord. But, in so far as every Name, regarded as a meaningful word, signifies just one attribute of God, no devotee can keep himself confined to just one *Nām* throughout his life. To illustrate, *Rāma* means 'That which permeates all that is there'; *Rahim,* 'the gracious or the merciful'; *ek Omkar,* 'the one life-principle'; and *Akāl Purukh* signifies the supreme Person who is beyond the trammels and ravages of time. But in the varying situations of life who does not feel the need to think of God as available everywhere and in every situation (*Rāma*); as merciful (*Karīm*); and as eternal and beyond decay and death, or as *Akāl Purukh*? A true *bhakta,* indeed, is respectful towards all the Names of God. Thus see the following:

> *balihārī jāu jete terey nāu hai.*[17]

Yet, I repeat, some specific holy Name is essential for every religion. Just as in daily life names are meant to facilitate our dealings with one another, so *Nām* is necessary for prayer. Indeed, how otherwise can God be addressed? Yet there is a difference between the two cases. When we use names in addressing, or referring to, people in everyday life we *assume* that they exist. In prayer, on the other hand, the utterance of *Nām* is often an attempt to *deepen* one's faith in His reality and attributes in spite of His being an invisible, spiritual reality.

Of course, no Name or aggregate of Names can capture His total reality which is infinite. Yet, to help our contemplation of His reality we have to use various Names as standing for His different attributes. It is indeed *Nām* which enables us to secure a kind of foothold in His Reality. An idol serves the same purpose, more or less. But if we compare the two, a *Nām* and an idol, the former seems to be clearly preferable in one respect. An idol may easily tend to keep the devotee's attention confined to its own inert and sensuous form. *Nām*, on the other hand, leaves the mind free to *think* of His attributes and of the many ways they are seen to work for our good in life's varying situations. However, though *Nām* does enable one to contemplate God directly, the relation thus provided is perhaps not so intimate as that which is involved in the use of *Thou* or *Tū*.

On the other hand, it would be wrong to suppose that if during prayer we use only *Nām*, and not *Thou* or *Tū*, the heart must remain totally untouched. The truth rather is that, speaking quite generally, a *Nām* itself does not make a whole prayer; that any regular prayer includes a good deal of verbal material which accords, in spirit, with the meaning of the specific *Nām* chosen, and also (we may add) with the praying person's present attitudes; and that, therefore, the utterance of a *Nām*—as embedded in its appropriate context—can be very soulful. Consider, for instance, two well-known devotional songs or *bhajans* which (individually) open as follows:

Hari tum haro jan kī pīr (Mīra)
tū dayāl dīn ḥoun-tū dātā houn bhikhārī. (Tulsidās)

Here, in the first prayer, God is addressed as *Hari* because He is requested to *relieve the sufferings* of people; and, in the second, as *dayāl*—that is, the Merciful—because the devotee who prays for relief is *dīn* or pitiable. As for the Sikh scriptures, just a single prayer from them should be enough to bear out the point being made:

tū merā pitā tū hai merā mātā.
tū merey jīa prāṇ sukhdātā.
tū merā thākur hau dās terā.
tujh binu avaru nahī ko merā.
kari kirpā karahu prabh dāti.
tumarī ustati karahu din rāti.[18]

In this prayer God is addressed as *Thākur* or the Lord; and what the word in question means is heightened not only by the devotee's referring to himself as a mere *dāsa* of His, but by his emphasis—say, in terms of the child-parent image—that his dependence on Him is entire and exclusive.

The point I am here seeking to make is that when, during the act of praying, such a Name is used as is accordant with the textual content of the prayer, it tends to *explicitly deepen* the faith that He is there and that He really possesses the attributes that the various names ascribe to Him. We say 'deepen', because a minimal measure of faith is (in principle) already there at the very outset of prayer.

It may here be added that at the deeper level of faith, where the devotee turns to God with childlike sincerity, the Name is not regarded as a mere pointer *to* God, but *as God Himself*:

> *satigur main ṣabad,*
> *ṣabad main satgur.*

This may not be dismissed as odd; for, as Susanne Langer has pointed out, the human mind has a natural tendency to identify a symbol with what it symbolizes. Thus, when a little girl points to the globe, she says: 'Look this *is* the earth'; she does not say: 'This *symbolizes* the earth'[19]. Similarly, when a mother takes the name of her own child, it is no mere utterance of a word referring to something beyond itself, but at once the loving visualization of a real individual. For her, indeed, the child's name is almost the same thing as the child itself.

Objectively, the identification of the symbol with what it signifies, or of *Nām* with God, facilitates the faith that *Nām* is the original creator and sustainer of the universe: *jetā kītā tetā Nau.*[20] It should now be easy to see the point of utterances such as the following:

> 'In the beginning was the Word, and the Word was with God and Word was God. The same was in the beginning with God. All things were made by Him, and without Him was not anything made that was made. In Him was life; and the life was the light of man. And the light shineth in darkness, and the darkness comprehendeth it not.'[21]

At this point, some thought may be given to the way *Nām* has been regarded in Sikhism as a metaphysical principle. Consider, for instance, the following:

> a. *hirdai nāmu sadā dhuni nihchal ghatai na kīmati pāi.*[22]

b. "*Nām* may be described as 'life-impulse' or 'conscious principle'. When it *begins* to vibrate, it provides melodious sound, which is termed *śabda.* The sound current proceeding from the deep silence of the Formless *kutasth* is (also) responsible for all forms and colours, visible and invisible to the naked eye. All life hangs on this life-principle. It is . . . the Essence and at once both the material and efficient cause of the endless universe."[23]

c. *Śabda* (Holy word) is the Primordial sound which was the manifestation of God Himself. This was the primordial Energy through which the universe came into existence. This sound (*anhad Śabda*) still reverberates in this universe. Divine persons are able to hear it by concentration. Along with it they can see the Light (*jot*) which too was the manifestation of God. The original energy of Sound and Light brought into existence the entire material universe which is ultimately resolvable into it. Holy persons who hear this Sound and see the Light wish to acquaint the common man with it; they wish to tell him what its nature is. The medium of communication at their disposal is speech. The description of this primordial Energy, which is God Himself, is called *Nām.*"[24]

In line with the third extract just cited it has been suggested that 'the Name in Sikhism is not a mere collection of momentary sounds, (but is rather) . . . the sabda Brahman (*anahad nāda*) of the grammarians and the Śaivās'.[25] However, from the purely rational point of view, as distinguished from that of mystical experience, I would like to explain the above utterances as follows:

Recitation of *Nām* is both an utterance *and* an earnest and hopeful looking to God. As mere utterance, it is sound and vibration. Vibrations are present, if not manifestly, in whatever is there; that is, in every detail of given reality; they may, therefore, be regarded as the very material of reality:

Nāmahi te sabh kuchh baṇiyā khaṇḍ brahmaṇḍ sarīr.[26]

On the other hand, as an utterance of faith or as prayer, *Nām* is also a speech-act of addressing the Lord Himself with the faith that He is the *efficient* cause of whatever there is, and of everything that happens, including the redress of our pain and suffering in response to prayer:

sad suṇdā sad vekhdā sabadi rahiyā bharpūri.[27]

Considering the two sides together, *Nām* may be said to be singular in the sense that *It* alone is both an essential and pervasive constituent of reality *and* an invocation of, as also a means to the attainment of, the supreme Reality itself:

kirat surat mukati ik nāi.
tā hī Niranjan rahiyā samāī.[28]

As utterance of the Name of the Lord, when it *begins* to vibrate in the heart of the devotee—that is, in a setting of intense and self-effacing love of God—it feels as melodious sound (*śabd*) and proceeds from the very depths of our soul or the formless *kutasth.* In its aspect of mere sound or vibrations, on the other hand, It may be said to be responsible for 'all forms and colours', that is, as much for physical reality as for our sentient life. It may further be suggested that when *Nām* is said to be (*already*) *reverberating* in all hearts, It is taken as vibrations without which neither physical reality nor conscious and embodied life is possible; and where It is said to *begin to* vibrate, *Nām* is to be looked on as prayerful utterance of His Name marking the *dawn* of devotion.

Personal prayer is, of course, not the only way of being related to *Nām.* The more important other ways are *sunan* (or *śravana*), *manan, kīrtan*; and, above all, the company of saints who provide a living verification of the life-giving power of the Name. But the most significant gains from our concern with *Nām* are to be had only through our own proper relatedness to it, or through *nāmajapa,* that is, devout and regular recitation of the Name. This is why we are commanded to:

jab lagu jobani sāsu hai tabu lagu nāmu dhiāi
chaldiā Hari chalsī Hari ante laye chhadāī.[29]

But, it is obvious, such a supremely helpful recitation of *Nām* cannot be the parrot-like repetition of a mere word. Instead, it has got to be the index of an evergrowing dependence on the Lord, which means that a single anguished utterance of the Name *can* be more rewarding as an experienced moment of faith, humility and prayer than a leisurely contemplation of His attributes as projected in a whole song. Indeed, our relation with *Nām* has to be very sincere. The way we utter It should not be a mere act of speech; it must rather be felt as a moment of yearning and trust, for only then can it make for our final liberation:

mukhahu Hari Hari sabh kahai viralai hirdai vasāiyā.
Nanak jinkai hirdai vasiā mokh mukati tin pāiyā.[30]

On the outer side, the mere writing, utterance, or inscription of a Name of God is not true *Nām*. Here It becomes a spiritual power only in the truthful words of a *gurū*, because *his* utterance of the Name springs from the depth of his personal realization. It is indeed the *gurū* who makes us receptive to the idea that a fathomless and invisible reality can yet have a Name:

Nām niranjan agam agochar satgur diyā bujhāi.[31]

At this point, we should also be able to see the philosophical secret of the adoration of the *Guru Granth Sahib*. The Sikh position is a little similar to that of the *Mimāṃsakas* who believe that a *mantra* possesses the power of making a deity incarnate. What is more, an analysis of Sikhism yields a philosophy of language which, on the one hand, agrees with the Vedic tradition of Śruti; and is, on the other hand, similar to the philosophy of mystic sound developed in the non-Vedic traditions like *Śaivāgama, Buddhist, Tantra* and *Sahajyāna*.[32]

c. But when so much has been said *for Nām*, one question still remains. How are we to verify the power or excellences attributed to It? What are the distinguishing marks of the being of a man who is rightly related to *Nām*? Questions such as these may be answered as follows:

A person who is truly committed to the Name comes to acquire quite a few admirable qualities. He becomes humble, for love of the Name naturally tends to destroy egoity:

haumai Nāvai nāli varodhu hai dui na vasahi ik thāi.[33]

Further, the individual in question is enabled to overcome the heat of passions, and so grows tranquil at heart.[34] And in case his circumstances require him to take up arms, he is seen to fight as a warrior with perfect forbearance and intelligence. Generally, he is blissful and healthy; perfectly non-attached to the material world; and steadfast in *sahaj* meditation, and so serene. The man who is perfectly devoted to *Nām* is successful in whatever he undertakes to do. Above all, though never inactive, he is ever released:

sūrvīr dhīraj mati pūrā
sahaji samādhi dhuni gahir gambhīrā.
sagal sūkh ānand ārog.
samdarṣī pūran nirjog.
āi na jāi doley kat nāhī.
jā kai nāmu vasai man māhī.
sadā mukatu tā ke pūre kām
jā kai riday vasai Hari Nām.[35]

I must, however, admit that everything that is said about *Nām* in the Sikh scriptures is not as clear to me as what I have said so far; and this section cannot be brought to an end without an attempt to deal with some difficult utterances of the various *gurus* on the subject:

> In *Nām*, we are told, there is perfect food, both for the eyes and the ears.[36] On the other hand, it is also emphasized, in a different context, that contact with Nām can take place only in a region *beyond the domain of senses* and sensory organs.[37] In this connection it is even asserted that 'Nām is not the subject of the eyes'.[38] Now, how are we to reconcile the two sides?

It seems to me that the key to meet the difficulty I have just posed is provided by the words 'perfect food'. Our everyday food is *im* perfect in so far as it satisfies our appetite only for a short time, after which hunger and the need for food appear anew. 'Perfect food', by contrast, would be that which satisfies the hunger of the senses, be it that of the tongue or of the eyes and ears, permanently. Now, a perfect or abiding transcendence of the craving of the senses for contact with their normal objects can be achieved only when *Nām* comes to really grip our hearts. By way of theoretical support, reference may here be made to the *Gītā* view, which Gandhi finds verified in the light of his own experience, that *rasa,* or craving for a relish of sense-objects, disappears only after a direct experience of God.

Another seeming contradiction occurs in the following passage:

a. Hari ke nām binu jhuṭhey sagal pāsāre.

b. Nām rahio sādhū rahio rahio gur Gobind.[39]

Here, again, (a) seems to clash with (b); for if Nām *alone* is of permanent value, how can *three other things* also be said to be 'eternal and lasting'? The difficulty, however, disappears the moment we reflect that, as a man of practical religion, the writer (himself a *gurū*) is not concerned with the mere concept of *Nām*, but with the recitation of the Name *by human beings*, in which relation alone Its value becomes manifest. This recitation, as actual utterance, *involves* the following: sound current; the inspiring, yet only generally helpful, example of those *sādhus* who are committed to the Name; the personal and graded guidance of one's individual *gurū;* and, of course, God or *Gobind* of whom the *Nām* is an inseparable symbol. In other words, *as an active force for human good*, the Nām is not a barren singleness, but a configuration of four inter-related factors. Therefore, I conclude, (a) really includes, instead of being opposed to, (b); and so no contradiction is involved.

IV. SOME PRAYERS ANALYSED

Generally, however, the more popular way of establishing a personal relationship with God is not mere *Nām*, but the Name as incorporated in whole prayers with an elaborate textual content. So, some select Sikh prayers may now be analyzed. This is necessary also because in so far as they were not *philosophers* of religion, the Sikh *gurus* have not expressely formulated their views on prayer in a systematic way, which means that *we* have to find out what prayer meant to them through careful analysis of their songs of devotion. Every individual prayer that I am now going to cite will be followed by some interpretative comments:

kirat karam ke bīchhuḍe kari kirpā melahu Rām.
chāri kunt dah dis bhramey thaki āye prabh ki sām.
dhenu dudhai te bāharī kittai na āvai kām.
jal binu sākh kumlāvatī upjahi nāhī dām.
Hari nāh na miliye sājanai kat pāiye bisrām.
jiṭu ghari Hari kantu na pragtaī bhathi nagar se grām.
sarab sīgār tambol ras saṇu dehā sabh khām.
prabh suāmī kant vihūṇiā mīt sajan sabhi jām.
Nanak kī benantiā kari kirpā dījai nāmu.[40]

Attention to the text of this prayer enables me to make the following points:

Ordinarily, petitionary prayer, which is usually an entreaty for some empirical gain, is thought to be inferior in value to prayers of thanksgiving and praise. But where, as in the present prayer, the petition is for such an exalted and purely spiritual end as union with God—and where, what is more, the surpassing value of the Lord is also openly acknowledged, as is freely done in prayers of thanksgiving and praise—the petitionary kind of prayer cannot be rated lower than the other kinds of prayer.

What I have just said also makes it clear that though for purposes of understanding we often draw a clear distinction between the different kinds of prayer, a whole, actual prayer is not necessarily one of petition only, but may also contain, as the present one does, a clear measure of praise to the Lord.

From this it follows that a real prayer is not as simple a matter as it may seem to be from the merely intellectual point of view. Nor is it a kind of relation *only* between God and Man. The world too is here vitally involved. Thus, in the prayer being discussed, the suggestion is quite clear that a man turns to God with earnestness only when he has realized, as a matter of personal experience, that none of the various directions of his empirical activity is able to give him abiding peace and satisfaction: see here the words, '*chāri kunt dah dis bhramey thaki āye prabh kī sām*' which may be translated thus, 'having wandered in all directions, tired and worn out, we have come to Thy feet'. (The 'objective' relevance of prayer should now be clear.)

Further, prayer is not a merely cognitive direction of attention at a clearly apprehended object. It is rather a kind of somewhat blind but avid insistence, so to say, for union with God in sheer desperation, love and longing. Here the devotee does not feel like arguing that because he has been able to gather enough of moral merit, he deserves to be united with God; instead, he only insists that because he is *thaki āye* or worn out, he must somehow be taken 'unto Thee again' (*prabh kī sām*) in spite of his 'own deeds' (*kirat karam*) which, one may add, are often directed to wrong ends.

As admission of the poor quality of one's own deeds or general living, humility is in fact an essential pre-condition of genuine prayer. (Such admission, we may add, is by no means easy. It calls for a continually self-critical way of living. So, the surrender which prayer demands is itself the result of effort, and is partly felt as healthy self-assessment rather than as a loss of dignity.) Indeed, the devotee who prays is not discouraged by the thought that there is a great gulf between his (so far) incorrigible vileness and God's own unmixed purity, and that therefore union with Him is impossible. He rather feels borne aloft on the very intenseness of his recoil from the things and pursuits of the world—towards a God who demands not a scholarly insight into His nature, but just a surrender to His feet. It is the recoil (*vīrakti*), and no mere understanding, which puts life and substance into our yearning for God.

Here, I may add, a point of some theoretical value could be made. Intellectually, the finite is merely opposed to the infinite. But this mere opposition becomes a vital and creative tension in the personality of a devotee. When he *realizes*, not merely *thinks* of, the ultimate futility of his worldly pursuits and of his own weaknesses, he turns to God not so much by way of thought and planned endeavour, as in love, renunciation, longing, and trust.

The devotee is worthless in his own view, not because he is literally without any merit, but because in his present state of estrangement from God he cannot find abiding peace. No external embellishment of the body can make up for the lack of inner tranquillity. The fact rather is that without a realization of God as *antaryāmī*—which awareness is the only source of peace imperturbable—involvement with outer, empirical ends only conduces to our perdition, by keeping us confined to what is insubstantial and perishable.

Finally, whereas a clear understanding of the nature and ways of God is for ever denied to us, a soulful utterance of His Name, exactly like a child's agonized cry for its mother's lap, is available to us all. (Heartfelt, yet *humble* praying to God becomes possible precisely because we do not understand *how* He can help, but only have the faith *that* He is bound to help.) Be it noted, however, that our becoming *gurmukh* or godward depends not only on our passing dissatisfaction with the world, but also on our original and abiding kinship with God, so that the prayer for 'union' is for being taken 'Unto Thee *again*'.

The suggestion, made during my discussion of the first prayer, that the same prayer may be directed at different ends, is also borne out by close attention to the prayer I am now going to dwell upon. This prayer is, primarily, a prayer for the resignation to the Will of God; and, secondarily, yet necessarily, also a prayer for humility, love and contentment (thus providing some answer to the question, earlier listed as a philosophical problem, as to how prayer can make for egolessness). What is further noteworthy about the prayer I am about to discuss is its identification of wisdom with love of God. This love, one may argue in accordance with the prayer in question (cited below), is the highest wisdom because it alone makes for realization of the three ends which are of supreme value to those who are committed to a spiritual life: that is, humility, purity and contentment:

kirpānidhi basahu ṛidai Hari nīt.
taisī budhi karahu pargāsā lagai prabh sangi prīti.
dās tumārai kī pāvau dhūrā.
mastak le le lāvau.
mahā patit te hot punītā Hari kīrtan gun gāvau.
āgiyā tumārī mīthī lāgau kīo tuhāro bhāvau
jo tu dehi tāhī ihu tripati ān na kathū dhāvau
sadahi nikati jānau prabh suāmī sagal raiṇ hoi rahiye.
sādhū sangati hoi parāpati tā prabhu apunā lahiye.
sadā sadā hum chhohrey tumrey tū prabh hamro mīrā.
Nanak bārik tum māt pitā mukhi nāmu tumāro khīrā.[41]

Some other truths of the good life which are suggested in the above prayer may be put as follows:

First, what is here prayed for is no empirical end, but only some attitudes which are essential for one's progress in the life of religion; love of God, and resignation to His Will. Such praying, we may at once add, is bound to temper egoity (or *haumai*).

Second, some such assertions are also made in the prayer as do not merely state what they mean, but are at once an exercise in some highly desirable attitudes (because, I assume, they are made in all earnestness). Thus, when the writer-devotee says: *mahā patit te hot punītā Hari kīrtan gun gāvau,* it is a direct exercise of the faith in His redemptive power; and when he declares: '*sadā sādā hum chhohre tumre tū prabh hamro mīrā*' or '*Nanak bārik tum māt pitā*' the utterances may be taken as expressing moments of *felt* humility in relation to, and of dependence on God.

Thirdly, a subtle truth of the good life seems to be implicit in the following line:

'*dās tumārey kī pāvau dhūrā mastak lai lai lāvau.*'

If this line is taken along with the writer's admission of his own fallenness (*mahā patit*), we get the thought that a devotee who is clearly conscious of his own depravity, and who at the same time feels the continuous presence of God by His side, cannot but be determined in practice by an implicit argument which may be put thus: 'If God, the most exalted Reality, is always with His devotee in spite of the latter's seemingly incorrigible vileness, why should not the devotee himself ever be close and helpful to the meanest of His servants'?

An excellent example of a truly spiritual prayer is provided by the following one, because the ends here prayed for are all clearly spiritual: union with and ceaseless remembrance of God; steadfastness in faith; surpassing commitment to the Name; and unremitting singing of the praises of the Lord:

1. *prabhajī milu merey prān.*
   bisaru nahī nimakh hīarey te apne bhagat kau pūran dān.
2. *khovahu bharamu rākhu merey prītam antarjāmī sughaḍ sujān.*
3. *koti rāj nām dhanu merey.*
4. *amrit dṛṣti dhārahu prabh mān.*
   āth pahar rasnā guṇ gāvai jasu pūri aghāvahi samrath kān.
5. *terī ṣarṇi jīān ke dāte sadā sadā Nanak kurbān.*[42]

What is here specially noteworthy is that where the surpassing value of the nectarine glance of the Lord (*amrit dṛṣti*) is accepted by the devotee, the inner determinant is his desire not merely to live long, but to pack every moment of the course of his life with *kīrtan* of His glory(4).

It is, of course, common knowledge that a devotee is required to cultivate an unwinking sense of the presence of God. But in the following prayer we are offered the additional thought that, however definite and pervasive be this sense, it is not as satisfying to the devotee as a 'blessed *vision*' of the Lord. For one who loves God intensely, *darśana* is superior to the mere faith in His omnipresence, however, unwavering it be:

darṣan pekhat manu āghāvai
sad balihār jāiye kurbānā.
jali thali pūri rahiā miharvānā . . .
rākhi līye sagley prabh āpe
utar gaye sabh sog santāpe.
Nām japat manu tanu hariyāvalu
prabh Nanak nadari nihāre jeo.[43]

What kind of seeing could this 'vision' be? It cannot be sense-perception of the ordinary kind, Guru Arjan declares:

'Nanak se akhiyā bianni jini disando mā piri'[44]

But if this is so—that is, if the vision in question is not what *we* know as seeing—how are we to interpret the words: 'my eyes may *behold Thy gracious form*'? Could we say that 'the blessed vision' sought is akin to the 'inner' seeing of the *svarūpa* of a god or goddess which is said to be accessible to those who are trained in the meditative practices of Yoga? Or are we to suppose, on the basis of Gandhi's experiences of fellowship with God, that the 'vision' in question is the overpowering sense of being commanded or guided by God *without* the preception, inner or outer, or any identifiable figure? This interpretation, however, would clash with the natural meaning of: 'behold Thy gracious form'. So, at this point I may only regret my inability to be definite.

This is, however, certain that in a person who loves God, the sense of creatureliness produces the feeling of gratitude; and that, therefore, the devotee, instead of complaining that the Infinite (or God) is incomprehensible, only revels in His plenitude (which *is* perhaps some answer, we may say, to the philosophic wonder as to how a Reality that defies understanding can at all be worshipped). This is the big idea in the following prayer:

> *tum māt pitā hum bārik terey.*
> *koi nā jāṇe tumrā unt. tumri gati miti tum hi jānī.*
> *Nanak dās sadā kurbāni.*[45]

The child-parent image is here instructive. The child does not seek to *understand* its mother before turning to her for help; it does so instinctively and directly in moments of need. Why can't it be so even in the case of the devotee-deity relation? To be sure, this relation is quite different from the one that obtains between participants in a seminar where discussion is a give-and-take between those who are equals, more or less; and where the emphasis is (in principle) on understanding. The devotee does not seek to match his wits with the Lord; his is only to depend on, and to draw sustenance from Him in the way of love, and surely not in that of servitude to an alien power. All this is borne out by the following prayer:

> *tū merā prītamu tum sungi hītu . . .*
> *tujh binu nimakhu na jāi rahaṇā . . .*
> *tū merī sobhā tum sangi rachiā.*
> *tū meri oat tū hai merā takiā.*
> *mun tan antari tuhī dhiāiyā.*
> *maramu tumārā gur te pāiā.*[46]

The love that the devotee here speaks of is exclusive and self-effacing; and, what is more, it involves his entire personality ('I worship Thee in my mind and body'). But the point of pivotal value, here, is that the experience of deep love is at once *a sense of losing oneself happily* in what is (for the time being) felt to be infinite ('I am absorbed in Thy love').

It must, however, be added that the devotee's yearning for God is not only determined by the intensity of his love and devotion, but is also, in a way, softened by his experienced humility in relation to God, so that what he pines for is not a bold and steadfast encounter with God, much less a comprehensive understanding of His reality and nature, but just a fleeting glimpse of His glory. I say so in the light of the following prayer:

kiā guṇ terey sāri samhālī mohi nirgun ke dātāre
. . . ihu jeu pindu sabhu thāre.
lāl rangīle prītam manmohan terey darṣan kau hum bāre . . .
kitu pāvau darsāre?
miti nahi pāiye antu na lahiye manu tarsey charṇāre.[47]

It should now be quite clear that a single prayer can comprise various attitudes, and so may not be characterizable as a prayer of praise *or* of petition alone. The truth indeed is that when in the course of praying the devotee contemplates the metaphysical attributes of God—may be, in negative terms such as 'Unreachable', 'Unknowable'—he also finds it necessary to relate Him to human life and existence, and so to dwell upon His moral attributes. What is more, contemplation of the moral attributes of God may assume the form of grateful acknowledgement, and not that of a mere petition for some empirical end; and the acknowledgment of His help can be as clearly a source of felt truthfulness in prayer as the making of a petition for relief in distress. The following prayer illustrates all this clearly:

tudhu binu dūjā nāhī koi. tu kartāru karahi so hoi.
terā joru teri mani tek. sadā sadā japi Nanak ek.
sabh ūpari pārbraham dātāru. teri tek terā ādhāru.
hai tu hai tu hovanhār. agam, agādh, ūch, apār.
jo tudhu sevahi tin bhau dukhu nāhī. gurparsādi Nanak gun gāhī.
jo dīsai so terā rūpu. guṇ nidhān gobind anūp.
simari simari simari jan soi. Nanak karam parāpati hoi.
jini japiā tis kau balihār. tis kai sangi tarai sansār.
kahu Nanak prabh lochā pūri. sant janā kī bāchhau dhūri.[48]

It is here important to see how the devotee's contemplation even of the metaphysical attributes of God can influence his attitude to his fellow beings. To illustrate, when a man reflects on the inexhaustible excellences of God he may find it easy to see that devotion to God is no monopoly of his; that His infinite qualities admit of contemplation by many devotees; and that, therefore, he should not regard himself superior to others merely because of his own truthful devotion to God. This is indeed the evidence of the following prayer:

tū thākuro bairāgro mai jehi ghaṇcheri Rām.
tū sāgro ratnāgro hau sār na jāṇā teri Rām.
sār na jāṇā ṭū vad dānā kari miharmanti sāin.
kirpā kījai sā mati dījai āth pahar tudhu dhiāi.
garabu na kījai raiṇu hovijai tā gati jiarey terī.
sabh ūpari Nanak kā thākuru main jehī ghaṇ cheri Rām.[49]

Why do the Sikh *gurus*, one may here ask, lay so much stress on humility and keep on characterizing themselves as mere dust? A part answer to this question may be given by inviting attention to an attitude which is indeed typical of the man of faith. Whereas the outsider—that is, a man who is not *in* faith—is often seen to complain as to why it should at all be necessary, if God is all-knowing, to pray to Him for the redress of our needs and difficulties, the prayer of the man who is *in* faith can assume the form of a quite different question: 'When, as *antaryāmin*, Thou knowest me through and through, why should not Thou eradicate my deep-seated faults straightway?' And the question is, with him, insistent; for he knows that it is his failings that bar the way to a closer approximation to God whom he burns to realize.

To pray for closeness to God, the *gurus* believe, is not to ask for what is merely one of the many important ends of life, but for an experience (or state) which alone is the most fundamental need of man. This is borne out by the following prayer:

jal bihūn mīn kat jīvan dūdh binā rahanu kat bāro.
jan Nanak piās charan kamlanh kī pekhi darasu piāsī sukh sāro.[50]

The relations here referred to—that is, of an infant to milk, and of a fish to the water in which it breathes—alike convey the idea of utter dependence; and, indeed, a prominent detail of prayer as visualized by the Sikh *gurus* is the emphasis they put on the thought that what is needed for a vital relationship with God is no merit on our part, but simply the attitude of implicit and exclusive dependence on Him. So says Nanak:

> *sunahu benantiā suāmi merey Rām.*
> *binvanti Nanak dāsu Hari kā prabh jīa prān adhārī.*[51]

It would here be relevant to point out that a devotee's contemplation of God's metaphysical attributes during prayer is never merely impersonal. He cannot help relating them to his own personal life. It is verily this relation that lends sincerity to prayer. Thus, in the following prayer, though the greatness of God as the creator and sustainer of all life is repeatedly emphasized, the *bhakta* also feels impelled to declare that an important manifestation of God's greatness lies in the fact that it is He who has elevated him, a poor helpless fellow, from 'a very low birth' to the status of a man of wisdom who realizes the indescribable greatness and providence of God:

> *Prabh ji mohi kavanu anāthu bichārā.*
> *kavan mūl te mānukh kariā ihu partāp tuhārā.*
> *jīa prān sarab ke dāte gun kahey na jāhi apārā.*
> *sabh ke prītam sarab pratipālak sarab ghatā ādhārā.*[52]

It is important to see how authentic prayer is a manifold exercise in the awareness of man-God relation. The man who prays sincerely does not merely ask for relief in distressful situations. Nor does he only feel steadied by the thought that *he* is able to pray truly, and so may be sure of receiving His grace. What distinguishes his praying is also the fact that *the contemplation of God's own attributes* is done in such a way that it at once tends to steady the praying man himself. Thus, when the devotee says to himself: 'It is in Thy very nature to love Thy devotees and to lift them up, however lowly they be', the purpose is not merely to describe God objectively, but also to steady his own being with the thought that *tujh binu nāhi koi binau mohi sāria.*[53] In so far as a prayer is, in the main, an attempt to establish or deepen an intimate relation with God regarded as the supreme personal reality, its true value lies not so much in the text of the prayer as in the present *attitudes* of the praying person. The truth indeed is that unless these are taken into account, some details of the text of a prayer may well appear a little odd to us. Consider, for instance, the following:

satgur āio sarani tuhārī.
milai sūkhu nāmu Hari sobhā chintā lāhi hamārī.
avar na sūjhai dūji thāhar hāri pariyo tau duārī.
lekhā chhodi alekhai chhūtah hum nirgun lehu ubāri.
sad bakhsindu sadā miharvānā sabhnā dei adhārī.
Nanak dās sant pāchhey pario rākhi lehu ihu bārī.[54]

In the above prayer, it is obvious, there are quite a few details which are not easy to make out. One may really wonder as to what exactly could be meant by *sūkh nāmu, and* whether it is literally true for the praying person to say: *hum nirgun.* A name may well enable us to direct our attention to its bearer. But how could it be blissful? And could it be literally true that the author of this prayer, himself an acknowledged saint, is quite without merit? But both these oddities disappear the moment we reflect that the attitude which animates the entire prayer is one of exclusive and self-effacing love of God:

'avar na sūjhai dūji thāhar'
'hum nirgun'.

It is because the Name is taken as an expression of such absolute and sanguine dependence and humility that every utterance of It becomes a breath of bliss; and again it is because of these attitudes, which do not see ultimate value anywhere except in God—or, we may say, because of an overwhelming sense of the surpassing greatness of God ('*sadā miharvānā sabhnā dei adhārī*')—that *the devotee's own relative lack of merit is magnified by contrast.*

Some impact on the devotee's own self, if not an explicit reference to it, is indeed a necessary feature of prayer; and I here feel like repeating, what I have said at the very outset, that prayer is an attempt to re-awaken the original relation between man and God. This is exactly why the actual recitation of a genuine prayer is hardly ever a characterization of, or speaking to, God alone; it is also, as a rule, a source of influence on the praying person too. Thus, when the devotee openly declares his keenness to sing the praises *of the Lord,* it is at once an expression also of his keenness to saturate his own being with the sense of the sovereignty of God, or to deepen his faith. This is why we find that in the same prayer lines like the following:

'Grant that I may be singing Thy praises day and night', go along with such open affirmations of faith:

tū merā pitā tū hai merā mātā.
tū merey jīa prān sukhdātā.
tū merā thākur hau dās terā.
tujh binu avar nahī ko merā.[55]

By way of additional illustration, reference may here be made to the following prayer too:

prabh kījai kirpā nidhān
hum Hari gun gāvahige.
. . . hum bārik mughadh iān.[56]

The contemplation of God's glory or attributes during prayer, we may note, is a quite different experience from a merely abstract enquiry into their meaning. Thus, when the praying devotee dwells in his mind upon the surpassing greatness of God, he does not fret at His incomprehensibleness; he rather rejoices, because of his devotion to God, to think *that such an exalted reality is so close and accessible to him.* This is illustrated by the following prayer:

sajaṇu tu hai saiṇu tu mai tujh ūpari bahu māṇiyā
. . . kitī lakh karoḍi piriye rom na pujani teriā.
sahiā tau asankh manjahu habhi vadhāṇiā.[57]

This is not merely a prayer of praise, but also a happy acknowledgement of one's own kinship with God.

Prayer can indeed be quite rich and complex in its inner content, if only because there are many ends for which we commonly pray. The Sikh scriptures, however, highlight a special object of prayer, namely, a chance to serve the saints, the servants of the Lord. But what exactly is the point in praying for this end? The answer, as suggested in Sikh religious literature, may be put thus. The saints sing the praises of the Lord, and this makes the man of prayer happy. What is more, in serving the saints without any narrow self-interest, the individual in question gets a chance to verify and deepen, if indirectly, his own love of God:

hau māgau tujhai daiyāl kari dāsā goliā.
amrit nāmu nidhānu dāsā ghari ghaṇā.
tin kai sangi nihālu sravanī jasu ghaṇā.
kamāvā tin kī kār sarīru pavitu hoi.
pakhā pāṇī pīsi bigsā pair dhoi.

āpahu kachhu na hoi prabh nadari nihāliye.
mohi nirgun dichai thau sant dharamsāliye.[58]

Further, the saints not only keep éulogizing the Lord in song, but radiate peace and joy from their faces. They therefore serve as a visible proof, so to say, of the value of a life of love of God, and thereby deepen the faith of the man who joins their company. I say so on the basis of prayers such as the following:

prabh ihai manorathu merā.
kirpānidhān daiyāl mohi dījai kari santan kā cherā.
prātahkāl lāgau jan charnī nisbāsur darasu pāvau.
tanu manu arapi karau jan sevā rasanā Hari gun gāvau.
sāsi sāsi simrau prabh apunā sant sangi nit rahiye.
eku adhāru nāmu dhanu morā anadu Nanak ihu lahiye.[59]

V. A PARADIGM OF PRAYER: ARDĀS

Let me, in the end, give a little thought to the standard prayer of the Sikhs: *Ardās.* My aim, here, will be to show that the *disposition* of the various thoughts and images in this prayer is not random, but accords with the logic of what the good life really is, and so may be expected to lead us—through a network of necessary relations between ideas, feelings and attitudes—evermore on the path of religiousness. But let me first cite the text of the prayer:

The Text of Prayer[60]

1. ੴ *(Ek Onkar) Śrī Vāhegurū jī kī Fateh*
2. *Śrī bhagauti jī sahāi*
   vār Śrī bhagauti jī kī pātshāhī ੧੦
3. *pratham bhaguati simari kai gur Nanak lāi dhiāyi.*
4. *phir Angad gur te Amardāsu Rāmdāsai hoi sahāi.*
5. *Arjan Harigobind no simrau Śrī Hari Rāi.*
6. *Śrī Harikrisan dhiāiye jis ditthai sabhi dukh jāi.*
7. *Teg Bahādur simariye ghar navnidhi āvai dhāi.*
8. *sabh thāin hoī sahāī.*
9. *dasvain Pātṣāh Śrī guru Gobind Singh Sāhib jī, sab thāin hoi sahāi.*

A. *dasān Pātṣāhiān dī joti Śrī Guru Granth Sāhib jī de pāth dīdār dā dhiān dhar ke bolo ji Vāheguru.*

B. *panjān piāriān, chohān sāhibzādiān, chālian muktiān, hathiān, japiān, tapiān, jinnā Nām japiā, vand chhakiā, deg chalāī, tegh vāhī, dekh kai andith kītā, tinna piāriān, sachiārian dī kamāi dā dhyān dhar ke, khālsā jī bolo jī Vāhegurū.*

C. *jinā singhān singhaniān ne dharam het sīs ditte, bund bund katāe, khopariān luhāiān, charkhaḍiān te chaḍey, āriān nāl chīrey gaye, Gurduārian dī sevā laī kurbānian kītiyān, dharam nahī hāriyā, Sikhi kesān suāsān nāl nibhāī, tinā di kamāī dā dhiān dhar ke, khālsāji Bolo ji Vāhegurū!*

D. *punjān takhtān, sarbat Gurduāriān dā dhiān dhar ke bolo ji Vāhegurū.*

E. *prathmey sarbat Khālsā ji ki ardās haiji, sarbat Khalsā ji ko Vāheguru, Vāheguru, Vāheguru, chit āvai, chit āvan kā sadkā sarab sukh hovai. jahān jahān Khālsā ji Sāhib tahān tahān rachhiā riait, deg teg phateh, birad kī paij, panth kī jīt Śrī Sāhib ji sahai. Khālsājī ke bol bāle, boloji Vāheguru!*

F. *Sikhān nu Sikhi dān, kes dān, rahit dān, vivek dān, visāh dān, bharosa dān dānā sir dān, Nām dān Śrī Amritsar ji de darshan ishnān, chaukiān, jhandey, bungey, jugojug atal, dharam kā jaikār, bolo ji Vāhegurū. Sikhān dā mun nīvā, mati ūnchī, mati pati dā rākhā āp Vāheguru!*

G. *hey Akāl Purukh apṇey panth de sadā sahāi dātār jeo. Śrī Nankānā Sāhib te hor gurduārian, gurdhāmā de, jinā to panth nu vichhoḍiā gayā hai, khuley darshan dīdar te sevā sambhāl dā dān Khālsāji nu baksho.*

H. *soi piyārey mel jinā miliān āp dā nām chit avai.*

I. *hey nimāṇiān de māṇ, nitāṇiān de tāṇ, niotian di oat, sachchey pitā Vāheguru. āp de huzur (Here the leader of the prayer mentions in suitable terms the specific occasion for which the prayer is offered or the purpose for which the blessings are sought).*

J. *akhar vādhā ghātā bhul chuk māf karni sarbat de kāraj rās kaney.*

K. *Nanak Nām chad dī kalā*
āpde bhāṇe sarbat dā bhalā

L. *Vāheguru ji dā Khālsā*
Vāheguru ji di fateh.

Now, the first two lines adumbrate a necessary relation between our specific conception of God and our attitude towards Him. The Lord is here acclaimed as *Vāheguru*. These words are commonly translated as: 'One wonderful God'[6T], the word 'one' being demanded by È with which the prayer really opens. It seems to me, however, that the translation is not quite apt. A thing or reality which only appears wonderful to us may well excite the instinct of curiosity and the impulse to understand, or the theoretic attitude. But the line (2) which immediately follows the one containing the words in question speaks of *submission*, and not of any inquisitiveness, on the part of the devotee. I therefore propose to interpret 'Vāhe Gurū' differently, and on the solid basis of how the word 'Vāhe' is used in daily conversation. Whenever we utter the words *vāh vāh*, in respect of an object, our attitude is not merely one of wonderment at the surpassing excellence of the object, but also one of admiration, love and joy. Indeed, whatever be the occasion of our use of these exclamatory words, the thing, person or achievement to which they refer is necessarily one which makes us feel happy, and a little elevated because of the very excellence that the object projects and gives us a chance to contemplate; and is also one which excites the impulse to communion, so that we would like *to be with* the 'object', in fact or in idea. Therefore, when the devotee seeks to invoke the blessings of the Lord by addressing Him as *Vāhe Gurū* his attitude is not one of mere wonderment, but a quite complex one, comprising joy, love, wonderment, and the attitude of feeling both subdued and elevated. A God who is the object of such an attitude can only excite the impulse to surrender, not the instinct of curiosity; and this indeed is why the second line expresses a prayer for protection by the Lord.

But what kind of *protection* is here sought? It seems to me, however, that the very phrasing of this question is somewhat improper. For, the word in the text which has been translated as 'protection' is *sahāi* which really means 'help' or rather 'help us'. And I think it necessary to press this difference because whereas 'protection' suggests the verbal supplement: protection *from* 'this or that', the word 'help' requires us to think thus: 'help *in* doing this or that'. The moment we see this difference and decide to interpret *sahāi* in the suggested (or second) sense, we get a clue to answer the question I have posed, provided we also take into account the lines that follow (3–7). *These* lines speak of the great *gurus* all of whom had to face difficulties of various kinds, and some of whom had even to sacrifice their very lives, in the act of holding on to their *dharma* or path of righteousness. So if, as is only reasonable to suppose, we are required to draw inspiration from the example of the great men listed in the prayer, the protection that is sought in the second line cannot be *from* the trials and tribulations of life, but only *in* treading the path of religion and morality. There is a good deal in the succeeding parts of the prayer—specially in paras c. and d.—which should bear out what I have said in regard to the 'protection' in question. But let me first look at the lines which immediately follow the second line, that is, lines 3 to 9.

In these lines (3–9) we are required to contemplate the lives and personalities of the great *gurus* all of whom share a common attitude,—that is, intense and self-effacing love of both God and religion of their choice. But, at the same time, the contemplation (or remembrance) enjoined is not said to be productive of moral gains alone, but also conducive to material welfare (*ghar nav nidhi āvai dhāi*). In other words, according to the prayer being analyzed, love of God is not incompatible with material welfare, though it may well be said to be capable of attenuating our *attachment* to worldly riches. Para (A) emphasizes the value of *Guru Granth Sāhib* as a source of spiritual instruction. But, it is important to note, here we are also forthwith required to utter *Vāhe Gurū.* This clearly suggests that, though the *Granth* is certainly the embodiment of the spiritual wisdom of the *gurus,* its importance lies essentially in its being conducive to the love of the Lord.

In para (B) we are required to recall the lives of some such dedicated men as have been known not only for their unfaltering devotion to God in their chosen way, but also for their social concern and forbearance. But here, again, it is the *Lord* who is to be praised for bestowing such varied excellences on those who have been devoted to Him: so, once again, we must utter *Vāheguru, Vāheguru, Vāheguru.* At the same time, care is taken to suggest that our devotion to God should not become a kind of inert self-contained feeling, but should rather work as an active impulse to help the needy, so that worshipping the Name and running a free kitchen for the hungry may both go together. In para (F), again, His grace is invoked not only for our success in defence of righteousness, but also for the continued serviceability of the cooking-pots. However, what this prayer aims at is not merely a blend of the spiritual and the quite simply secular, but a heightened awareness of collective interest. Remembering the glorious deeds of the great *gurus* is not only expected to inspire us with thoughts of righeousness and sacrifice, but is also meant to express our *collective* gratitude to those to whom we (the Sikhs) owe our very existence as a distinct community. Again, it is because they are expected to serve as places of *congregation* and reciting the Name of the lord that the four *Takhts* are given the great importance (para, D) that they command to this day.

The collective aspect of the prayer is again manifest in 'para E' where it is clearly said that the praying is being done for, and on behalf of, the entire community.

Para F, emphasizes the moral pre-conditions of proper praying, such as humility, detachment towards things of sense, and freedom from ignoble desire and anger.

In the end, attention may be drawn to some such details of the prayer as are likely to be missed. This prayer, it is interesting to mark, is not meant to be sung; and this indeed is why, to provide against a possible sickening of interest during the act of praying, the recurring triple utterance of *Vāhegūru* is meant to serve as a kind of refrain, and so to provide a suggestion of song-like form or organized structure. Further, our interest is kept up also by the *dramatic quality* of what we are required to recall, that is, the glorious deeds of valour and self-sacrifice done by the *gurus* and their great followers. Indeed, if it is rightly done, this prayer can serve as a source not only of peace and spiritual tranquillity, but also of the requisite zeal and courage for treading the path of service and righteousness.

VI. KINDS OF PRAYER IN SIKHISM

After this analysis of some select prayers from *Gurbāni* I may now consider some others from the same source, but from the viewpoint of the commonly accepted classification of prayers as of petition, confession, thanksgiving and adoration. In so far as the best known Sikh prayer of praise, Guru Nanak's *Ārti*, is to be done separately, I may omit eulogistic prayers in my present discussion.

A. To begin with petitionary prayer, it may be regarded as the very essence of religion; for, as William James has pointed out, 'however our opinion of prayer's effects may come to be limited by criticism, religion . . . in the vital sense . . . must stand or fall by the persuasion that effects of some sort genuinely do occur . . .'[62]

It must, however, be forthwith added that all petitionary prayers are not for the production of changes in the world or in one's individual fortune. In fact, in its most exalted form, petitionary prayer seeks the grace of God for continued devotion to Him through 'the way things go'[63], whether frustrating or rewarding by common standards. But a little more has to be said about such prayer, taken generally, before we turn to see how it appears in the Sikh scriptures. To begin with, like every other kind of prayer, a petitionary prayer too is generally offered by an individual. Here, however—that is, in the case of the scriptures we are concerned with—the individual who offers the prayer is a man of exalted religiousness, a recognized *gurū*. This deserves notice, for the quality of one who prays cannot but determine *what is prayed for*, which is another distinct detail of petitionary prayer. Further, though he who prays is generally one person, what is prayed for may not relate to him alone, but to mankind in general. Here, again, the *gurus* have a clear edge over ordinary mortals, partly because freedom from egoity is one clear objective for which they freely pray. The *gurus*, to be sure, cannot be expected to pray for narrow selfish ends. Another necessary detail of petitionary prayer is the consideration on the strength of which the petition is made and is expected to bear fruit. Finally, in so far as a petitionary prayer is offered to secure something which is of great importance to the praying person, the *intensity* with which one prays is also an important element of petitionary prayer. It may here be added that in so far as the existence of God and His sensitiveness to our needs are not as *directly* verifiable as other aspects of a petitionary prayer, in the prayers of Sikh *gurus* the details which dominate whole prayers are subjective intensity, universal relevance of what is prayed for, and the mind's dwelling on His own grace or mercy, in so far as—because of our obvious proneness, if not actual subjection, to every kind of weakness—we can never claim to *deserve* what we want, but can only pray that it be granted to us *in spite of our weaknesses* which He may ignore in His magnanimity. What I have just said is amply borne out by the following prayers:

a. *tumh karahu daiyā merey sāin.*
aisi mat dīje merey Thākur sadā sadā tudhu dhiāī.[64]

b. *jagatu jalandā rakhi lai apnī kirpā dhāri.*
jitu duārai ubarai titte lehu ubār.[65]

c. *Hari kirpā karke bakhasi laihu hau pāpī vad gunahgāru.*[66]

d. *jetā samundu sāgaru nīri bhariā tetey avagun hamārey.*
daiyā karahu kichhu mihar upāvahu dubdey patthar tārey.[67]

e. *hā hā prabh rākhi lehu. hum te kichhu*
na hoi merey suāmī kari kirpā apunā nāmu dehu.[68]

f. *kirat karam ke vīchhude kari kirpā melahu Rām.*
chāri kunt dah dis bhramey thaki āye prabh kī sām.[69]

g. *hum mūrakh mugadh agiān matī sarnāgati purakh ajanamā.*
karī kirpā rākhi levahu merey Thākur hum pāthar hīn akarmā.[70]

Now, in all the above prayers the petition is made on the strength of faith in the compassion or mercy of the Lord. Again, barring 'c', all the prayers listed aim at some spiritual objective, whether it be commitment to the contemplation of the Lord, or to the Name, or to the supreme purpose of being united to Him or being 'saved', that is, liberated. What is more, excluding the one that is embodied in the first prayer, all the petitions made are for the good of the whole world or of humanity in general. As for their subjective intensity, it is manifest in such thoughts and images as 'My Lord' (*merey Thākur*), open confession of (our) weaknesses or sinfulness, and of incapacity for quite independent endeavour; the felt anguish of alienation from God (*kirat karam ke bīchhude*); and the earnestness and humility of surrender (*chāri kunt dah dis bhramey thaki āye prabh ki sām*).

B. It should now be clear that a petitionary prayer may easily include an *admission of his* (or *her*) *weaknesses* on the part of the praying person. However, there are some prayers in which this detail *dominates*, and which may therefore be called prayers of confession. Some such prayers from Sikh religious literature may be cited before we turn to analyse them:

1. *kuchil kathor kapat khal kāmī. jeu jānahi tiu tāri suāmī.*
   tū samrathu saraṇi jogu tū rākhahi apnī kal dhāri.
   jāp tāp nem suchi sanjam nāhī in bidhī chhutkār.
   garat ghor andh te kādahu Prabh Nanak nadari nihāri.[71]
2. *haun aprādhī gunehgār haun bemukhmandā chor jār*
   johāriā pari ghar jo handā.
   nindak, duṣt, harāmkhor, thagdesh thagandā
   kām, krodh, mud, labh, mohu, hunkār karandā
   viṣvāsghāt akiratghan mohe ko nā rakhandā
   simar murīdā dhādiā Satgur bakhṣindā.[72]

A look at the above reveals the following about the essential structure of a confessional prayer:

> First, the individual who offers the prayer must grow clearly conscious of the various moral defects which beset his being. Such self-awareness serves, on the one hand, to make him clearly aware of what exactly is to be rooted out; and, on the other hand,

of the depth and enormity of the defects in question. Both these revelations of the confession are of help. The one can give better direction to the individual's own moral endeavour; and the second can evoke in him the requisite creaturely feeling that, in so far as the evil he has to fight against is very deeply entrenched, he cannot make the right kind of eradicative effort entirely on his own, and that therefore he must invoke the grace of God. Again, the confession, we may note, is not made at the behest of an alien authority, but of one's own free will; and, what is more, because of the intense inner urge to somehow rise above the unrest and uncertainty of the world, and to attain to the true haven of peace. Nor is the confession in question a mere listing of one's own weaknesses in a coolly cognitive way. Rather, it is necessarily, if in part, a felt revulsion against them; and what turns this movement *away* from one's weaknesses into yearning *for* God's mercy is the clear realization that one has so far failed to overcome these weaknesses by one's own efforts, and that therefore one has to be rescued by God in whatever way—we do not know which—He may choose to adopt. A prayer of confession is, therefore, at once an exercise in deeply felt humility, and also a surrender to His mercy. Yet, it is obvious, no humiliation is here felt; for, I repeat, the confession is done quite freely and for the kindly notice of One in whose benevolence we have implicit faith, and who has never been suspected of using our disclosures of weakness for the purpose of black mailing or humiliating us. It is common knowledge that we happily admit our weaknesses in the presence of only those whom we love deeply and trust implicitly. Therefore, a prayer of confession is not merely an exercise in humility, but also an expression of, or a plea for, deeper faith.

In the end, it may be pointed out that the weaknesses 'admitted' in the above prayers of confessions are all common human defects; they are not individual idiosyncrasies. This is what makes these prayers relevant to one and all.

C. Prayers of thanksgiving, on the other hand, are of general interest because they often appeal to *the very conditions of human existence.* This is borne out by prayers such as the following one from *Sukhmani Sāhib*:

jih prasādi dhar ūpari sukhi basahi.
sut bhrāt mīt banitā sangi hasahi

jih prasādi pīvahi sītal jalā.
sukhdāi pāvanu pāvaku amulā.
jih prasādi bhogahi sabhi rasā.
sagal samagrī sangi sāthi basā.
dīney hasat pāv karan netra rasnā.
tisahi tiāgi avar sangi rachnā.
aise dokh mūd andh biāpe.
Nanak kādhi lehu prabh āpe.[73]

Even a little close attention to this prayer brings out the following main points, indicating, incidentally, how a *single* prayer may influence a man's *whole* life:

a. The Lord is here thanked not for any particular blessing received on some special occasion, but for the very basic conditions and conveniences of life, such as the comforting setting of a family, limbs and organs of the body, and the elements without which no life is possible. In so far as these are all co-extensive with the whole course of one's life, such a prayer of thanksgiving can easily make for a prayerful *way of life*, as distinguished from mere episodic *acts* of prayer. It may also be expected to help the cultivation of a sense of the presence of God as a pervasive source of sustenance.
b. Further, if our embodied life itself is regarded as a package of facilities received gratuitously from God, two highly desirable attitudes are likely to follow. First, because the body is here taken as a facility provided by a kindly God, we cannot but be impelled to use it very carefully, out of love and grateful regard; and, second, because it is not only given by Him, but also sustained by the conditions He provides, and so is really His, our care of the body should (in principle) proceed in a spirit of non-attachment, so that at the moment of death, or when the 'facility' in question is to be returned to its rightful owner[74]—separation from the body may not cause too much anguish to the individual. This indeed is the full meaning of the famous utterance of the saint poet, Kabir, that he has put aside the *chadariyā* exactly as it was when received (as a gift[75]). My suggestion that acceptance of bodily life itself as but a gratuitous provision from God is likely to make for a non-indulgent or non-attached kind of living is supported by the consideration that a man is expected to pray not only in the way

of thanksgiving, but also by petitioning for release from lust, egoity, and desire for sense-indulgence taken generally. It may here be added, in passing, that the *theoretical* requirement to distinguish the different kinds of prayer should not be allowed to bedim our common *practical* need to offer quite a few different kinds of prayers in varying situations.

c. An additional suggestion would here be relevant. It seems that a close reading of the prayer under review provides material for a new and interesting way of looking at the problem of evil and suffering. There is no doubt as to the seriousness of this problem. But man is *not born* with the sense of evil and suffering. What he is born into is essentially a network of kindly human relationships and an environment of elements that serve to keep him alive. What is more, he is born with some organs and faculties which give him the power to make the most of what he is born into. So, what the very beginning of a man's life may be said to demand, quite generally, is *gratefulness* for what we have called the package of gratuitous facilities. In case a man is really able to adopt and retain this attitude he will not easily feel inclined to regard the evil and suffering that he may see in the world as a proof against the existence and goodness of God. His impulse would rather be to avail of His power and goodness in reducing the extent and impact of the ugly realities in question. In saying so we do not, of course, provide a rational solution of the problem, but we *are* able to argue for an alternative way of looking at it, say, the way of practice and righteous endeavour. And this way is by no means inferior to the demands of theory. After all, whether we succeed or fail in reconciling the fact of evil and suffering with the nature and existence of God, the sting of the problem—that is, the pain and repulsiveness of actual suffering and evil—will continue and keep clamouring for practical remedial measures, as against mere understanding.

d. Fourthly, we may note that though nothing is here expressly asked for, such a prayer of thanksgiving necessarily secures for the person who offers it the additional gifts of religious humility, detachment and contentment with what one has, though not with one's present moral quality. In the light of this truth it sure seems possible to enlarge the following line in the famous prayer of St. Francis of Assissi: 'It is in giving . . . that we receive' as: 'It is in giving (thanks to God for the very gift of life) that we receive (the spiritual gifts of humility, abstinence and the unwinking sense of the presence of God).

e. Finally, it does not seem too much to suggest that a sense of continual gratefulness to God is likely to impel us to think of doing something for Him in return; and that, in so far as *He* does not need anything, our expression of gratitude may well take the course of serving *His creatures.*

This indeed is the evidence of the way the Sikh *gurus* lived. They sought to serve the lowliest of men by way of worshipping the one sovereign Lord. Humility is an essential condition of devotion:

> Humility considered as a special virtue, . . . mainly concerns a man's subjection to God for whose sake he also submits himself to others.[76]

VII. THE RESPLENDENT ADORATION: ĀRTI[77]

To a man of devotion, however, the sovereignty of God is no mere matter of unchallengeable might; it is also a reflex of his faith that He is the true source of all loveliness and variety of form, colour and sound, and the real impulse behind Man's spiritual quickening. This is nowhere so manifest as in Guru Nanak's splendid *ārti* to which I now turn. But there, again, I have first to cite the full text of the prayer before attempting to analyze it. I will have to do a bit of arguing as well, specially because I find it difficult to accept every detail of the standard translations of this prayer. Such argument, however, will be put within brackets, so that the substance of the prayer may nowhere seem broken to the reader.

Text of Ārti[78]

1. *gagan mai thāl.*
2. *ravi chand dīpak baney,*
3. *tarikā mandal janak moti.*
4. *dhūpu malianalo,*
5. *pavan chavro karey.*
6. *sagal banrāi,*
7. *foolant joti.*
8. *kaisī Ārti hoi,*
9. *bhavkhandanā teri ārti.*
10. *anhata sabad vājant bheri.*
11. *sahas tav nain.*
12. *nan nain hai tohi kau.*
13. *sahas mūrati.*
14. *Nanā ek tohī.*

15. *sahas pad bimal.*
16. *nan ek pad.*
17. *gandh binu,*
18. *sahas tav gandh,*
19. *iv Chalat mohī.*
20. *sabh mahi joti,*
21. *joti hai soi.*
22. *tis kai chanaṇ,*
23. *sabh mahi chānaṇ hoi.*
24. *gur sākhī,*
25. *joti pargatu hoī.*
26. *jo tisu bhāvai,*
27. *su Ārti hoi.*
28. *Hari charan kamal,*
29. *makrand lobhit.*
30. *mano andino mohi āhi piāsa.*
31. *kirpā jal dehi Nanak,*
32. *sāring kau.*
33. *hoi jāte tere nāi vāsā.*

Now, it is easy to see that this prayer is a blend of two distinct attitudes, the objective and the subjective. It is also an adoration of God as both transcendent and immanent. The first eighteen lines visualize God as the one essence of the manifold outer world. Here, the emphasis is on the devotee's rapture evoked by contemplation of God as the non-attached ground of the whole of *outer* nature. In the second half of this *ārti* (19-33) the focus is on the immanence of God; and so the emotions here projected are those of individual love, faith and humility in relation to God.

Now, to turn to a detailed understanding of the prayer, the meaning of the first eight lines is obvious. To the intensely prayerful mind of Guru Nanak, the heavens and the woods, the winds and the flowers, all seem to offer their light and beauty in homage to the Lord. But in the ninth line the word *Bhav* presents a difficulty. All the recognized translators interpret it as 'fear'; and, therefore, the words *bhav khandanā* as: 'He who dispels all fear'. But I prefer to translate these words as: 'He who destroys, or liberates us from the *birth-death cycle*'. (My argument here may be put as follows: The contemplation of what Kant calls the 'free' beauties of Nature—that is, of the heavens and the woods—cannot but have an *elevating and liberating* effect on the mind. This is, it appears, exactly what Carlyle meant, when he spoke of the sky as 'the daily bread of the soul'). Therefore, in my view (I repeat) the words *bhav khandanā* mean: 'He who *liberates* us from the *narrow* attachments of the world'. This interpretation, I may add, would go well with the images of the unrestricted or 'free' beauties of nature with which this *ārti* opens, on the one hand; and with the next (or the tenth) line which speaks of a music that is *free from* dependence on the impact of repeated individual strokes, on the other.

As for the next six lines (11-16), they may be summarized quite simply, as follows:

All visibility, all forms and every kind of movement, are there because of Him. But He Himself is non-physical, formless and motionless. The next (or the seventeenth) line, however, again presents a problem. Here, the word *gundh* has been commonly translated as 'nose'[79]. But I would like to take it in the sense of smell or fragrance. I say so because the natural and most common meaning of *gundh* is 'smell'. (In the Gītā too, we may note, where *gundh* is related to the Lord, what is meant is fragrance; the reference here is to the 9th verse of the VII chapter which runs thus: 'I am the sweet fragrance in earth and the brilliance in fire, the life in all beings, and I am austerity in the austere')[80]. In case the word in question is interpreted as *nose*, the reader's imagination as it follows what the prayer visualizes, will not be happily affected by the image of the facial proturberance which a nose is. Nor will *this* interpretation prepare the way to the *inner* aspect of our being which is referred to in line 20: '*in* every heart there is light'. On the other hand, the meaning I have given to the word *gundh* will at once make for the transition required, that is, from things or objects (or limbs) to what is at once an affection of the inside, so to say.

The transition in question is also helped by the 'bewitchment' of the devotee (-writer) brought about by his contemplation of the beauty of nature (as an aspect of God), and of His playfulness as registered by the devotee's awareness that, though He is the basis of all that is there in the physical world, He Himself is, in a way, untouched by the sensible manifold that our living in the world is. And once the mood of bewitchment and love is induced, the devotee grows introspective; and affirms—in part on the basis of his own experience—that God is immanent *in*, and illuminates, every heart. But, he adds, again on the evidence of his own experience, that the individual as such has no power to make this Light manifest; and that the manifestation in question is brought about by the grace and guidance of the *Satgurū* who may well be identified with God for the practical purposes of devotion. It is the *gurū* who enables the pupil to establish a personal relation of longing with the Lord; and, we may say, this humble offering of a soulful love is itself good enough *Ārti* for him, for what can please the Lord of mercy more than a prayer for His mercy,—a prayer which Nanak himself offers in the last six lines?

These closing lines are a personal testament of faith. It may be noted that they highlight the images of sucking ('the nectar of the flowers') and drinking ('only rain drops'). What is more, the image of His 'lotus feet' which is projected in the 28th line may be said to be implicit also in the 12th and 15th lines where the writer speaks respectively, of eyes and feet; because the word *kamal* is freely associated with these bodily parts, say, as *kamal nayan* and *charan kamal*. We may also note that whenever the word *kamal* is used in such contexts, the thoughts of purity and beauty, *and* of bowing to what is possessed of these qualities, is generally present, if implicitly. We may therefore conclude that the Lord is here thought of not as merely merciful, but also as the supremely pure and beautiful; and that the devotee's attitude in this *ārti* is not one of mere adoration *of God*, but of saturating *his own self* with a sense of the awesome beauty, sovereignty and inexplicable singleness of God. Contemplation and fervour here blend as the vision and warmth of religious experience.

Is it at all possible, one may wonder, to put such a rich view of prayer within the confines of a single definition? I demur to say 'yes' at once, partly because definition is not an important concern of an *analytic* study which this work has all along striven to be. Yet, by way of gathering the key ideas projected so far in my treatment of the Sikh view of prayer, which is by no means wholly otherwordly, the following definition may be proposed:

> As a conscious act, prayer is an attempt on the part of man to saturate himself ever better with the sense of the reality and attributes of the One Supreme God, importantly (though not necessarily) with the help of a true teacher (*Satgurū*), and by means of such acts and attitudes as the three-fold discipline (comprising *simran, bhajan* and *dhyān*); worshipful contemplation of the glories of nature; and service of saints in particular, and of His creatures quite generally, in terms of acts that make for fellowship in daily life, such as gathering to attend a religious discourse (*saṅgat*) or for the purely secular purpose of eating together without any sense of distinction between the high and low (*paṅgat*).

Be it noted, however, that the definition put forth applies only to the *conscious* act of praying. It does not cover the unseen quickening of prayer by the working of His grace.

NOTES

1. *The Confessions of St. Augustine*, tr. by Rex Warner, A Mentor—Omega Book, 1963, pp.182-83.
2. D. Z. Phillips: *The Concept of Prayer*, Routledge and Kegan Paul, London, 2nd impression, 1968, p.119.
3. K. Barth: *Church Dogmatics*, Translated by G.T. Thomson, Vol. I, Part I, T and T Clark, 1936, p.155.
4. A. J. Ayer: *Language, Truth and Logic*, London, 1946, 2nd edition, p.188.
5. Simone Weil: *Waiting on God*, tr. by Emma Craufurd, Collins Fount Paperbacks, 1950, pp.72–73.
6. Newman: *Grammar of Assent*, Longmans, 1947, p.24.
7. *Ādi Granth*, M.5, p.44.
8. Ibid., M.5, p.187.
9. Ibid., M.5, p.714.
10. Ibid., M.5, p.289.
11. Ibid., p.265.
12. Ibid., M.1, p.1232.
13. Ibid., M.5, p.265.
14. Ibid., M.5, p.266.
15. Ibid., M.3, p.565.
16. Ibid., M.3, p.560.
17. Ibid., M.1, p.1168.
18. Ibid., M.5, p.1144.
19. S.K. Langer: *Problems of Art*, Routledge and Kegan Paul, London, 1957, pp.20-21.
20. *Ādi Granth*, M.1, p.4.
21. St. John 1:1–5.
22. *Ādi Granth*, M.1, p.1232.
23. Kirpal Singh, *Nām or Word*, The Sant Bani Press, Tilton, New Hampshire, 1974, p.24.
24. Pritam Singh Gill, *Concepts of Sikhism*, New Academic Publishing Co., Jullundur, 1979, p.14.
25. R.C. Pandeya: *The Philosophy of Name*, included in *Perspectives on Guru Nanak* (Seminar Papers), edited by Harbans Singh, Department of Religious Studies, Punjabi University, Patiala, 1975, p.80.
26. M.1, Sri Guru Nanak Prakash, p.54.
27. *Ādi Granth*, M.3, p.429.
28. Ibid., M.1, p.221.
29. Ibid., M.4, p.82.
30. Ibid., M.3, p.565.
31. Ibid., M.3, p.585.

32. *The Philosophy of Name*, p:82.
33. *Ādi Granth*, M.3, p.560.
34. Ibid., M.5, p.287, *Also see*: Ibid, M.1, p.1127.
35. Ibid., M.5, pp.890–91.
36. Ibid., M.1, p.1009.
37. Ibid., M.1, pp.1034–35.
38. Ibid., M.1, pp.1041–42.
39. Ibid., Bhagat Ravidas, p.694. *Also see*: Ibid, M.9, p.1429.
40. *Ādi Granth*, M.5, p.133. As translated by Shri Kirpal Singh in his book: *Prayer—Its Nature & Technique*, The Sant Bani Press, Tilton, New Hampshire, United State of America, fourth Printing, 1974.
41. *Ādi Granth*, M.5, p.712–13.
42. Ibid., p.716.
43. *Ādi Granth*, M.5, p.105, as translated in *Prayer—Its Nature & Technique.*
44. *Ādi Granth*, M.5, pp.1099–1100.
45. Ibid, M.1, p.268.
46. Ibid., M.5, p.181.
47. Ibid., M.5, p.738.
48. Ibid., M.5, pp.723–24.
49. Ibid., p.779.
50. Ibid., p.829.
51. Ibid., p.547.
52. Ibid., p.1220.
53. Ibid., M.5, p.709.
54. Ibid., p.713.
55. Ibid., M.5, p.1144.
56. Ibid., M.4, p.1321.
57. *Ādi Granth*, M.5, p.761.
58. Ibid., p.518.
59. Ibid., p.533.
60. Standard Ardās as approved by Shiromani Gurdwārā Parbandhak Committee, Amritsar, Numbering of lines and paragraphs has been done by me to facilitate reference.
61. Gandā Singh, *Sikh and Sikhism*, p.57.
62. William James: *The Varieties of Religious Experience*, p.446.
63. D. Z. Phillips: *The Concept of Prayer*, pp.120–21.
64. *Ādi Granth*, M.5, p.673 as translated in *Prayer—Its Nature & Technique.*
65. Ibid., M.3, p.853.
66. Ibid., p.1416.
67. Ibid., M.1, p.156.
68. *Ādi Granth*, M.5, p.675.
69. Ibid, M.5, p.133.
70. Ibid, M.4, p.799.

71. *Ādi Granth,* M.5, p.1301.
72. Bhai Gurdas, War 36, Pauri 28; cited in *Prayer—Its Nature & Technique,* p.90.
73. *Ādi Granth,* M.5, p.267.
74. Cf. 'God gave me being in order that I should give it back to Him'. Simone Weil: *Gravity and Grace,* p.35. Also see: 'Everything without exception which is of value in me comes from somewhere other than myself, not as a gift but as a loan which must be ceaselessly renewed.' Ibid, p.27.
75. *dās kabir jatan sion odhī*
    jyon ki tyon dhar dinī chadariyā—Kabīrdās.
76. Thomas Aquinas: *Summa Theologia,* Vol.44, p.93.
77. *Ādi Granth,* M.1, p.663.
78. Translation of the *Ārti* as given in *Sikh Review,* Sikh Cultural Centre, Park Street, Calcutta, September 1967, p.45. The lines have been numbered, to facilitate reference.
79. See, here, translation of *Ādi Granth* by Mr. Manmohan Singh and Dr. Gopal Singh.
80. *The Holy Geeta,* Commentary by Swami Chinmayananda, Central Chinmaya Mission Trust, Bombay, p.431.

TRANSLATIONS OF THE PASSAGES FROM *Ādi Granth* CITED IN THE BOOK[1]

[NOTE: In what follows **P.** stands for *page number* (of the present work), **Ref.** for the number of the *reference* as it occurs in the book and **N.** for *notes* at the end of each chapter.]

P.13

Ref. 1: Most fortunate, indeed, are those who have faith in the Lord and who have a genuine *thirst for God.* When they come to be blessed with commitment to the Name, their thirst is duly answered (though not quite satisfied); they become tranquil in spirit; and their virtues get a chance to blossom in the congenial company of saints.

Ref. 2: Those who pin their faith in the Name of the Lord *do not let their minds dwell upon anything else.* Even if the whole earth is transformed into gold and offered to them, they would not be attracted to it if it cannot, in some way, be related to Nām.

Ref. 3: It is only with the kindly guidance of the *Satgurū* that faith bears fruit, sorrow is transcended, and one becomes saturated with the love of God.

Ref. 4: It is only when his discrimination has been purified by the *Satgurū* that the devotee's spiritual yearning is rewarded with what it pines for, and his faith is consummated.

Ref. 5: *My faith is perfected,* O Thou kindly life of the world, as I feel suffused with devotion *at the darṣana than hast granted to me.*

Ref. 6: Those who listen (to His glories) with faith and devotion are *redeemed by His Grace.*

---

1. Following, at places, Manmohan Singh's translation of Guru Granth Sahib (*Ādi Granth*). Pretty often, however, I have had to go by my own translations. *Where I thought it necessary to disagree with Mr. Singh's translation at the foot of it I have just written the words, 'Note: See the relevant p. of the book'.* In the Chapter on 'Prayer' I have consulted translation of selected prayers by Sri Kirpal Singh in his book: *Prayer—Its Nature and Technique.* Translation of Ardās has been taken from Ganda Singh's book *Sikhs and Sikhism,* published by Sikh Cultural Centre, Patna, 1968, pp. 57-61. Notice has also been taken of the translation of Ārti as given in *Sikh Review,* September 1967 issue.

P.14

Ref. 1: I wandered from village to village and through all the cities, but through the Lord's slaves I found God in my very mind.

Faith and confidence have welled up within me and the Great *Gurū* has emancipated and blended me with the Lord:

Ref.2(a): God is realized through faith.

Ref.3(b): Faith and devotional service are pleasing to my Master's mind and He safeguards the honour of His serfs.

Ref. 4: Whenever I remember my Lord, I feel supremely blessed.

P.15

Ref. 1: It is only the supremely lucky ones who are able to saturate themselves with the nectar of faith by singing, hearing and reciting the glories of the Lord.

Ref. 2: O Lord Master, the Life of the world, Show Thou mercy unto me and instill in me faith in Thy Name.

Ref. 3: Thou Thyself createst faith in Man.

Ref. 4: For my Lord Master I have spread the bedding of faith. I can abandon not my Lord, as within my mind there is immense affection for Him.

Ref. 5: Permeating my mind and body is the love of the Infinite Lord. An overpowering faith wells up in my mind incessantly.

Ref. 6: O my merciful Lord Supreme! take pity on me, so that I may never forsake the World Cherisher from my mind . . . . O Lord, fulfil Thou Thy slave Nanak's desire.

Ref. 7: I am attached in faithful love to my Beloved. Without Him, I cannot abide even for an instant.

P.16

Ref. 1: (According to the man of faith) Agriculture and business (which are the basic material conditions of human existence) flourish under the shelter of the Name. This provision, however, is but a neutral possibility (*beej*) of vice and virtue. But, because his being is riddled with the innate defects of desire and anger, what the human individual generally tends to choose is a life of utter indifference to the Name, so that when he passes away his state of being is, so to say, freckled with impurity.

P.18

Ref. 1: Very difficult to cross is the sea of worldliness. It shoves the mortals like the violent blowing of wind. My mind is terrified to hear that the Righteous judge is very strict.

Our (foster-) home—that is, the world—is like a (blind) well which appears to be quite without an escape—route; and what is worse, all afire (with passions that threaten to consume our moral being).

NOTE: Here, the thought that the world is only our foster-home has been borrowed from Wordsworth's 'Ode to Immortality'.

Nanak says: I have been able to secure the support of the saints and so I now contemplate the Lord (unceasingly).

Ref. 2: Ever-stable art Thou, O my Creator-Lord I lean on Thee alone.

Ref. 3: Smitten with virtue, ego is stilled; and imbued with the Name, the soul develops hate for the world.

P.19

Ref. 1: Being absorbed in True love the soul gets blended with what it has sprung from.

Ref. 2: Other shelters have I seen all. Thy shelter alone remains for me.

Ref. 3: My associates and comrades have all left me. None has remained with me to the last.

Says Nanak, in this calamity, the Lord alone is my support.

Ref. 4: Thou art my Sumer mountain, O Lord. I have grasped Thy protection.
Thou shakest not, nor do I fall.
Thou, O Lord, hast preserved my honour.

Now and then and here and hereafter there is but Thee.

By Thine grace, O my Master, I am ever in peace.

P.20

Ref. 1: Seek the protection of the kind god who is the Master of the world and the Cherisher of the universe. The Lord's service is profitable.

Ref. 2: God's Name is the support of His slave.

Ref. 3: With the devotees God's Name is an article of everyday use.

It gives peace to the hearts of holy persons.

God's Name is the support of His slave.

By God's Name, millions of men have been saved.

Ref. 4: Without Thee, there is no other,
O Creator! Thou art my support and protection.

Ref. 5: Powerful is the refuge of the Lord's feet; so my dependence on the people is all past.

Ref. 6: O reverend Master, the Lord of the world, Thou art the only support of mine.
Thou, O Omnipotent Lord, art the Giver of protection . . . . The man who embraces Thine meditation, O Lord, him no anxiety befalls.

PP.20–21

Ref. 1: I utter God's Name in the early morn. Thereby I have made a shelter for myself both here and hereafter.

Ever, ever contemplate thou the Lord's Name, so that thy mind's desires may be fulfilled.

NOTE: See the relevant p. in the book.

P.21

Ref. 1: I sing Thine praises with my every breath,
O Lord! Nanak has sought the refuge of the *Gurū's* feet.

NOTE: See the relevant p. in the book.

Ref. 2: Thou art my Beloved and Thou the support of my very life.
Seeing, seeing Thee, my soul has blossomed.

Wandering, wandering, wandering through many existences I have grown weary.

I have now grasped the refuge of the saints' congregation.

Thou, O Lord, art Inaccessible, Incomprehensible, Invisible and Infinite.

Day and night, Nanak meditates on Thee, O God.

NOTE: See the relevant p. in the book.

PP.21–22

Ref. 3: Without Thee, O Lord, I have no other second.
Thou alone art in my mind.

Thou, O Lord, art my friend and comrade. Why should my soul be afraid?

Thou art my refuge and Thou my hope.

Sitting, standing, sleeping, waking, breathing or eating,—may I never forget Thee, O Lord! Protect, protect me, O Lord, I have entered Thine Sanctuary. Dreadful is the ocean of fire.

The True *Gurū*, is the giver of peace to Nanak.
I am Thy child, O the world-cherisher.

NOTE: See the relevant p. in the book.

P.22

Ref. 1: I have grasped the protection of the merciful Lord, the Treasure of grace.

Ref. 2: The Lord Master is unseen; one, yet many. His protection Nanak has grasped.

Ref. 3: Nanak has entered the sanctuary of the Divine feet of the Infinite Lord and is holding fast to their protection.

Ref. 4: The entire cleverness of my mind is ended.

The Lord is the Doer and the Inciter; Nanak has clung to His refuge.

NOTE: See the relevant p. in the book.

P.23

Ref. 1: Lord's lotus feet abide within his mind and with his every breath and morsel, he repeats Lord's Name.

NOTE: See the relevant p. in the book.

Ref. 2: The Lord is the purifier of the sinners, the Lover of His saints, the Destroyer of dread and a boat to ferry across.

My eyes are satiated, seeing the Lord's vision and my ears are sated hearing His praise.

I, the meek one, seek the protection of the Beneficent Lord of the world, who is the support of my vital breath and the Patron of the patronless.

God is the Fulfiller of hope and the Destroyer of pain. Nanak has grasped the refuge of His holy feet.

NOTE: See the relevant p. in the book.

Ref. 3: He alone realizes Thee, whom Thou makest realize.

NOTE: See the relevant p. in the book.

Ref. 4: O the Lord of wealth, grant me such understanding that I may serve only the saints and seek their feet's protection.

Ref. 5: By Thy grace do I understand Thee. Thou art my covert and Thou art my honour.

NOTE: See the relevant p. in the book.

P.24

Ref. 1: Thou art my father, Thou art my mother . . . Thou art my cover and Thou art my honour.

Ref. 2: I have sought the protection of my Lord, the Cherisher of the universe. I have entered the sanctuary of the Perfect Lord and my bonds are all broken.

Ref. 3: I grasped the Lord's protection and then was I emancipated.
By saints' grace, when I sang the Lord God Master's praise, then were removed my sins and ailments.

Ref. 4: O my soul, seek thou the shelter of God's Name remembering which thy evil intellect shall be dispelled and thou shall obtain the status of supreme bliss.

NOTE: See the relevant p. in the book.

P.25

Ref. 1: It operates through covetuousness, the basic malady.
The mammon affects not in many ways. Under Thy protection, O Lord, the saints pass their life unaffected by the dreadful ocean of fire.

NOTE: See the relevant p. in the book.

Ref. 2: I am quite without good qualities, and merits I have none (positively) I am unwise, attached (to the worldly), ignorant, and thoughtless . . . . I do not know anything (truly); and my judgment is deficient.

A prayerful Nanak puts himself entirely under Thy wings.

Ref. 3: How can such a man be evef led astray who puts himself in Thy care?

Ref. 4: Discard all (human) ways and means, and take shelter under Him who controls all life and never deserts anything.

Ref. 5: Thou art Omnipotent, and Thou alone art my Master.

Everything flows from Thee, Thou art the Inner knower.

The Perfect Transcendent Lord is the support of his serf.

Seeking Thine shelter millions of persons are saved, O Master.

P.26

Ref. 1: The persons who hold fast to Thy protection, O Lord Master, they are happy in Thine sanctuary. The men who forget the Creator Lord, they are counted amongst the miserable ones.

Ref. 2: All are suffering in the world. He alone is happy who makes Name his stronghold.

Ref. 3: Only that person is to be acknowledged as a saint who remembers His Name with every breath and every morsel of food. Indeed only such a person is blessed and is a perfect saint. (Guru Granth Kosh, p. 120)

Ref. 4: Associating with the saints and seeking the supreme Lord's protection, O Nanak, the mortal becomes immaculate.

Ref. 5: The True *Gurū* has imparted instruction unto me.

My soul, body and the whole world belong to God.

Whatever I do, that is per Thy might.

Thou art my refuge and Thou art my court.

P.27

Ref. 1: He whose protection seek I; on Him alone is pinned my hope.

Ref. 2: O God, I know not of another support, Thou alone art my support and hope.

Ref. 3: Thou, O True Creator, art the support of the devotees and Thou the shelter of the saints.

Ref. 4: The World-Lord is my sole support. I have relinquished other hopes.

Lord, the Perfect Treasure of virtues is powerful over all. The Name is the prop of the Lord's slave who has sought His refuge. In their heart, the saints have the support of the supreme Lord.

Ref. 5: My associates and comrades have all left me. None has remained with me to the last. Says Nanak, in this calamity, the Lord alone is my support.

Ref. 6: It is useless to depend on worldly resources.

My Lord, My Master, Thou art my sole anchor.

P.28

Ref. 1: As is the stick in the hand of the blind, so is the God's Name with me.

Night, day and morn Lord God's Name is my support.

Ref. 2: No hurdle bars the way of the man who surrenders himself to God in prayer; for He is the reliever of all the three types of suffering and pain, and the repository of happiness. Nanak says: it is He who works as the grace of saints, and as the curative power of physicians. He is also the sole cause and agent of all that is; and the giver of strength, wisdom, and perfect happiness. Hari is, indeed, the ultimate refuge.

Ref. 3: Lord Master's Name is the support of the life of His slaves.

P.29

Ref. 1: Thy Name alone saves the world.

This alone is my hope and mainstay.

Ref. 2: One man says that there are many arms of his brothers to support him.

Another says that he can depend on his abundant material resources.

But I, the meek and lonely depend only on Hari alone.

Ref. 3: Thou art my Father, Thou my Mother and Thou my Friend, well-wisher and Brother.

Thou art my family and Thou my mainstay. Thou alone art the Giver of life and the vital breath to me.

Ref. 4: With the Name, I have entered into dealings.

The Name alone is the prop of this soul.

Ref. 5: The Pervading God gives support to all the hearts.

Ref. 6: Why waverest thou, O mortal. The Creator shall protect Thee.

He, who gave thee birth, will provide thee with sustenance.

P.30

Ref. 1: I have the support of the Lord's Name alone.

Ref. 2: The True Name is my only support.

Ref. 3: The Nectar-Name is the mainstay of my soul.

Ref. 4: The *Gurū* is my vital breath and the *Gurū* is my mainstay. The *Gurū* is my way of life and the *Gurū* is my family.

Ref. 5: I supplicate my True *Gurū* to bless me with the sustenance of the Lord's Name.

Ref. 6: My Sire Master, Thou art the support of my life.

I make obeisance and prostration to Thee and many a time am a sacrifice unto Thee . . . . Whatever Thou doest, that I deem good. Seeing Thine lotus feet, peace wells up in me.

Ref. 7: Thine shelter and support.

P.31

Ref. 1: I have now obtained the Lord's support.

Whoever seek the refuge of the Treasure of mercy, they all are ferried across the world ocean.

Ref. 2: Lord's slaves have faith in the Lord.

Meditating on the Name all the anxieties are annulled.

Ref. 3: Thou art my hope and Thou my faith. I take and enshrine Thy Name in my mind.

My power flows from Thee and in Thine association am I embellished. Whatever Thou biddest, that alone I do, O my Lord.

Ref. 4: When it pleases Him, then, He has His order obeyed and causes this boat to float over.

Ref. 5: Keep me under Thy patronage.

Ref. 6: Peace-giving ever is the Lord's Name.

By remembering which Ajāmal was redeemed and the courtesan Ganika liberated. Daropadi, the Princess of the King of Panchali, remembered the Lord's Name in the royal court.

God, the Embodiment of mercy, removed her suffering and enhanced His own glory.

The man who hymns the praise of God, the Treasure of compassion, Him the Lord succours.

Says Nanak, relying on this, I have come and sought the Lord's protection.

Ref. N: Four sources of power are available to man: self-effort, self-discipline, physical prowess, and money: and where all these become unavailing, it is the Lord who becomes our source of strength.

P.48

Ref. 1: I see Thy grace in (the proper working of) my body and mind.

P.49

Ref. 1: It is Thou, O Lord, who preserveth the life in the womb.

Ref. 2: Thoroughly imbued in the Lord's love, they sing His praises.

Ref. 3: Through the True *Gurbāni,* he sings God's praise and becomes happy with the kind glance of the kind Lord.

Note: See the relevant p. in the book.

Ref. 4: Meditating on the Name, the soul and body are rendered ever-green and with gracious glance the Lord looks on the mortal, O Nanak!

Note: See the relevant p. in the book.

P.50

Ref. 1: If the Lord extends His mercy, the Name abides in the mind, pure become the mortal's body and soul and pure becomes his speech.

Note: See the relevant p. in the book.

Ref. 2: (It is only) when the Lord bestows His grace (that) goodness becomes incarnate. (Thereupon) God is assured and truth is deservedly won.

Ref. 3: He alone comes to know the right way who is blessed with His grace.

Ref. 4: They alone attain to the life everlasting whose mind dwells on the feet of the Lord. Further, says Nanak, the sense of grace comes to grip their heart; and thus becoming Godward the individual comes to dwell in (or realize) the natural state of the self.

Ref. 5: Some sleep in luxury (on wadded covers); others (less fortunate ones) only wait on them. Nanak says: (this disparity is explained by the fact that) they alone prosper who come to receive His grace.

P.53

Ref. 1: He alone achieves true peace who is able to gain access to a True *Gurū.*

(This is so because) in the heart of such a person God's Name gets firmly embedded. Saith Nanak! he alone realizes the Lord who is favoured with His mercy. He secures freedom both from dependence on, and anxiety in respect of worldly fortune. The reason of this dual emancipation partly is that his egoistical concern in burnt out by (faith which issues from) devout recitation of the Name.

P.54

Ref. 1: When the Perfect *Gurū* instructs, man's intellect becomes sublime.

From within he is cooled and pacified and through the Lord's Name he obtains happiness.

If the Lord God casts His merciful glance, then alone the Perfect *Gurū* is met.

Ref. 2: We recognize the Lord by *Gurū's* guidance, when He Himself casts His merciful glance.

Ref. 3: When the Lord Himself casts His merciful glance, then alone is this fleeting mind restrained.

Ref. N: By His grace, God blesses man with his love and he ponders over *Gurbāni.*

Ref. 4: If the Lord shows mercy, man meets with the Perfect *Gurū* and the tyrant Death's courier strikes him not.

He flowers like the lotus flower in water and instinctively remembers God with glee.

Ref. 5: He, to whom the Perfect *Gurū* extends his mercy, Him the chivalrous *Gurū* unites with the Name through his instruction.

P.55

Ref. 1: In this world of mundane attachment, none is another's comrade or friend. Without the *Gurū*-God, who has ever obtained peace?

Ref. 2: He alone is the Giver, the True Master.

He, the True Lord, is with thee.

Obtain a direct vision of the Lord by means of the *Gurū's* grace. A man's life becomes accursed if he forgets his true spouse (that is, God). But if he gives due thought to his *Gurū's* instructions, the Lord takes pity on him and prevents him from forgetting the Maker.

P.56

Ref. 1: It is only when he is favoured with the grace of God that a man is able to find a true *Gurū,* and to cross (with the latter's help) the dreadful world-ocean.

Ref. 2: The cup of Truth is passed on to him all, too spontaneously, on whom is the Lord's grace, and he who deals in this Nectar loveth not the worldly wines.

NOTE: See the relevant p. of the book

Ref. 3: As far as it lies in thy power, drink thou not at all the false wine.

Nanak, he whom the True *Gurū* approaches and meets, obtains the true wine by God's grace.

Ref. 4: By drinking which intellect departs, madness enters the brain, man distinguishes not between mine and thine, and is baffled by the master.

Ref. 5: It is as an exercise of His grace that God cancels illusory beliefs.

Truth is attained only on realizing His Will.

P.57

Ref. 1: O brother! (even in the case of men) Truth and purity always go together; but He alone is truly (or perfectly) pure. God is realized only by those on whom He bestows His grace.

Ref. 2: Ṇanak says: 'Right listening to recitation of the Name (*Sravan*) naturally tends to purify both mind and body; and (in so far as I do such listening day in and day out), my being is suffused with love of the Name.'

Ref. 3: They, on whom God casts His kind glance, suffer neither torture nor pain and punishment.

Nanak, they who are pleasing to the Lord, become perfectly successful.

Ref. 4: He who eating dry bread remembers God, with his eyes sees the Lord within and without.

Ref. 5: Nanak! they who are bereft of God's gracious glance, cherish not fondness for charity and the Name.

Ref. 6: The months, days, and moments are good for those on whom the Lord casts His merciful glance.

P.58

Ref. 1: Falsehood has vanished, love for duality has run away; and they are perfectly brimful with truth.

They serve the supreme Lord Master and place the unique One in their heart.

NOTE: See the relevant p. in the book.

P.59

Ref. 1: God shows favour (unto) or (in) him whose soul is contented with truthfulness.

Ref. N: Save me, as it pleases Thee, O Saviour.

Except Thee, with mine eyes, I have not seen any other.

Ref. 2: He on whom the Lord casts His merciful glance, is blessed with truth, contentment, gnosis and devout contemplation.

Ref. 3: The mind, which has a natural tendency to flit from one object to another, is controlled only when the Lord casts His merciful glance.

P.60

Ref. 1: A mortal (human) being is taken care of by the Lord Himself once He chooses to bless him with His look of mercy.

Ref. 2: It is only by God's grace that one gets a chance to serve his *Gurū* (a man of Realization); and it is, again, by His grace that selfless service becomes possible.

It is by God's grace that this (flitting) mind is controlled; and it is, again, by His grace that purity of mind is attained.

Ref. 3: Nanak says: 'My soul has retained its pristine purity even in the midst of this world which naturally tends to corrupt human souls. The reason is that the formula (*gur*) of the love of the Name (*mahāmantra*) has gripped my heart. This (completeness) of surrender to the *mahāmantra* has itself become possible because I have heard a lot about the wondrous potency of the Name. The Lord has condescended to cast a look of grace on me. This is why I am wedded to His feet, and have been granted the bliss of love and devotion, and a very close fellowship with the saints.'

P.61

Ref. 1: There are some who renounce the world and sit lost in rapt communion with God. Still others who aim at the same goal (who aim at the same spiritual end and renounce the world) are Yogis, men of self-control, scholars and thinkers (with the same end in view), still others repair to graveyards or structures that overlay mortal remains, and forests.

But all these persons, when they arise from their meditation, find that (though they have physically left the world) attachment to the world still clings to them.

(On the other hand), He whose attachment to the world is severed by the Lord Himself, enshrines His Name within his heart. (This, prompts him to get in touch with holy men.) It is indeed the company of saints that enables men to secure emancipation. But Nanak has secured liberation primarily because of His look of Grace. (This, we may note, reiterates the idea with which the present extract opens.)

Ref. 2: I cool them with a fan, carry water for them, grind their corn and am overjoyed by washing their feet.

On my own I can do nothing. My Master, look Thou towards me with Thy merciful glance.

Bless me, a sinner, with a seat in the saints' place of piety, O Lord.

NOTE: See the relevant p. in the book.

P.62

Ref. 1: My task is to make a supplication, and Thine to shower benediction. Thou art the Lord who hast created Thine own self.

When Thou, O Lord caused me to speak, then alone did I repeat the Name.

NOTE: See the relevant p. in the book.

Ref. 2: Those maids, on whom the Lord casts His look of favour, become happy wives.

NOTE: See the relevant p. in the book.

P.63

Ref. 1: Guided by mere self-interest, he who goes on doing (and becoming) evil day in and day out cannot escape the inexorable law: 'As you sow, so you reap'.

It is only through His grace that the self-seekers come to see the evil in themselves. (And thus get set on the road to salvation.)

Ref. 2: If Thou look with favour on me, then alone can I know Thy Truth.

When Thou Thyself instructest me, then alone do I know Thy Truth.

Ref. 3: The Name itself is both diamond and ruby.

In other words, It is the sole locus of value Supreme.

It alone possesses a mind that is pure like a pearl. That is to say, the mind that is thoroughly imbued with love of the Name becomes perfectly pure.

Further, says Nanak, if he is able to test (as Nanak is) the thoroughness with which his own heart is imbued with love of the Name, it is only by virtue of His look of grace which blesseth one and all.

Ref. 4: The bliss of (contemplating) the Name gives me a sense of security and shelter, exactly as houses and mansions do; and it also provides a sense of fellowship in the way of a family.

P.64

Ref. 1: Those who (devotedly) wait on the Lord are very close of His heart, and He keeps them gratified (with the sense that they are well taken care of) by His look of grace.

Ref. 2: Condescending to let me hold onto the hem of His garment, the Lord has ferried me across the world-ocean of fear and suffering. O my friend! His look of grace keeps me overwhelmed with an infinite sense of joy and gratitude.

Ref. 3: Ye saints, see with the searching glance that God abides close by and is fully pervading everywhere.

NOTE: See the relevant p. in the book.

Ref. 4: O Nanak—the kindly Lord makes us feel blessed by (the sense that we are enfolded by) His look of grace.

P.65

Ref. 1: They alone dance who are pleasing to thee; and they, the *Guruwards*, who ponder on the Name.

Ref. 2: Says Nanak, they on whom is Thine grace bestowed, obtain celestial peace.

When God casts His merciful glace the mortal sings His praises then; and by His grace merges in truth.

Ref. 3: Those who are devoted to the feet of the Lord remain ever awake (in respect of their devotion) and (this is why) their inner being keeps reverberating with bliss.

The Lord has favoured me with His look of grace which is the source of all happiness and saves a person here in this life and beyond it.

In all humility, Nanak urges one and all to recite His Name regularly, because it is He who sustains both body and the indwelling spirit.

Ref. 4: What matters if whether, he, on whom God casts His merciful glance, be a swan or a crane?

If it pleases Him, O Nanak, He changes a crow into a swan.

Ref. 5: Where the poor are looked after, there does rain the look of Thy grace, O Lord!

Ref. 6: By good actions the physical robe is obtained, and by the Lord's benediction the gate of salvation.

P.66

Ref. 1: False is the uttering of praise by those who love falsehood.

Nanak, God alone is true and He Himself casts His favourable glance.

Ref. 2: It is only by means of his own independent thinking that a man can try to assess the value of the Name. (In other words, a man must become genuinely interested in determining the value of the Name.) But success in this effort can come quite easily under the guidance of a teacher of complete realization. The *Gurū's* help, however, will come only if the devotee puts his faith in him (the teacher) steadfastly and sincerely. The way in which spiritual guidance is given by a teacher of true realization is clear.

Authentic grace—that is the grace of a person of genuine realization—is a sure redeemer of the devotee whose devotion to the teacher is exclusive.

P.67

Ref. 1: He, the Creator-Lord, Himself abides all the ages through.

If the Master casts His gracious glance, then alone one meets with Him.

Ref. 2: The mortal is redeemed at the bidding of him on whom is the Lord's grace.

The Lord Himself sends and recalls the mortals. There is none else to counsel Him.

He Himself demolishes, constructs and creates. He, the Lord, knows everything.

Nanak, the Name is the gift, which the Merciful Master makes unto him to whom He extends His mercy.

Ref. 3: O Lord of deities and men, Infinite and Unborn, Thy true palace is unrivalled.

O Life of the world, bestow peace unto Nanak and save him by Thine gracious glance.

Note: See the relevant p. in the book.

P.68

Ref. 1: Just as, after giving birth to a son, the mother nurtures him, keeps an eye on him, feeds him whenever she approaches or leaves him (for a while), fondles him repeatedly, in the same way God looks after him who puts himself under His care.

P.69

Ref. 1: I am but a child, and God is my caring Father.

Ref. 2: Almighty art Thou, a worthy refuge; for we are all sheltered under the wings of Thy might.

Recitation (of the Name), penance, moral disciplines and unblemished self-control—none of these is by itself able to secure liberation for us. Nanak, therefore, prays that he be blessed with His grace so that he may be redeemed from the blind dungeon of sinfulness.

Ref. 3: By Thy gracious glance (O Lord), Nanak has attained the blessed state by reflecting on Thy Name.

Those who are ego-centred are led astray, and so they perish; (on the other hand), those who meditate on the Name of the Lord secure liberation (by His grace). Unspeakable is the lot of those on whom His grace does not descend.

P.70

Ref. 1: Nanak says: Let Truth be revealed to me through the mouth of the *Gurū*.

I have no one else to depend on. So, be pleased to bestow Thy look of grace on me.

Ref. 2: Within me is the *Gurū*—given gnosis of the Lord, the Gem, which leads to emancipation.

Nanak says: he alone who is favoured with His grace gets some insight into Truth and is adjudged as passable at His doorstep (for a fuller glimpse of Truth).

Ref. 3: As borax liquifies gold (beautiful in itself), so desire and anger dissipate the body (which is, in principle, a means to God-realization). It is only when the metal is tested at the touchstone, after being put through fire which purifies, that the metal assumes the lustrous shape which finds favour with the goldsmith.

P.71

Ref. 1: He who is blessed with even a single glance of His grace at once becomes immune to sinning.

Ref. 2: Whosoever overwhelms his mind, realizes death in life.
Nanak, through His grace, the Gracious Lord is recognized.

NOTE: See the relevant p. in the book.

Ref. 3: Ever and ever the genuine coins are taken care of. With them true merchandise is purchased.

The false ones are not seen in Lord's treasury. They are seized and cast into fire again.

NOTE: See the relevant p. in the book.

Ref. 4: It is only by virtue of the descent of His grace that the Name comes to grip one's heart. Thereupon, all illusory beliefs are dispelled.

Ref. 5: (However, this suffusion with love of the Name is not itself a realization of God. That realization comes when) by the grace of God one is able to gain access to a true *Gurū*! Only then is one enabled to discover the indwelling spirit, the *Antaryāmin* within one's own heart.

Ref. 6: Nanak reassures: O my dear fellow beings! it is only His grace which releases one from the soul-killing grip of fiery passions like lust and wrath.

P.72

Ref. 1: My heart is suffused with love of my Lord.

He is the axis around which my whole life moves, in utter self-abandonment. Bless me, O Lord with (at least) a passing look of Thy grace.

Ref. 2: If Thou, O Lord, showest mercy and savest me, then alone can I be saved. O compassionate to the poor, bless Thou me with Thy True Name.

Prays Nanak, Thou art the Cherisher of all the beings, O Lord; and I am the slave of Thine slaves.

NOTE: See the relevant p. of the bóok.

Ref. 3: Ever praise thou that True Lord.

By whose grace peace ever results.

P.73

Ref. 1: He looks with His eye of grace on all alike, but as is one's love for Him, so is the fruit he obtains.

NOTE: See the relevant p. in the book.

Ref. 2: My merciful Master, the searcher of hearts,
behold Thou Thy slave with Thy eye of grace.

O Lord, show Thou mercy unto me, and bless me with this bounty, that Nanak may live contemplating Thy Name.

NOTE: See the relevant p. in the book.

Ref. 3: Without God's grace, the Name is not obtained.

It can be obtained only through perfect destiny.

Nanak, if the Lord casts His gracious glance, then, by *Gurū's* instruction, the mortal merges in union with Him.

NOTE: See the relevant p. in the book.

P.74

Ref. 1: Supremely difficult is the service of the *Gurū* and the spiritual guides, but in it is the essence of bliss.

He, on whom the Lord casts His merciful glance, him He inspires with His love and affection.

NOTE: See the relevant p. in the book.

Ref. 2: Out of sheer mercy, the Lord establishes His devotion in him and for His slave's sake, He saves the world.

The Lord Master is all by Himself and the Lord Himself beautifies the world.

Of Himself, the Lord is pervading everywhere, O slave Nanak; and showing His mercy, He Himself emancipates the mortals.

P.75

Ref. 1: My Lord is the most high of the high. Showing His mercy He blends the mortal with Himself.

P.76

Ref. 1: The *Gurū* is the friend of the Lord, who is there since the very commencement and beginning of ages.

The Lord mercifully pardons the sins committed by man, and emancipates him in His court.

Ref. 2: Beholding with His eye of mercy, He has dispelled the pains of his slave.

God's serf, the *Gurū* God has saved. Taking me to His bosom, the compassionate and forgiving Lord has wiped away all my sins.

P.77

Ref. 1: When such Divine comprehension wells up, then God shows His vision and mercifully enters into the mortal's own house.

Ref. 2: Having showered His benediction, my Lord has entered my house of Himself and has met me.

Ref. 3: The Merciful Master has graciously made me meet the *Gurū* and by *Gurū's* teaching, I, the stone, am saved.

Ref. 4: God is the Treasure of mercy and the Deliverer of the sinners.

I have wandered through millions of births and suffered pain.

The *Gurū* has implanted the Name within me and I am now in utter peace, O Nanak.

P.78

Ref. 1: The Lord preserves man's soul, body and wealth; and mercifully protects his very life.

The lofty Lord Master is man's pardoner. He washes off all his sins, O Nanak!

Ref. 2: He has created the soul and body and has mercifully granted us the very life.

Ref. N: Wandering through many existences, in several births I suffered torture again and again.

By Thy grace, I have obtained the human body. Now, grant me Thine view, O my God, the King.

O my Omniparous Lord, have Thou mercy upon me. Wondrous are Thine bounties.

All the sentient beings are created by Thee, O Lord, and all the hearts contemplate Thee.

Thine state and extent, Thou alone knowest. The worth of Thy Omnipotence can be ascertained not.

Ref. 3: Wandering and roaming about I have grown weary. Adapting various ways I have searched the Lord.

PP.78–79

Says Nanak, the Lord has shown mercy unto me, and I have gained the treasure of saints' society.

The Lord is the desire-fulfilling gem and embodiment of mercy.

The lofty Lord is merciful to the meek who attain peace by meditating on Him.

The knowledge of the Immortal Lord is beyond comprehension.

By hearing His praise, millions of sins are effaced.

O Master, the Treasure of benevolence, show mercy, unto Nanak, that he may repeat the Lord God's Name.

P.80

Ref. 1: When the ego is gone, then man becomes the Lord Himself, and seeks the shelter of the Treasure of mercy.

Ref. 2: Except the True *Gurū*, no one is man's friend.

Here and hereafter, He, the Lord, alone is the mortal's saviour.

Showing His mercy, the *Gurū* blesses man with the Lord's Name and he merges in Him as water does with water.

P.81

Ref. 1: Have mercy on me, O Beneficent to the meek; and consider not at all my merits and demerits.

How can the dust be washed? Such is the state of the man, O my Lord.

Ref. 2: Give pied cuckoo Nanak, the water of Thine mercy, O God! so that he may have an abode in Thy Name.

P.82

Ref. 1: Show mercy, O Lord! and save me; there is no other shower of mercy.

Without Thee, O God! to live is to roll in dust. To whom shall I narrate my wail of distress?

Ref. 2: I have no understanding, intellect and cleverness. Mercifully attach me to Thine feet, O Lord.

Ref. 3: Show Thou Thy mercy; mercy, mercy unto me, O my Love, that I may suck the Lord's elixir through the *Gurū's* word.

The body—village is the beauteous village in which the business of God's nectar is transacted.

Ref. 4: Everything in great abundance God has produced.

Showing His mercy the Lord has satiated all.

P.83

Ref. 1: When Thou givest gifts, O my Bestower, the mortals and other sentient beings are all gratified.

Ref. 2: O Lord God! I, the meek one, have sought Thine refuge. Take Thou pity, pity on me and unite me with Thine beloved slaves.

Says Nanak, the slave of Thine slaves, O Lord, I am the water-carrier of Thine attendants.

Ref. 3: I hear, Thy Name is nectar. If Thou showest mercy unto me, then alone can I drink it.

Like the sparrow hawk for the rain-drop
I hope and thirst for Thee, O my Groom.

Says Nanak, my soul is a sacrifice unto
Thee, Bless me Thou with Thy vision, O Lord.

P.84

Ref. 1: O Master of the Universe, the Patron of the poor. My Beloved Lord, mercifully hear my prayer. Grasp me by the hand, O Nanak's Lord. My soul and body are all Thine property.

P.85

Ref. 1: Lord God Himself tests and assays those unto whom He extends His mercy.

Nanak, Lord's plays are not known. No one can understand them.

NOTE: See the relevant p. in the book.

Ref. 2: They alone are delivered in the world, whom the True Lord preserves.

I live by beholding the faces of those who taste God's Nectar.

Lust, wrath, avarice and worldly love are burnt down in the saints' congregation.

Lord God Himself tests and assays those unto whom He extends His mercy. Nanak, Lord's plays are not known. No one can understand them . . . Nanak, beautiful is the day when the Lord comes into the mind.

But accursed is the day and season, however pleasant, when the supreme Lord is forgotten.

P.86

Ref. 1: Various means, artifices and efforts succeed not. When the Lord is merciful, then alone is He met, O man.

My kind and compassionate Lord is the Treasure of mercy. Slave Nanak is the dust of the saints' feet.

Ref. 2: Mercifully bless Thou me with such an understanding that I may contemplate Thee, during the eight watches of the day.

O man, be not proud, become thou the dust of all, and then alone shalt thou be emancipated.

Over the heads of all is the Lord of Nanak.
He has good many handmaidens like me.

P.87

Ref. 1: Shower Thine benediction. O Lord! that I may blend with the dust of Thine slaves' feet.

As Thou keepest me so do I live. I wear and eat what Thou givest me.

Grant me the enterprise, O Lord! by which I may sing Thine praises on meeting the saints.

Ref. 2: The fruit of virtue, adoration, Divine comprehension, meditation, and all service is obtained by him, O Nanak, whom the kind True *Gurū* graciously meets.

PP.87–88

Ref. 3: By means of saints' kindness my doubts are removed.

The whole truth of faith is to have a bath in the dust of saintly *Gurū's* feet.

When the Saint is merciful, compassionate becomes the Master of the Universe.

This life of mine abides in the (midst of) Saints.

P.88

Ref. 1: Thou, Unfathomable, exceedingly great and Omnipresent Lord, art an ocean of mercy and a mine of jewels.

Mumper Nanak asks for the Lord God's Name and rests his forehead at the feet of his Lord.

Ref. N: Wandering and roaming about I have grown weary. I have searched the Lord in various ways.

Says Nanak, The Lord has shown mercy unto me, and I have gained the treasure of Saints' society.

Ref. N: By Thy grace, O Lord, the Name is repeated.

By Thy grace, the seat is obtained in Thine court.

Except Thee, O Supreme Lord, there is no other.

By Thy grace, everlasting peace is procured.

If Thou abidest in the mind, misery overtakes not the mortal, then.

By Thine grace, doubt and fear run away.

P.89

Ref. 1: Thou, O Lord, art my Father and Thou my mother.

Thou art the Giver of peace to my soul and very life.

Thou art my Lord and I am Thy serf.

Without Thee, no one else is mine.

O Lord, in Thine mercy, bless me Thou with this boon, that day and night I may hymn Thy praise.

Ref.N. (a): Says Nanak, my Lord has shown mercy unto me and with every breath and morsel of mine, I now ponder over my Lord Master.

Ref.N. (b): My Lord God, show Thou mercy unto Nanak, that he may contemplate Thee with his every breath.

Ref. 2: Nanak, this mode of life is obtained by Lord's grace.

P.90

Ref. 1: They to whom the peace-giving Lord shows mercy, grasping the saints' feet, they weave them into their mind.

Ref. 2: When the Reverend Lord bestows His mercy, then merge I in the *Gurū's* word.

Ref. 3: O Sire, preserve the dignity of Thy Name. With Thee, I am hand and glove.

Have mercy on me and show me thy vision, O *Gurū*, through the Name, I have burnt down my ego.

Ref. 4: O brother, by the grace of the *Gurū*, Lord's devotional service is performed.

Ref. 5: By God's grace, one becomes God's devotee. The entire world ought to be saved by seeing the face of the Lord's pious person.

Ref. 6: He, unto whom the Lord shows mercy, remains dead in life, and joining the society of saints, crosses the sea of (love of) mammon.

Nanak, that man is exonerated in God's court.

P.91

Ref. 1: The thirsty wayfarer's mind is attached to the *Gurū*-Tank to obtain the spiritual water.

Slave Nanak loves to see the Lord's vision; and the Lord, in His mercy, has blessed him with it.

Ref. 2: O Ram! Let your grace enable those to be re-united with Thee who were estranged because of the (misdeeds) done by them.

We have put ourselves under Thy wings (after seeking for lasting peace) in all the four corners of the world and in all the ten directions.

Ref. 3: By means of His grace I have been able to secure the bliss of authentic emancipation. In spite of all that has been said to the contrary, no one has been able to realize God without the assistance of a true *Gurū*.

Ref. 4: I prostrate myself at the feet of the *Gurū* who has dispelled all my illusory beliefs. Now (for a positive vision of Reality), I pray for the grace of the Lord who creates and preserves the realm of Truth.

Ref. 5: The True Lord showers His benediction on him. How can such a slave be afraid of death?

Ref. 6: By showing His mercy, He has blended me with His own self.

P.92

Ref. 1: Showing his mercy, the *Gurū* reveals the Lord's mansion, within man's own house.
Nanak, effacing the ego, the *Gurū* unites man with the Master.

Ref. 2: Like this, venerable Lord, as the consort enjoys his wife.

The good brides are pleasing to Thee.
O Lord! by Thine grace Thou decoratest them.

Ref. N: His fear of birth and death departs and he obtains the dignity of eternal life.

Nanak, the Commandment gives this rank to him, to whom He shows His mercy.

Ref. 3: He whom the Master mercifully makes His own, sublime is his word.

They alone are emancipated through the saints' society O Nanak, who are imbued with (love of) their detached Lord.

Ref. 4: My True Lord is ever brand new. By the *Gurū's* grace, I ever utter His Name.

The Lord is my protector, My Mother and Father, through whose meditation one comes not to grief.

Ref. N: Some call the Lord, *Ram, Ram* and some *Khudā*.

P.93

Ref. 1: My Lord, I have come to Thee. Thine refuge I have sought.

Placing faith in Thee and Thine mercy,
I have come; come to Thee. O my Lord.

As Thou willest, so Thou save me, O Lord.
The *Gurū* has put me on Thy path.

Ref. 2: God shows mercy to him who meets with the True God and the Nectar-Name becomes the support.

Ref. 3: Nanak has sought the protection of God, the treasure and ocean of compassion; and his subservience to others is ended.

Ref. 4: Showing his benediction, the *Gurū* attuned my mind to the Lord.

The True *Gurū* has caused me to understand the One Master.

P.94

Ref. 1: O Transcendent Lord, my Master, take pity on me and free me of these bonds.

The sinking blind mortals, O Nanak, the Lord redeems by uniting them with the society of pious persons.

Ref. N: O Father, O Lord of the universe, show Thou only mercy unto me and make me the water-carrier of the slaves of Thine slaves.

Sublime is their intellect, and sublime their honour, within whose mind the flower-girt Lord dwells.

My God-Lord, yoke Thou me to their service. Contemplating Thee in their association I shall be emancipated.

Ref. 2: He, in whose heart the Lord mercifully plants meekness, O Nanak, he obtains salvation here and peace hereafter.

Ref. 3: He to whom the Lord is compassionate and shows mercy, performs His service.

The servant, whom the Lord causes to abide by His order, serves Him.

P.95

Ref. 1: Invoking the great *Gurū*, I am blessed with eternal peace.

The Master, merciful to the meek, has become compassionate unto me; and he of himself has made me utter His Name.

Ref. 2: They unto whom the Beloved becomes merciful, they endure the unendurable bliss of the Lord's Name.

Ref. 3: Showing His mercy, the Lord has made me His own and within me has welled up the thirst to see His sight.

Ref. 4: If He, the Lord, shows mercy, I would laud Him.

In the entire world, is the light of the Name jewel.

To the *Guruward, Gurbāni* tastes sweet.

His heart blooms, and night and day his attention remains centred on it.

P.96

Ref. 1: When the World-Lord becomes merciful.

On meeting the True *Gurū*, I have obtained peace, wealth and the fruit of God's Name.

Ref. 2: O perfect Lord, the ocean of peace, I seek Thy refuge. In Thine mercy, bless Thou me with this gift.

Nanak lives by contemplating his Lord and in this way his self-conceit is also eradicated.

Ref. 3: The Lord has become merciful unto His serf and his this world and the yonder one are taken care of.

Ref. 4: If He keeps me at home, I deem it as peace and pleasure; and if He asks me to quit it, then therefrom I run to vacate it.

Ref. 5: Says Nanak, he on whom is Lord's grace, is saintly and divine.

P.97

Ref. 1: Showering His benediction the Lord causes His saints to be renowned.

Joining the society of the saints I have repeated God's Name and my ailment of indolence has disappeared.

NOTE: See the relevant p. in the book.

P.98

Ref. 1: When I obtained Lord's favour, I easily had a vision of Him and now I am imbued with Lord's love.

By serving the saints, I imbibed love and affection for my beloved Master.

Ref. 2: Merciful, merciful is the Lord. Merciful is my Master.

He blesses all the beings with His bounties.

P.99

Ref. 1: Remembering and contemplating my Beneficent Lord, I enjoy all the comforts.

I have become renowned throughout the whole world and the canopy of the Lord's grace is stretched over me.

Ref. 2: Infinite are our sins, like the waters that overrun the seas and oceans.

Commiserate us, O Lord! and favour us with Thy grace so that our hardened selves, sinking in sinfulness, may be saved. Our selves are burning (with passions) and ripping (with savage impulses). Saith Nanak, the way to incessant happiness lies in acknowledging His Will, in absolute self-surrender.

Ref. 3: He on whom is Thine grace, O Master his ego is stilled.

Ref. 4: If the Lord shows His mercy, man forgets Him not even for a moment.

Ref. 5: O Lord, shower Thou Thine benediction and take care of all the beings.

Produce Thou plenty of corn and water; and, ridding them of pain and penury, ferry them across the world-ocean.

The beneficent Lord heard my prayer and the world has been comforted.

My Lord, take Thou me into Thine embrace and banish all my misery.

Nanak meditates on the Lord's Name, for the House of the Lord is the Giver of boons.

P.100

Ref. 1: God Himself is the *Sat Gurū*, Himself the Lord, and He Himself grants to man union with Him.

Making man follow the great true *Gurū*, the Lord mercifully blends him with Himself.

In this world, the Lord Himself is the life of the entire universe. Like water blending with water, O Nanak! God's slave gets absorbed in God.

Ref. 2: The hearts of those chaste happy wives were moved to pity and they said:

The words of the true *Gurū's* love partake of Lord's ambrosia, and are known to the great and exceedingly fortunate.

This elixir of God is contained in forest, straw and the whole universe; but the unfortunate are not able to partake of it.

P.102

Ref. 1: My beneficent Master, Thou art my compassionate Lord of mercy. What are these poor beings before Thee?

The emancipated and the bound are all from Thee.
It is meet to say and speak thus:

He who turns *Guruwards* is termed as emancipated and the helpless and the egocentric are bound down.

That man alone is emancipated who enshrines affections for the One Lord and ever abides with the Lord.

NOTE: See the relevant p. in the book.

Ref. 2: Thou, O unapproachable, kind and wise Lord, art the great Bestower.

I see none as great as Thee. Thou, O wise Lord, art pleasing to my mind.

P.104

Ref. 1: His saints, the Lord glorifies in the whole world; and for them the Lord infuses the sentiments of kindness in (human) beings.

Hugging to His bosom, the Lord saves His slave and allows not even the hot wind to touch him.

Ref. 2: The light of the Lord's Name is permeating all. The *Guruward* automatically comes to perceive the unperceivable.

God has become merciful unto the meek Nanak, who through His loving adoration has been absorbed in His Name.

Ref. 3: The Lord has kept imbedded (the Name-) diamond in my mind.

Ever sensitive to our needs, the Lord has helped me in gaining access to the true *Gurū* and it is as a result of this meeting that I have been able to realize the value of the (Name-) diamond.

P.105

Ref. 1: God, God, God, God's Name is Nectar.
He alone drinks it whom the Lord makes drink.

Showing His mercy, he whom the merciful Master of Himself

makes meet the True *Gurū*, that man tastes the Name-Nectar of the Lord God.

Ref. N: I am ignorant and thoughtless and know not the Lord's state and measure. The *Gurū* has made me wise and a man of understanding. The Lord, merciful to the meek, has owned me; and my mind now utters the Lord God's Name.

Ref. 2: The generous *Gurū* is merciful. He ever feels compassion.

The True *Gurū* is uninimical from within and beholds that unique Lord everywhere.

Ref. 3: God Himself is the relish of God's Name and Himself is the Divine elixir.

Showing His mercy, God Himself gives the Name Nectar to the virtuous and trickles it into his mouth.

P.106

Ref. 1: If it please Thee, I sing Thy *Gurbāni* then.

If it please Thee, I tell the truth then.

If it please Thee, true *Gurū's* grace is upon me, then.

All the peace is in Thy grace, O, my Lord.

Whatever pleases Thee, that is the pure deed.

That which pleases Thee, that is the true faith.

The treasure of all the excellences is with Thee.

Thou art the Lord. Thy servant makes supplication before Thee.

Ref. 2: Alluring are the feet of the Lord, and His saints are (naturally) drawn to them. They shed off their self-concern, so become fit to serve; and sing His glory ecstatically. They hope and thirst for nothing but a vision of the Lord; and nothing else is of interest to them. But everything (specially the actual having of the vision) depends upon your mercy, O Lord! What can the poor creature's (or human) judgement do in the matter? Nanak, therefore, surrenders himself to Thee in loving and happy self-effacement.

P.107

Ref. 1: Effacing self-conceit, they attain God's profit and meet the Spouse, long separated from them.

The Unique, Inaccessible and Infinite Lord showers His benediction and holding them by the arm makes them His own.

Supplicates Nanak, ever immaculate are they who hymn the praise of the True Name.

Ref. 2: The minstrel utters a cry and the Lord hears that in His mansion.

Within his mind is composure and he obtains the Perfect Lord.

What destiny is writ by the Lord, those deeds he does.

When the Master becomes merciful, then he obtains Master's mansions as his own home.

That Lord of mine is exceedingly grand. Through the *Gurū*, is he met.

P.108

Ref. 1: If Lord God Himself mercifully grants, then alone man partakes of God's immortalizing elixir.

Ref. 2: Through Thine mercy, O my world-Lord, I have obtained Thine Name. Slave Nanak has entered Thy Sanctuary.

P.109

Ref. 1: The Lord's praise, man obtains through His grace. Showing mercy, He Himself bestows it.

Nanak, through the *Gurū*, the Lord God is obtained, by night and day remembering the Name.

Ref. 2: The merciful Lord God showered His benediction and with my soul, body and mouth, I utter God's Name.

Through the *Gurū* I have acquired a very fast and deep colour, and my body jacket is drenched with God's love.

P.110

Ref. 1: He who deserves to be called a true disciple of the *Gurū* lives in the following disciplined way. As he gets up in the morning he contemplates the Name, shakes off lethargy and bestirs himself for the daily round of activities; takes a bath in the holy tank at Amritsar, relieving himself of all vices and sinfulness; sings *Gurbāni,* as the day advances; and takes His Name all the while as he moves about. Indeed only that disciple of the *Gurū* pleases Hari who contemplates the Name with every breath of his and with every intake of food. However, only that pupil is blessed with such words of wisdom (as listed above) through the teacher's mouth to whom my Lord is merciful. Nanak, a mere serf of the Lord, pines for the dust of the feet of those disciples who make a habit of reciting the Name themselves and show others the way to do the same.

Ref. 2: I repair and submit to the *Gurū's* protection. By his grace he unites me with that Lord.

Through mind's obstinacy none has obtained the Lord. All have grown weary of making efforts.

By adapting thousands of clevernesses the mortals have failed. The dry mind is insensitive to Lord's love.

Through falsehood and deceit no one has gained God. Whatever one sows that he eats.

P.111

Ref. 1: Through the *Gurū* I have come to learn (and acknowledge), the truth that Thou art the fashioner of life and death. This has freed me from all fear, also because I know that Thou art merciful and superviseth everything compassionately. It also serves to relieve (the sting of) my pain and suffering.

P.112

Ref. 1: O my Unfathomable, Compassionate and Beneficent Lord of grace, showering Thine benediction save Thou us all.

O Lord, Thou alone art the vital breath of all the beings and the world. Sustain me, Thy slave Nanak.

Ref. 2: My Lord is dyed in surpassing beauty.

My soul-charmer Beloved is merciful to the meek, very flavorous and of deep red dye.

Ref. 3: Those who have compassion as their deity and forgiveness as rosary, are the most sublime persons.

P.113

Ref. 1: Compassion is the root of religion, even as conceit is the mainspring of sin. Tulasi therefore says: one should not abjure compassions as long as one lives.

Ref. 2: On the twelfth lunar day—man should know how to practise compassion and charity, and ought to restrain his outgoing mind.

He alone is the true faster who observes the austerity of rendering selfless service.

The mortal ought to embrace speechless meditation and utter the Name with his mouth.

The one Lord permeating the three worlds knows all.

Purity and continence are all contained in knowing the true Lord.

Ref. 3: Forsake thou thy wisdom and great cleverness.

O man, sans the Lord's Name, there is no place of rest.

The Lord Master has taken pity on me.

Nanak has sought the protection of the Lord's Name.

P.114

Ref. 1: On me, the unwise and ignorant one, O Lord take Thou pity that I may ever abide in Thy refuge.

Says Nanak, fruitless are the worldly affairs. By the *Gurū's* grace, some rare one is blessed with the Nectar-Name.

Ref. 2: Through Thine mercy, O, my world-Lord, I have obtained the Name. Slave Nanak has entered Thy sanctuary.

Ref. 3: Happy are they who are imbued with the Lord's true Name.

O Merciful Lord of the poor, take Thou pity on me.

It is on Him alone that I depend.
So let Him keep me as He wishes.

The *Gurū*-God is pleasing unto my mind.

I cannot live without seeing the Lord's vision. If the *Gurū* puts me on the way to union with the Lord, I shall easily meet Him.

P.115

Ref. 1: O my most Darling Beloved, shower Thine benediction and pay me a visit.

The bride supplicates Thee, to adorn her with the True Name.

Ref. 2: Pleasant is Baisakh, when the tree-bough adorns itself anew.

The bride is anxious to receive God at her door, 'Come my Love, come. Take Thou pity on me.'

Come home, O my Beloved and ferry me across the difficult world-ocean. Without Thee I am not worth even a shell.

Ref. 3: O my Master, take Thou pity on me.

Bless me with such understanding, O my Lord, that I may ever meditate on Thee.

Ref. 4: If Thou so blesseth, O Merciful Master, the crane is again transformed into the swan.

Ref. 5: O my great *Sat-Guru*, I, the slave of the Lord and the True Person, make a supplication before Thee. I am an insect and a worm, and have sought thy shelter. Mercifully bestow on me the light of God's Name, O true *Gurū*.
I have entered into the sanctuary of saints and have placed before them my soul, life and wealth.
I know nothing of Thine service and gnosis.
My Master, take Thou pity on me, a mere worm of Thine.

P.116

Ref. 1: Priceless are Thine merits. O Lord!
and priceless Thy dealings.

Priceless are Thine dealers and priceless Thy treasures.

Priceless are they who come to Thee and priceless they who purchase and fetch goods from Thee.

Priceless is Thy affection and priceless the absorption in Thee.

Priceless is Thy Divine law and priceless Thy court.

Priceless are Thy scales and priceless Thine weights.

Priceless are Thy gifts, and wondrous are the ways in which they are bestowed on us, (wondrous because they are not easy to read or anticipate).

Priceless is Thy benevolence and priceless Thy order. Beyond price and invaluable, the Lord's greatness cannot be expressed. Those who continually speak to Thee, remain absorbed in Thy love.

P.117

Ref. 1: Thou art kind, and the cherisher of refugees. I beg Thee to grant me the gift of Thy Love, O God.

Ref. 2: O Brahman, thou worshippest and propitiatest the stone-god and deemest it a good act to wear the rosary of sweet basil.
Build thou the boat of the meditation on the Lord's Name and pray, 'O Merciful Master, Take Thou pity on me.'

Ref.N.1: God, the destroyer of Madh demon, and the Lord of wealth, is my very life.

The Lord's Nectar-Name is sweet to my heart and body.

My Lord and Master, take pity on me and lead me on to the *Gurū*. He himself is the immaculate Lord.

Ref.N.2: The Munificent Master or Lord takes pity on the ignorant bride or the unenlightened soul, and helps her meet a person who is a true *Gurū* or a man of realization.

Nanak, with peace and poise the *Gurū* unites with the Lord the mortals who have been separated from Him since many births.

Ref. 3: O, Lord Master, I make a supplication, show mercy unto me, that I may meditate on Thee.

Serf Nanak asks for the dust of the feet of those who have obtained the true *Gurū*.

Ref. 4: Show mercy, and enable me to gain thine sight, O God, within my soul and body. This is the great yearning.

P.118

Ref. 1: O my Lord of life, show me mercy and compassion. Patronless, I have entered Thine Sanctuary, O Master.

From within the blind well take me out by giving Thy hand. I have no wisdom and device whatever.

Ref. 2: In thy mind remember the One Pervading Lord, who has one form and many manifestations.

He is the World-Cherisher, the Holder of Universe in His belly, kind and humble, destroyer of pain and perfectly merciful. Remember, remember the Name over and over again. Nanak, it is the only support of the soul.

Ref. 3: Meet, meet me, O my mates and utter to me the Lord's discourse.

The True *Gurū* has mercifully united me with my Lord.

Chopping off my head, I offer it to him.

P.119

Ref. 1: In every hair, mind and body of mine, I feel the pang of separation. Without seeing my Lord, I can not sleep.

Ref. 2: (a) Showering His benediction, the Lord has made me His own.

(b) Catching me by the arm, God has pulled me out of the mire.

(c) Blessed me with the saints' congregation.

(d) Meditating on God, all my sins and sufferings are burnt off.

(e) My tongue utters the Name of the one Lord and my soul and body are drenched in God's Name.

(f) Nanak, whomsoever the Lord unites with Himself, he becomes adept in all the virtues.

P.120

Ref. 1: The Lord Himself has shown mercy unto Nanak and has made him the slave of the slaves of His slaves.

Ref. 2: Show mercy unto me, O my Lord, that I may ever forsake them (the passions) from my mind.

Applying the dust of saints' feet to my face and forehead, I burn off the poison of lust and wrath.

The lowest of all, I deem my own self.
This way I install peace within my mind.

Ref. 3: Exercising His natural benevolence, the Sovereign Lord has taken me under His wing. All illusory beliefs have been shown the door.

Ref. 4: Bear that God in thy mind, by whose grace thou eatest the thirty-six delicacies.

Thou shalt obtain the supreme dignity by remembering Him, by whose favour thou appliest perfume to thy body . . . the heart lotus blooms.

Ref. 5: By whose grace I have found the nine treasures.

That Lord, my mind forgets not.

P.121

Ref. 1: Who from a senseless man, made me into a sensible one.

Ref. 2: (In respect of purifying power) Thou, O Lord, are as potent as a dip in the Holy Ganges in Varanasi. It is bathing in the (love of) Thy Name alone which befits the soul (*Rāo*), in the sense that it alone can rule all our mental and bodily powers.

If day and night I am able to enshrine affection for Thee, then *that* will be my true ablution.

Some barley-balls are meant for ancestors and others for gods. But it is really the Pandit who kneads and eats them.

Nanak, the rice-balls of Lord's gift are never exhausted.

P.122

Ref. 1: In an instant He can exalt a grovelling worm into a king.

The transcendent Lord is the patron of the humble.

Him, who is totally obscure, the Lord can at once render famous in ten directions.

The Lord of the world takes not the account of him on whom He bestows His favours.

Soul and body are all His capital.
Every heart, the Perfect Lord illumines.

His own handiwork, He has Himself made.

Nanak lives by beholding His greatness.

P.123

Ref. 1: Some obtain gifts through His order and some through His order are ever made to wander in transmigration.

All are subject to His fiat and none is exempt from it.

O Nanak! if man were to understand Lord's fiat, then no one would be proud.

Ref. 2: One Lord is the bestower of all. He Himself bestows bounties.

He gives unto him with whom He is pleased. No one has any say in it.

Nanak, God is obtained through the *Gurū*.
He Himself understands His own self.

Ref. N: The Beloved Himself is the Merciful Master, O slave Nanak; forgiving the mortal He blends him with Himself.

Ref. 3: The Lord Himself sends and recalls the mortals.
There is none else to counsel Him.

He Himself demolishes, constructs and creates.
He, the Lord, knows everything.

Nanak, the Name is the gift, which the Merciful Master makes unto him to whom He extends His mercy.

P.124

Ref. 1: When Thou revealest Thyself, only then can any one know Thee.
He then repeats the Name given by Thee.

Thou are wondrous, and astounding is Thy Omnipotence, O Lord.

Thou Thyself art the cause and Thyself the Doer.

In Thy will is birth; and in Thy will, death.

The Name is the support of my soul and body.

For the slave Nanak, this is a gift of Thine, O Lord.

P.125

Ref. 1: Nanak seeks the company of those who are of low caste among the lowly, nay, rather the lowest of the low. (He has no desire to) nor (does he) rival the lofty. Where the poor are looked after, there does rain the look of Thy grace, O Lord!

Ref. 2: Thou alone art my high official.

I perform Thine service with the support of the *Gurū*.

By various devices I found Thee not.

Taking hold of me, the *Gurū* has employed me as Thy slave.

I have annihilated the five oppressors.

By *Gurū's* grace, I have vanquished the army of evil.

I have received the one Name as Lord's bounty.

In peace, equipoise, and bliss is my abode, now.

P.126

Ref. 1: Dealing in this true merchandise, the man ever earns the profit of the unrivalled Name.

In this very world of poison, the Name Nectar becomes manifest. By the Lord's grace alone it is quaffed.

Nanak, praise thou the True Lord. Blessed is He, the Embellisher of the mortals.

Ref. 2: They whose destiny Thou hast so preordained, O Lord, are attached to Thy Name.

Says Nanak, they obtain peace and in their home plays the celestial strain.

Ref. 3: By Thine grace, man obtains the mark of honour which cannot be effaced by effacing.

P.127

Ref. 1: Truth overtops everything, but truthful conduct is even higher.

Call everyone exalted, none appears to be base.

The One Lord has fashioned the pots and

One Light is pervading the three worlds.

Through God's grace Truth is attained to.

None can efface the primordial gift.

Ref. 2: In what way can one appraise God's worth?

By *Gurū's* instruction some rare person meets the Infinite, Unapproachable and Incomprehensible Lord.

Through the *Gurū*, a few know Lord's worth.

Some solitary one becomes the recipient of Lord's grace.

With the sublime *Gurbāni*, one becomes sublime.

Through the *Gurū*, a few repeat God's Name.

P.128

Ref. 1: Without the True Lord, how can one be released?

The jewel of God's praise is attained through His grace alone.

If He Himself liberates, then alone one is liberated. He Himself is our great Master.

When the Lord Himself shows mercy, one is emancipated by *Gurū's* grace.

The glories are in the Lord's own hand.
He blesses with them the mortal with whom He is pleased.

Ref. 2: As Thy servant, I beg for a chance to serve the masses. However, it is only through Thy grace that such a chance can be had.

This is the prayer of Nanak: 'O Lord, may I see the vision of Thine saints.'

P.129

Ref. 1: Thou art the Peace-giving Lord of all beings. It is through perfect destiny that Thou art contemplated.

Ref. 2: I, Thy slave, perform Thy service and supplicate before Thee, O Lord.

Thou seatest me close to Thee and unites me with Thyself.

PP.129–30

Ref. 3: He whose power is my Lord, all his heart's desires are fulfilled and to him no sorrow clings.

What sustains me in life is listening to the stories of such devotees who have established a personal relation of love with God.

However (because closeness to God is no body's monopoly) we should all struggle to obtain a glimpse of God. If we do so, we are bound to receive His grace.

P.131

Ref. 1: It is by *Gurū's* grace that one is able to renounce wickedness and banish his heart's (ignoble) desires.

Ref. 2: He who enjoys his Lord's love by *Gurū's* grace, his lust, wrath and ego are wiped off; and by the *Gurū's* grace, he is ferried across the world-ocean.

Ref. 3: It is by His grace that I have been able to rid myself of erroneous beliefs (in many gods) and in my present state I see the one God in every direction that my eye takes.

Ref. 4: Kabir says: By God's grace I will easily rise above the hold of this world in which this body is located.

P.132

Ref. 1: All your problems will be solved when you come to realize the value of the grace of God.

I (too) have established a personal relation of vassalage with the Lord who is known in every household as *Niranjan,* that is, as one whose love is not confined to any particular person or group of persons.

Without *Gurū's* instruction one is not emancipated. See and reflect upon this.

Though man may perform lacs of rituals, without the *Gurū* it is all dark.

Ref. 2: Searching, searching and searching, ultimately the mortal succeeds.

Ref. 3: The filth of falsehold and fraud attaches not to those who by *Gurū's* grace remain wakeful night and day.

The immaculate Name abides in their hearts and their lights merge with the light of God.

Ref. 4: Only those persons are saved who by *Gurū's* grace run towards and enter God's sanctuary.

Ref. 5: By *Gurū's* grace, I have found the abode of bliss.

The darkness is dispelled and the moon of wisdom has risen.

P.133

Ref. 1: I have sought the refuge of the Lord who has created the world-ocean.

By *Gurū's* grace, I contemplate my Lord and Death's courier dare not say anything to me.

Ref. 2: By *Gurū's* grace man obtains eternal peace.

He does true deeds and bears love for truth.

Very fortunate are they who serve the True *Gurū.*

Stilling their ego, they embrace love for the True Lord.

Ref. 3: It is with God's grace that the mind of the devotee becomes purified and he obtains surpassing bliss.

Ref. 4: He alone is the essence of life. He is immanent in every heart.

By the grace of the *Gurū* He has lit up my own home (or rather my own heart). We have only to set our own affairs in order—that is, to regulate our efforts; the bliss of success will be given by God, the Giver Supreme.

By the grace of the teacher I have realized God in my own home (or heart) and this has extinguished the fire of all my passions.

P.134

Ref. 1: The Lord is dear to those who are pleasing to the Lord.

By *Gurū's* grace Nanak has spoken of the Indescribable One.

Ref. 2: Meditating on my Lord, I obtain exactly that which I wish for; and my hopes and desires are fulfilled.

By *Gurū's* grace the Lord is enshrined in Nanak's mind; and knowing Him, he does not grieve in distress.

Ref. 3: The world-fascinating mammon I have discarded and dispelled. I have met the Absolute Lord and congratulations are pouring in on me. It is all so charming that it captivates the soul.

It affects man on the way and wharf and in the home, jungle and wilderness.

To the mind and body, the experience tastes sweet.

By *Gurū's* grace, I have perceived it, though it is subtle.

Ref. 4: True *jog* (or renunciation) does not consist in deserting the family and wandering all over.

In the body-home itself is the Lord God's Name. By *Gurū's* grace, thou shalt find thy Lord Master right there.

P.135

Ref. 1: He, who by *Gurū's* grace, subdues his evil self, fixes his love on God.

Nanak says, he whose life is directed towards God goes on gaining in truthfulness and progress on the path to life Eternal. On the other hand, he who continues to be guided by self-will remains entangled in the cycle of life and death.

Ref. 2: With the help of *Gurū's* grace a man is able to nourish himself with what is not a common man's source of sustenance: that is, riches of the spirit. This is so because the teacher's grace awakens the pupil's sense of discrimination (viveka).

I here feel tempted to refer to a more or less similar thought in the Gitā: 'A man of self-control is asleep in respect of things (that is, objects of self-indulgence) which keep an ordinary man awake. Further, a temperate man is wide awake in respect of those things and activities which are of no concern at all to the average man; that is, activities relating to righteous living.

Ref. 3: O my Venerable Lord of mammon, he who mixes with the society of saints is surely saved.

By *Gurū's* grace, he obtains the supreme status and the dry wood blossoms forth.

Ref. 4: Such is the glory of the Name that by *Gurū's* grace, man ceases to petition any one other than God.

O Sire, many men wear various religious garbs for begging and for filling their bellies.

P.136

Ref. 1: By *Gurū's* grace my mind is attached to God's Name.

Asleep for many births, it has now awakened.

Ref. 2: By *Gurū's* grace, I am attached to the relish of the Lord's Name.

Why wastest thou thy life in enmity and strife?

Ref. 3: They whose tongue instinctively tastes God's ambrosia, by *Gurū's* grace, get absorbed in the True Lord.

The tongue which is imbued with truth, and ponders over *Gurū's* hymns, quaffs Nectar of the pure stream of God's Name.

P.137

Ref. 1: By *Gurū's* grace, my mind ever remains imbued with Him.

Thine slaves live by remembering, remembering Thee and merge in Thee, O Unique Lord.

Ref. 2: By Perfect *Gurū's* grace, mine eyes have seen like this that without the Name, dominions, property, riches and youth are all vain.

Ref. 3. By *Gurū's* favour some rare person is able to describe Him.

True, true, true is He who has created all.

Out of millions, scarcely any one really knows Him.

Beautiful, beautiful, beautiful is Thine form, O Lord.

Thou art exceedingly beauteous, limitless and incomparable.

P.138

Ref. 1: Manifest unto me is the Beloved Lord, the World Cherisher; and in the society of saints I repeat His Name.

I have seen the wondrous Lord. He sprinkles Nectar on me. By *Gurū's* grace I have known Him.

Ref. 2: By *Gurū's* grace he (the devotee) attains to the Supreme status.

His heart is pure and pure is his speech.
God's praises he instinctively sings.

Ref. 3: By *Gurū's* grace, I have obtained the supreme status and great has become my glory.

Whoever, sings the praise of the True Lord night and day, he merges in the True one.

Ref. 4: Lord's slave sings His excellences and praises.
By *Gurū's* favour, he obtains the reward, O Nanak.

P.139

Ref. 1: By *Gurū's* grace some rare one understands it. There are the nectareal tanks of Lord's sermons. He who has access to them takes and quaffs the Nectar.

Ref. N: By *Gurū's* grace, I speak of the Indescribable one and utter what the Lord makes me utter.

Ref. 2: Nanak says, my only support is God, who is ever merciful to the needy. I do not look up to any one else.

PP.139–40

Ref. 3: O people, my brethren, see a strange thing. By slaying duality, the Lord has come to be enshrined in my mind.

The priceless Name is not obtained in any other wise.

By *Gurū's* grace it comes to abide within man's mind.

He, the unique Lord, abides amongst all.

By *Gurū's* instruction, He becomes manifest in the mind.

P.140

Ref. 1: I have seen the perfect, inaccessible, wondrous, Exalted Lord Master.

By the grace of the perfect *Gurū*, Nanak has made God's Name his (real) wealth.

P.141

Ref. 1: By *Gurū's* grace, the Lord abides within my mind and I obtain what is predestined for me.

Says Nanak, the body of one who attaches his mind to the True *Gurū*, becomes acceptable (to the Lord).

P.142

Ref. 1: He who (by *Gurū's* grace) deems weal and woė alike, beholds the Lord in every heart.

Ref. 2: By *Guru's* grace, the heart is touched by Divine love.

In this association with God, there is no death.

NOTE: See the relevant p. in the book.

Ref.N.1: With the help of *Gurū's* grace I have realized God, who is Omnipresent and the true owner of everything. It is unto such a God that my life is a ceaseless sacrifice.

Ref.N.2: When it pleases Him, it is then that man comes to embrace love for the Lord, and the error of superstition departs from within him.

Equipoise is produced and the intellect awakens to Divine Knowledge.

P.143

Ref. 1: By *Gurū's* grace, I have meditated on the Lord and my doubt is stilled.

Trouble, ignorance and fear have left me; and my misdeeds are at an end.

Ref. 2: (Those) whose doubt is dispelled by *Gurū's* grace; in them, O Nanak, is this firm faith (rooted).

P.144

Ref. 1: By *Gurū's* grace one recognizes the Lord's will, restrains the wandering mind, and brings it back to the One Lord's Abode.

Imbued with the Name, he ever remains detached; and the Name jewel is enshrined within his mind. He, the One Lord, is present in the whole world.

By *Gurū's* grace, He becomes manifest.

The grace of God has manifested itself (as Ṣabad). And they alone are pure who praise the Scriptures; and it is only in their hearts that God may be said to abide.

Ref. 2: He who, by *Gurū's* grace knows himself, blooms the lotus of his mind.

Ref. 3: By *Gurū's* favour through *Gurbāni,* I praise Thee O Lord.

In (submission to) Thine Will the Nectar abides and by Thy Will Thou makest man quaff the Nectar.

P.145

Ref. 1: They who are satiated with God's elixir, they merge in the Lord; and their glory cannot be uttered with the mouth.

They, O Nanak, are satisfied by *Gurū's* grace, and, remembering and contemplating the Lord's Name, are emancipated.

Ref. 2: By *Gurū's* word, a good many silent sages are emancipated and they even surpass Indra, Brahma, and their like.

Sanak, Sanandan, and many penitent persons have been delivered by the *Gurū's* grace.

Ref. 3: He who, by *Gurū's* grace, knows the Lord's will comes to realize the (true) way of life of all the ages.

Ref. 4: By *Gurū's* grace, Thou hast summoned me to Thine presence, and as Thou art, so hast Thou shown Thyself to me.

Says Nanak, the entire screen (of duality) is rent, and I have become Thine and Thou art enshrined within my mind.

By *Gurū's* grace, this understanding is attained. Slave Nanak has merged in the lap of the Lord.

P.146

Ref. 1: Thou art known by the grace of the *Gurū,* through whom Thou revealest Thyself.

They (the devotees) are easily absorbed in the True Lord.

Ref. 2: My Intimate is carefree.

By *Gurū's* grace I have come to bear Him love.

My Intimate is the Searcher of hearts.

My Master is the Omnipresent Person and the Supreme Lord.

I am Thine Serf, and Thou art my Lord.

My Honour and glory are all Thine gifts O Lord.

NOTE: See the relevant p. in the book.

P.147

Ref. 1: My True Lord is ever new.

By *Gurū's* grace, I ever utter His Name.

The Lord is my Protector, my Mother and Father, and contemplating Him one never comes to grief.

Ref. 2: By *Gurū's* grace, sing thou the praise of the Infinite Lord.

The Divine light shall shine in thy mind and within the collyrium of gnosis, thy spiritual ignorance shall be dispelled.

Such is the Lord to whose greatness there is no limit.

His glory is boundless and Infinite.

Many are His wondrous plays, which cannot be counted.

P.148

Ref. 1: By *Gurū's* favour, my soul and body are rendered pure and the immaculate Name do I meditate upon.

From birth to death I have dedicated my entire life to Thine service, O Lord!

Thou givest glory to him who Thou forgivest. O Nanak!

Ref. 2: By *Gurū's* grace, man realizes the Name.

When the Infinite Lord abides in man's mental firmanent, he sings the Lord's praise and dwells in celestial peace.

P.149

Ref. 1: By *Gurū's* grace, man's mind and body are gratified with the Name.

Uttering the Lord's Name, the tongue is drenched in delight. Through the Lord's affection, one obtains celestial bliss.

Ref. 2: By *Gurū's* grace, it (the Name) shall be enshrined in thy mind and thou shalt swim across the terrible world-ocean.

It is only when the mind contemplates, without wavering, the riches of the Name that Māyā (or attachment to worldly charms) loses its hold upon the individual.

Ref. 3: By *Gurū's* grace (alone) is God's Name repeated.

Says Nanak, the man, within whose mind the Illustrious Lord abides, becomes acceptable (to Him).

P.150

Ref. 1: It is by *Gurū's* grace, that the immortal, unapproachable and unfathomable Beloved is obtained.

The Beloved Himself hears and sees all and Himself speaks through the mouths of all.

Ref. 2: By *Gurū's* grace, my foolish soul has been propitiated.

The *Gurū* is the Creator and the *Gurū* is capable of doing everything.

God, the teacher Supreme, truly is and will ever abide.

Says Nanak, this is what the Lord has made me understand.

Without the *Gurū*, salvation is not obtained, O brother.

P.151

Ref. 1: It is only by the grace of the teacher that some rare souls have been able to relish, as a personal experience, the sweetness of the Name.

Without the Name, accursed and doomed is the proud person who performs many religious rites and good actions.

O, slave Nanak, he is bound in chains, and is entangled in mammon's noose; but he is released by receiving Divine light through the *Gurū*.

P.152

Ref. 1: The man on whom the grace of the *Gurū* descends understands the way to this.

Nanak, he blends with the world-Lord, as water mingles with water.

Ref. 2: Through the *Gurū's* grace my speech has become Nectar sweet.

Ref. 3: By *Gurū's* grace, I have vanquished the army of evil.

I have received the Name as Lord's bounty.

In peace, equipoise, and bliss is my abode now.

Nanak says: resplendent are the faces of those who wait upon the Lord befittingly.

P.153

Ref. 1: By virtue of *Gurū's* grace, God, who is Himself a lover of His devotees, comes to suffuse the innermost recesses of the heart as a quite natural happening.

Eradicating ego from within himself when man worships Him, then he meets with the True Lord.

His saints ever look beauteous at the Lord God's door.

By loving the *Gurū*, they cultivate love and affection for the True Lord.

Ref. 2: My Immaculate Master is immanent in all.
By *Gurū's* grace, the mortal enters into union with God.
The servant of God's servants attains peace.
My Lord, God, is obtained in this way.
It is by His own grace, that man sings the praise of God.

PP.154–55

Ref. 1: At His (own) pleasure the Lord has staged a play.
By *Gurū's* grace, I have obtained the supreme status.
Says Nanak, Lord alone destroys and creates all.
So know it thou. Let no one stray into doubt.

P.156

Ref. 1: The fear of God is mighty and of great weight. Egoism is worthless and just . . . (loudmouthed). Walk under the weight of such fear; and through Divine grace obtain knowledge of God.

(Trans. by Dr. Gopal Singh)

P.157

Ref. 1: My heart is attached to the world, but the world is of no avail (when the heart aches). Yes, he alone liveth detached whose destiny is awake. When the night is young, it yieldeth flower; when old, the fruit. Yea, they who keep ever awake in God, alone are blest. All bounties are God's; but one cannot force God. Some attain them not, while awake; while the others He wakes up and blesses! O thou in search of a spouse, something is amiss in thee; for they who are wedded to God look not out and within. Make the inner patience thy arrow; and patience thy bow, and then aim at thy life-object; and lo, thou winnest, by God's grace. Men of patience burn off their sense of self, and so they are near God, (but) they do not share their mystery with another. O man, if thou art firmly rooted in patience, Yea, if this be thy object in life, then thou growest like a mighty river and breakest not off as a mere offshoot. Thou lovest, O Farid, if thy love is buttered, but hard it is to be a *Darvesh.* Yea, rare is the God's man who goeth the way of God.

(Trans: by Dr. Gopal Singh)

P.159

Ref. 1: Sense-control is the furnace (where our instinctive passions are burnt out); patience is the goldsmith (or the agency or medium through which alone our nature is properly moulded); discrimination is the anvil (that is, the solid block or ground *on the basis of which* our nature is hammered into proper shape); Vedas are the hammer (that is, it is the authentic utterances of the Vedas that lend the power of faith to our efforts at self-improvement); penance is the fire in which the evil in our being is burnt. ***Tapasyā*** or penance is the means by which the persistent residue (or ***khalā***) (in our being) of fear and uncertainty (*bhau*) is burnt out and *abhaya* attained. (It may be pointed out that in the Gitā, ***abhaya*** heads the list of riches of the spirit.) Our intentions are the utensils (which are to be suitably shaped by patient and earnest endeavour). It is only in these utensils (of good intentions) that *amrit* (or nectar of love of the Name of God) can be put. All this shaping of our nature is, however, possible only through devotion to the Holy Word which alone is the true mint (where coins that serve in the spiritual life are made).

P.160

Ref. 1: O Nanak! the compassionate Lord, by His grace, bestows gifts.
So many are His bounties that they cannot be recorded.

NOTE: See the relevant p. in the book.

Ref. 2: Some are blest by the Will of the Giver.
Some are lost in girdling the cycle for ever.

(Trans. by Pritam Singh)

Ref. 3: Actions may earn you a birth, but emancipation is obtained by His Grace. (Trans. by Harbans Singh)

P.182

Ref. 1: I pray to Him who is the bestower of all blessings, and saviour from all ills,

Shower Thy mercy, O Merciful!

For then (alone) will my efforts be well directed.

Ref. 2: Remember the One and sing thou His praises, Chant His holy name and keep Him ensconced in thy heart.

Ceaselessly meditate on His endless attributes, and serve Him with all thy heart and soul. God is one, peerless and precious, complete in Himself,

All-pervasive and permeating,
Creator of the vast creation is that One,
Worship then the One and none besides,
Be saturated, body and mind, in His love,
O Nanak! through the Grace of the Master,
is that One realised.

Ref. 3: 'God, Thou art the dispeller of all evils and bestower of peace, whosoever prays unto Thee, can have no ills.'

P.183

Ref. 1: Thou, O Lord, art my only shelter, mine only prop.
Nanak asks for Thy excellent Name, my Master.

Ref. 2: There is nothing equal to God's Name.

Ref. 3: Without the Name, every one is a pauper.
The True *Gurū* has imparted this understanding unto me.

Ref. 4: This Name of God is the Elysian tree.
The singing of Lord God's praise is the milch-cow of the gods.

P.184

Ref. 1: Of all the religions, the best religion is to repeat God's Name and to do pious deeds.

Ref. 2: Nanak, they within whose mind dwells the Lord, they alone attain to deliverance and emancipation.

Ref. 3: I revere each of Thy Names, O God!

P.185

Ref. 1: 'O great Redeemer! redeem the common people from their suffering.' (Meera)

Ref. 2: 'Thou art the dispenser of pity, I am pitiable; Thou art the Giver supreme, I am a mere beggar.' (Tulsidas)

Ref. 3: Thou, O Lord, art my Father and Thou my Mother.

Thou art the Giver of peace to my soul and my very life.

Thou art my Lord and I am Thy serf.

Except Thee, no one else is mine.

O Lord, in Thine mercy, bless me Thou with this boon, that day and night I may hymn Thy praise.

P.186

Ref. 1: 'The Nām (sound principle) reverberating as It is in all hearts, does not diminish or increase, and is unchanging permanence.'

P.187

Ref. 1: Nām alone is the source of everything; of the universe and its various worlds, and of the human body.

P.188

Ref. 1: Ever He hears, ever He beholds and thoroughly immanent is He in the world.

Ref. 2: Celebrity, Beauty and Salvation are all contained in one Name.
In that very Name, the Pure one remains pervasively.

Ref. 3: 'Commune with Nām till the last breath of life, (for) this brings proximity to God and He saves (us) in the end.'

P.189

Ref. 1: From the mouth every one repeats God's Name, but only a few enshrine It in their mind.

Nanak, they within whose mind dwells the Lord, they alone attain to deliverance and are emancipated.

Ref. 2: The True *Gurū* has made me realize the Name of the Immaculate, Unreachable and Unperceivable Lord.

Ref. 3: Pride is at variance with the Name.
The two dwell not at one place.

P.190

Ref. 1: He alone is valiant, fortitudinous, perfectly intelligent, attuned to primordial trance, profound, unfathomable and ever emancipated; and his affairs are all well managed within whose mind abides God's Name.

Ref. 2: (a) Excepting the True Nām, the rest is all trash.
(b) Four things alone are eternal and lasting: *Nām* or Sound current, *Sādhu* or disciplined soul well established in the Word; *Gurū* or Word-personified, with a divine commission to . . . (put others in touch) with the Nām; and lastly, Gobind or the Lord, God—the Eternally Formless One.

P.191

Ref. 1: We are severed from Thee through our own deeds:
Show mercy and take us unto Thee again.
Having wandered in all directions, tired and worn out, we have come to Thy feet.

Just as a dry cow is of no consequence and vegetables without moisture go stale and become valueless, so we, the worthless, have no peace without our Beloved. If the Beloved reveals Himself not in the house (body), the house, nay the very town where one lives, is like a desert; and all the make-up and ornamentation of the body becomes useless.

In the absence of the Beloved, my friends and relations appear like angels of death (*Yamadūtas*).

Nānak prayeth: Kindly grant me the gift of Thy Holy Word.

P.194

Ref. 1: O Ocean of Mercy! always reside in my heart.

Grant me the wisdom that may make me love the Lord.

I ask for the dust of Thy servants' feet, That I may rub it over and over again on my forehead.

Fallen though I am to the lowest depths,
I am sure that I will be purified
by singing Thy praises.

Let Thy will be sweet unto me, and
Whatever Thou doest be pleasant for me;
Whatever Thou givest I should accept
with good grace and not wish for anything else.

Knowing Thee to be always near me,
I wish to be the dust of Thy servants.

If we get the company of saints then
alone can we attain the Lord.

We are always Thy boy-servants, and
Thou art our Master.

Nanak saith: I am a child and Thou art my
Father and Mother,
And Thy Nām in my mouth is just like
exhilarating nectar.

P.195

Ref. 1: 'It is through Thee that I live, forsake me not even for a moment.

Ref. 2: O grant me but one gift; remove my doubts and protect me, my Beloved, Thou the knower of all secrets.

Ref. 3: The wealth of the Word is more than millions of earthly kingdoms.

Ref. 4: The nectar of Thy glance is the highest honour for me; O Omnipotent Beloved! grant me the power to sing Thy praises all the time.

Ref. 5: O Benefactor of all souls, I take shelter with Thee. Nanak lovingly sacrifices himself at Thy feet.'

Ref. 6: Be gracious, my Lord, (so) that *my eyes may behold Thy Gracious Form*, . . .

The Lord permeates water, earth, ether
and everything besides; and *I see Him everywhere*,

All doubts and delusions have vanished,
I see the Lord as the nearest of the near,

O Lord! be merciful to Nanak, that he
may have *Thy blessed vision*.

Ref. 7: O Nanak; the eyes that behold the Lord are quite different from those with which we see the world.

P.196

Ref. 1: Thou art mother and father to us, and we are Thine children . . .
Nobody knows Thy greatness . . .

Thou alone knowest

Nanak, a slave of Thine is ever a sacrifice unto Thee.

Ref. 2: Thou art my Beloved and my love goes only to Thee . . .
And I cannot live without Thee, even for a while . . .
Thou art my honour and I am *immersed in* Thy love.
Thou art my shelter and Thou my support;
I worship Thee in my mind and body,
after having got this secret from the *Gurū*.

P.197

Ref. 1: O Benefactor of this unworthy soul!
My life, body and mind are all Thine.

How can one gauge Thy greatness
. . . All my body and soul are Thine.

O most beautiful and attractive Beloved!
I shall give all that I have for a
glimpse of Thee . . .
How can I have Thy *darshan* (a look at Thee)?

We cannot know Thy Greatness,
Nor thine Existence Infinite:
My mind is yearning just for a glimpse of Thee.

Ref. 2: There is none beside Thee, Thou the creator,
and all happens as Thou desireth,
All my strength is from Thee and Thou art the support
Of my mind, . . . Thou art and Thou shalt ever be:

Unreachable, Unknowable, the Highest and the Endless.

Those who serve Thee are freed from fear and pain.
Nanak says: (in so far as) my yearning for God is total, I long for the dust (of the feet) of saints.

P.198

Ref. 1: Thou art a most loving Lord
With many disciples like me,

Thou art an Ocean of Jewels, with depths *immeasurable,*
Thou, O Supreme Wisdom! be merciful unto me,
and give me understanding to meditate on Thee all the time,

O my self, do not be vain and proud,
but humble like dust; for that is the
way to liberation,

The Lord of Nanak is the highest of all,
and *many like Nanak serve His Will.*

Ref. 2: . . . How can a fish live without water?
And how an infant without milk?
Nanak is thirsty for the light of Thy lotus feet:
A glimpse of Thee brings in all the happiness that one needs.

P.199

Ref. 1: . . . O Lord! do hear Nanak's prayer.
Save me, for I am Thy disciple.

. . . Nanak prayeth: I am the slave of Hari:
The Lord is the support of my breath.

Ref. 2: My Lord, what a poor helpless fellow am I!

Thou hast raised me into a man from a very low birth,

and therein lies Thy greatness. Thou art the Lord of all,
the Giver of soul and the life-breath,
And none can describe Thy numerous attributes,
Beloved of all, Thou providest nourishment to all,
Thou the sustainer of all life.

P.200

Ref. 1: *Satgurū,* I have come to Thy feet:
Give me the bliss of Nām for Divine
honour and free (me) from all anxieties.
I cannot think of any other place of rest;
and, as a last resort, I am at Thy door.
Whether I deserve it or not, O save me as
Thou wilt, for merit I have none.
Thou art ever forgiving, ever kind and sustaineth all,
Nanak hath taken his refuge with the saints: kindly protect him this time.

P.201

Ref. 1: 'Thou art my Father,
Thou art my Mother,
Thou art my soul and life, . . .!
Thou art my Master and
I am Thy slave,
And apart from Thee nothing is (truly) mine.'

Ref. 2: O Lord! be kind and grant that we may sing Thy praises, . . . we are children without wisdom and are steeped in stark ignorance.

Ref. 3: Thou art my (real) friend and relation, and I am highly proud of Thee . . .
Millions of suns and moons cannot equal
the glory of Thy one hair;
Thou art the greatest of the Great:
the Indescribable and the Ineffable.

PP.201–2

Ref. 4: O merciful One, I ask of Thee to make
me a slave of Thy servants: . . .
The treasure of Nām-nectar abounds
in the house of the Lord's devotees.
I feel elated in their company, for
there I hear His praises, . . .
I bring water for them, fan them, grind
their corn, and grow happy by washing

their feet, . . . Show me Thy Grace,
O Lord!

Give me a place to live with the divine Saints.

P.202

Ref. 1: O Lord! I have just one desire:
O Treasure of mercy and benevolence,
Make me a disciple of Thy saints;
I may make obeisance unto them
at early morning hours,
And reverently look at *their beaming faces* day and night,
And dedicate myself, body and mind, to their service;
I may ever sing praises of the Lord with my tongue.
And with each breath of my life, let
me remember The Lord, and let me
live with the saints from day to day.
My only food and wealth is Thy Divine Nām,
Thus Nanak enjoys the real bliss.

PP.202–3

Ref. 2: Translated by Gandā Singh in his book: *Sikh and Sikhism,* Sikh Cultural Centre, Patna, 1968, pp. 57–61. I have taken only those translated portions which are required for Standard Ardās as approved by Shiromani Gurdwara Prabandhak Committee. Numbering of lines and paragraphs has been done by me, to facilitate reference.

1. Victory to the one wonderful God.
2. May the Almighty Lord protect us.
   Ode to the Lord by the Tenth Guru Gobind Singh.
3. Having first of all invoked the Almighty
   God, think of Gurū Nanak;
4. Then think of Gurū Angad, Amar Das,
   Rām Das; May they help us;
5. Remember Gurū Arjan, Hargobind and
   the great Hari Rai;
6. Think of the great Har Krishan whose
   sight dispels all pains and sorrows;
7. Remember Tegh Bahadur, and the nine
   treasures shall come hastening to our homes.
8. May they help us at all places!
9. May the great Gurū Gobind Singh, the Tenth
   Master, protect us everywhere.

A. (Then) concentrate on the sight and sound of the holy *Guru Granth Sahib,* the spirit (embodied in the visible word) of the Ten Masters and utter *Vāheguru* (wonderful is the Lord)!

B. Think of the glorious deeds of the Five Beloved ones, the four sons of the Master, the forty saved ones and of other steadfast, meditating and devout souls who worshipped the Name, shared their food in companionship with others, ran a free kitchen (for the needy) and plied the sword (in defence of the helpless) and overlooked the faults of others—think of those dear and true ones, O Khālsā, and utter *Vāheguru* (wonderful is the Lord)!

C. Think of those Singhs, men and women, who sacrificed their lives at the altar of *dharma* (duty enjoined by Sikhism), who were cut up joint by joint, suffered their scalps to be scrapped, were broken on the wheel, were sawn or flayed alive, and who abjured not their faith and perjured not their soul, but lived in devotion to Sikhism with their hair intact to the last breath of their lives—think of those great martyrs, O Khālsa, and utter *Vāheguru* (wonderful is the Lord)!

D. Think of the four *Takhts*—the seats of holy authority—and of the various *gurudwārās* and utter *Vāheguru* (wonderful is the Lord)!

E. We pray, in the first instance, for and on behalf of the *Sarbat Khālsa,* the entire community. May they bring to their mind the holy Name of the wonderful Lord! And through His grace, may they be blessed with peace and happiness!

F. May His protection be extended to the Khālsā wherever they are! May success attend their cooking-pots (for the service of the needy) and victory come to their swords (in defence of their righteousness). May God preserve His form and image in the *Khālsā*! May the *Panth* be ever victorious! May the great Sword be ever helpful and may the Khālsā always triumph and prosper! Utter *Vāheguru* (wonderful is the Lord)!

G. Grant to the Sikhs, O Lord, the gift of a life of discipline and discipleship—Sikhism—the gift of unshorn hair, the gift of good conduct, the gift of discrimination, faith and confidence; and, above all, the gift of Thy Name, and of unhampered *darshan* and dip in the holy tank of Amritsar.

May the choirs, banners and mansions of the Sikhs abide for ever and ever! And may righteousness triumph! Utter *Vāheguru* (wonderful is the Lord)!

May the Khālsā be humble in mind and exalted in understanding! May the Timeless Lord Himself guide their intellect and protect their honour!

H. O Merciful Almighty Lord, the Honour of the unhonoured, the strength of the weak and the shelter of the shelterless, standing in Thy presence we offer our prayer. Forgive our sins and errors and fulfil the wishes of all . . . (Here the leader of the prayer mentions in suitable terms the specific occasion for which the prayer is offered or the purpose for which the blessings of God are sought).

I. Through Nanak, may Thy Name, Thy Glory,
be for ever on the increase!

J. And, in Thy Will, may peace and prosperity
come to one and all in the world.

K. The Khālsā belongs to God
To God belongs victory.

PP.207–8

Ref. a: O God, be merciful to me,
And bless me with the wisdom that
I may ever dwell upon Thee.

Ref. b: The entire world is being consumed
In the invisible flames of hellfire,
Save us all with Thy loving grace
in whatever way it may be possible.

Ref. c: O Lord! forgive us in Thy Grace, for we are inveterate sinners.

Ref. d: We are as full of faults as the sea is full of water. Please take pity on us and bless us with Thy grace (we are hopeful as we pray thus, for) Thou hast redeemed even those who were hardened sinners and were threatened with drowning because of the weight of sinfulness.

Ref. e: O Lord! take us under the shadow of Thy protective wings.
We are unable to do anything on our own. Graciously give us Thy Name.

Ref. f: For ages upon ages have we been separated, unite us unto Thee,
O Lord, through sheer compassion, if Thou wilt
We have wandered high and low in all the points of the compass,
Now keep us O Thou under the shadow of Thy holy wings.

Ref. g: We the ignorant, insensate and devoid of all virtues, have taken refuge with Thee, O Primal Being.

Through Thy boundless Grace, O Lord! save us, in spite of all our shortcomings.

P.208

Ref. 1: Full of deadly sins and tormented by lusts of the flesh I cry,

Rescue me by Thy Grace, as best Thou may, O Great and Compassionate One! I am at Thy mercy,

With austerities and penances one cannot escape,

But with Thy glance of Grace, take Nanak out of the blind well.

Ref. 2: I am a depraved sinner and a heretic,

A thief, a gambler and a housekeeper,

A thug that lives on illicit gains,

A constant prey to all kinds of lusts,

A slave to the five passions, viz., lust, anger, greed, attachment and egoism,

A betrayer, an ungrateful wretch, abhorred by all.

O Ye, with all these faults, and still more, Remember the *Satgurū*, for He is compassionate indeed.

PP.209–10

Ref. 1: By whose grace, thou enjoyest in peace on earth, And revellest with thy sons, brothers, friends, wife,

By whose Grace thou drinkest fresh and cool water,
And breathest the life-giving air and enjoyeth the precious warmth of fire,

By whose Grace thou enjoyest all joys,
And livest with all thy Treasures;

He, who gave thee hands, feet, ears, eyes, tongue;

Such is the ignorance of this wild fool,

O Lord,
Pull him thou out of the muck, of Thyself.

Ref. N: Saith Kabir, I have worn this body-apparel with great care.
And I am putting it aside exactly as it was, intact and unharmed. (Kabirdas)

PP.212–13

Ref. : Translation of the Ārti as given in *Sikh Review,* Sikh Cultural Centre, Park Street, Calcutta, September 1967, p.45. The lines have been numbered, to facilitate reference.

ĀRTI—THY ADORATION

1. The firmament is Thy Salver.
2. The sun and the moon Thy lamps.
3. The galaxy of stars are as pearls scattered.
4. The woods of sandal are Thy incense.
5. The breezes blow Thy royal fan.
6. The flowers of the forests,
7. Lie as offerings at thy feet.

8. What wonderful worship with lamps is this.
9. O Thou destroyer of fear.
10. Unstruck music is the sound of Thy temple drums.
11. Thousands are Thine eyes,
12. And yet Thou has no eyes.
13. Thousands are Thy shapes,
14. And yet Thou hast no shape.
15. Thousands are Thy pure feet,
16. And yet Thou has not one foot.
17. Thousands are Thy noses,
18. And yet Thou hast no nose.
19. All this is Thy play that bewitches me.
20. In every heart there is light,
21. That light art Thou.
22. By the light that is of God Himself,
23. Is every soul illumined.
24. But this divine Light becomes manifest,
25. Only by the *Gurū's* teachings.
26. What is pleasing to Thee, O Lord!
27. Is the best *ārti* (worship with the lamps).
28. O Lord, my mind yearns for Thy lotus feet,
29. As the honey-bee for the nectar of the flowers.
30. Night and day, Lord, I am athirst for Thee.
31. Give water of Thy mercy to Nanak.
32. He is like the *sārang*: the hawk-cuckoo that drinks only rain drops.
33. So that he may dwell forever in the peace of Thy Name.

ORIGINAL *GURMUKHI* PASSAGES CITED IN THE BOOK

FAITH

		ਆਦਿ ਗ੍ਰੰਥ ਪੰਨਾ
P. 13	ਹਰਿ ਜਨ ਕੇ ਵਡਭਾਗ ਵਡੇਰੇ ਜਿਨ ਹਰਿ ਹਰਿ ਸਰਧਾ ਹਰਿ ਪਿਆਸ ॥ ਹਰਿ ਹਰਿ ਨਾਮੁ ਮਿਲੈ ਤ੍ਰਿਪਤਾਸਹਿ ਮਿਲਿ ਸੰਗਤਿ ਗੁਣ ਪਰਗਾਸਿ ॥[13]	492
P. 13	ਜਿਨ ਸਰਧਾ ਰਾਮ ਨਾਮਿ ਲਗੀ ਤਿਨ੍ ਦੂਜੈ ਚਿਤੁ ਨ ਲਾਇਆ ਰਾਮ ॥ ਜੇ ਧਰਤੀ ਸਭ ਕੰਚਨੁ ਕਰਿ ਦੀਜੈ ਬਿਨੁ ਨਾਵੈ ਅਵਰੁ ਨ ਭਾਇਆ ਰਾਮ ॥[14]	444
P. 13	ਸਤਿਗੁਰੂ ਹੋਏ ਦਇਆਲੁ ਤਾ ਸਰਧਾ ਪੂਰੀਐ ਸਤਿਗੁਰੁ ਹੋਇ ਦਇਆਲ ਨ ਕਬਹੂੰ ਝੂਰੀਐ ॥ ਸਤਿਗੁਰੁ ਹੋਇ ਦਇਆਲੁ ਤਾ ਦੁਖੁ ਨਾ ਜਾਣੀਐ ॥[15]	149
P. 13	ਏਕੁ ਅਰਾਧਿ ਪਰਾਛਤ ਗਏ ॥ ਮਨ ਤਨ ਅੰਤਰਿ ਏਕੁ ਪ੍ਰਭੁ ਰਾਤਾ ॥ ਗੁਰ ਪ੍ਰਸਾਦਿ ਨਾਨਕ ਇਕੁ ਜਾਤਾ ॥[16]	289
P. 13	ਮੇਰੀ ਸਰਧਾ ਪੂਰਿ ਜਗਜੀਵਨ ਦਾਤੇ ਮਿਲਿ ਹਰਿ ਦਰਸਨਿ ਮਨੁ ਭੀਜੈ ਜੀਉ ॥[17]	95
P. 13	ਜੋ ਜਨੁ ਸੁਣੈ ਸਰਧਾ ਭਗਤਿ ਸੇਤੀ ਕਰਿ ਕਿਰਪਾ ਹਰਿ ਨਿਸਤਾਰੇ ॥[18]	493
P. 14	ਗ੍ਰਾਮ ਗ੍ਰਾਮ ਨਗਰ ਸਭ ਫਿਰਿਆ ਰਿਦ ਅੰਤਰਿ ਹਰਿ ਜਨ ਭਾਰੇ ॥ ਸਰਧਾ ਸਰਧਾ ਉਪਾਇ ਮਿਲਾਏ ਮੋ ਕਉ ਹਰਿ ਗੁਰ ਗੁਰਿ ਨਿਸਤਾਰੇ ॥[20]	983
P. 14	ਚੀਤਿ ਆਵੈ ਤਾਂ ਸਰਧਾ ਪੂਰੀ ॥[27]	1141

P. 15	ਗਾਵਤ ਸੁਨਤ ਸੁਨਾਵਤ ਸਰਧਾ ਹਰਿ ਰਸੁ ਪੀ ਵਡਭਾਗੇ ।।[29]	1206
P. 15	ਹਰਿ ਹਰਿ ਕ੍ਰਿਪਾ ਕਰਹੁ ਜਗਜੀਵਨ ਮੈ ਸਰਧਾ ਨਾਮਿ ਲਗਾਵੈਗੋ ।।[30]	1310
P. 15	..... ਤੂੰ ਆਪੇ ਸਰਧਾ ਲਾਇਹਿ ।।[31]	749
P. 15	ਹਰਿ ਹਰਿ ਸਰਧਾ ਸੇਜ ਵਿਛਾਈ ਪ੍ਰਭੁ ਛੋਡਿ ਨ ਸਕੈ ਬਹੁਤੁ ਮਨਿ ਭਈਆ ।।[32]	836
P. 15	ਮੈ ਮਨਿ ਤਨਿ ਪ੍ਰੇਮੁ ਅਗਮ ਠਾਕੁਰ ਕਾ ਖਿਨੁ ਖਿਨੁ ਸਰਧਾ ਮਨਿ ਬਹੁਤੁ ਉਠਈਆ ।।[33]	836
P. 15	ਕਰਿ ਕਿਰਪਾ ਪਾਰਬ੍ਰਹਮ ਦਇਆਲ ।। ਮਨ ਤੇ ਕਬਹੁ ਨਾ ਬਿਸਰੁ ਗੋਪਾਲ।। ਤੇਰੇ ਦਾਸ ਕੀ ਹੋਵਾ ਧੂਰ।। ਨਾਨਕ ਕੀ ਪ੍ਰਭ ਸਰਧਾ ਪੂਰਿ ।।[34]	893
P. 15	ਸਰਧਾ ਲਾਗੀ ਸੰਗਿ ਪ੍ਰੀਤਮੈ ਇਕੁ ਤਿਲੁ ਰਹਣੁ ਨ ਜਾਇ ।।[35]	928
P. 16	ਖੇਤੀ ਵਣਜੁ ਨਾਵੈ ਕੀ ਓਟ ।। ਪਾਪੁ ਪੁੰਨੁ ਬੀਜ ਕੀ ਪੋਟ ।। ਕਾਮੁ ਕ੍ਰੋਧੁ ਜੀਅ ਮਹਿ ਚੋਟ ।। ਨਾਮੁ ਵਿਸਾਰਿ ਚਲੇ ਮਨਿ ਖੋਟ ।।[37]	152
P. 18	ਮਹਾ ਦੁਤਰੁ ਮਾਇਆ ।। ਜੈਸੇ ਪਵਨੁ ਝੁਲਾਇਆ ।। ਸੁਨਿ ਸੁਨਿ ਹੀ ਡਰਾਇਆ ।। ਕਰਰੋ ਧ੍ਰਮਰਾਇਆ ।। ਗ੍ਰਿਹ ਅੰਧ ਕੂਪ ਕੂਪਾਇਆ ।। ਪਾਵਕੁ ਸਗਰਾਇਆ ।। ਗਹੀ ਓਟ ਸਾਧਾਇਆ ।। ਨਾਨਕ ਹਰਿ ਧਿਆਇਆ ।। ਅਬ ਮੈ ਪੂਰਾ ਪਾਇਆ ।।[40]	746
P. 18	ਅਸਥਿਰੁ ਕਰਤਾ ਤੂ ਧਣੀ ਤਿਸ ਹੀ ਕੀ ਮੈ ਓਟ ।।[41]	936
P. 18	ਗੁਣ ਕੀ ਮਾਰੀ ਹਉ ਮੁਈ ਸਬਦਿ ਰਤੀ ਮਨਿ ਚੋਟ ।।[42]	936

P. 19	ਜਹ ਤੇ ਉਪਜੀ ਤਹ ਮਿਲੀ ਸਚੀ ਪ੍ਰੀਤਿ ਸਮਾਹੁ ।।[43]	135
P. 19	ਅਵਰ ਓਟ ਮੈ ਸਗਲੀ ਦੇਖੀ ਇਕ ਤੇਰੀ ਓਟ ਰਹਾਈਐ ।।[45]	625
P. 19	ਸੰਗ ਸਖਾ ਸਭਿ ਤਜਿ ਗਏ ਕੋਊ ਨ ਨਿਬਹਿਓ ਸਾਥਿ ।।	1429
	ਕਹੁ ਨਾਨਕ ਇਹ ਬਿਪਤਿ ਮੈ ਟੇਕ ਏਕ ਰਘੁਨਾਥ ।।[46]	
P. 19	ਤੂੰ ਮੇਰੋ ਮੇਰੁ ਪਰਬਤੁ ਸੁਆਮੀ ਓਟ ਗਹੀ ਮੈ ਤੇਰੀ ।।	969
	ਨਾ ਤੁਮ ਡੋਲਹੁ ਨਾ ਹਮ ਗਿਰਤੇ ਰਾਖਿ ਲੀਨੀ ਹਰਿ ਮੇਰੀ ।।	
	ਅਬ ਤਬ ਜਬ ਕਬ ਤੁਹੀ ਤੁਹੀ ।।	
	ਹਮ ਤੁਅ ਪਰਸਾਦਿ ਸੁਖੀ ਸਦ ਹੀ ।।[47]	
P. 20	ਓਟ ਗੋਵਿੰਦ ਗੋਪਾਲ ਰਾਇ	135
	ਸੇਵਾ ਸੁਆਮੀ ਲਾਹੁ ।।[48]	
	ਹਰਿ ਕਾ ਨਾਮੁ ਦਾਸ ਕੀ ਓਟ ।।[49]	264
P. 20	ਭਗਤਿ ਜਨਾ ਕੀ ਬਰਤਨਿ ਨਾਮੁ ।।	
	ਸੰਤ ਜਨਾ ਕੋਇ ਸਨਿ ਬਿਸ੍ਰਾਮ ।।	
	ਹਰਿ ਕਾ ਨਾਮੁ ਦਾਸ ਕੀ ਓਟ ।।	264
	ਹਰਿ ਕੈ ਨਾਮਿ ਉਧਰੇ ਜਨ ਕੋਟਿ ।।[50]	
P. 20	ਤੁਧੁ ਬਿਨੁ ਅਵਰੁ ਨ ਕੋਈ ਕਰਤੇ	107
	ਮੈ ਧਰ ਓਟ ਤੁਮਾਰੀ ਜੀਉ ।।[51]	
P. 20	ਹਰਿ ਚਰਣ ਕੀ ਓਟ ਸਤਾਣੀ ।।	622
	ਸਭ ਚੂਕੀ ਕਾਣਿ ਲੋਕਾਣੀ ।।[52]	
P. 20	ਪ੍ਰਭ ਜੀ ਤੇਰੀ ਓਟ ਗੁਸਾਈ ।।	630
	ਤੂ ਸਮਰਥੁ ਸਰਨਿ ਦਾ ਦਾਤਾ ਆਠ ਪਹਰ ਤੁਮ੍ ਧਿਆਈ ।। ਰਹਾਉ ।।	
	ਜੋ ਜਨੁ ਭਜਨੁ ਕਰੇ ਪ੍ਰਭ ਤੇਰਾ ਤਿਸੈ ਅੰਦੇਸਾ ਨਾਹੀ ।।[53]	
P. 20	ਪ੍ਰਾਤਹਕਾਲਿ ਹਰਿ ਨਾਮੁ ਉਚਾਰੀ ।।	743

ਈਤ ਊਤ ਕੀ ਓਟ ਸਵਾਰੀ ।।
ਸਦਾ ਸਦਾ ਜਪੀਐ ਹਰਿ ਨਾਮ ।।
ਪੂਰਨ ਹੋਵਹਿ ਮਨ ਕੇ ਕਾਮ ।।[54]

P. 21 ਸਾਸ ਸਾਸ ਤੇਰੇ ਗੁਣ ਗਾਵਾ 100
ਓਟ ਨਾਨਕ ਗੁਰ ਚਰਣਾ ਜੀਓ ।।[55]

P. 21 ਤੂੰ ਪ੍ਰੀਤਮ ਤੂੰ ਪ੍ਰਾਨ ਅਧਾਰੇ ।। 740
ਤੁਮ ਹੀ ਪੇਖਿ ਪੇਖਿ ਮਨੁ ਬਿਗਸਾਰੇ ।। ਰਹਾਉ ।।
ਅਨਿਕ ਜੋਨਿ ਭ੍ਰਮਿ ਭ੍ਰਮਿ ਭ੍ਰਮਿ ਹਾਰੇ ।।
ਓਟ ਗਹੀ ਅਬ ਸਾਧ ਸੰਗਾਰੇ ।।
ਅਗਮ ਅਗੋਚਰੁ ਅਲਖ ਅਪਾਰੇ ।।
ਨਾਨਕੁ ਸਿਮਰੈ ਦਿਨੁ ਰੈਨਾਰੇ ।।[56]

P. 21 ਤੁਝ ਬਿਨੁ ਅਵਰੁ ਨਾਹੀ ਮੈ ਦੂਜਾ 378
ਤੂੰ ਮੇਰੇ ਮਨ ਮਾਹੀ ।।
ਤੂੰ ਸਾਜਨੁ ਸੰਗੀ ਪ੍ਰਭੁ ਮੇਰਾ
ਕਾਹੇ ਜੀਅ ਡਰਾਹੀ ।।
ਤੁਮਰੀ ਓਟ ਤੁਮਾਰੀ ਆਸਾ ।।
ਬੈਠਤ ਊਠਤ ਸੋਵਤ ਜਾਗਤ
ਵਿਸਰੁ ਨਾਹੀ ਤੂੰ ਸਾਸ ਗਿਰਾਸਾ ।। ਰਹਾਉ ।।
ਰਾਖੁ ਰਾਖੁ ਸਰਣਿ ਪ੍ਰਭ ਅਪਨੀ
ਅਗਨਿ ਸਾਗਰ ਵਿਕਰਾਲਾ ।।
ਨਾਨਕ ਕੇ ਸੁਖਦਾਤੇ ਸਤਿਗੁਰ
ਹਮ ਤੁਮਰੇ ਬਾਲ ਗੁਪਾਲਾ ।।[57]

P. 22 ਓਟ ਗਹੀ ਗੋਪਾਲ ਦਇਆਲ ਕ੍ਰਿਪਾ ਨਿਧੇ ।।[57] 456
ਪ੍ਰਭ ਏਕ ਅਨਿਕ ਅਲਖ ਠਾਕੁਰ
ਓਟ ਨਾਨਕ ਤਿਸੁ ਗਹੀ ।।[59] 458

P. 22 ਹਰਿ ਚਰਣ ਸਰਣ ਅਪਾਰ ਪ੍ਰਭ 502
ਕੇ ਦ੍ਰਿੜੁ ਗਹੀ ਨਾਨਕ ਓਟ ।।[60]

P. 22 ਮਨ ਸਗਲ ਸਿਆਨਪ ਰਹੀ ।। 529
ਕਰਨ ਕਰਾਵਨਹਾਰ ਸੁਆਮੀ ਨਾਨਕ ਓਟ ਗਹੀ ।।[61]

P. 23 ਚਰਨ ਕਮਲ ਬਸਿਆ ਰਿਦ ਭੀਤਰਿ ਸਾਸਿ ਗਿਰਾਸਿ ਉਚਾਰਿਓ ।। 534
ਨਾਨਕ ਓਟ ਗਹੀ ਜਗਦੀਸੁਰ ਪੁਨਹ ਪੁਨਹ ਬਲਿਹਾਰਿਓ ।।[62]

P. 23 ਪਤਿਤ ਪਾਵਨੁ ਭਗਤਿ ਬਛਲੁ ਭੈ ਹਰਨ ਤਾਰਨ ਤਰਨ ।। ਰਹਾਉ ।। 1306
ਨੈਨ ਤਿਪਤੇ ਦਰਸੁ ਪੇਖਿ ਜਸੁ ਤੋਖਿ ਸੁਨਤ ਕਰਨ ।।
ਪ੍ਰਾਨ ਨਾਥ ਅਨਾਥ ਦਾਤੇ ਦੀਨ ਗੋਬਿਦ ਸਰਨ ।।
ਆਸ ਪੂਰਨ ਦੁਖ ਬਿਨਾਸਨ ਗਹੀ ਓਟ ਨਾਨਕ ਹਰਿ ਚਰਨ ।।[63]

P. 23 ਜਿਸਹਿ ਜਨਾਵਹੁ ਤਿਨਹਿ ਤੁਮ ਜਾਤੇ ।।[64] 563

P. 23 ਮਾਧਵੇ ਐਸੀ ਦੇਹੁ ਬੁਝਾਈ ।।
ਸੇਵਉ ਸਾਧ ਗਹਉ ਓਟ ਚਰਨਾ ਨਾ ਬਿਸਰੈ ਮੁਹਤੁ ਚਸਾਈ ।।[65] 609

P. 23 ਤੁਮਰੀ ਕ੍ਰਿਪਾ ਤੇ ਤੁਧੁ ਪਛਾਣਾ ।।
ਤੂੰ ਮੇਰੀ ਓਟ ਤੂੰਹੈ ਮੇਰਾ ਮਾਣਾ ।।[66] 103

P. 24 ਤੂੰ ਮੇਰਾ ਪਿਤਾ ਤੂੰਹੈ ਮੇਰਾ ਮਾਤਾ ।। 103
ਤੂੰ ਮੇਰੀ ਬੰਧਪ ਤੂੰ ਮੇਰਾ ਮਾਣਾ ।।[67]

P. 24 ਤਾ ਤੇ ਮੋਹਿ ਧਾਰੀ ਓਟ ਗੋਪਾਲ ।। 676
ਸਰਨਿ ਪਰਿਓ ਪੂਰਨ ਪਰਮੇਸੁਰ
ਬਿਨਸੇ ਸਗਲ ਜੰਜਾਲ ।।[68]

P. 0 ਪ੍ਰਭ ਕੀ ਓਟ ਗਹੀ ਤਉ ਛੂਟੋ ।। 673
ਸਾਧ ਪ੍ਰਸਾਦਿ ਹਰਿ ਹਰਿ ਹਰਿ ਗਾਏ
ਬਿਖੈ ਬਿਆਧਿ ਤਬ ਹੂਟੋ ।।[69]

P. 24 ਰੇ ਮਨ ਓਟ ਲੇਹੁ ਹਰਿ ਨਾਮਾ ।। 901
ਜਾ ਕੈ ਸਿਮਰਨਿ ਦੁਰਮਤਿ ਨਾਸੈ ਪਾਵਹਿ ਪਦੁ ਨਿਰਬਾਨਾ ।।[70]

P. 25	ਮੂਲੁ ਬਿਆਧੀ ਬਿਆਪਸਿ ਲੋਭਾ ।। ਮਾਇਆ ਬਿਆਪਤ ਬਹੁ ਪਰਕਾਰੀ ।। ਸੰਤ ਜੀਵਹਿ ਪ੍ਰਭੁ ਓਟ ਤੁਮਰੀ ।।[71]	182
P. 25	ਮੈ ਨਿਰਗੁਨ ਗੁਣੁ ਨਾਹੀ ਕੋਇ ।। ਕਰਨ ਕਰਾਵਨਹਾਰ ਪ੍ਰਭ ਸੋਇ ।। ਰਹਾਉ ।। ਮੂਰਖ ਮੁਗਧ ਅਗਿਆਨ ਵੀਚਾਰੀ ।। ਨਾਮ ਤੇਰੇ ਕੀ ਆਸ ਮਨਿ ਧਾਰੀ ।। ਜਪੁ ਤਪੁ ਸੰਜਮੁ ਕਰਮ ਨ ਸਾਧਾ ।। ਨਾਮੁ ਪ੍ਰਭੂ ਕਾ ਮਨਹਿ ਅਰਾਧਾ ।। ਕਿਛੂ ਨ ਜਾਨਾ ਮਤਿ ਮੇਰੀ ਥੋਰੀ ।। ਬਿਨਵਤਿ ਨਾਨਕ ਓਟ ਪ੍ਰਭ ਤੋਰੀ ।।[73]	388
P. 25	ਤਾ ਕਉ ਧੋਖਾ ਕਹਾ ਬਿਆਪੈ ਜਾ ਕਉ ਓਟ ਤੁਹਾਰੀ ।।[74]	711
P. 25	ਸਰਬ ਜੀਅ ਹਹਿ ਜਾ ਕੈ ਹਾਥਿ ।। ਕਦੇ ਨ ਬਿਛੁੜੈ ਸਭ ਕੈ ਸਾਥਿ ।। ਉਪਾਵ ਛੋਡਿ ਗਹੁ ਤਿਸ ਕੀ ਓਟ ।। [75]	177
P. 25	ਤੂੰ ਸਮਰਥੁ ਤੂੰਹੈ ਮੇਰਾ ਸੁਆਮੀ ।। ਸਭੁ ਕਿਛੁ ਤੁਮ ਤੇ ਤੂੰ ਅੰਤਰਜਾਮੀ ।। ਪਾਰਬ੍ਰਹਮ ਪੂਰਨ ਜਨ ਓਟ ।। ਤੇਰੀ ਸਰਣਿ ਉਧਰਹਿ ਜਨ ਕੋਟਿ ।।[76]	193
P. 26	ਜਿਹ ਜਨ ਓਟ ਗਹੀ ਪ੍ਰਭ ਤੇਰੀ ਸੇ ਸੁਖੀਏ ਪ੍ਰਭ ਸਰਣੇ ।। ਜਿਹ ਨਰ ਬਿਸਰਿਆ ਪੁਰਖੁ ਬਿਧਾਤਾ ਤੇ ਦੁਖੀਆ ਮਹਿ ਗਨਣੇ ।।[77]	613
P. 26	ਨਾਨਕ ਦੁਖੀਆ ਸਭੁ ਸੰਸਾਰੁ ।। ਮੰਨੇ ਨਾਉ ਸੋਈ ਜਿਣਿ ਜਾਇ ।।[78]	954
P. 26	ਜਿਨਾ ਸਾਸ ਗਿਰਾਸਿ ਨਾ ਵਿਸਰੈ	319

ਹਰਿ ਨਾਮਾਂ ਮਨਿ ਸੰਤੁ
ਧੰਨੁ ਸਿ ਸੋਇ ਨਾਨਕਾ
ਪੂਰਨਿ ਸੋਈ ਸੰਤੁ ।।[79]

P. 26 ਨਿਰਮਲੰ ਸੰਤ ਸੰਗੇਣ ਓਟ ਨਾਨਕ ਪਰਮੇਸੁਰਹ ।।[80] 709

P. 26 ਸਤਿਗੁਰਿ ਮੋ ਕਉ ਦੀਆ ਉਪਦੇਸੁ ।। 371
ਜੀਉ ਪਿੰਡੁ ਸਭੁ ਹਰਿ ਕਾ ਦੇਸੁ ।।
ਜੋ ਕਿਛੁ ਕਰੀ ਸੁ ਤੇਰਾ ਤਾਣੁ ।।
ਤੂੰ ਮੇਰੀ ਓਟ ਤੂੰਹੈ ਦੀਬਾਣੁ ।।[81]

P. 27 ਜਿਸ ਕੀ ਓਟ ਤਿਸੈ ਕੀ ਆਸਾ ।।[82] 1144

P. 27 ਅਵਰ ਓਟ ਮੈ ਕੋਇ ਨ ਸੂਝੈ ਇਕ ਹਰਿ ਕੀ ਓਟ ਮੈ ਆਸ ।।[83] 1304

P. 27 ਭਗਤਾ ਕੀ ਟੇਕ ਤੂੰ ਸੰਤਾ ਕੀ ਓਟ ਤੂੰ ਸਚਾ ਸਿਰਜਨਹਾਰਾ ।।[84] 746

P. 27 ਏਕ ਟੇਕ ਗੋਵਿੰਦ ਕੀ ਤਿਆਗੀ ਅਨ ਆਸ ।। 812
ਸਭ ਊਪਰਿ ਸਮਰਥ ਪ੍ਰਭ ਪੂਰਨ ਗੁਣਤਾਸ ।।
ਜਨ ਕਾ ਨਾਮੁ ਅਧਾਰੁ ਹੈ ਪ੍ਰਭ ਸਰਣੀ ਪਾਹਿ ।।
ਪਰਮੇਸਰ ਕਾ ਆਸਰਾ ਸੰਤਨ ਮਨ ਮਾਹਿ ।।[85]

P. 27 ਸੰਗ ਸਖਾ ਸਭਿ ਤਜਿ ਗਏ ਕੋਊ ਨ ਨਿਬਹਿਓ ਸਾਥਿ ।। 1429
ਕਹੁ ਨਾਨਕ ਇਹ ਬਿਪਤਿ ਮੈ ਟੇਕ ਏਕ ਰਘੁਨਾਥ ।।[86]

P. 27 ਬਿਰਥਾ ਭਰਵਾਸਾ ਲੋਕ ।। ਠਾਕੁਰ ਪ੍ਰਭ ਤੇਰੀ ਟੇਕ ।।[87] 896

P. 28 ਜਿਉ ਅੰਧੁਲੈ ਹਥਿ ਟੋਹਣੀ ਹਰਿ ਨਾਮੁ ਹਮਾਰੈ ।। 422
ਰਾਮ ਨਾਮੁ ਹਰਿ ਟੇਕ ਹੈ ਨਿਸਿ ਦਉਤ ਸਵਾਰੈ ।।[89]

P. 28 ਤੀਨੇ ਤਾਪ ਨਿਵਾਰਣਹਾਰਾ ਦੁਖ ਹੰਤਾ ਸੁਖ ਰਾਸਿ ।। 714
ਤਾ ਕਉ ਬਿਘਨੁ ਕੋਊ ਲਾਗੈ ਜਾ ਕੀ ਪ੍ਰਭ ਆਗੈ ਅਰਦਾਸਿ ।।

ਸੰਤ ਪ੍ਰਸਾਦਿ ਬੈਦ ਨਾਰਾਇਣ ਕਰਣ ਕਾਰਣ ਪ੍ਰਭ ਏਕ ।।
ਬਾਲ ਬੁਧਿ ਪੂਰਨ ਸੁਖਦਾਤਾ ਨਾਨਕ ਹਰਿ ਹਰਿ ਟੇਕ ।।[90]

P. 28 ਹਰਿ ਹਰਿ ਨਾਮੁ ਜਨ ਪ੍ਰਾਨ ਅਧਾਰੁ ।।[91] 183

P. 29 ਤੇਰਾ ਏਕੁ ਨਾਮੁ ਤਾਰੇ ਸੰਸਾਰੁ ।। 24
ਮੈ ਏਹਾ ਆਸ ਏਹੋ ਆਧਾਰੁ ।।1।।[92]

P. 29 ਕਿਨਹੀ ਕਹਿਆ ਬਾਹ ਬਹੁ ਭਾਈ ।। 913
ਕੋਈ ਕਹੈ ਮੈ ਧਨਹਿ ਪਸਾਰਾ ।।
ਮੋਹਿ ਦੀਨ ਹਰਿ ਹਰਿ ਅਧਾਰਾ ।।[93]

P. 29 ਤੁਮਹਿ ਪਿਤਾ ਤੁਮ ਹੀ ਫੁਨਿ ਮਾਤਾ 1215
ਤੁਮਹਿ ਮੀਤ ਹਿਤ ਭ੍ਰਾਤਾ ।।
ਤੁਮ ਪਰਵਾਰ ਤੁਮਹਿ ਆਧਾਰਾ
ਤੁਮਹਿ ਜੀਅ ਪ੍ਰਾਨਦਾਤਾ ।।[94]

P. 29 ਨਾਮ ਸੰਗਿ ਕੀਨੋ ਬਿਉਹਾਰੁ ।। 863
ਨਾਮੋ ਹੀ ਇਸੁ ਮਨ ਕਾ ਅਧਾਰੁ ।।[95]

P. 29 ਰਮਤ ਰਾਮ ਘਟ ਘਟ ਆਧਾਰ ।।[96] 897

P. 29 ਤੂ ਕਾਹੇ ਡੋਲਹਿ ਪ੍ਰਾਣੀਆ ਤੁਧੁ ਰਾਖੈਗਾ ਸਿਰਜਣਹਾਰੁ ।। 724
ਜਿਨਿ ਪੈਦਾਇਸਿ ਤੂ ਕੀਆ ਸੋਈ ਦੇਇ ਆਧਾਰੁ ।।[97]

P. 30 ਹਰਿ ਕੇ ਨਾਮ ਕੋ ਆਧਾਰੁ ।।[98] 112

P. 30 ਸਾਚਾ ਨਾਮੁ ਮੇਰਾ ਆਧਾਰੋ ।।[99] 917

P. 30 ਅੰਮ੍ਰਿਤ ਨਾਮੁ ਮਨਹਿ ਆਧਾਰੋ ।।[100] 1215

P. 30 ਗੁਰੁ ਮੇਰੀ ਜੀਵਨਿ ਗੁਰੁ ਆਧਾਰੁ ।। 1270

ਗੁਰੁ ਮੇਰੀ ਵਰਤਣਿ ਗੁਰੁ ਪਰਵਾਰੁ ॥[101]

P. 30 ਸਤਿਗੁਰ ਪਾਸਿ ਬੇਨੰਤੀਆ ਮਿਲੈ ਨਾਮੁ ਆਧਾਰਾ ॥[102] 746

P. 30 ਪ੍ਰਭ ਜੀ ਤੂ ਮੇਰੇ ਪ੍ਰਾਨ ਅਧਾਰੈ ॥ 820
ਨਮਸਕਾਰ ਡੰਡਉਤਿ ਬੰਦਨਾ ਅਨਿਕ ਬਾਰ ਜਾਉ ਬਾਰੈ ॥ ਰਹਾਉ ॥
....ਜੋ ਤੁਮ ਕਰਹੁ ਸੋਈ ਭਲ ਹਮਰੈ ਪੇਖਿ ਨਾਨਕ ਸੁਖ ਚਰਨਾਰੈ ॥[103]

P. 30 ਤੇਰੀ ਸਰਣਿ ਤੇਰੈ ਭਰਵਾਸੈ ਪੰਚ ਦੁਸਟ ਲੈ ਸਾਧਹਿ ॥[104] 750

P. 31 ਅਬ ਮੋਹਿ ਰਾਮ ਭਰੋਸਉ ਪਾਏ ॥ 1204
ਜੋ ਜੋ ਸਰਣਿ ਪਰਿਓ ਕਰੁਣਾਨਿਧਿ
ਤੇ ਤੇ ਭਵਹਿ ਤਰਾਏ ॥[105]

P. 31 ਰਾਮ ਜਨਾ ਕਉ ਰਾਮ ਭਰੋਸਾ ॥ 194
ਨਾਮੁ ਜਪਤ ਸਭੁ ਮਿਟਿਓ ਅੰਦੇਸਾ ॥[106]

P. 31 ਮਾਨੁ ਮਹਤੁ ਤੁਮ੍ਹਾਰੇ ਊਪਰਿ ਤੁਮ੍ਹਰੀ ਓਟ ਤੁਮ੍ਹਾਰੀ ਸਰਨਾ ॥ ਰਹਾਉ ॥ 1299
ਤੁਮ੍ਹਰੀ ਆਸ ਭਰੋਸਾ ਤੁਮ੍ਹਰਾ
ਤੁਮਰਾ ਨਾਮੁ ਰਿਦੈ ਲੈ ਧਰਨਾ ॥
ਤੁਮਰੋ ਬਲੁ ਤੁਮ ਸੰਗਿ ਸੁਹੇਲੇ
ਜੋ ਜੋ ਕਹਹੁ ਸੋਈ ਸੋਈ ਕਰਨਾ ॥

P. 31 ਜਾ ਤਿਸੁ ਭਾਵੈ ਤਾ ਹੁਕਮੁ ਮਨਾਵੈ ॥[108] 337

P. 31 ਕਰਹੁ ਅਨੁਗ੍ਰਹੁ ਪਤਿਤ ਉਧਾਰਨ ਰਾਖੁ ਸੁਆਮੀ ਆਪ ਭਰੋਸੇ ॥[109] 829

P. 31 ਹਰਿ ਕੋ ਨਾਮੁ ਸਦਾ ਸੁਖਦਾਈ ॥ 1008
ਜਾ ਕਉ ਸਿਮਰਿ ਅਜਾਮਲੁ ਉਧਰਿਓ ਗਨਿਕਾ ਹੂ ਗਤਿ ਪਾਈ ॥ ਰਹਾਉ ॥
ਪੰਚਾਲੀ ਕਉ ਰਾਜ ਸਭਾ ਮਹਿ ਰਾਮ ਨਾਮ ਸੁਧਿ ਆਈ ॥
ਤਾ ਕੋ ਦੂਖੁ ਹਰਿਓ ਕਰੁਣਾ ਮੈ ਅਪਨੀ ਪੈਜ ਬਢਾਈ ॥
ਜਿਹ ਨਰ ਜਸੁ ਕਿਰਪਾ ਨਿਧਿ ਗਾਇਓ ਤਾ ਕਉ ਭਇਓ ਸਹਾਈ ॥
ਕਹੁ ਨਾਨਕ ਮੈ ਇਹੀ ਭਰੋਸੈ ਗਹੀ ਆਨਿ ਸਰਨਾਈ ॥[110]

GRACE

		ਆਦਿ ਗ੍ਰੰਥ ਪੰਨਾ
P. 48	ਮਨ ਤਨ ਅੰਤਰਿ ਤੁਧੁ ਨਦਰਿ ਨਿਹਾਲੀ ।।[20]	132
P. 50	ਨਦਰਿ ਕਰੇ ਸਬਦੁ ਘਟ ਮਹਿ ਵਸੈ ਵਿਚਹੁ ਭਰਮੁ ਗਵਾਏ ।। ਤਨੁ ਮਨੁ ਨਿਰਮਲੁ ਨਿਰਮਲ ਬਾਣੀ ਨਾਮੋੁ ਮੰਨਿ ਵਸਾਏ ।।[26]	944
P. 50	ਨਦਰਿ ਕਰੇ ਪ੍ਰਭੁ ਆਪਣੀ ਗੁਣ ਅੰਕਿ ਸਮਾਵੈ ।। ਨਾਨਕ ਮੇਲੁ ਨ ਚੂਕਈ ਲਾਹਾ ਸਚੁ ਪਾਵੈ ।।[27]	228-29
P. 50	ਜਿਸ ਨੋ ਨਦਰਿ ਕਰੇ ਸੋਈ ਬਿਧਿ ਜਾਣੈ ।।[28]	1330
P. 50	ਓਇ ਸਦਾ ਸਦਾ ਜਨ ਜੀਵਤੇ ਜੋ ਹਰਿ ਚਰਣੀ ਚਿਤਿ ਲਾਹਿ ।। ਨਾਨਕ ਨਦਰੀ ਮਨਿ ਵਸੈ ਗੁਰਮੁਖਿ ਸਹਜਿ ਸਮਾਹਿ ।।[29]	508
P. 50	ਇਕਿ ਨਿਹਾਲੀ ਪੈ ਸਵਨ੍ਹਿ ਇਕਿ ਉਪਰਿ ਰਹਨਿ ਖੜੇ ।। ਤਿਨ੍ਹਾ ਸਵਾਰੇ ਨਾਨਕਾ ਜਿਨ੍ਹ ਕਉ ਨਦਰਿ ਕਰੇ ।।[30]	475
P. 53	ਸਤਿਗੁਰੁ ਭੇਟੇ ਸੋ ਸੁਖੁ ਪਾਏ ।। ਹਰਿ ਕਾ ਨਾਮੁ ਮੰਨਿ ਵਸਾਏ ।। ਨਾਨਕ ਨਦਰਿ ਕਰੇ ਸੋ ਪਾਏ ।। ਆਸ ਅੰਦੇਸੇ ਤੇ ਨਿਹਕੇਵਲੁ ਹਉਮੈ ਸਬਦਿ ਜਲਾਏ ।।[31]	468

P. 54 ਪੂਰੈ ਗੁਰਿ ਸਮਝਾਇਆ ਮਤਿ ਊਤਮ ਹੋਈ ।। 424
ਅੰਤਰੁ ਸੀਤਲੁ ਸਾਂਤਿ ਹੋਇ ਨਾਮੇ ਸੁਖੁ ਹੋਈ ।।
ਪੂਰਾ ਸਤਿਗੁਰੁ ਤਾਂ ਮਿਲੈ ਜਾਂ ਨਦਰਿ ਕਰੇਈ ।।[32]

P. 54 ਗੁਰ ਕੈ ਸਬਦਿ ਪਛਾਣੀਐ ਜਾ ਆਪੇ ਨਦਰਿ ਕਰੇਇ ।।[33] 37

P. 54 ਇਹੁ ਮਨੁ ਧਾਵਤੁ ਤਾ ਰਹੈ ਜਾ ਆਪੇ ਨਦਰਿ ਕਰੇਇ ।।[34] 30

P. 54 ਨਦਰਿ ਕਰੇ ਪੂਰਾ ਗੁਰੁ ਭੇਟੈ ।। 1036
ਜਮ ਜੰਦਾਰੁ ਨ ਮਾਰੈ ਫੇਟੈ ।।
ਜਿਉ ਜਲ ਅੰਤਰਿ ਕਮਲੁ ਬਿਗਾਸੀ
ਆਪੇ ਬਿਗਸਿ ਧਿਆਇਦਾ ।।[35]

P. 54 ਜਿਸ ਕਉ ਨਦਰਿ ਕਰੇ ਗੁਰੁ ਪੂਰਾ ।। 1043
ਸਬਦਿ ਮਿਲਾਏ ਗੁਰਮਤਿ ਸੂਰਾ ।।[36]

P. 55 ਮੋਹ ਪਸਾਰ ਨਹੀ ਸੰਗਿ ਬੇਲੀ 1043
ਬਿਨੁ ਹਰਿ ਗੁਰ ਕਿਨਿ ਸੁਖੁ ਪਾਇਆ ।।[38]

P. 55 ਏਕੋ ਹੈ ਦਾਤਾਰੁ ਸਚਾ ਆਪਿ ਧਣੀ ।। 755
ਸੋ ਸਚੁ ਤੇਰੈ ਨਾਲਿ ਹੈ ਗੁਰਮੁਖਿ ਨਦਰਿ ਨਿਹਾਲਿ ।।
ਆਪੇ ਬਖਸੇ ਮੇਲਿ ਲਏ ਸੋ ਪ੍ਰਭੁ ਸਦਾ ਸਮਾਲਿ ।।
ਮਨੁ ਮੈਲਾ ਸਚੁ ਨਿਰਮਲਾ ਕਿਉ ਕਰਿ ਮਿਲਿਆ ਜਾਇ ।।
ਪ੍ਰਭੁ ਮੇਲੇ ਤਾ ਮਿਲਿ ਰਹੈ ਹਉਮੈ ਸਬਦਿ ਜਲਾਇ ।।
ਸੋ ਸਹੁ ਸਚਾ ਵੀਸਰੈ ਧ੍ਰਿਗੁ ਜੀਵਣੁ ਸੰਸਾਰਿ ।।
ਨਦਰਿ ਕਰੇ ਨਾ ਵੀਸਰੈ ਗੁਰਮਤੀ ਵੀਚਾਰਿ ।।[39]

P. 56 ਨਦਰਿ ਕਰੇ ਤਾ ਸਤਿਗੁਰੁ ਮਿਲੈ ।। 35
ਪ੍ਰਣਵਤਿ ਨਾਨਕੁ ਭਵਜਲੁ ਤਰੈ ।।[40]

P. 56 ਪੂਰਾ ਸਾਚੁ ਪਿਆਲਾ ਸਹਜੇ ਤਿਸਹਿ ਪੀਆਏ ਜਾ ਕਉ ਨਦਰਿ ਕਰੇ ।। 360
ਅੰਮ੍ਰਿਤ ਕਾ ਵਾਪਾਰੀ ਹੋਵੈ ਕਿਆ ਮਦਿ ਛੂਛੈ ਭਾਉ ਧਰੇ ।।[41]

P. 56	ਝੂਠਾ ਮਦੁ ਮੂਲਿ ਨ ਪੀਚਈ ਜੇ ਕਾ ਪਾਰਿ ਵਸਾਇ ॥ ਨਾਨਕ ਨਦਰੀ ਸਚੁ ਮਦੁ ਪਾਈਐ ਸਤਿਗੁਰੁ ਮਿਲੈ ਜਿਸੁ ਆਇ ॥[42]	554
P. 56	ਜਿਤ ਪੀਤੇ ਮਤਿ ਦੂਰਿ ਹੋਇ ਬਰਲੁ ਪਾਵੈ ਵਿਚਿ ਆਇ ॥ ਅਪਣਾ ਪਰਾਇਆ ਨਾ ਪਛਾਣਈ ਖਸਮਹੁ ਧਕੇ ਖਾਹਿ ॥[43]	554
P. 56	ਨਦਰਿ ਕਰੇ ਤਾਂ ਭਰਮੁ ਚੁਕਾਏ ॥ ਹੁਕਮੈ ਬੂਝੈ ਤਾਂ ਸਾਚਾ ਪਾਏ ॥[44]	1169
P. 57	ਸਚੁ ਸਦਾ ਹੈ ਨਿਰਮਲਾ ਭਾਈ ਨਿਰਮਲ ਸਾਚੇ ਸੋਇ ॥ ਨਦਰਿ ਕਰੇ ਜਿਸ ਆਪਣੀ ਭਾਈ ਤਿਸੁ ਪਰਾਪਤਿ ਹੋਇ ॥[45]	609
P. 57	ਖੇਦੁ ਨ ਦੁਖੁ ਨਾ ਡਾਨ ਤਿਹ ਜਾ ਕਉ ਨਦਰਿ ਕਰੀ ॥[47]	253
P. 57	ਹਰਿ ਰੁਖੀ ਰੋਟੀ ਖਾਇ ਸਮਾਲੇ॥ ਹਰਿ ਅੰਤਰਿ ਬਾਹਰਿ ਨਦਰਿ ਨਿਹਾਲੇ ॥[48]	105
P. 57	ਨਾਨਕ ਨਦਰੀ ਬਾਹਰੇ ਰਾਚਹਿ ਦਾਨਿ ਨ ਨਾਇ ॥[49]	15
P. 57	ਮਾਹ ਦਿਵਸ ਮੂਰਤ ਭਲੇ ਜਿਸ ਕਉ ਨਦਰਿ ਕਰੇ ॥[50]	136
P. 58	ਕੂੜ ਗਏ ਦੁਬਿਧਾ ਨਸੀ ਪੂਰਨ ਸਾਚਿ ਭਰੇ ॥ ਪਾਰਬ੍ਰਹਮ ਪ੍ਰਭੁ ਸੇਵਦੇ ਮਨਿ ਅੰਦਰਿ ਏਕ ਧਰੇ ॥[50]	136
P. 59	ਇਹੁ ਮਨੁ ਸਾਚਿ ਸੰਤੋਖਿਆ ਨਦਰਿ ਕਰੇ ਤਿਸੁ ਮਾਹਿ ॥[53]	19
P. 59	ਸਤੁ ਸੰਤੋਖੁ ਗਿਆਨੁ ਧਿਆਨੁ ਪਿਆਰੇ ਜਿਸ ਨੋ ਨਦਰਿ ਕਰੇ ॥[54]	641
P. 59	ਇਹੁ ਮਨੁ ਧਾਵਤੁ ਤਾ ਰਹੈ ਜਾ ਆਪੇ ਨਦਰਿ ਕਰੇਇ ॥[55]	30
P. 60	ਨਦਰਿ ਕਰਹਿ ਜੇ ਆਪਣੀ ਤਾਂ ਆਪੇ ਲੈਹਿ ਸਵਾਰਿ ॥[56]	1420
P. 60	ਨਦਰੀ ਸਤਗੁਰੁ ਸੇਵੀਐ ਨਦਰੀ ਸੇਵਾ ਹੋਇ ॥ ਨਦਰੀ ਇਹੁ ਮਨੁ ਵਸਿ ਆਵੈ ਨਦਰੀ ਮਨੁ ਨਿਰਮਲੁ ਹੋਇ ॥[57]	558

P. 60 ਕਾਜਰ ਕੋਠ ਮਹਿ ਭਈ ਨ ਕਾਰੀ 384
ਨਿਰਮਲ ਬਰਨੁ ਬਨਿਓ ਰੀ ॥
ਮਹਾ ਮੰਤ੍ਰ ਗੁਰ ਹਿਰਦੈ ਬਸਿਓ
ਅਚਰਜ ਨਾਮੁ ਸੁਨਿਓ ਰੀ ॥
ਕਰਿ ਕਿਰਪਾ ਪ੍ਰਭ ਨਦਰਿ ਅਵਲੋਕਨ
ਅਪੁਨੈ ਚਰਣਿ ਲਗਾਈ ॥
ਪ੍ਰੇਮ ਭਗਤਿ ਨਾਨਕ ਸੁਖੁ ਪਾਇਆ
ਸਾਧੂ ਸੰਗਿ ਸਮਾਈ ॥[58]

P. 61 ਹੋਇ ਅਉਧੂਤ ਬੈਠੇ ਲਾਇ ਤਾਰੀ ॥ ਜੋਗੀ ਜਤੀ ਪੰਡਿਤ ਬੀਚਾਰੀ ॥ 1004
ਗ੍ਰਿਹਿ ਮੜੀ ਮਸਾਣੀ ਬਨ ਮਹਿ ਬਸਤੇ
ਊਠਿ ਤਿਨਾ ਕੈ ਲਾਗੀ ਪਲੀਆ ॥
ਕਾਟੇ ਬੰਧਨ ਠਾਕੁਰਿ ਜਾ ਕੇ ॥
ਹਰਿ ਹਰਿ ਨਾਮੁ ਬਸਿਓ ਜੀਅ ਤਾ ਕੈ ॥
ਸਾਧਸੰਗਿ ਭਏ ਜਨ ਮੁਕਤੇ ਗਤਿ ਪਾਈ ਨਾਨਕ ਨਦਰਿ ਨਿਹਲੀਆ ॥[59]

P. 61 ਪਖਾ ਪਾਣੀ ਪੀਸਿ ਬਿਗਸਾ ਪੈਰ ਧੋਇ ॥ 518
ਆਪਹੁ ਕਛੂ ਨ ਹੋਇ ਪ੍ਰਭ ਨਦਰਿ ਨਿਹਾਲਿਐ ॥[60]

P. 62 ਨਦਰਿ ਤੁਧੁ ਅਰਦਾਸਿ ਮੇਰੀ ਜਿੰਨੀ ਆਪੁ ਉਪਾਇਆ ॥ 566
ਤਾ ਮੈ ਕਹਿਆ ਕਹਣੁ ਜਾ ਤੁਝੈ ਕਹਾਇਆ ॥[61]

P. 62 ਸੇ ਸਹੀਆ ਸੋਹਾਗਣੀ ਜਿਨ ਕਉ ਨਦਰਿ ਕਰੇਇ ॥[62] 38

P. 63 ਇਕਨ੍ਾ ਅੰਦਰਿ ਖੋਟੁ ਨਿਤ ਖੋਟੁ ਕਮਾਵਹਿ 303
ਓਹੁ ਜੇਹਾ ਬੀਜੇ ਤੇਰਾ ਫਲੁ ਖਾਏ ॥
ਜਾ ਸਤਿਗੁਰੁ ਸਰਾਫੁ ਨਦਰਿ ਕਰਿ ਦੇਖੈ
ਸੁਆਵਗੀਰ ਸਭਿ ਉਘੜਿ ਆਏ ॥[63]

P. 63 ਨਦਰਿ ਕਰਹਿ ਤਾ ਸਾਚੁ ਪਛਾਣਾ ॥ 567
ਸਾਚੋ ਪਛਾਣਾ ਤਾਮਿ ਤੇਰਾ ਜਾਮਿ ਆਪਿ ਬੁਝਾਵਹੇ ॥[64]

P. 63	ਹੀਰਾ ਨਾਮੁ ਜਵੇਹਰ ਲਾਲੁ ।। ਮਨੁ ਮੋਤੀ ਹੈ ਤਿਸ ਕਾ ਮਾਲੁ ।। ਨਾਨਕ ਪਰਖੈ ਨਦਰਿ ਨਿਹਾਲੁ ।।[65]	414
P. 63	ਘਰ ਮੰਦਰ ਖੁਸੀ ਨਾਮ ਕੀ ਨਦਰਿ ਤੇਰੀ ਪਰਵਾਰੁ ।।[66]	16
P. 64	ਦਾਸ ਰਖੇ ਕੰਠਿ ਲਾਇ ਨਦਰਿ ਨਿਹਾਲਿਓਨੁ ।।[67]	653
P. 64	ਅੰਚਲਿ ਲਾਇ ਤਰਾਇਆ ਭਾਈ ਭਉਜਲੁ ਦੁਖੁ ਸੰਸਾਰੁ ।। ਕਰਿ ਕਿਰਪਾ ਨਦਰਿ ਨਿਹਾਲਿਆ ਭਾਈ ਕੀਤੋਨੁ ਅੰਗੁ ਅਪਾਰੁ ।।[68]	640
P. 64	ਹਰਿ ਸੰਤਹੁ ਦੇਖਹੁ ਨਦਰਿ ਕਰਿ ਨਿਕਟਿ ਵਸੈ ਭਰਪੂਰਿ ।।[69]	27
P. 64	ਸੰਤਹੁ ਦੇਖਹੁ ਹਰਿ ਨਦਰਿ ਕਰਿ ਨਿਕਟਿ ਵੇਸਾਹਿ ਭਰਪੂਰਿ ।।[71]	27
P. 65	ਸੇਈ ਨਾਚਹਿ ਜੋ ਤੁਧੁ ਭਾਵਹਿ ਜਿ ਗੁਰਮੁਖਿ ਸਬਦੁ ਵੀਚਾਰੀ ।। ਕਹੁ ਨਾਨਕ ਸੇ ਸਹਜ ਸੁਖੁ ਪਾਵਹਿ ਜਿਨ ਕਉ ਨਦਰਿ ਤੁਮਾਰੀ ।।[72]	506
P. 65	ਨਦਰਿ ਕਰੇ ਤਾ ਹਰਿ ਗੁਣ ਗਾਵੈ ਨਦਰੀ ਸਚਿ ਸਮਾਵਣਿਆ ।।[73]	119
P. 65	ਗੁਰੂ ਚਰਣ ਲਾਗੇ ਸਦਾ ਜਾਗੇ ਮਨਿ ਵਜੀਆ ਵਾਧਾਈਆ ।। ਕਰੀ ਨਦਰਿ ਸੁਆਮੀ ਸੁਖਹ ਗਾਮੀ ਹਲਤੁ ਪਲਤੁ ਸਵਾਰਿਆ ।। ਬਿਨਵੰਤਿ ਨਾਨਕ ਨਿਤ ਨਾਮੁ ਜਪੀਐ ਜੀਉ ਪਿੰਡ ਜਿਨਿ ਧਾਰਿਆ ।।[74]	782
P. 65	ਕਿਆ ਹੰਸੁ ਕਿਆ ਬਗੁਲਾ ਜਾ ਕਉ ਨਦਰਿ ਧਰੇ ।। ਜੇ ਤਿਸੁ ਭਾਵੈ ਨਾਨਕਾ ਕਾਗਹੁ ਹੰਸੁ ਕਰੇ ।।[75]	1384
P. 65	ਜਿਥੈ ਨੀਚ ਸਮਾਲੀਅਨਿ ਤਿਥੈ ਨਦਰਿ ਤੇਰੀ ਬਖਸੀਸ ।।[76]	15
P. 65	ਕਰਮੀ ਆਵੈ ਕਪੜਾ ਨਦਰੀ ਮੋਖੁ ਦੁਆਰੁ ।।[77]	2
P. 66	ਕੂੜੀ ਕਰਨਿ ਵਡਾਈਆ ਕੂੜੇ ਸਿਉ ਲਗਾ ਨੇਹੁ ।। ਨਾਨਕ ਸਚਾ ਆਪਿ ਹੈ ਆਪੇ ਨਦਰਿ ਕਰੇਇ ।।[78]	311

P. 66 ਆਪੁ ਵੀਚਾਰੈ ਸੁ ਪਰਖੇ ਹੀਰਾ ।। 413
ਏਕ ਦ੍ਰਿਸਟਿ ਤਾਰੇ ਗੁਰ ਪੂਰਾ ।।
ਗੁਰੁ ਮਾਨੈ ਮਨ ਤੇ ਮਨੁ ਧੀਰਾ ।।
ਐਸਾ ਸਾਹੁ ਸਰਾਫੀ ਕਰੈ ।।
ਸਾਚੀ ਨਦਰਿ ਏਕ ਲਿਵ ਤਰੈ ।।[79]

P. 67 ਆਪੇ ਕਰਤਾ ਜੁਗਿ ਜੁਗਿ ਸੋਇ ।। ਨਦਰਿ ਕਰੇ ਮੇਲਾਵਾ ਹੋਇ ।।[80] 664

P. 67 ਛੁਟੈ ਤਾ ਕੈ ਬੋਲਿ ਸਾਹਿਬ ਨਦਰਿ ਜਿਸੁ ।। 729
ਘਲੇ ਆਣੇ ਆਪਿ ਜਿਸੁ ਨਾਹੀ ਦੂਜਾ ਮਤੈ ਕੋਇ ।।
ਢਾਹਿ ਉਸਾਰੇ ਸਾਜਿ ਜਾਣੈ ਸਭ ਸੋਇ ।।
ਨਾਉ ਨਾਨਕ ਬਖਸੀਸ ਨਦਰੀ ਕਰਮੁ ਹੋਇ ।।[81]

P. 67 ਸੁਰਿ ਨਰ ਨਾਥ ਬੇਅੰਤ ਅਜੋਨੀ ਸਾਚੈ ਮਹਲਿ ਅਪਾਰਾ ।। 489
ਨਾਨਕ ਸਹਜਿ ਮਿਲੇ ਜਗਜੀਵਨ ਨਦਰਿ ਕਰਹੁ ਨਿਸਤਾਰਾ ।।[82]

P. 68 ਜਿਉ ਜਨਨੀ ਸੁਤੁ ਜਣਿ ਪਾਲਤੀ ਰਾਖੈ ਨਦਰਿ ਮਝਾਰਿ ।। 168
ਅੰਤਰਿ ਬਾਹਰਿ ਮੁਖਿ ਦੇ ਗਿਰਾਸੁ ਖਿਨੁ ਖਿਨੁ ਪੋਚਾਰਿ ।।
ਤਿਉ ਸਤਿਗੁਰ ਗੁਰਸਿਖ ਰਾਖਤਾ ਹਰਿ ਪ੍ਰੀਤਿ ਪਿਆਰਿ ।।[83]

P. 69 ਹਮ ਬਾਰਿਕ ਹਰਿ ਪਿਤਾ ਪ੍ਰਤਿਪਾਲੀ ।।[84] 1134

P. 69 ਤੂ ਸਮਰਥੁ ਸਰਨਿ ਜੋਗੁ ਤੂ ਰਾਖਹਿ ਅਪਨੀ ਕਲ ਧਾਰਿ ।। 1301
ਜਾਪ ਤਾਪ ਨੇਮ ਸੁਚਿ ਸੰਜਮ ਨਾਹੀ ਇਨ ਬਿਧੇ ਛੁਟਕਾਰ ।।
ਗਰਤ ਘੋਰ ਅੰਧ ਤੇ ਕਾਢਹੁ ਪ੍ਰਭ ਨਾਨਕ ਨਦਰਿ ਨਿਹਾਰਿ ।।[85]

P. 69 ਨਦਰਿ ਤੇਰੀ ਸੁਖੁ ਪਾਇਆ ਨਾਨਕ ਸਬਦੁ ਵੀਚਾਰਿ ।। 937
ਮਨਮੁਖ ਭੂਲੇ ਪਚਿ ਮੁਏ ਉਬਰੇ ਗੁਰ ਬੀਚਾਰਿ ।।
ਜਿ ਪੁਰਖੁ ਨਦਰਿ ਨ ਆਵਈ ਤਿਸ ਕਾ ਕਿਆ ਕਰਿ ਕਹਿਆ ਜਾਇ ।।[86]

P. 70 ਨਾਨਕੁ ਮੰਗੈ ਸਚੁ ਗੁਰਮੁਖਿ ਘਾਲੀਐ ।। 420
ਮੈ ਤੁਝ ਬਿਨੁ ਅਵਰੁ ਨ ਕੋਇ ਨਦਰਿ ਨਿਹਾਲੀਐ ।।[87]

P. 70	ਅੰਤਰਿ ਗੁਰ ਗਿਆਨੁ ਹਰਿ ਰਤਨੁ ਹੈ ਮੁਕਤਿ ਕਰਾਵਣਹਾਰਾ ।। ਨਾਨਕ ਜਿਸ ਨੋ ਨਦਰਿ ਕਰੇ ਸੋ ਪਾਏ ਸੋ ਹੋਵੈ ਦਰਿ ਸਚਿਆਰਾ ।।[88]	593
P. 70	ਕਾਮੁ ਕ੍ਰੋਧੁ ਕਾਇਆ ਕਉ ਗਾਲੈ ।। ਜਿਉ ਕੰਚਨ ਸੋਹਾਗਾ ਢਾਲੈ ।। ਕਸਿ ਕਸਵਟੀ ਸਹੈ ਸੁ ਤਾਉ ।। ਨਦਰਿ ਸਰਾਫ ਵੰਨੀਸਚੜਾਉ ।।[89]	932
P. 71	ਕੀਚੜਿ ਹਾਥੁ ਨ ਬੂਡਈ ਏਕਾ ਨਦਰਿ ਨਿਹਾਲਿ ।।[90]	1411
P. 71	ਮਨੁ ਮਾਰੇ ਜੀਵਤ ਮਰਿ ਜਾਣੁ ।। ਨਾਨਕ ਨਦਰੀ ਨਦਰਿ ਪਛਾਣੁ ।।[91]	1343
P. 71	ਨਿਤ ਨਿਤ ਖਰਾ ਸਮਾਲੀਐ ਸਚੁ ਸਉਦਾ ਪਾਈਐ ।। ਖੋਟੇ ਨਦਰਿ ਨ ਆਵਨੀ ਲੇ ਅਗਨਿ ਜਲਾਈਐ ।।[92]	421
P. 71	ਨਦਰਿ ਕਰੇ ਸਬਦੁ ਘਟ ਮਹਿ ਵਸੈ ਵਿਚਹੁ ਭਰਮੁ ਗਵਾਏ ।। [93]	944
	ਨਦਰਿ ਕਰੇ ਤਾ ਸਤਿਗੁਰੁ ਮੇਲੇ ਤਾ ਨਿਜ ਘਰਿ ਵਾਸਾ ਇਹੁ ਮਨੁ ਪਾਏ ।।[94]	945
	ਕਾਮ ਕ੍ਰੋਧ ਬਿਖੁ ਅਗਨਿ ਨਿਵਾਰੇ ਨਾਨਕ ਨਦਰਿ ਪਿਆਰੇ ।।[95]	943
P. 72	ਮੈਡਾ ਮਨੁ ਰਤਾ ਆਪਨੜੇ ਪਿਰ ਨਾਲਿ ।। ਹਉ ਘੋਲਿ ਘੁਮਾਈ ਖੰਨੀਐ ਕੀਤੀ ਹਿਕ ਭੋਰੀ ਨਦਰਿ ਨਿਹਾਲਿ ।।[96]	1014
P. 72	ਨਦਰਿ ਕਰਹਿ ਤੂ ਤਾਰਹਿ ਤਰੀਐ ਸਚੁ ਦੇਵਹੁ ਦੀਨ ਦਇਆਲਾ ।। ਪ੍ਰਣਵਤਿ ਨਾਨਕ ਦਾਸਨਿ ਦਾਸਾ ਤੂ ਸਰਬ ਜੀਆ ਪ੍ਰਤਿਪਾਲਾ ।।[97]	1112
P. 72	ਭੀ ਸਾਲਾਹਿਹੁ ਸਾਚਾ ਸੋਇ ।। ਜਾ ਕੀ ਨਦਰਿ ਸਦਾ ਸੁਖੁ ਹੋਇ ।।[98]	595

P. 73	ਏਕ ਨਦਰਿ ਕਰਿ ਵੇਖੈ ਸਭ ਊਪਰਿ ਜੇਹਾ ਭਾਉ ਤੇਹਾ ਫਲੁ ਪਾਈਐ ।।[99]	602
P. 73	ਅੰਤਰਜਾਮੀ ਪ੍ਰਭ ਦਇਆਲ ।। ਅਪਣੇ ਦਾਸ ਕਉ ਨਦਰਿ ਨਿਹਾਲਿ ।। ਕਰਿ ਕਿਰਪਾ ਮੋਹਿ ਦੇਹੁ ਦਾਨੁ ।। ਜਪਿ ਜੀਵੈ ਨਾਨਕੁ ਤੇਰੋ ਨਾਮੁ ।।[100]	1183
P. 73	ਬਿਨੁ ਕਰਮੈ ਨਾਉ ਨ ਪਾਈਐ ਪੂਰੈ ਕਰਮਿ ਪਾਇਆ ਜਾਇ ।। ਨਾਨਕ ਨਦਰਿ ਕਰੇ ਜੇ ਆਪਣੀ ਤਾ ਗੁਰਮਤਿ ਮੇਲਿ ਮਿਲਾਇ ।।[101]	648
P. 74	ਗੁਰ ਪੀਰਾਂ ਕੀ ਚਾਕਰੀ ਮਹਾਂ ਕਰੜੀ ਸੁਖ ਸਾਰੁ ।। ਨਦਰਿ ਕਰੇ ਜਿਸੁ ਆਪਣੀ ਤਿਸੁ ਲਾਏ ਹੇਤ ਪਿਆਰੁ ।।[103]	1422
P. 74	ਕ੍ਰਿਪਾ ਕ੍ਰਿਪਾ ਕਰਿ ਭਗਤਿ ਦ੍ਰਿੜਾਏ ਜਨ ਪੀਛੈ ਜਗੁ ਨਿਸਤਾਰੇ ।। ਆਪਨ ਆਪਿ ਆਪਿ ਪ੍ਰਭੁ ਠਾਕੁਰੁ ਪ੍ਰਭੁ ਆਪੇ ਸ੍ਰਿਸਟਿ ਸਵਾਰੇ ।। ਜਨ ਨਾਨਕ ਆਪੇ ਆਪਿ ਸਭੁ ਵਰਤੈ ਕਰਿ ਕ੍ਰਿਪਾ ਆਪਿ ਨਿਸਤਾਰੇ ।।[104]	982
P. 75	ਮੇਰਾ ਪ੍ਰਭੁ ਅਤਿ ਊਚੋ ਊਚਾ ਕਰਿ ਕਿਰਪਾ ਆਪਿ ਮਿਲਾਵਣਿਆ ।।[105]	112
P. 76	ਓਹੁ ਆਦਿ ਜੁਗਾਦੀ ਰਾਮ ਸਨੇਹੀ ।। ਦਰਗਹ ਮੁਕਤਿ ਕਰੇ ਕਰਿ ਕਿਰਪਾ ਬਖਸੇ ਅਵਗੁਣ ਕੀਨਾ ਹੇ ।।[106]	1027-28
P. 76	ਕ੍ਰਿਪਾ ਕਟਾਖ੍ਹ ਅਵਲੋਕਨੁ ਕੀਨੋ ਦਾਸ ਕਾ ਦੂਖੁ ਬਿਦਾਰਿਓ ।। ਹਰਿ ਜਨ ਰਾਖੇ ਗੁਰ ਗੋਵਿੰਦ ।। ਕੰਠਿ ਲਾਇ ਅਵਗੁਣ ਸਭਿ ਮੇਟੇ ਦਇਆਲ ਪੁਰਖ ਬਖਸੰਦ ।।[107]	681
P. 77	ਊਗਵਿਆ ਅਸਰੂਪੁ ਦਿਖਾਵੈ ।। ਕਰਿ ਕਿਰਪਾ ਅਪੁਨੈ ਘਰਿ ਆਵੈ ।।[108]	930

P. 77 ਕਰਿ ਕਿਰਪਾ ਘਰਿ ਆਇਆ ਆਪੇ ਮਿਲਿਆ ਆਇ ।।[109] 32

P. 77 ਕ੍ਰਿਪਾ ਕ੍ਰਿਪਾ ਕਰਿ ਗੁਰੂ ਮਿਲਾਏ ਹਮ ਪਾਹਨ ਸਬਦਿ ਗੁਰ ਤਾਰੇ ।।[110] 981

P. 77 ਹਰਿ ਕ੍ਰਿਪਾ ਨਿਧਿ ਪਤਿਤ ਉਧਾਰਨ ।। 1301
ਕੋਟਿ ਜਨਮ ਦੂਖ ਕਰਿ ਪਾਇਓ ।।
ਸੁਖੀ ਨਾਨਕ ਗੁਰਿ ਨਾਮੁ ਦ੍ਰਿੜਾਇਓ ।।[112]

P. 78 ਜੀਅ ਪ੍ਰਾਣ ਤਨੁ ਧਨੁ ਰਖੇ 46
ਕਰਿ ਕਿਰਪਾ ਰਾਖੀ ਜਿੰਦੁ ।।
ਨਾਨਕ ਸਗਲੇ ਦੋਖ ਉਤਾਰਿਅਨੁ
ਪ੍ਰਭੁ ਪਾਰਬ੍ਰਹਮ ਬਖਸਿੰਦੁ ।।[113]

P. 78 ਜੀਉ ਪਿੰਡੁ ਜਿਨਿ ਸਾਜਿਆ ਕਰਿ ਕਿਰਪਾ ਦਿਤੀਨੁ ਜਿੰਦੁ ।।[114] 137

P. 79 ਭ੍ਰਮਤੋ ਭ੍ਰਮਤੋ ਹਾਰਿਆ ਅਨਿਕ ਬਿਧੀ ਕਰਿ ਟੋਰੈ ।। 212
ਕਹੁ ਨਾਨਕ ਕਿਰਪਾ ਭਈ ਸਾਧਸੰਗਤਿ ਨਿਧਿ ਮੋਰੈ ।।
ਚਿੰਤਾਮਣਿ ਕਰੁਣਾ ਮਏ ।। ਰਹਾਉ ।। ਦੀਨ ਦਇਆਲਾ ਪਾਰਬ੍ਰਹਮ ।।
ਜਾ ਕੈ ਸਿਮਰਣਿ ਸੁਖ ਭਏ ।।
ਅਕਾਲ ਪੁਰਖ ਅਗਾਧਿ ਬੋਧ ।।
ਸੁਨਤ ਜਸੋ ਕੋਟਿ ਅਘ ਖਏ ।।
ਕਿਰਪਾ ਨਿਧਿ ਪ੍ਰਭ ਮਇਆ ਧਾਰਿ ।।
ਨਾਨਕ ਹਰਿ ਹਰਿ ਨਾਮ ਲਏ ।।[115]

P. 80 ਆਪੁ ਗਇਆ ਤਾ ਆਪਹੀ ਭਾਏ ।। 202
ਕ੍ਰਿਪਾ ਨਿਧਾਨ ਕੀ ਸਰਨੀ ਪਏ ।।[116]

P. 80 ਸਤਿਗੁਰ ਬਾਝੁ ਨ ਬੇਲੀ ਕੋਈ ।। 1031-32
ਐਥੈ ਓਥੈ ਰਾਖਾ ਪ੍ਰਭੁ ਸੋਈ ।।
ਰਾਮ ਨਾਮੁ ਦੇਵੈ ਕਰਿ ਕਿਰਪਾ
ਇਉ ਸਲਲੈ ਸਲਲ ਮਿਲਾਤਾ ਹੇ ।।[117]

P. 81 ਕਿਰਪਾ ਕਰਹੁ ਦੀਨ ਕੇ ਦਾਤੇ 882
ਮੇਰਾ ਗੁਣੁ ਅਵਗਣੁ ਨ ਬੀਚਾਰਹੁ ਕੋਈ ॥
ਮਾਟੀ ਕਾ ਕਿਆ ਧੋਪੈ ਸੁਆਮੀ ਮਾਣਸ ਕੀ ਗਤਿ ਏਹੀ ॥[118]

P. 81 ਕ੍ਰਿਪਾ ਜਲੁ ਦੇਹਿ ਨਾਨਕ ਸਾਰਿੰਗ ਕਉ ਹੋਇ ਜਾ ਤੇ ਤੇਰੈ ਨਾਇ ਵਾਸਾ ॥[119] 13

P. 82 ਕਰਿ ਕਿਰਪਾ ਪ੍ਰਭ ਰਾਖਿ ਲੇਹੁ ਹੋਰੁ ਨਾਹੀ ਕਰਣ ਕਰੇਣ ॥ 136
ਹਰਿ ਤੁਧੁ ਵਿਣੁ ਖਾਕੂ ਰੂਲਣਾ ਕਹੀਐ ਕਿਥੈ ਵੈਣ ॥[120]

P. 82 ਸੁਰਤਿ ਮਤਿ ਨਾਹੀ ਚਤੁਰਾਈ ॥ 750
ਕਰਿ ਕਿਰਪਾ ਪ੍ਰਭ ਲਾਵਹੁ ਪਾਈ ॥[121]

P. 82 ਕ੍ਰਿਪਾ ਕ੍ਰਿਪਾ ਕਿਰਪਾ ਕਰਿ ਪਿਆਰੇ ਗੁਰ ਸਬਦੀ ਹਰਿ ਰਸੁ ਪੀਜੈ ॥ 1323
ਕਾਇਆ ਨਗਰੁ ਹੈ ਨੀਕੋ ਵਿਚਿ ਸਉਦਾ ਹਰਿ ਰਸੁ ਕੀਜੈ ॥[122]

P. 82 ਸਭੁ ਕਿਛੁ ਬਹੁਤੋ ਬਹੁਤੁ ਉਪਾਇਆ ॥ 104
ਕਰਿ ਕਿਰਪਾ ਪ੍ਰਭਿ ਅਪਿ ਰਜਾਇਆ ॥[123]

P. 83 ਦਤਿ ਕਰਹੁ ਮੇਰੇ ਦਾਤਾਰਾ ਜੀਅ ਜੰਤ ਸਭਿ ਧ੍ਰਾਪੇ ਜੀਉ ॥[124] 104

P. 83 ਕ੍ਰਿਪਾ ਕ੍ਰਿਪਾ ਕਰਿ ਦੀਨ ਪ੍ਰਭ ਸਰਨੀ ਮੋ ਕਉ 981-82
ਹਰਿ ਜਨ ਮੇਲਿ ਪਿਆਰੇ ॥
ਨਾਨਕ ਦਾਸਨਿ ਦਾਸੁ ਕਹਤੁ ਹੈ
ਹਮ ਦਾਸਨ ਕੇ ਪਨਿਹਾਰੇ ॥[125]

P. 83 ਅੰਮ੍ਰਿਤ ਨਾਮੁ ਸੁਨੀਜੈ ਤੇਰਾ ਕਿਰਪਾ ਕਰਹਿ ਤਾ ਪੀਵਾ ॥ 1117
ਆਸ ਪਿਆਸੀ ਪਿਰ ਕੈ ਤਾਈ ਜਿਉ ਚਾਤ੍ਰਿਕੁ ਬੂੰਦੇਰੇ ॥
ਕਹੁ ਨਾਨਕ ਜੀਅੜਾ ਬਲਿਹਾਰੀ ਦੇਹੁ ਦਰਸੁ ਪ੍ਰਭ ਮੇਰੇ ॥[126]

P. 84 ਕਰਿ ਕਿਰਪਾ ਗੋਬਿੰਦ ਪ੍ਰਭ ਪ੍ਰੀਤਮ ਦੀਨਾ ਨਾਥ ਸੁਨਹੁ ਅਰਦਾਸਿ ॥ 204
ਕਰੁ ਗਹਿ ਲੇਹੁ ਨਾਨਕ ਕੇ ਸੁਆਮੀ
ਜੀਉ ਪਿੰਡੁ ਸਭੁ ਤੁਮਰੀ ਰਾਸਿ ॥[127]

P. 85 — 318

1. ਕਰਿ ਕਿਰਪਾ ਪ੍ਰਭਿ ਆਪਣੀ
   ਹਰਿ ਆਪਿ ਪਰਖੇ ॥
2. ਨਾਨਕ ਚਲਤ ਨ ਜਾਪਨੀ
   ਕੋ ਸਕੈ ਨ ਲਖੇ ॥[128]

P. 86 — 1307

ਜਤਨ ਜਤਨ ਅਨਿਕ ਉਪਾਵ ਰੇ ਤਉ ਮਿਲਿਓ ਜਉ ਕਿਰਪਾਈ ॥
ਪ੍ਰਭੂ ਦਇਆਰ ਕ੍ਰਿਪਾਰ ਕ੍ਰਿਪਾ ਨਿਧਿ ਜਨ ਨਾਨਕ ਸੰਤ ਰੇਨਾਈ ॥[131]

P. 86 — 779

ਕਿਰਪਾ ਕੀਜੈ ਸਾ ਮਤਿ ਦੀਜੈ ਆਠ ਪਹਰ ਤੁਧੁ ਧਿਆਈ ॥
ਗਰਬੁ ਨ ਕੀਜੈ ਰੇਣ ਹੋਵੀਜੈ ਤਾ ਗਤਿ ਜੀਅਰੇ ਤੇਰੀ ॥
ਸਭ ਊਪਰਿ ਨਾਨਕ ਕਾ ਠਾਕੁਰੁ ਮੈ ਜੇਹੀ ਘਣ ਚੇਰੀ ਰਾਮ ॥[132]

P. 87 — 137

ਕਰਿ ਕਿਰਪਾ ਪ੍ਰਭ ਆਪਣੀ
ਜਨ ਧੂੜੀ ਸੰਗਿ ਸਮਾਉ ॥
ਜਿਉ ਤੂੰ ਰਾਖਹਿ ਤਿਉ ਰਹਾ
ਤੇਰਾ ਦਿਤਾ ਪੈਨਾ ਖਾਉ ॥
ਉਦਮੁ ਸੋਈ ਕਰਾਇ
ਪ੍ਰਭ ਮਿਲਿ ਸਾਧੂ ਗੁਣ ਗਾਉ ॥[133]

P. 87 — 187

ਗੁਣ ਪੂਜਾ ਗਿਆਨ ਧਿਆਨ ਨਾਨਕ ਸਗਲ ਘਾਲ ॥
ਜਿਸ ਕਰਿ ਕਿਰਪਾ ਸਤਿਗੁਰੁ ਮਿਲੈ ਦਇਆਲ ॥[135]

P. 87 — 183

ਸੰਤ ਕ੍ਰਿਪਾ ਤੇ ਮਿਟੇ ਮੋਹ ਭਰਮ ॥
ਸਾਧ ਰੇਣ ਮਜਨ ਸਭਿ ਧਰਮ ॥
ਸਾਧ ਕ੍ਰਿਪਾਲ ਦਇਆਲ ਗੋਵਿੰਦੁ ॥
ਸਾਧਾ ਮਹਿ ਇਹ ਹਮਰੀ ਜਿੰਦੁ ॥
ਕਿਰਪਾ ਨਿਧਿ ਕਿਰਪਾਲ ਧਿਆਵਉ ॥
ਸਾਧਸੰਗਿ ਤਾ ਬੈਠਣ ਪਾਵਉ ॥[136]

P. 88 — 1301

ਤੂ ਅਥਾਹੁ ਅਤਿ ਬਡੋ ਸੁਆਮੀ ਕ੍ਰਿਪਾ ਸਿੰਧੁ ਪੂਰਨ ਰਤਨਾਗੀ ॥
ਨਾਨਕੁ ਜਾਚਕੁ ਹਰਿ ਹਰਿ ਨਾਮੁ ਮਾਂਗੈ
ਮਸਤਕੁ ਆਨਿ ਧਰਿਓ ਪ੍ਰਭ ਪਾਗੀ ॥[137]

P. 89 ਤੂ ਮੇਰਾ ਪਿਤਾ ਤੂਹੈ ਮੇਰਾ ਮਾਤਾ ।। 1144
ਤੂ ਮੇਰੇ ਜੀਅ ਪ੍ਰਾਨ ਸੁਖਦਾਤਾ ।।
ਤੂ ਮੇਰਾ ਠਾਕੁਰ ਹਉ ਦਾਸਾ ਤੇਰਾ ।।
ਤੁਝ ਬਿਨੁ ਅਵਰੁ ਨਹੀ ਕੋ ਮੇਰਾ ।।
ਕਰਿ ਕਿਰਪਾ ਕਰਹੁ ਪ੍ਰਭ ਦਾਤਿ ।।
ਤੁਮ੍ਰੀ ਓਸਤਤਿ ਕਹਹੁ ਦਿਨ ਰਾਤਿ ।।[139]

P. 89 ਨਾਨਕ ਇਹੁ ਸੰਜਮੁ ਪ੍ਰਭ ਕਿਰਪਾ ਪਾਈਐ ।।[140] 299

P. 90 ਜਿਨ ਕਉ ਕ੍ਰਿਪਾ ਕਰੀ ਸੁਖਦਾਤੇ।। ਤਿਨ ਸਾਧੂ ਚਰਣ ਲੈ ਰਿਦੈ ਪਰਾਤੇ ।।[141] 1083

P. 90 ਹਰਿ ਜੀ ਕ੍ਰਿਪਾ ਕਰੇ ਜਉ ਅਪਨੀ ਤੌ ਗੁਰ ਕੇ ਸਬਦਿ ਸਮਾਵਹਿਗੇ ।।[142] 1103

P. 90 ਐ ਜੀ ਰਾਖਹੁ ਪੈਜ ਨਾਮ ਅਪੁਨੇ ਕੀ 504
ਤੁਝ ਹੀ ਸਿਉ ਬਨਿ ਆਈ ।।
ਕਰਿ ਕਿਰਪਾ ਗੁਰ ਦਰਸੁ ਦਿਖਾਵਹੁ ਹਉਮੈ ਸਬਦਿ ਜਲਾਈ ।।[143]

P. 90 ਭਾਈ ਰੇ ਗੁਰ ਕਿਰਪਾ ਤੇ ਭਗਤਿ ਠਾਕੁਰ ਕੀ ।।[144] 504-5

P. 90 ਹਰਿ ਕਿਰਪਾ ਤੇ ਹੋਆ ਹਰਿ ਭਗਤੁ 550
ਹਰਿ ਭਗਤ ਜਨਾ ਕੈ ਮੁਹਿ ਡਿਠੈ
ਜਤਗੁ ਤਰਿਆ ਸਭੁ ਲੋੜੀਐ ।।[145]

P. 90 ਮਨ ਬਿਖੈ ਹੀ ਮਹਿ ਲੁਝੀ ਹੇ ।। 213
ਜਾ ਕਉ ਰੇ ਕਿਰਪਾ ਕਰੈ ਜੀਵਤ ਸੋਈ ਮਰੈ ਸਾਧਸੰਗਿ ਮਾਇਆ ਤਰੈ ।।
ਨਾਨਕ ਸੋ ਜਨੁ ਦਰਿ ਹਰਿ ਸਿਝੀ ਹੇ ।।[146]

P. 91 ਪਥਿਕ ਪਿਆਸ ਚਿਤ ਸਰੋਵਰ ਆਤਮ ਜਲੁ ਲੈਨ ।। 1272
ਹਰਿ ਦਰਸ ਪ੍ਰੇਮ ਜਨ ਨਾਨਕ ਕਰਿ ਕਿਰਪਾ ਪ੍ਰਭ ਦੈਨ ।।[147]

P. 91 ਕਿਰਤ ਕਰਮ ਕੇ ਵੀਛੁੜੇ ਕਰਿ ਕਿਰਪਾ ਮੇਲਹੁ ਰਾਮ ।। 133
ਚਾਰਿ ਕੁੰਟ ਦਹ ਦਿਸ ਭ੍ਰਮੇ ਥਕਿ ਆਏ ਪ੍ਰਭ ਕੀ ਸਾਮ ।।[148]

P. 91 ਕਿਰਪਾ ਤੇ ਸੁਖੁ ਪਾਇਆ ਸਾਚੇ ਪਰਥਾਈ ।। 420
ਗੁਰ ਬਿਨੁ ਕਿਨੈ ਨ ਪਾਇਓ ਕੇਤੀ ਕਹੈ ਕਹਾਏ ।।[149]

P. 91 ਪਾਇ ਪਰਹ ਸਤਿਗੁਰੂ ਕੈ ਜਿਨਿ ਭਰਮੁ ਬਿਦਾਰਿਆ ।। 399
ਕਰਿ ਕਿਰਪਾ ਪ੍ਰਭਿ ਆਪਣੀ ਸਚੁ ਸਾਜਿ ਸਵਾਰਿਆ ।।[150]

P. 91 ਸਾਚਾ ਸਾਹਿਬੁ ਕਿਰਪਾ ਕਰੈ ।। ਸੋ ਸੇਵਕੁ ਜਮ ਤੇ ਕੈਸਾ ਡਰੈ ।।[151] 661

P. 91 ਕਿਰਪਾ ਕਰਿ ਕੈ ਆਪਣੀ ਆਪੇ ਲਏ ਸਮਾਇ ਜੀਉ ।।[152] 73

P. 92 ਕਰਿ ਕਿਰਪਾ ਘਰੁ ਮਹਲੁ ਦਿਖਾਇਆ ।। 153
ਨਾਨਕ ਹਉਮੈ ਮਾਰਿ ਮਿਲਾਇਆ ।।[153]

P. 92 ਕਰਿ ਕਿਰਪਾ ਜੋ ਅਪੁਨਾ ਕੀਨੋ ਤਾ ਕੀ ਊਤਮ ਬਾਣੀ ।। 1220
ਸਾਧਸੰਗਿ ਨਾਨਕ ਨਿਸਤਰੀਐ ਜੋ ਰਾਤੇ ਪ੍ਰਭ ਨਿਰਬਾਣੀ ।।[155]

P. 92 ਹਰਿ ਜੀਉ ਹਉ ਹਉ ਰਾਵੈ ਨਾਰਿ ।। 54
ਤੁਧੁ ਭਾਵਨਿ ਸੋਹਾਗਣੀ ਅਪਣੀ ਕਿਰਪਾ ਲੈਹਿ ਸਵਾਰਿ ।।[156]

P. 92 ਸਚੁ ਪਰਮੇਸਰੁ ਨਿਤ ਨਵਾ ।। ਗੁਰ ਕਿਰਪਾ ਤੇ ਨਿਤ ਚਵਾ ।। 1183
ਪ੍ਰਭ ਰਖਵਾਲੇ ਮਾਈ ਬਾਪ ।। ਜਾ ਕੈ ਸਿਮਰਣਿ ਨਹੀ ਸੰਤਾਪ ।।[156]

P. 93 ਤਉ ਮੈ ਆਇਆ ਸਰਨੀ ਆਇਆ ।। 746
ਭਰੋਸੈ ਆਇਆ ।। ਕਿਰਪਾ ਆਇਆ ।।
ਜਿਉ ਭਾਵੈ ਤਿਉ ਰਾਖਹੁ ਸੁਆਮੀ
ਮਾਰਗੁ ਗੁਰਹਿ ਪਠਾਇਆ।।[158]

P. 93 ਸਤਿਗੁਰਿ ਮਿਲਿਐ ਕਿਰਪਾ ਕੀਨੀ ਅੰਮ੍ਰਿਤ ਨਾਮੁ ਅਧਾਰਾ ।।[159] 635

P. 93 ਨਾਨਕ ਸਰਣਿ ਕ੍ਰਿਪਾ ਨਿਧਿ ਸਾਗਰ ਬਿਨਸਿਓ ਆਨ ਨਿਹੋਰ ।।[160] 1228

P. 93 ਕਰਿ ਕਿਰਪਾ ਮੇਰਾ ਚਿਤੁ ਲਾਇਆ ।। 223
ਸਤਿਗੁਰਿ ਮੋ ਕਉ ਏਕੁ ਬੁਝਾਇਆ ।।[161]

P. 94 ਕਰਿ ਕਿਰਪਾ ਪਾਰਬ੍ਰਹਮ ਸੁਆਮੀ ਇਹ ਬੰਧਨ ਛੁਟਕਾਰੀ ।। 681
ਬੂਡਤ ਅੰਧ ਨਾਨਕ ਪ੍ਰਭ ਕਾਢਤ ਸਾਧ ਜਨਾ ਸੰਗਾਰੀ ।।[162]

P. 94 ਕਰਿ ਕਿਰਪਾ ਜਿਸ ਕੈ ਹਿਰਦੈ ਗਰੀਬੀ ਬਸਾਵੈ ।। 278
ਨਾਨਕ ਈਹਾ ਮੁਕਤੁ ਆਗੈ ਸੁਖੁ ਪਾਵੈ ।।[163]

P. 94 ਸਾਹਿਬੁ ਹੋਇ ਦਇਆਲੁ ਕਿਰਪਾ ਕਰੇ ਤਾ ਸਾਈ ਕਾਰ ਕਰਾਇਸੀ ।। 471
ਸੋ ਸੇਵਕੁ ਸੇਵਾ ਕਰੇ ਜਿਸ ਨੋ ਹੁਕਮੁ ਮਨਾਇਸੀ ।।[164]

P. 95 ਗੁਰੁ ਗੁਰੁ ਕਰਤ ਸਦਾ ਸੁਖੁ ਪਾਇਆ ।। 1341
ਦੀਨ ਦਇਆਲ ਭਏ ਕਿਰਪਾਲਾ ਅਪਣਾ ਨਾਮੁ ਆਪਿ ਜਪਾਇਆ ।।[165]

P. 95 ਜਾ ਕਉ ਭਇਓ ਕ੍ਰਿਪਾਲੁ ਬੀਠੁਲਾ 1206
ਤਿਨਿ ਹਰਿ ਹਰਿ ਅਜਰ ਜਰਨ ।।[166]

P. 95 ਕਰਿ ਕਿਰਪਾ ਲੀਨੇ ਕਰਿ ਅਪੁਨੇ ਉਪਜੀ ਦਰਸ ਪਿਆਸ ।।[167] 1228

P. 95 ਕਿਰਪਾ ਕਰਹਿ ਗਾਵਾ ਪ੍ਰਭੁ ਸੋਇ ।। 232
ਨਾਮ ਰਤਨੁ ਸਭ ਜਗ ਮਹਿ ਲੋਇ ।।
ਗੁਰਮੁਖਿ ਬਾਣੀ ਮੀਠੀ ਲਾਗੀ ।।
ਅੰਤਰੁ ਬਿਗਸੈ ਅਨਦਿਨੁ ਲਿਵ ਲਾਗੀ ।।[168]

P. 96 ਜਉ ਕਿਰਪਾ ਗੋਬਿੰਦ ਭਈ ।। 402
ਸੁਖ ਸੰਪਤਿ ਹਰਿ ਨਾਮ ਫਲ ਪਾਏ ਸਤਿਗੁਰ ਮਿਲਈ ।।[169]

P. 96 ਤੇਰੀ ਸਰਨਿ ਪੂਰਨ ਸੁਖ ਸਾਗਰ 1221
ਕਰਿ ਕਿਰਪਾ ਦੇਵਹੁ ਦਾਨ ।।
ਸਿਮਰਿ ਸਿਮਰਿ ਨਾਨਕ ਪ੍ਰਭ ਜੀਵੈ
ਬਿਨਸਿ ਜਾਇ ਅਭਿਮਾਨ ।।[170]

P. 96 ਭਇਓ ਕ੍ਰਿਪਾਲੁ ਠਾਕੁਰੁ ਸੇਵਕ ਕਉ ਸਵਰੇ ਹਲਤ ਪਲਾਤਾ ।।[171] 1000

P. 96	ਕਹੁ ਨਾਨਕ ਕਿਰਪਾ ਭਈ ਭਗਤੁ ਗਿਆਨੀ ਸੋਇ ॥[172]	251
P. 97	ਕਰਿ ਕਿਰਪਾ ਭਗਤੀ ਪ੍ਰਗਟਾਇਆ ॥ ਸੰਤਸੰਗਿ ਮਿਲਿ ਹਰਿ ਹਰਿ ਜਪਿਆ ਬਿਨਸੇ ਆਲਸ ਰੋਗਾ ਜੀਉ ॥[173]	108
P. 98	ਕਿਰਪਾ ਪਾਏ ਸਹਜਾਏ ਦਰਸਾਏ ਅਬ ਰਾਤਿਆ ਗੋਵਿੰਦ ਸਿਉ ॥ ਸੰਤ ਸੇਵਿ ਪ੍ਰੀਤਿ ਨਾਥ ਰੰਗੁ ਲਾਲਨ ਲਾਏ ॥[174]	408
P. 98	ਮਿਹਰਵਾਨੁ ਸਾਹਿਬੁ ਮਿਹਰਵਾਨੁ ॥ ਸਾਹਿਬੁ ਮੇਰਾ ਮਿਹਰਵਾਨੁ ॥ ਜੀਅ ਸਗਲ ਕਉ ਦੇਇ ਦਾਨੁ ॥[176]	724
P. 99	ਸਿਮਰਿ ਸਿਮਰਿ ਦਾਤਾਰੁ ਸਭਿ ਰੰਗ ਮਾਣਿਆ ॥ ਪਰਗਟੁ ਭਇਆ ਸੰਸਾਰਿ ਮਿਹਰ ਛਾਵਾਣਿਆ ॥[177]	1291
P. 99	ਜੇਤਾ ਸਮੁੰਦੁ ਸਾਗਰੁ ਨੀਰਿ ਭਰਿਆ ਤੇਤੇ ਅਉਗਣ ਹਮਾਰੇ ॥ ਦਇਆ ਕਰਹੁ ਕਿਛੁ ਮਿਹਰ ਉਪਾਵਹੁ ਡੁਬਦੇ ਪਥਰ ਤਾਰੇ ॥ ਜੀਅੜਾ ਅਗਨਿ ਬਰਾਬਰਿ ਤਪੈ ਭੀਤਰਿ ਵਗੈ ਕਾਤੀ ॥ ਪ੍ਰਣਵਤਿ ਨਾਨਕੁ ਹੁਕਮੁ ਪਛਾਣੈ ਸੁਖੁ ਹੋਵੈ ਦਿਨੁ ਰਾਤੀ ॥[178]	156
P. 99	ਜਿਸ ਨੋ ਤੇਰੀ ਮਿਹਰ ਸੁ ਤੇਰੀ ਬੰਦਿਗੀ ॥[179]	961
P. 99	ਮਿਹਰ ਕਰੇ ਜੇ ਆਪਣੀ ਚਸਾ ਨ ਵਿਸਰੈ ਸੋਇ ॥[180]	49
P. 99	ਸਭੇ ਜੀਅ ਸਮਾਲਿ ਅਪਣੀ ਮਿਹਰ ਕਰੁ ॥ ਅੰਨੁ ਪਾਣੀ ਮੁਚੁ ਉਪਾਇ ਦੁਖ ਦਾਲਦੁ ਭੰਨਿ ਤਰੁ ॥ ਅਰਦਾਸਿ ਸੁਣੀ ਦਾਤਾਰਿ ਹੋਈ ਸਿਸਟਿ ਠਰੁ ॥ ਲੇਵਹੁ ਕੰਠਿ ਲਗਾਇ ॥ ਅਪਦਾ ਸਭ ਹਰੁ ॥ ਨਾਨਕ ਨਾਮੁ ਧਿਆਇ ਪ੍ਰਭ ਕਾ ਸਫਲੁ ਘਰੁ ॥[181]	1251
P. 100	ਆਪੇ ਸਤਿਗੁਰੁ ਆਪਿ ਹਰਿ ਆਪੇ ਮੇਲਿ ਮਿਲਾਇ ॥	41

ਆਪਿ ਦਇਆ ਕਰਿ ਮੇਲਸੀ
ਗੁਰ ਸਤਿਗੁਰ ਪੀਛੈ ਪਇ ।।
ਸਭੁ ਜਗਜੀਵਨੁ ਜਗਿ ਆਪਿ ਹੈ
ਨਾਨਕ ਜਲੁ ਜਲਹਿ ਸਮਾਇ ।।[182]

P. 100 ਗੁਰਮੁਖੀਆ ਸੋਹਾਗਣੀ ਤਿਨ ਦਇਆ ਪਈ ਮਨਿ ਆਇ ।। 41
ਸਤਿਗੁਰ ਵਚਨੁ ਰਤਨੁ ਹੈ ਜੋ ਮੰਨੇ ਸੁ ਹਰਿ ਰਸੁ ਖਾਏ ।।
ਸੇ ਵਡਭਾਗੀ ਵਡ ਜਾਣਅਹਿ ਜਿਨ ਹਰਿ ਰਸੁ ਖਾਧਾ ਗੁਰੂ ਭਾਇ ।।
ਇਹ ਹਰਿ ਰਸ ਵਣਿ ਤ੍ਰਿਣਿ ਸਭਤੁ ਹੈ ਭਾਗਹੀਣ ਨਹੀ ਖਾਏ ।।[183]

P. 102 ਤੂ ਦਇਆਲੁ ਦਇਆਪਤਿ ਦਾਤਾ ਕਿਆ ਏਹਿ ਜੰਤ ਵਿਚਾਰੇ ।। 796
ਮੁਕਤ ਬੰਧ ਸਭਿ ਤੁਝ ਤੇ ਹੋਏ ਐਸਾ ਆਖਿ ਵਖਾਣੇ ।।
ਗੁਰਮੁਖਿ ਹੋਵੈ ਸੋ ਮੁਕਤੁ ਕਹੀਐ ਮਨਮੁਖ ਬੰਧ ਵਿਚਾਰੇ ।।
ਸੋ ਜਨੁ ਮੁਕਤੁ ਜਿਸੁ ਏਕ ਲਿਵ ਲਾਗੀ
ਸਦਾ ਰਹੈ ਹਰਿ ਨਾਲੇ ।।[185]

P. 102 ਤੂ ਸਾਹਿਬੁ ਅਗਮ ਦਇਆਲੁ ਹੈ ਵਡ ਦਾਤਾ ਦਾਣਾ ।। 305
ਤੁਧੁ ਜੇਵਡੁ ਮੈ ਹੋਰੁ ਕੋ ਦਿਸਿ ਨਾ ਆਵਈ
ਤੂਹੈਂ ਸੁਘੜੁ ਮੇਰੈ ਮਨਿ ਭਾਣਾ ।।[187]

P. 104 ਜੈ ਜੈ ਕਾਰੁ ਕੀਨੋ ਸਭ ਜਗ ਮਹਿ ਦਇਆ ਜੀਅਨ ਮਹਿ ਪਾਇਓ ।। 1270
ਕੰਠਿ ਲਾਇ ਅਪੁਨੋ ਦਾਸੁ ਰਾਖਿਓ ਤਾਤੀ ਵਾਉ ਨ ਲਾਇਓ ।।[188]

P. 104 ਰਾਮ ਨਾਮੁ ਹੈ ਜੋਤਿ ਸਬਾਈ ਗੁਰਮੁਖਿ ਆਪੇ ਅਲਖੁ ਲਖਈਆ ।। 833
ਨਾਨਕ ਦੀਨ ਦਇਆਲ ਭਏ ਹੈ ਭਗਤਿ ਭਾਇ ਹਰਿ ਨਾਮਿ ਸਮਈਆ ।।[189]

P. 104 ਮੇਰੈ ਮਨਿ ਗੁਪਤ ਹੀਰੁ ਹਰਿ ਰਾਖਾ ।। 696
ਦੀਨ ਦਇਆਲਿ ਮਿਲਾਇਓ ਗੁਰੁ ਸਾਧੂ ਗੁਰਿ ਮਿਲਿਐ ਹੀਰੁ ਪਰਾਖਾ ।।[190]

P. 105 ਹਰਿ ਦਾ ਨਾਮੁ ਅੰਮ੍ਰਿਤੁ ਹਰਿ ਹਰਿ ਹਰੇ 1202
ਸੋ ਪੀਐ ਜਿਸੁ ਰਾਮੁ ਪਿਆਸੀ।।
ਹਰਿ ਆਪਿ ਦੋਇਆਲੁ ਦਇਆ ਕਰਿ ਮੇਲੈ

ਜਿਸੁ ਸਤਿਗੁਰੂ ਸੋ ਜਨੁ ਹਰਿ
ਹਰਿ ਅੰਮ੍ਰਿਤ ਨਾਮੁ ਚਖਾਸੀ ।।[191]

P. 105 ਸਤਿਗੁਰੁ ਦਾਤਾ ਦਇਆਲੁ ਹੈ ਜਿਸ ਨੋ ਦਇਆ ਸਦਾ ਹੋਇ ।। 302
ਸਤਿਗੁਰੁ ਅੰਦਰਹੁ ਨਿਰਵੈਰੁ ਹੈ ਸਭੁ ਦੇਖੈ ਬ੍ਰਹਮੁ ਇਕੁ ਸੋਇ ।।[192]

P. 105 ਹਰਿ ਹਰਿ ਹਰਿ ਰਸੁ ਆਪਿ ਹੈ ਆਪੇ ਹਰਿ ਰਸੁ ਹੋਇ ।। 41
ਆਪਿ ਦਇਆ ਕਰਿ ਦੇਵਸੀ ਗੁਰਮੁਖਿ ਅੰਮ੍ਰਿਤੁ ਚੋਇ ।।[193]

P. 106 ਤੁਧੁ ਭਾਵੈ ਤਾ ਗਾਵਾ ਬਾਣੀ ।। 180
ਤੁਧੁ ਭਾਵੈ ਤਾ ਸਚੁ ਵਖਾਣੀ ।।
ਤੁਧੁ ਭਾਵੈ ਤਾ ਸਤਿਗੁਰ ਮਇਆ ।।
ਸਰਬ ਸੁਖਾ ਪ੍ਰਭ ਤੇਰੀ ਦਇਆ ।।
ਜੋ ਤੁਧੁ ਭਾਵੈ ਸੋ ਨਿਰਮਲ ਕਰਮਾ ।।
ਜੋ ਤੁਧੁ ਭਾਵੈ ਸੋ ਸਚੁ ਧਰਮਾ ।।
ਸਰਬ ਨਿਧਾਨ ਗੁਣ ਤੁਮ ਹੀ ਪਾਸਿ ।।
ਤੂੰ ਸਾਹਿਬੁ ਸੇਵਕ ਅਰਦਾਸਿ ।।[194]

P. 106 ਠਾਕੁਰ ਚਰਣ ਸੁਹਾਵੇ ।। ਹਰਿ ਸੰਤਨ ਗਾਵੇ ।। ਰਹਾਉ ।। 407
ਆਪੁ ਗਵਾਇਆ ਸੇਵ ਕਮਾਇਆ ਗੁਨ ਰਸਿ ਰਸਿ ਗਾਵੇ ।।
ਏਕਹਿ ਆਸਾ ਦਰਸ ਪਿਆਸਾ ਆਨ ਨ ਭਾਵੇ ।।
ਦਇਆ ਤੁਹਾਰੀ ਕਿਆ ਜੰਤ ਵਿਚਾਰੀ ਨਾਨਕ ਬਲਿ ਬਲਿ ਜਾਵੇ ।।[195]

P. 107 ਹਰਿ ਲਾਭੁ ਪਾਇਆ ਆਪੁ ਮਿਟਾਇਆ 545
ਮਿਲੇ ਚਿਰੀ ਵਿਛੁੰਨਿਆ ।।
ਗਹਿ ਭੁਜਾ ਲੀਨੇ ਦਇਆ ਕੀਨ੍ਹੇ
ਪ੍ਰਭ ਏਕ ਅਗਮ ਅਪਾਰੋ ।।
ਬਿਨਵੰਤਿ ਨਾਨਕ ਸਦਾ ਨਿਰਮਲ
ਸਚੁ ਸਬਦੁ ਗੁਣ ਝੁਣਕਾਰੋ ।।[196]

P. 107 ਢਾਢੀ ਕਰੇ ਪੁਕਾਰ ਪ੍ਰਭੂ ਸੁਣਾਇਸੀ ।। 510
ਅੰਦਰਿ ਧੀਰਕ ਹੋਇ ਪੂਰਾ ਪਾਇਸੀ ।।

ਜੋ ਧੁਰਿ ਲਿਖਿਆ ਲੇਖੁ ਸੇ ਕਰਮ ਕਮਾਇਸੀ ॥
ਜਾ ਹੋਵੈ ਖਸਮੁ ਦਇਆਲੁ ਤਾ ਮਹਲੁ ਘਰੁ ਪਾਇਸੀ ॥
ਸੋ ਪ੍ਰਭੁ ਮੇਰਾ ਅਤਿ ਵਡਾ ਗੁਰਮੁਖਿ ਮੇਲਾਇਸੀ ॥[197]

P. 108 ਹਰਿ ਹਰਿ ਆਪਿ ਦਇਆ ਕਰਿ ਦੇਵੈ 170
ਤਾ ਅੰਮ੍ਰਿਤੁ ਹਰਿ ਰਸੁ ਚਖੀਐ ॥[198]

P. 108 ਹਰਿ ਨਾਮੁ ਦਇਆ ਕਰਿ ਪਾਇਆ ਮੇਰੇ 174
ਗੋਵਿੰਦਾ ਜਨ ਨਾਨਕੁ ਸਰਣਿ ਤੁਮਾਰੀ ਜੀਉ ॥[199]

P. 109 ਵਾਹੁ ਵਾਹੁ ਕਰਮੀ ਪਾਈਐ ਆਪਿ ਦਇਆ ਕਰਿ ਦੇਇ ॥ 515-16
ਨਾਨਕ ਵਾਹੁ ਵਾਹੁ ਗੁਰਮੁਖਿ ਪਾਈਐ ਅਨਦਿਨੁ ਨਾਮੁ ਲਏਇ ॥[200]

P. 109 ਹਰਿ ਦਇਆਲਿ ਦਇਆ ਪ੍ਰਭਿ ਕੀਨੀ 168
ਮੇਰੈ ਮਨਿ ਤਨਿ ਮੁਖਿ ਹਰਿ ਬੋਲੀ ॥
ਗੁਰਮੁਖਿ ਰੰਗੁ ਭਇਆ ਅਤਿ ਗੂੜਾ
ਹਰਿ ਰੰਗਿ ਭੀਨੀ ਮੇਰੀ ਚੋਲੀ ॥[201]

P. 110 ਗੁਰ ਸਤਿਗੁਰ ਕਾ ਜੋ ਸਿਖੁ ਅਖਾਏ 305-6
ਸੁ ਭਲਕੇ ਉਠਿ ਹਰਿ ਨਾਮੁ ਧਿਆਵੈ ॥
ਉਦਮੁ ਕਰੇ ਭਲਕੇ ਪਰਭਾਤੀ
ਇਸਨਾਨੁ ਕਰੇ ਅੰਮ੍ਰਿਤ ਸਰਿ ਨਾਵੈ ॥
ਉਪਦੇਸਿ ਗੁਰੂ ਹਰਿ ਹਰਿ ਜਪੁ ਜਾਪੈ
ਸਭਿ ਕਿਲਵਿਖ ਪਾਪ ਦੋਖ ਲਹਿ ਜਾਵੈ ॥
ਫਿਰਿ ਚੜੈ ਦਿਵਸੁ ਗੁਰਬਾਣੀ ਗਾਵੈ
ਬਹਦਿਆ ਉਠਦਿਆ ਹਰਿ ਨਾਮੁ ਧਿਆਵੈ ॥
ਜੋ ਸਾਸਿ ਗਿਰਾਸਿ ਧਿਆਏ ਮੇਰਾ ਹਰਿ ਹਰਿ
ਸੋ ਗੁਰਸਿਖੁ ਗੁਰੂ ਮਨਿ ਭਾਵੈ ॥
ਜਿਸ ਨੋ ਦਇਆਲੁ ਹੋਵੈ ਮੇਰਾ ਸੁਆਮੀ
ਤਿਸੁ ਗੁਰਸਿਖ ਗੁਰੂ ਉਪਦੇਸੁ ਸੁਣਾਵੈ ॥
ਜਨੁ ਨਾਨਕ ਧੂੜਿ ਮੰਗੈ ਤਿਸੁ ਗੁਰਸਿਖ ਕੀ
ਜੋ ਆਪਿ ਜਪੈ ਅਵਰਹ ਨਾਮੁ ਜਪਾਵੈ ॥[202]

P. 110 ਹਉ ਗੁਰ ਸਰਣਾਈ ਢਹਿ ਪਵਾ ਕਰਿ ਦਇਆ ਮੇਲੇ ਪ੍ਰਭੁ ਸੋਇ ॥ 39-40
ਮਨਹਠਿ ਕਿਨੈ ਨ ਪਾਇਆ ਕਰਿ ਉਪਾਵ ਥਕੇ ਸਭੁ ਕੋਇ ॥
ਸਹਜ ਸਿਆਣਪ ਕਰਿ ਰਹੇ ਮਨਿ ਕੋਰੈ ਰੰਗੁ ਨ ਹੋਇ ॥
ਕੂੜਿ ਕਪਟਿ ਕਿਨੈ ਨ ਪਾਇਓ ਜੋ ਬੀਜੈ ਖਾਵੈ ਸੋਇ ॥[203]

P. 110 ਤੁਝ ਹੀ ਕੀਆ ਜੰਮਣ ਮਰਣਾ ॥ ਗੁਰ ਤੇ ਸਮਝ ਪੜੀ ਕਿਆ ਡਰਣਾ ॥ 1022
ਤੂ ਦਇਆਲੁ ਦਇਆ ਕਰਿ ਦੇਖਹਿ ਦੁਖੁ ਦਰਦੁ ਸਰੀਰਹੁ ਜਾਈ ਹੇ ॥[204]

P. 112 ਤੂ ਅਗਮ ਦਇਆਲ ਦਇਆ ਪਤਿ ਦਾਤਾ 1326
ਸਭ ਦਇਆ ਧਾਰਿ ਰਖਿ ਲੀਜੈ ॥
ਸਰਬ ਜੀਆ ਜਗਜੀਵਨੁ ਏਕੋ ਨਾਨਕ ਪ੍ਰਤਿਪਾਲ ਕਰੀਜੈ ॥[206]

P. 112 ਮੇਰਾ ਪ੍ਰਭੁ ਰਾਂਗਿ ਘਣੌ ਅਤਿ ਰੂੜੌ ॥ 1331
ਦੀਨ ਦਇਆਲ ਪ੍ਰੀਤਮ ਮਨਮੋਹਨੁ ਅਤਿ ਰਸ ਲਾਲ ਸਗੂੜੌ ॥[207]

P. 112 ਦਇਆ ਦੇਵਤਾ ਖਿਮਾ ਜਪਮਾਲੀ ਤੇ ਮਾਣਸ ਪਰਧਾਨ ॥[208] 1245

P. 113 ਦੁਆਦਸੀ ਦਇਆ ਦਾਨੁ ਕਰਿ ਜਾਣੈ ॥ 840
ਬਾਹਰਿ ਜਾਤੋ ਭੀਤਰਿ ਆਣੈ ॥
ਬਰਤੀ ਬਰਤ ਰਹੈ ਨਿਹਕਾਮ ॥
ਅਜਪਾ ਜਾਪੁ ਜਪੈ ਮੁਖਿ ਨਾਮ ॥
ਤੀਨਿ ਭਵਣ ਮਹਿ ਏਕੋ ਜਾਣੈ ॥
ਸਭਿ ਸੁਚਿ ਸੰਜਮ ਸਾਚੁ ਪਛਾਣੈ ॥[209]

P. 113 ਛੋਡਿ ਸਿਆਣਪ ਬਹੁ ਚਤੁਰਾਈ ॥ 891
ਮਨ ਬਿਨੁ ਹਰਿ ਨਾਵੈ ਜਾਇ ਨ ਕਾਇ ॥
ਦਇਆ ਧਾਰੀ ਗੋਵਿਦ ਗੋੁਸਾਈ ॥
ਹਰਿ ਹਰਿ ਨਾਨਕ ਟੇਕ ਟਿਕਾਈ ॥[210]

P. 114 ਮੈ ਮੂਰਖ ਮੁਗਧ ਊਪਰਿ ਕਰਹੁ ਦਇਆ ॥ 1170
ਤਉ ਸਰਣਾਗਤਿ ਰਹਉ ਪਇਆ ॥
ਕਹਤੁ ਨਾਨਕੁ ਸੰਸਾਰ ਕੇ ਨਿਹਫਲ ਕਾਮਾ ॥

ਗੁਰ ਪ੍ਰਸਾਦਿ ਕੋ ਪਾਵੈ ਅੰਮ੍ਰਿਤ ਨਾਮਾ ।।[211]

P. 114 ਹਰਿ ਨਾਮੁ ਦਇਆ ਕਰਿ ਪਾਇਆ ਮੇਰੇ ਗੋਵਿੰਦਾ 174
ਜਨ ਨਾਨਕੁ ਸਰਣਿ ਤੁਮਾਰੀ ਜੀਉ ।।[212]

P. 114 ਰਾਤੇ ਸਾਚਿ ਹਰਿ ਨਾਮਿ ਨਿਹਾਲਾ ।। 1172
ਦਇਆ ਕਰਹੁ ਪ੍ਰਭ ਦੀਨ ਦਇਆਲਾ ।।
ਤਿਸੁ ਬਿਨੁ ਅਵਰੁ ਨਹੀ ਮੈ ਕੋਇ ।।
ਜਿਉ ਭਾਵੈ ਤਿਉ ਰਾਖੈ ਸੋਇ ।।
ਗੁਰ ਗੋਪਾਲ ਮੇਰੈ ਮਨਿ ਭਾਏ ।।
ਰਹਿ ਨ ਸਕਉ ਦਰਸਨ ਦੇਖੇ ਬਿਨੁ
ਸਹਜਿ ਮਿਲਉ ਗੁਰੁ ਮੇਲਿ ਮਿਲਾਏ ।।[213]

P. 115 ਆਵਹੁ ਦਇਆ ਕਰੇ ਜੀਉ ਪ੍ਰੀਤਮ ਅਤਿ ਪਿਆਰੇ ।। 245
ਕਾਮਣਿ ਬਿਨਉ ਕਰੇ ਜੀਉ ਸਚਿ ਸਬਦਿ ਸੀਗਾਰੇ ।।[214]

P. 115 ਵੈਸਾਖੁ ਭਲਾ ਸਾਖਾ ਵੇਸ ਕਰੇ ।। 1108
ਧਨ ਦੇਖੈ ਹਰਿ ਦੁਆਰਿ ਆਵਹੁ ਦਇਆ ਕਰੇ ।।
ਘਰਿ ਆਉ ਪਿਆਰੇ ਦੁਤਰ ਤਾਰੇ ਤੁਧੁ ਬਿਨੁ ਅਢੁ ਨ ਮੋਲੋ ।।[215]

P. 115 ਤੁਮ੍ ਕਰਹੁ ਦਇਆ ਮੇਰੇ ਸਾਈ ।। 673
ਐਸੀ ਮਤਿ ਦੀਜੈ ਮੇਰੇ ਠਾਕੁਰ
ਸਦਾ ਸਦਾ ਤੁਧੁ ਧਿਆਈ ।।[216]

P. 115 ਬਗੁਲੇ ਤੇ ਫੁਨਿ ਹੰਸੁਲਾ ਹੋਵੈ ਜੇ ਤੂ ਕਰਹਿ ਦਇਆਲਾ ।। 1171
ਪ੍ਰਣਵਤਿ ਨਾਨਕੁ ਦਾਸਨਿ ਦਾਸਾ ਦਇਆ ਕਰਹੁ ਦਇਆਲਾ ।।[217]

P. 115 ਹਰਿ ਕੇ ਜਨ ਸਤਿਗੁਰ ਸਤ ਪੁਰਖਾ 492
ਹਉ ਬਿਨਉ ਕਰਉ ਗੁਰ ਪਾਸਿ ।।
ਹਮ ਕੀਰੇ ਕਿਰਮ ਸਤਿਗੁਰ ਸਰਣਾਈ
ਕਰਿ ਦਇਆ ਨਾਮੁ ਪਰਗਾਸਿ ।।
ਮੇਰੇ ਮੀਤ ਗੁਰਦੇਵ ਮੋ ਕਉ ਰਾਮ ਨਾਮੁ ਪਰਗਾਸਿ।।[218]

P. 116 ਅਮੁਲ ਗੁਣ ਅਮੁਲ ਵਾਪਾਰ ।। 5
ਅਮੁਲ ਵਾਪਾਰੀਏ ਅਮੁਲ ਭੰਡਾਰ ।।
ਅਮੁਲ ਆਵਹਿ ਅਮੁਲ ਲੈ ਜਾਹਿ ।।
ਅਮੁਲ ਭਾਇ ਅਮੁਲਾ ਸਮਾਹਿ ।।
ਅਮੁਲੁ ਧਰਮੁ ਅਮੁਲੁ ਦੀਬਾਣੁ ।।
ਅਮੁਲੁ ਤੁਲ ਅਮੁਲੁ ਪਰਵਾਣੁ ।।
ਅਮੁਲੁ ਬਖਸੀਸ ਅਮੁਲੁ ਨੀਸਾਣੁ ।।
ਅਮੁਲੁ ਕਰਮੁ ਅਮੁਲੁ ਫੁਰਮਾਣੁ ।।
ਅਮੁਲੋ ਅਮੁਲੁ ਆਖਿਆ ਨ ਜਾਇ ।।
ਆਖਿ ਆਖਿ ਰਹੇ ਲਿਵ ਲਾਇ ।।[219]

P. 116 ਤੁਮ ਦਇਆਲ ਸਰਣਿ ਪ੍ਰਤਿਪਾਲਕ 169
ਮੋ ਕਉ ਦੀਜੈ ਦਾਨੁ ਹਰਿ ਹਮ ਜਾਚੇ ।।[220]

P. 116 ਸਾਲ ਗ੍ਰਾਮ ਬਿਪ ਪੂਜਿ ਮਨਾਵਹੁ 1170-71
ਸੁਕ੍ਰਿਤੁ ਤੁਲਸੀ ਮਾਲਾ ।।
ਰਾਮ ਨਾਮੁ ਜਪਿ ਬੇੜਾ ਬਾਂਧਹੁ
ਦਇਆ ਕਰਹੁ ਦਇਆਲਾ ।।[221]

P. 117 ਹਰਿ ਦਇਆ ਧਾਰਿ ਪ੍ਰਭ ਬੇਨਤੀ ਹਰਿ ਹਰਿ ਚੇਤਾਇਆ ।। 163
ਜਨ ਨਾਨਕੁ ਮੰਗੈ ਧੂੜਿ ਤਿਨ ਜਿਨ ਸਤਿਗੁਰੁ ਪਾਇਆ ।।[222]

P. 117 ਦਇਆ ਕਰਹੁ ਹਰਿ ਦਰਸੁ ਦਿਖਾਵਹੁ 170
ਮੇਰੈ ਮਨਿ ਤਨਿ ਲੋਚ ਘਣੇਰੀ ।।[223]

P. 118 ਦਇਆ ਮਇਆ ਕਰਿ ਪ੍ਰਾਨਪਤਿ ਮੋਰੇ 208
ਮੋਹਿ ਅਨਾਥ ਸਰਣਿ ਪ੍ਰਭ ਤੋਰੀ ।।
ਅੰਧ ਕੂਪ ਮਹਿ ਹਾਥ ਦੇ ਰਾਖਹੁ
ਕਛੂ ਸਿਆਨਪ ਉਕਤਿ ਨ ਮੋਰੀ ।।[225]

P. 118 ਚਿਤਿ ਚਿਤਵਹੁ ਨਾਰਾਇਣ ਏਕ ।। 295
ਏਕ ਰੂਪ ਜਾ ਕੇ ਰੰਗ ਅਨੇਕ ।।
ਗੋਪਾਲ ਦਾਮੋਦਰ ਦੀਨ ਦਇਆਲ ।।

ਦੁਖ ਭੰਜਨ ਪੂਰਨ ਕਿਰਪਾਲ ।।
ਸਿਮਰਿ ਸਿਮਰਿ ਨਾਮੁ ਬਾਰੰ ਬਾਰ ।।
ਨਾਨਕ ਜੀਅ ਕਾ ਇਹੈ ਅਧਾਰ ।।[226]

P. 118 ਮਿਲੁ ਮਿਲੁ ਸਖੀ ਹਰਿ ਕਥਾ ਸੁਨਈਆ ।। 836
ਸਤਿਗੁਰੁ ਦਇਆ ਕਰੇ ਪ੍ਰਭੁ ਮੇਲੇ
ਮੈ ਤਿਸੁ ਆਗੈ ਸਿਰੁ ਕਟਿ ਕਟਿ ਪਈਆ ।।[227]

P. 119 ਰੋਮਿ ਰੋਮਿ ਮਨਿ ਤਨਿ ਇਕ ਬੇਦਨ 836

P. 120 ਮੈ ਪ੍ਰਭ ਦੇਖੇ ਬਿਨੁ ਨੀਦ ਨ ਪਈਆ ।।[228] 443
ਨਾਨਕ ਆਪਿ ਅਨੁਗ੍ਰਹੁ ਕੀਆ ਹਮ ਦਾਸਨਿ ਦਾਸਾ ।।[230]
ਕਰਹੁ ਅਨੁਗ੍ਰਹੁ ਸੁਆਮੀ ਮੇਰੇ ਮਨ ਤੇ ਕਬਹੁ ਨ ਡਾਰਉ ।।

P. 120 ਸਾਧੂ ਧੂਰਿ ਲਾਈ ਮੁਖਿ ਮਸਤਕਿ ਕਾਮ ਕ੍ਰੋਧ ਬਿਖੁ ਜਾਰਉ ।। 531-32
ਸਭ ਤੇ ਨੀਚੁ ਆਤਮ ਕਰਿ ਮਾਨਉ ਮਨਿ ਮਹਿ ਇਹੁ ਸੁਖ ਧਾਰਉ ।।[231]

P. 120 ਧਾਰਿ ਅਨੁਗ੍ਰਹੁ ਪਾਰਬ੍ਰਹਮਿ ਰਾਖੇ ਭ੍ਰਮ ਕੇ ਖੁਲ੍ਹੇ ਕਪਾਟ ।।[232] 1269

P. 120 ਜਿਹ ਪ੍ਰਸਾਦਿ ਛਤੀਹ ਅੰਮ੍ਰਿਤ ਖਾਹਿ ।। 269
ਤਿਸੁ ਠਾਕੁਰ ਕਉ ਰਖੁ ਮਨ ਮਾਹਿ ।।
ਜਿਹ ਪ੍ਰਸਾਦਿ ਸੁਗੰਧਤ ਤਨਿ ਲਾਵਹਿ ।।[233]

P. 120 ਜਿਸੁ ਪਰਸਾਦਿ ਨਵੈ ਨਿਧਿ ਪਾਈ ।। 177
ਸੋ ਪ੍ਰਭੁ ਮਨ ਤੇ ਬਿਸਰਤ ਨਾਹੀ ।।[234]

P. 121 ਗੰਗ ਬਨਾਰਸਿ ਸਿਫਤਿ ਤੁਮਾਰੀ ਨਾਵੈ ਆਤਮ ਰਾਉ ।। 358
ਸਚਾ ਨਾਵਣੁ ਤਾਂ ਥੀਐ ਜਾਂ ਅਹਿਨਿਸਿ ਲਾਗੈ ਭਾਉ ।।
ਇਕ ਲੋਕੀ ਹੋਰੁ ਛਮਿਛਰੀ ਬ੍ਰਾਹਮਣੁ ਵਟਿ ਪਿੰਡੁ ਖਾਇ ।।
ਨਾਨਕ ਪਿਡੁ ਬਖਸੀਸ ਕਾ ਕਬਹੂੰ ਨਿਖੂਟਸਿ ਨਾਹਿ ।।[236]

P. 122 ਖਿਨ ਮਹਿ ਨੀਚ ਕੀਟ ਕਉ ਰਾਜ ।। 277

ਪਾਰਬ੍ਰਹਮ ਗਰੀਬ ਨਿਵਾਜ ।।
ਜਾ ਕੀ ਦ੍ਰਿਸਟਿ ਕਛੂ ਨ ਆਵੈ ।।
ਤਿਸੁ ਤਤਕਾਲ ਦਹ ਦਿਸ ਪ੍ਰਗਟਾਵੈ ।।
ਜਾ ਕਉ ਅਪੁਨੀ ਕਰੈ ਬਖਸੀਸ ।।
ਤਾ ਕਾ ਲੇਖਾ ਨ ਗਨੈ ਜਗਦੀਸ ।।
ਜੀਉ ਪਿੰਡੁ ਸਭ ਤਿਸ ਕੀ ਰਾਸਿ ।।
ਘਟਿ ਘਟਿ ਪੂਰਨ ਬ੍ਰਹਮ ਪ੍ਰਗਾਸ ।।
ਅਪਨੀ ਬਣਤ ਆਪਿ ਬਨਾਈ ।।
ਨਾਨਕ ਜੀਵੈ ਦੇਖਿ ਬਡਾਈ ।।[237]

P. 123 ਇਕਨਾ ਹੁਕਮੀ ਬਖਸੀਸ ਇਕਿ ਹੁਕਮੀ ਸਦਾ ਭਵਾਈਅਹਿ ।। 1
ਹੁਕਮੈ ਅੰਦਰਿ ਸਭੁ ਕੋ ਬਾਹਰਿ ਹੁਕਮ ਨ ਕੋਇ ।।
ਨਾਨਕ ਹੁਕਮੈ ਜੇ ਬੁਝੈ ਤ ਹਉਮੈ ਕਹੈ ਨ ਕੋਇ ।।[239]

P. 123 ਸਭਨਾ ਕਾ ਦਾਤਾ ਏਕੁ ਹੈ ਆਪੇ ਬਖਸ ਕਰੇਇ ।। 30
ਕਹਣਾ ਕਿਛੂ ਨ ਜਾਵਈ ਜਿਸੁ ਭਾਵੈ ਤਿਸੁ ਦੇਇ ।।
ਨਾਨਕ ਗੁਰਮੁਖਿ ਪਾਈਐ ਆਪੇ ਜਾਣੈ ਸੋਇ ।।[240]

P. 123 ਛੂਟੈ ਤਾ ਕੈ ਬੋਲਿ ਸਾਹਿਬ ਨਦਰਿ ਜਿਸੁ ।। 729
ਘਲੇ ਆਣੇ ਆਪਿ ਜਿਸੁ ਨਾਹੀ ਦੂਜਾ ਮਤੈ ਕੋਇ ।।
ਢਾਹਿ ਉਸਾਰੇ ਸਾਜਿ ਜਾਣੈ ਸਭ ਸੋਇ ।।
ਨਾਉ ਨਾਨਕ ਬਖਸੀਸ ਨਦਰੀ ਕਰਮੁ ਹੋਇ ।।[241]

P. 124 ਤੂ ਜਾਣਾਇਹਿ ਤਾ ਕੋਈ ਜਾਣੈ ।। 563-64
ਤੇਰਾ ਦੀਆ ਨਾਮੁ ਵਖਾਣੈ ।।
ਤੂ ਅਚਰਜੁ ਕੁਦਰਤਿ ਤੇਰੀ ਬਿਸਮਾ ।।
ਤੁਧੁ ਆਪੇ ਕਾਰਣੁ ਆਪੇ ਕਰਣਾ ।।
ਹੁਕਮੇ ਜੰਮਣੁ ਹੁਕਮੇ ਮਰਣਾ ।।
ਨਾਮੁ ਤੇਰਾ ਮਨ ਤਨ ਆਧਾਰੀ ।।
ਨਾਨਕ ਦਾਸੁ ਬਖਸੀਸ ਤੁਮਾਰੀ ।।[242]

P. 125 ਨੀਚਾ ਅੰਦਰਿ ਨੀਚ ਜਾਤਿ ਨੀਚੀ ਹੂ ਅਤਿ ਨੀਚੁ ।। 15

ਨਾਨਕੁ ਤਿਨ ਕੈ ਸੰਗਿ ਸਾਥਿ ਵਡਿਆ ਸਿਉ ਕਿਆ ਰੀਸ ॥
ਜਿਥੈ ਨੀਚ ਸਮਾਲੀਅਨਿ ਤਿਥੈ ਨਦਰਿ ਤੇਰੀ ਬਖਸੀਸ ॥[243]

P. 126 ਦੀਬਾਨੁ ਹਮਾਰੋ ਤੁਹੀ ਏਕ ॥ 210
ਸੇਵਾ ਥਾਰੀ ਗੁਰਹਿ ਟੇਕ ॥
ਅਨਿਕ ਜੁਗਤਿ ਨਹੀ ਪਾਇਆ ॥
ਗੁਰਿ ਚਾਕਰ ਲੈ ਲਾਇਆ ॥
ਮਾਰੇ ਪੰਚ ਬਿਖਾਦੀਆ ॥
ਗੁਰ ਕਿਰਪਾ ਤੇ ਦਲੁ ਸਾਧਿਆ ॥
ਬਖਸੀਸ ਵਜਹੁ ਮਿਲਿ ਏਕੁ ਨਾਮ ॥
ਸੂਖ ਸਹਜ ਆਨੰਦ ਬਿਸ੍ਰਾਸ ॥[244]

P. 126 ਸਚਾ ਸਉਦਾ ਲਾਭੁ ਸਦਾ ਖਟਿਆ ਨਾਮੁ ਅਪਾਰੁ ॥ 646
ਵਿਖੁ ਵਿਚਿ ਅੰਮ੍ਰਿਤ ਪ੍ਰਗਟਿਆ ਕਰਮਿ ਪੀਆਵਣਹਾਰੁ ॥
ਨਾਨਕ ਸਚੁ ਸਲਾਹੀਐ ਧੰਨੁ ਸਵਾਰਣਹਾਰੁ ॥[246]

P. 126 ਧੁਰਿ ਕਰਮਿ ਪਾਇਆ ਤੁਧੁ ਜਿਨ ਕਉ ਸਿ ਨਾਮਿ ਹਰਿ ਕੈ ਲਾਗੇ ॥ 917
ਕਹੈ ਨਾਨਕੁ ਤਹ ਸੁਖੁ ਹੋਆ ਤਿਤੁ ਘਰਿ ਅਨਹਦ ਵਾਜੇ ॥[247]

P. 127 ਕਰਮਿ ਪਵੈ ਨੀਸਾਨੁ ਨ ਚਲੈ ਚਲਾਇਆ ॥[248] 150

P. 127 ਸਚਹੁ ਓਰੈ ਸਭੁ ਕੋ ਉਪਰਿ ਸਚੁ ਆਚਾਰੁ ॥ 62
ਸਭੁ ਕੋ ਊਚਾ ਆਖੀਐ ਨੀਚੁ ਨ ਦੀਸੈ ਕੋਇ ॥
ਇਕਨੈ ਭਾਂਡੇ ਸਾਜਿਐ ਇਕੁ ਚਾਨਣੁ ਤਿਹੁ ਲੋਇ ॥
ਕਰਮਿ ਮਿਲੈ ਸਚੁ ਪਾਈਐ ਧੁਰਿ ਬਖਸ ਨ ਮੇਟੈ ਕੋਇ ॥[249]

P. 127 ਹਰਿ ਕੀ ਕੀਮਤਿ ਕਿਨ ਬਿਧਿ ਹੋਇ ॥ 361
ਹਰਿ ਅਪਰੰਪਰੁ ਅਗਮ ਅਗੋਚਰੁ ਗੁਰ ਕੈ ਸਬਦਿ ਮਿਲੈ ਜਨੁ ਕੋਇ ॥
ਗੁਰਮੁਖਿ ਕੀਮਤਿ ਜਾਣੈ ਕੋਇ ॥
ਵਿਰਲੇ ਕਰਮਿ ਪਰਾਪਤਿ ਹੋਇ ॥
ਊਚੀ ਬਾਣੀ ਊਚਾ ਹੋਇ ॥
ਗੁਖਮੁਖਿ ਸਬਦਿ ਵਖਾਣੈ ਕੋਇ ॥[250]

P. 128 ਬਿਨੁ ਸਾਚੇ ਕਿਉ ਛੂਟੀਐ ਹਰਿ ਗੁਣ ਕਰਮਿ ਮਣੀ ।। 934
ਆਪਿ ਛਡਾਏ ਛੂਟੀਐ ਵਡਾ ਆਪਿ ਧਣੀ ।।
ਗੁਰ ਪਰਸਾਦੀ ਛੂਟੀਐ ਕਿਰਪਾ ਆਪਿ ਕਰੇਇ ।।
ਅਪਣੇ ਹਾਥਿ ਵਡਾਈਆ ਜੈ ਭਾਵੈ ਤੈ ਦੇਇ ।।[251]

P. 128 ਸੇਵਕੁ ਜਨ ਕੀ ਸੇਵਾ ਮਾਗੈ 802
ਪੂਰੈ ਕਰਮਿ ਕਮਾਵਾ ।।
ਨਾਨਕ ਕੀ ਬੇਨੰਤੀ ਸੁਆਮੀ
ਤੇਰੇ ਜਨ ਦੇਖਣੁ ਪਾਵਾ ।।[252]

P. 129 ਸਭਨਾ ਜੀਆ ਕਾ ਸੁਖਦਾਤਾ ਪੂਰੈ ਕਰਮਿ ਧਿਆਇਆ ।।[253] 1067

P. 129 ਸੇਵਕ ਸੇਵਹਿ ਕਰਹਿ ਅਰਦਾਸਿ ।। 1067
ਤੁ ਆਪੇ ਮੇਲਿ ਬਹਾਲਹਿ ਪਾਸਿ ।।[254]

P. 129 ਜਾ ਕੈ ਰਾਮ ਕੋ ਬਲੁ ਹੋਇ ।। 1223
ਸਗਲ ਮਨੋਰਥ ਪੂਰਨ ਤਾਹੂ ਕੇ
ਦੂਖੁ ਨ ਬਿਆਪੈ ਕੋਇ ।। ਰਹਾਉ ।।
ਜੋ ਜਨੁ ਭਗਤੁ ਦਾਸੁ ਨਿਜੁ ਪ੍ਰਭ ਕਾ
ਸੁਣਿ ਜੀਵਾਂ ਤਿਸੁ ਸੋਇ ।।
ਉਦਮੁ ਕਰਉ ਦਰਸਨੁ ਪੇਖਨ ਕੌ
ਕਰਮਿ ਪਰਾਪਤਿ ਹੋਇ ।।[255]

P. 131 ਗੁਰ ਪ੍ਰਸਾਦਿ ਬਿਖਿਆ ਪਰਹਰੈ ।। ਮਨ ਕੀ ਬਾਸਨਾ ਮਨ ਤੇ ਟਰੈ ।।[256] 274

P. 131 ਗੁਰ ਪਰਸਾਦੀ ਹਰਿ ਰੰਗੁ ਮਾਣੁ ।। 1339
ਬਿਨਸੇ ਕਾਮ ਕ੍ਰੋਧ ਅਹੰਕਾਰ ।।
ਨਾਨਕ ਗੁਰਮੁਖਿ ਉਤਰਹਿ ਪਾਰਿ ।।[257]

P. 131 ਗੁਰ ਪਰਸਾਦੀ ਦੁਰਮਤਿ ਖੋਈ ।। 357
ਜਹ ਦੇਖਾ ਤਹ ਏਕੋ ਸੋਈ ।।[258]

P. 131 ਇਹੁ ਬਸਤੀ ਤ ਬਸਤ ਸਰੀਰਾ ।। 481
ਗੁਰ ਪ੍ਰਸਾਦਿ ਸਹਜਿ ਤਰੇ ਕਬੀਰਾ ।।[259]

P. 132 ਗੁਰ ਪਰਸਾਦੀ ਬੂਝਿ ਲੇ ਤਉ ਹੋਇ ਨਿਬੇਰਾ ।। 229
ਘਰਿ ਘਰਿ ਨਾਮੁ ਨਿਰੰਜਨਾ ਸੋ ਠਾਕੁਰੁ ਮੇਰਾ ।।
ਬਿਨੁ ਗੁਰ ਸਬਦ ਨ ਛੂਟੀਐ ਦੇਖਹੁ ਵੀਚਾਰਾ ।।
ਜੇ ਲਖ ਕਰਮ ਕਮਾਵਹੀ ਬਿਨੁ ਗੁਰ ਅੰਧਿਆਹਾ ।।[260]

P. 132 ਸੋਧਤ ਸੋਧਤ ਸੋਧਤ ਸੀਝਿਆ ।। ਗੁਰ ਪ੍ਰਸਾਦਿ ਤਤੁ ਸਭੁ ਬੂਝਿਆ ।।[261] 281

P. 132 ਕੂੜੁ ਕੁਸਤੁ ਤਿਨਾ ਮੈਲੁ ਨ ਲਾਗੈ ।। 128
ਗੁਰ ਪਰਸਾਦੀ ਅਨਦਿਨੁ ਜਾਗੈ ।।
ਨਿਰਮਲ ਨਾਮੁ ਵਸੈ ਘਟ ਭੀਤਰਿ
ਜੋਤੀ ਜੋਤਿ ਮਿਲਾਵਣਿਆ ।।[262]

P. 132 ਗੁਰ ਪਰਸਾਦੀ ਸੇ ਨਰ ਉਬਰੇ ਜਿ ਹਰਿ ਸਰਣਾਗਤਿ ਭਜਿ ਪਇਆ ।।[263] 433
P. 132 ਗੁਰ ਪਰਸਾਦਿ ਸਹਜ ਘਰੁ ਪਾਇਆ ਮਿਟਿਆ ਅੰਧੇਰਾ ਚੰਦੁ ਚੜਿਆ ।।[264] 393

P. 133 ਸੰਸਾਰ ਸਾਗਰੁ ਜਿਨਿ ਉਪਾਇਓ ਸਰਣਿ ਪ੍ਰਭ ਕੀ ਗਹੀ ।। 1017
ਗੁਰ ਪ੍ਰਸਾਦੀ ਪ੍ਰਭੁ ਅਰਾਧੇ ਜਮਕੰਕਰੁ ਕਿਛੁ ਨ ਕਹੀ ।।[265]

P. 133 ਗੁਰ ਪਰਸਾਦੀ ਸਦਾ ਸੁਖੁ ਪਾਏ ।। 841
ਸਚੁ ਕਰਣੀ ਸਾਚਿ ਲਿਵ ਲਾਏ ।।
ਸਤਿਗੁਰੁ ਸੇਵਹਿ ਸੇ ਵਡਭਾਗੀ ।।
ਹਉਮੈ ਮਾਰਿ ਸਚਿ ਲਿਵ ਲਾਗੀ ।।[266]

P. 133 ਗੁਰ ਪਰਸਾਦਿ ਭਇਓ ਮਨੁ ਨਿਰਮਲੁ 496
ਸਰਬ ਸੁਖਾ ਸੁਖ ਪਾਇਅਉ ।।[267]

P. 133 ਸਭ ਮਹਿ ਜੀਉ ਜੀਉ ਹੈ ਸੋਈ 1273
ਘਟਿ ਘਟਿ ਰਹਿਆ ਸਮਾਈ।
ਗੁਰ ਪਰਸਾਦਿ ਘਰ ਹੀ ਪਰਗਾਸਿਆ ਸਹਜੇ ਸਹਜਿ ਸਮਾਈ ।।

ਅਪਨਾ ਕਾਜੁ ਸਵਾਰਹੁ ਆਪੇ ਸੁਖਦਾਤੇ ਗੋਸਾਂਈ ।।
ਗੁਰ ਪਰਸਾਦਿ ਘਰ ਹੀ ਪਿਰੁ ਪਾਇਆ
ਤਉ ਨਾਨਕ ਤਪਤਿ ਬੁਝਾਈ ।।[268]

P. 134 ਤਿਨ੍ਾ ਪਿਆਰਾ ਰਾਮੁ ਜੋ ਪ੍ਰਭ ਭਾਣਿਆ ।। 397
ਗੁਰ ਪਰਸਾਦਿ ਅਕਥੁ ਨਾਨਕਿ ਵਖਾਣਿਆ ।।[269]

P. 134 ਜੋ ਚਾਹਉ ਸੋਈ ਸੋਈ ਪਾਵਉ ਆਸਾ ਮਨਸਾ ਪੂਰਉ ਜਪਿ ਪ੍ਰਭ ਕਉ ।। 700
ਗੁਰ ਪ੍ਰਸਾਦਿ ਨਾਨਕ ਮਨਿ ਵਸਿਆ
ਦੂਖਿ ਨ ਕਬਹੂ ਝੂਰਉ ਬੁਝਿ ਪ੍ਰਭ ਕਉ ।।[270]

P. 134 ਜਗ ਮੋਹਨੀ ਹਮ ਤਿਆਗਿ ਗਵਾਈ ।। ਨਿਰਗੁਨੁ ਮਿਲਿਓ ਵਜੀ ਵਧਾਈ ।। 392
ਐਸੀ ਸੁੰਦਰਿ ਮਨ ਕਉ ਮੋਹੈ ।। ਬਾਟਿ ਘਾਟਿ ਗ੍ਰਿਹਿ ਬਨਿ ਬਨਿ ਜੋਹੈ ।।
ਮਨਿ ਤਨਿ ਲਾਗੈ ਹੋਇ ਕੈ ਮੀਠੀ ।। ਗੁਰ ਪ੍ਰਸਾਦਿ ਮੈ ਖੋਟੀ ਡੀਠੀ ।।[271]

P. 134 ਏਹੁ ਜੋਗੁ ਨ ਹੋਵੈ ਜੋਗੀ 909
ਜਿ ਕੁਟੰਬੁ ਛੋਡਿ ਪਰਭਵਣੁ ਕਰਹਿ ।।
ਗ੍ਰਿਹ ਸਰੀਰ ਮਹਿ ਹਰਿ ਹਰਿ ਨਾਮੁ
ਗੁਰ ਪਰਸਾਦੀ ਅਪਣਾ ਹਰਿ ਪ੍ਰਭੁ ਲਹਹਿ ।।[272]

P. 135 ਗੁਰ ਪਰਸਾਦੀ ਮਨੁ ਜਿਣੈ ਹਰਿ ਸੇਤੀ ਲਿਵ ਲਾਇ ।। 87
ਨਾਨਕ ਗੁਰਮੁਖਿ ਸਚੁ ਕਮਾਵੈ
ਮਨਮੁਖਿ ਆਵੈ ਜਾਇ ।।[273]

P. 135 ਗੁਰ ਪਰਸਾਦੀ ਸਿਵ ਘਰਿ ਜੰਮੈ ਵਿਚਹੁ ਸਕਤਿ ਗਵਾਇ।। 1276
ਅਚਰੁ ਚਰੈ ਬਿਬੇਕ ਬੁਧਿ ਪਾਏ ਪੁਰਖੈ ਪੁਰਖੁ ਮਿਲਾਇ ।।[274]

P. 135 ਮੇਰੇ ਮਾਧਉ ਜੀ ਸਤਸੰਗਤਿ ਮਿਲੇ ਸਿ ਤਰਿਆ ।। 495
ਗੁਰ ਪਰਸਾਦਿ ਪਰਮ ਪਦੁ ਪਾਇਆ ਸੂਕੇ ਕਾਸਟ ਹਰਿਆ ।।[275]

P. 135 ਗੁਰ ਪਰਸਾਦੀ ਹਰਿ ਪ੍ਰਭ ਜਾਚੇ ਐਸੀ ਨਾਮ ਬਡਾਈ ।। ਰਹਾਉ ।। 504
ਐ ਜੀ ਬਹੁਤੇ ਭੇਖ ਕਰਹਿ ਭਿਖਿਆ ਕਉ ਕੇਤੇ ਉਦਰੁ ਭਰਨ ਕੈ ਤਾਈ ।।[276]

P. 126 ਗੁਰ ਪਰਸਾਦਿ ਨਾਮਿ ਮਨੁ ਲਾਗਾ ॥ 184
ਜਨਮ ਜਨਮ ਕਾ ਸੋਇਆ ਜਾਗਾ ॥[277]

P. 136 ਗੁਰ ਪ੍ਰਸਾਦਿ ਲਾਗੇ ਨਾਮ ਸੁਆਦਿ ॥ 1176
ਕਾਹੇ ਜਨਮੁ ਗਵਾਵਹੁ ਵੈਰਿ ਵਾਦਿ ॥[278]

P. 136 ਰਸਨਾ ਹਰਿ ਰਸੁ ਚਾਖਿਆ ਸਹਜਿ ਸੁਭਾਇ ॥ 158
ਗੁਰ ਕਿਰਪਾ ਤੇ ਸਚਿ ਸਮਾਇ ॥
ਸਾਚੇ ਰਾਤੀ ਗੁਰ ਸਬਦੁ ਵੀਚਾਰ ॥
ਅੰਮ੍ਰਿਤੁ ਪੀਵੈ ਨਿਰਮਲ ਧਾਰ ॥[279]

P. 137 ਗੁਰ ਪਰਸਾਦਿ ਸਦਾ ਮਨੁ ਰਾਤਾ ॥ 1072
ਸਿਮਰਿ ਸਿਮਰਿ ਜੀਵਹਿ ਜਨ ਤੇਰੇ
ਏਕੰਕਾਰਿ ਸਮਾਈ ਹੇ ॥[280]

P. 137 ਐਸੀ ਪੇਖੀ ਨੇਤ੍ਰ ਮਹਿ ਪੂਰੇ ਗੁਰ ਪਰਸਾਦਿ ॥ 810
ਰਾਜ ਮਿਲਖ ਧਨ ਜੋਬਨਾ ਨਾਮੈ ਬਿਨੁ ਬਾਦਿ ॥[281]

P. 137 ਗੁਰ ਪਰਸਾਦਿ ਕਿਨੈ ਵਖਿਆਨੀ ॥ 279
ਸਚੁ ਸਚੁ ਸਚੁ ਸਭੁ ਕੀਨਾ ॥
ਕੋਟਿ ਮਧੇ ਕਿਨੈ ਬਿਰਲੈ ਚੀਨਾ ॥
ਭਲਾ ਭਲਾ ਭਲਾ ਤੇਰਾ ਰੂਪ ॥
ਅਤਿ ਸੁੰਦਰ ਅਪਾਰ ਅਨੂਪ ॥[282]

P. 138 ਪ੍ਰਗਟੇ ਗੁਪਾਲ ਗੋਬਿੰਦ ਲਾਲਨ 460
ਸਾਧਸੰਗਿ ਵਖਾਣਿਆ ॥
ਆਚਰਜੁ ਡੀਠਾ ਅਮਿਉ ਵੂਠਾ
ਗੁਰ ਪ੍ਰਸਾਦੀ ਜਾਣਿਆ ॥[283]

P. 138 ਗੁਰ ਪਰਸਾਦਿ ਪਰਮ ਪਦੁ ਪਾਇਆ ॥ 114
ਅੰਤਰੁ ਨਿਰਮਲੁ ਨਿਰਮਲ ਬਾਣੀ
ਹਰਿ ਗੁਣ ਸਹਜੇ ਗਾਵਣਿਆ ॥[284]

P. 138	ਗੁਰ ਪਰਸਾਦਿ ਪਰਮ ਪਦੁ ਪਾਇਆ ਵਡੀ ਵਡਿਆਈ ਹੋਈ ।। ਅਨਦਿਨੁ ਗੁਣ ਗਾਵੈ ਨਿਤ ਸਾਚੇ ਸਚਿ ਸਮਾਵੈ ਸੋਈ ।।[285]	1258
P. 138	ਗੁਨ ਗੋਬਿਦ ਕੀਰਤਨੁ ਜਨੁ ਗਾਵੈ ।। ਗੁਰ ਪ੍ਰਸਾਦਿ ਨਾਨਕ ਫਲੁ ਪਾਵੈ ।।[286]	285
P. 139	ਅਗਮ ਰੂਪ ਕਾ ਮਨ ਮਹਿ ਥਾਨਾ ।। ਗੁਰ ਪ੍ਰਸਾਦਿ ਕਿਨੈ ਵਿਰਲੈ ਜਾਨਾ ।। ਸਹਜ ਕਥਾ ਕੇ ਅੰਮ੍ਰਿਤ ਕੁੰਟਾ ।। ਜਿਸਹਿ ਪਰਾਪਤਿ ਤਿਸੁ ਲੈ ਭੁੰਚਾ ।।[287]	186
P. 139	ਮਨ ਤਨ ਅੰਤਰਿ ਏਕੁ ਪ੍ਰਭੁ ਰਾਤਾ ।। ਗੁਰ ਪ੍ਰਸਾਦਿ ਨਾਨਕ ਇਕੁ ਜਾਤਾ ।।[288]	289
P. 139	ਏਕ ਅਚਰਜੁ ਜਨ ਦੇਖਹੁ ਭਾਈ ।। ਦੁਬਿਧਾ ਮਾਰਿ ਹਰਿ ਮੰਨਿ ਵਸਾਈ ।। ਨਾਮੁ ਅਮੋਲਕੁ ਨ ਪਾਇਆ ਜਾਇ ।। ਗੁਰ ਪਰਸਾਦਿ ਵਸੈ ਮਨਿ ਆਇ ।। ਸਭ ਮਹਿ ਵਸੈ ਪ੍ਰਭੁ ਏਕੋ ਸੋਇ ।। ਗੁਰਮਤੀ ਘਟਿ ਪਰਗਟੁ ਹੋਇ ।।[289]	663
P. 140	ਪਾਰਬ੍ਰਹਮੁ ਪ੍ਰਭੁ ਦ੍ਰਿਸਟੀ ਆਇਆ ਪੂਰਨ ਅਗਮ ਬਿਸਮਾਦ ।। ਨਾਨਕ ਰਾਮ ਨਾਮੁ ਧਨੁ ਕੀਤਾ ਪੂਰੇ ਗੁਰ ਪਰਸਾਦਿ ।।[290]	320-21
P. 141	ਗੁਰ ਪਰਸਾਦੀ ਹਰਿ ਮੰਨਿ ਵਸਿਆ ਪੂਰਬਿ ਲਿਖਿਆ ਪਾਇਆ ।। ਕਹੈ ਨਾਨਕੁ ਏਹੁ ਸਰੀਰੁ ਪਰਵਾਣੁ ਹੋਆ ਜਿਨਿ ਸਤਿਗੁਰ ਸਿਉ ਚਿਤੁ ਲਾਇਆ ।।[291]	922
P. 141	ਗੁਰ ਪ੍ਰਸਾਦਿ ਸੁਖੁ ਦੁਖੁ ਸਮ ਜਾਣੈ ਘਟਿ ਘਟਿ ਰਾਮੁ ਹਿਆਲੀਐ ।।[292]	1019
P. 142	ਗੁਰ ਪ੍ਰਸਾਦਿ ਅੰਤਰਿ ਲਿਵ ਲਾਗੈ ।। ਇਤੁ ਸੰਗਤਿ ਨਾਹੀ ਮਰਣਾ ।।[293]	92

P. 143 ਗੁਰ ਪ੍ਰਸਾਦੀ ਪ੍ਰਭੁ ਧਿਆਇਆ ਗਈ ਸੰਕਾ ਤੂਟਿ ।। 501-2
ਦੁਖ ਅਨੇਰਾ ਭੈ ਬਿਨਾਸੇ ਪਾਪ ਗਏ ਨਿਖੂਟਿ ।।[297]

P. 143 ਗੁਰ ਪਰਸਾਦਿ ਭਰਮ ਕਾ ਨਾਸੁ ।। 294
ਨਾਨਕ ਤਿਨ ਮਹਿ ਏਹੁ ਬਿਸਾਸੁ ।।[298]

P. 144 ਗੁਰ ਪਰਸਾਦੀ ਹੁਕਮੁ ਪਛਾਣੈ ।। 1054
ਧਾਵਤੁ ਰਾਖੈ ਇਕਤੁ ਘਰਿ ਆਣੈ ।।
ਨਾਮੇ ਰਾਤਾ ਸਦਾ ਬੈਰਾਗੀ ਨਾਮੁ ਰਤਨੁ ਮਨਿ ਤਾਹਾ ਹੇ ।।
ਸਭ ਜਗ ਮਹਿ ਵਰਤੈ ਏਕੋ ਸੋਈ ।।
ਗੁਰ ਪਰਸਾਦੀ ਪਰਗਟੁ ਹੋਈ ।।
ਸਬਦੁ ਸਲਾਹਹਿ ਸੇ ਜਨ ਨਿਰਮਲ
ਨਿਜ ਘਰਿ ਵਾਸਾ ਤਾਹਾ ਹੇ ।[299]

P. 144 ਗੁਰ ਪਰਸਾਦੀ ਆਪੁ ਪਛਾਣੈ ਕਮਲੁ ਬਿਗਸੈ ਬੁਧਿ ਤਾਹਾ ਹੇ ।।[300] 1056

P. 145 ਗੁਰ ਪਰਸਾਦੀ ਸਬਦਿ ਸਲਾਹੀ ।। 119
ਤੇਰੇ ਭਾਣੇ ਵਿਚਿ ਅੰਮ੍ਰਿਤ ਵਸੈ
ਤੂੰ ਭਾਣੈ ਅੰਮ੍ਰਿਤੁ ਪੀਆਵਣਿਆ ।।[301]

P. 145 ਹਰਿ ਰਸਹਿ ਅਘਾਨੇ ਸਹਜਿ ਸਮਾਨੇ 1206
ਮੁਖ ਤੇ ਨਾਹੀ ਜਾਤ ਬਰਨ ।।
ਗੁਰ ਪ੍ਰਸਾਦਿ ਨਾਨਕ ਸੰਤੋਖੇ
ਨਾਮੁ ਪ੍ਰਭੂ ਜਪਿ ਜਪਿ ਉਧਰਨ ।।[302]

P. 145 ਗੁਰ ਕੈ ਸਬਦਿ ਤਰੇ ਮੁਨਿ ਕੇਤੇ ਇੰਦ੍ਰਾਦਿਕ ਬ੍ਰਹਮਾਦਿ ਤਰੇ ।। 1125
ਸਨਕ ਸਨੰਦਨ ਤਪਸੀ ਜਨ ਕੇਤੇ ਗੁਰ ਪਰਸਾਦੀ ਪਾਰਿ ਪਰੇ ।।[303]

P. 145 ਗੁਰ ਕਿਰਪਾ ਤੇ ਹੁਕਮੁ ਪਛਾਣੈ ।। ਜੁਗਹ ਜੁਗੰਤਰ ਕੀ ਬਿਧਿ ਜਾਣੈ ।।[304] 1027

P. 146 ਗੁਰ ਕਿਰਪਾ ਤੇ ਨੀਚੁ ਨਿਵਾਜਿਆ ।। 887
ਖੋਲਿ ਕਿਵਾਰਾ ਮਹਲਿ ਬੁਲਾਇਆ ।।

ਜੈਸਾ ਸਾ ਤੈਸਾ ਦਿਖਲਾਇਆ ।।
ਕਹੁ ਨਾਨਕ ਸਭੁ ਪੜਦਾ ਤੂਟਾ ।।
ਹਉ ਤੇਰਾ ਤੂ ਮੈ ਮਨਿ ਵੂਠਾ ।।[305]

P. 146 ਗੁਰ ਕਿਰਪਾ ਤੇ ਜਾਣਿਆ ਜਿਥੈ ਤੁਧੁ ਆਪੁ ਬੁਝਾਇਆ ।। 469
ਸਹਜੇ ਹੀ ਸਚਿ ਸਮਾਇਆ ।।[306]

P. 146 ਮੀਤੁ ਹਮਾਰਾ ਵੇਪਰਵਾਹਾ ।। 187-88
ਗੁਰ ਕਿਰਪਾ ਤੇ ਮੋਹਿ ਅਸਨਾਹਾ ।।
ਮੀਤੁ ਹਮਾਰਾ ਅੰਤਰਜਾਮੀ ।।
ਸਮਰਥ ਪੁਰਖੁ ਪਾਰਬ੍ਰਹਮੁ ਸੁਆਮੀ ।।
ਹਮ ਦਾਸੇ ਤੁਮ ਠਾਕੁਰ ਮੇਰੇ ।।
ਮਾਨੁ ਮਹਤੁ ਨਾਨਕ ਪ੍ਰਭੁ ਤੇਰੇ ।।[307]

P. 147 ਸਚੁ ਪਰਮੇਸਰੁ ਨਿਤ ਨਵਾ ।। 1183
ਗੁਰ ਕਿਰਪਾ ਤੇ ਨਿਤ ਚਵਾ ।।
ਪ੍ਰਭ ਰਖਵਾਲੇ ਮਾਈ ਬਾਪ ।।
ਜਾ ਕੈ ਸਿਮਰਣਿ ਨਹੀ ਸੰਤਾਪ ।।[308]

P. 147 ਗੁਰ ਕਿਰਪਾ ਤੇ ਗੁਨ ਗਾਇ ਅਪਾਰ ।। 1235
ਮਨ ਭੀਤਰਿ ਹੋਵੈ ਪਰਗਾਸੁ ।।
ਗਿਆਨ ਅੰਜਨੁ ਅਗਿਆਨ ਬਿਨਾਸੁ ।।
ਮਿਤਿ ਨਾਹੀ ਜਾ ਕਾ ਬਿਸਥਾਰੁ ।।
ਸੋਭਾ ਤਾ ਕੀ ਅਪਰ ਅਪਾਰ ।।
ਅਨਿਕ ਰੰਗ ਜਾ ਕੇ ਗਨੇ ਨ ਜਾਹਿ ।।[309]

P. 148 ਗੁਰ ਕਿਰਪਾ ਤੇ ਮਨੁ ਤਨੁ ਨਿਰਮਲੁ ਨਿਰਮਲ ਨਾਮੁ ਧਿਆਵਣਿਆ ।। 110
ਜੀਵਣੁ ਮਰਣਾ ਸਭੁ ਤੁਧੈ ਤਾਈ ਜਿਸੁ ਬਖਸੇ ਤਿਸੁ ਦੇ ਵਡਿਆਈ ।।[310]

P. 148 ਗੁਰਕਿਰਪਾ ਤੇ ਨਾਮ ਪਛਾਨਿਆ ।। 932
ਗਗਨ ਗੰਭੀਰੁ ਗਗਨੰਤਰ ਵਾਸੁ ।।
ਗੁਨ ਗਾਵਹਿ ਸੁਖ ਸਹਜਿ ਨਿਵਾਸੁ ।।[311]

P. 149 ਗੁਰ ਕਿਰਪਾ ਤੇ ਮਨੁ ਤਨੁ ਭੀਜੈ ।। 1064
ਰਸਨਾ ਨਾਮੁ ਧਿਆਏ ਰਸਿ ਭੀਜੈ
ਰਸ ਹੀ ਤੇ ਰਸੁ ਪਾਇਦਾ ।।[312]

P. 149 ਗੁਰ ਕਿਰਪਾ ਤੇ ਹਿਰਦੈ ਵਾਸੈ 891
ਭਉਜਲੁ ਪਾਰਿ ਪਰਲਾ ।। ਰਹਾਉ ।।
ਨਾਮੁ ਨਿਧਾਨੁ ਧਿਆਇ ਮਨ ਅਟਲ ।।
ਤਾ ਛੂਟਹਿ ਮਾਇਆ ਕੇ ਪਟਲ ।।[313]

P. 149 ਗੁਰ ਕਿਰਪਾ ਤੇ ਨਾਮੁ ਵਖਾਨੁ ।। 189
ਕਹੁ ਨਾਨਕ ਸੋ ਜਨੁ ਪਰਵਾਨੁ ।।
ਜਾ ਕੈ ਰਿਦੈ ਵਸੈ ਭਗਵਾਨੁ ।।[314]

P. 150 ਗੁਰ ਕਿਰਪਾ ਤੇ ਪਾਈਐ ਪਿਆਰਾ ਅੰਮ੍ਰਿਤੁ ਅਗਮ ਅਥਾਹ ।। 604
ਆਪੇ ਸੁਣਿ ਸਭ ਵੇਖਦਾ ਪਿਆਰਾ ਮੁਖਿ ਬੋਲੇ ਆਪਿ ਮੁਹਾਹੁ ।।[315]

P. 150 ਗੁਰ ਕਿਰਪਾ ਤੇ ਮੁਗਧ ਮਨੁ ਮਾਨਿਆ ।। 864
ਗੁਰੁ ਕਰਤਾ ਗੁਰੁ ਕਰਣੈ ਜੋਗੁ ।।
ਗੁਰੁ ਪਰਮੇਸਰੁ ਹੈ ਭੀ ਹੋਗੁ ।।
ਕਹੁ ਨਾਨਕ ਪ੍ਰਭਿ ਇਹੈ ਜਨਾਈ ।।
ਬਿਨੁ ਗੁਰ ਮੁਕਤਿ ਪਾਈਐ ਨ ਭਾਈ ।।[316]

P. 151 ਗਿਆਨੁ ਧਿਆਨੁ ਗੁਰ ਸਬਦੁ ਹੈ ਮੀਠਾ ।। 162
ਗੁਰ ਕਿਰਪਾ ਤੇ ਕਿਨੈ ਵਿਰਲੈ ਚਖਿ ਡੀਠਾ ।।
ਕਰਮ ਕਾਂਡ ਬਹੁ ਕਰਹਿ ਅਚਾਰ ।।
ਬਿਨੁ ਨਾਵੈ ਧ੍ਰਿਗੁ ਧ੍ਰਿਗੁ ਅਹੰਕਾਰ ।।
ਬੰਧਨਿ ਬਾਧਿਓ ਮਾਇਆ ਫਾਸ ।।
ਜਨ ਨਾਨਕ ਛੂਟੈ ਗੁਰ ਪਰਗਾਸ ।।[317]

P. 152 ਗੁਰ ਕਿਰਪਾ ਜਿਹ ਨਰ ਕਉ ਕੀਨੀ ਤਿਹ ਇਹ ਜੁਗਤਿ ਪਛਾਨੀ ।। 633-34
ਨਾਨਕ ਲੀਨ ਭਇਓ ਗੋਬਿੰਦ ਸਿਉ ਜਿਉ ਪਾਨੀ ਸੰਗਿ ਪਾਨੀ ।।[318]

P. 152 ਗੁਰ ਕਿਰਪਾ ਤੇ ਅੰਮ੍ਰਿਤ ਮੇਰੀ ਬਾਣੀ ।।[319] 239

P. 152 ਗੁਰ ਕਿਰਪਾ ਤੇ ਦਲੁ ਸਾਧਿਆ ।। 210-11
ਬਖਸੀਸ ਵਜਹੁ ਮਿਲਿ ਏਕੁ ਨਾਮ ।।
ਸੂਖ ਸਹਜ ਆਨੰਦ ਬਿਸ੍ਰਾਮ ।।
ਪ੍ਰਭ ਕੇ ਚਾਕਰ ਸੇ ਭਲੇ ।।
ਨਾਨਕ ਤਿਨ ਮੁਖ ਊਜਲੇ ।।[320]

P. 153 ਭਗਤਿ ਵਛਲੁ ਹਰਿ ਵਸੈ ਮਨਿ ਆਇ ।। 1173
ਗੁਰ ਕਿਰਪਾ ਤੇ ਸਹਜ ਸੁਭਾਇ ।।
ਭਗਤਿ ਕਰੇ ਵਿਚਹੁ ਆਪੁ ਖੋਇ ।।
ਤਦ ਹੀ ਸਾਚਿ ਮਿਲਾਵਾ ਹੋਇ ।।
ਭਗਤ ਸੋਹਹਿ ਸਦਾ ਹਰਿ ਪ੍ਰਭ ਦੁਆਰਿ ।।
ਗੁਰ ਕੈ ਹੇਤਿ ਸਾਚੈ ਪ੍ਰੇਮ ਪਿਆਰਿ ।।[321]

P. 153 ਮੇਰਾ ਪ੍ਰਭੁ ਨਿਰਮਲਾ ਸਭ ਤੈ ਰਹਿਆ ਸਮਾਇ ।। 233
ਗੁਰ ਕਿਰਪਾ ਤੇ ਮਿਲੈ ਮਿਲਾਇ ।।
ਹਰਿ ਦਾਸਨ ਕੋ ਦਾਸੁ ਸੁਖੁ ਪਾਏ ।।
ਮੇਰਾ ਹਰਿ ਪ੍ਰਭੁ ਇਨ ਬਿਧਿ ਪਾਇਆ ਜਾਏ ।।
ਹਰਿ ਕਿਰਪਾ ਤੇ ਰਾਮ ਗੁਣ ਗਾਏ ।।[322]

P. 154 ਕਰਿ ਪ੍ਰਸਾਦੁ ਇਕੁ ਖੇਲੁ ਦਿਖਾਇਆ ।। 1128
ਗੁਰ ਕਿਰਪਾ ਤੇ ਪਰਮ ਪਦੁ ਪਾਇਆ ।।
ਕਹਤ ਨਾਨਕੁ ਮਾਰਿ ਜੀਵਾਲੇ ਸੋਇ ।।
ਐਸਾ ਬੂਝਹੁ ਭਰਮਿ ਨ ਭੂਲਹੁ ਕੋਇ ।।[323]

P. 154 ਭਉ ਮੁਚੁ ਭਾਰਾ ਵਡਾ ਤੋਲੁ ।। 151
ਮਨ ਮਤਿ ਹਉਲੀ ਬੋਲੇ ਬੋਲੁ ।।
ਸਿਰਿ ਧਰਿ ਚਲੀਐ ਸਹੀਐ ਭਾਰੁ ।।
ਨਦਰੀ ਕਰਮੀ ਗੁਰ ਬੀਚਾਰੁ ।।[324]

P. 155 ਫਰੀਦਾ ਦਿਲੁ ਰਤਾ ਇਸੁ ਦੁਨੀ ਸਿਉ ਦੁਨੀ ਨ ਕਿਤੈ ਕੰਮਿ ।। 1183-84
ਮਿਸਲ ਫਕੀਰਾਂ ਗਾਖੜੀ ਸੁ ਪਾਈਐ ਪੂਰ ਕਰੰਮਿ ।।

ਪਹਿਲੈ ਪਹਰੈ ਫੁਲੜਾ ਫਲੁ ਭੀ ਪਛਾ ਰਾਤਿ ।।
ਜੋ ਜਾਗੰਨ੍ਹਿ ਲਹੰਨਿ ਸੇ ਸਾਈ ਕੰਨੋ ਦਾਤਿ ।।
ਦਾਤੀ ਸਾਹਿਬ ਸੰਦੀਆ ਕਿਆ ਚਲੈ ਤਿਸੁ ਨਾਲਿ ।।
ਇਕਿ ਜਾਗੰਦੇ ਨਾ ਲਹਨ੍ਹਿ ਇਕਨਾ ਸੁਤਿਆ ਦੇਇ ਉਠਾਲਿ ।।
ਢੂਢੇਦੀਆ ਸੁਹਾਗ ਕੂ ਤਉ ਤਨਿ ਕਾਈ ਕੋਰ ।।
ਜਿਨਾ ਨਾਉ ਸੁਹਾਗਣੀ ਤਿਨ੍ਹਾ ਝਾਕ ਨ ਹੋਰ ।।
ਸਬਰ ਮੰਝ ਕਮਾਣ ਏ ਸਬਰੁ ਕਾ ਨੀਹਣੋ ।।
ਸਬਰ ਸੰਦਾ ਬਾਣੁ ਖਾਲਕੁ ਖਤਾ ਨ ਕਰੀ ।।
ਸਬਰ ਅੰਦਰਿ ਸਾਬਰੀ ਤਨੁ ਏਵੈ ਜਾਲੇਨ੍ਹਿ ।।
ਹੋਨਿ ਨਜੀਕਿ ਖੁਦਾਇ ਦੈ ਭੇਤੁ ਨ ਕਿਸੈ ਦੇਨਿ ।।
ਸਬਰੁ ਏਹੁ ਸੁਆਉ ਜੇ ਤੂੰ ਬੰਦਾ ਦਿੜੁ ਕਰਹਿ ।।
ਵਧਿ ਥੀਵਹਿ ਦਰੀਆਉ ਟੁਟਿ ਨ ਥੀਵਹਿ ਵਾਹੜਾ ।।
ਫਰੀਦਾ ਦਰਵੇਸੀ ਗਾਖੜੀ ਚੋਪੜੀ ਪਰੀਤਿ ।।
ਇਕਨਿ ਕਿਨੈ ਚਾਲੀਐ ਦਰਵੇਸਾਵੀ ਰੀਤਿ ।।[325]

P. 159 ਜਤੁ ਪਾਹਾਰਾ ਧੀਰਜੁ ਸੁਨਿਆਰੁ ।। 8
ਅਹਰਣਿ ਮਤਿ ਵੇਦੁ ਹਥੀਆਰੁ ।।
ਭਉ ਖਲਾ ਅਗਨਿ ਤਪ ਤਾਉ ।।
ਭਾਂਡਾ ਭਾਉ ਅੰਮ੍ਰਿਤੁ ਤਿਤੁ ਢਾਲਿ ।।
ਘੜੀਐ ਸਬਦੁ ਸਚੀ ਟਕਸਾਲ ।।
ਜਿਨ ਕਉ ਨਦਰਿ ਕਰਮੁ ਤਿਨ ਕਾਰ ।।
ਨਾਨਕ ਨਦਰੀ ਨਦਰਿ ਨਿਹਾਲ ।।[327]

P. 160 ਨਾਨਕ ਨਦਰੀ ਕਰਮੀ ਦਾਤਿ ।। 5
ਬਹੁਤਾ ਕਰਮੁ ਲਿਖਿਆ ਨਾ ਜਾਇ ।।[329]

PRAYER

ਆਦਿ ਗ੍ਰੰਥ
ਪੰਨਾ

P. 182 ਸੁਖਦਾਤਾ ਭੈ ਭੰਜਨੋ ਤਿਸੁ ਆਗੈ ਕਰਿ ਅਰਦਾਸਿ ।। 44
ਮਿਹਰ ਕਰੇ ਜਿਸੁ ਮਿਹਰਵਾਨੁ ਤਾਂ ਕਾਰਜੁ ਆਵੈ ਰਾਸਿ ।।[7]

P. 182 ਰੇ ਮਨ ਮੇਰੇ ਤੂੰ ਤਾ ਕਉ ਆਹਿ ।। 187
ਜਾ ਕੈ ਊਣਾ ਕਛਹੂ ਨਾਹਿ ।।
ਹਰਿ ਸਾ ਪ੍ਰੀਤਮੁ ਕਰਿ ਮਨ ਮੀਤ ।।
ਪ੍ਰਾਨ ਅਧਾਰੁ ਰਾਖਹੁ ਸਦ ਚੀਤ ।।
ਰੇ ਮਨ ਮੇਰੇ ਤੂੰ ਤਾ ਕਉ ਸੇਵਿ ।।
ਆਦਿ ਪੁਰਖ ਅਪਰੰਪਰ ਦੇਵ ।।
ਤਿਸੁ ਊਪਰਿ ਮਨ ਕਰਿ ਤੂੰ ਆਸਾ ।।
ਆਦਿ ਜੁਗਾਦਿ ਜਾ ਕਾ ਭਰਵਾਸਾ ।।
ਜਾ ਕੀ ਪ੍ਰੀਤਿ ਸਦਾ ਸੁਖੁ ਹੋਇ ।।
ਨਾਨਕੁ ਗਾਵੈ ਗੁਰ ਮਿਲਿ ਸੋਇ ।।[8]

P. 182 ਤੀਨੇ ਤਾਪ ਨਿਵਾਰਣਹਾਰਾ ਦੁਖ ਹੰਤਾ ਸੁਖ ਰਾਸਿ ।। 714
ਤਾ ਕਉ ਬਿਘਨੁ ਨ ਕੋਊ ਲਾਗੈ ਜਾ ਕੀ ਪ੍ਰਭ ਆਗੈ ਅਰਦਾਸਿ ।।[9]

P. 183 ਏਕ ਓਟ ਏਕੋ ਆਧਾਰੁ ।। 289
ਨਾਨਕ ਮਾਗੈ ਨਾਮੁ ਪ੍ਰਭ ਸਾਰੁ ।।[10]

P. 183 ਨਾਮ ਤੁਲਿ ਕਛੁ ਅਵਰੁ ਨ ਹੋਇ ।।[11] 265

P. 183 ਬਿਨੁ ਨਾਵੈ ਸਭੁ ਕੋਈ ਨਿਰਧਨੁ ਸਤਿਗੁਰਿ ਬੂਝ ਬੁਝਾਈ ।।[12] 1232

P. 183 ਪਾਰਜਾਤੁ ਇਹੁ ਹਰਿ ਕੋ ਨਾਮ ।। 265
ਕਾਮਧੇਨ ਹਰਿ ਹਰਿ ਗੁਣ ਗਾਮ ।।[13]

P. 184	ਸਰਬ ਧਰਮ ਮਹਿ ਸ੍ਰੇਸਟ ਧਰਮੁ ॥ ਹਰਿ ਕੋ ਨਾਮੁ ਜਪਿ ਨਿਰਮਲ ਕਰਮੁ ॥[14]	266
P. 184	ਨਾਨਕ ਜਿਨ ਕੈ ਹਿਰਦੈ ਵਸਿਆ ਮੋਖ ਮੁਕਤਿ ਤਿਨ੍ ਪਾਇਆ ॥[15]	565
P. 184	ਬਲਿਹਾਰੀ ਜਾਉ ਜੇਤੇ ਤੇਰੇ ਨਾਵ ਹੈ ॥[17]	1168
P. 185	ਤੂ ਮੇਰਾ ਪਿਤਾ ਤੂਹੈ ਮੇਰਾ ਮਾਤਾ ॥ ਤੂ ਮੇਰੇ ਜੀਅ ਪ੍ਰਾਨ ਸੁਖਦਾਤਾ ॥ ਤੂ ਮੇਰਾ ਠਾਕੁਰੁ ਹਉ ਦਾਸੁ ਤੇਰਾ ॥ ਤੁਝ ਬਿਨੁ ਅਵਰੁ ਨਹੀ ਕੋ ਮੇਰਾ ॥ ਕਰਿ ਕਿਰਪਾ ਕਰਹੁ ਪ੍ਰਭ ਦਾਤਿ ॥ ਤੁਮ੍ਰੀ ਉਸਤਤਿ ਕਰਉ ਦਿਨ ਰਾਤਿ ॥[18]	1144
P. 186	ਹਿਰਦੈ ਨਾਮੁ ਸਦਾ ਧੁਨਿ ਨਿਹਚਲ ਘਟੈ ਨ ਕੀਮਤਿ ਪਾਈ ।[22]	1232
P. 187	ਨਾਮਹਿ ਸਭ ਕਛੁ ਬਨਿਆ ਖੰਡ ਬ੍ਰਹਮੰਡ ਸਰੀਰ ॥ ।[26]	1232
P. 188	ਸਦ ਸੁਣਦਾ ਸਦ ਵੇਖਦਾ ਸਬਦਿ ਰਹਿਆ ਭਰਪੂਰਿ ॥੧॥[27]	429
P. 188	ਕੀਰਤਿ ਸੂਰਤਿ ਮੁਕਤਿ ਇਕ ਨਾਈ ॥ ਤਾਹੀ ਨਿਰੰਜਨੁ ਰਹਿਆ ਸਮਾਈ ॥[28]	221
P. 188	ਜਬ ਲਗੁ ਜੋਬਨਿ ਸਾਸੁ ਹੈ ਤਬ ਲਗੁ ਨਾਮੁ ਧਿਆਇ ॥ ਚਲਦਿਆ ਨਾਲਿ ਹਰਿ ਚਲਸੀ ਹਰਿ ਅੰਤੇ ਲਏ ਛਡਾਇ ॥[29]	82
P. 189	ਮੁਖਹੁ ਹਰਿ ਹਰਿ ਸਭੁ ਕੋ ਕਹੈ ਵਿਰਲੈ ਹਿਰਦੈ ਵਸਾਇਆ ॥ ਨਾਨਕ ਜਿਨ ਕੈ ਹਿਰਦੈ ਵਸਿਆ ਮੋਖ ਮੁਕਤਿ ਤਿਨ੍ ਪਾਇਆ ॥[30]	565
P. 189	ਨਾਮੁ ਨਿਰੰਜਨੁ ਅਗਮੁ ਅਗੋਚਰੁ ਸਤਿਗੁਰਿ ਦੀਆ ਬੁਝਾਏ ॥[31]	585
P. 189	ਹਉਮੈ ਨਾਵੈ ਨਾਲਿ ਵਿਰੋਧੁ ਹੈ ਦੁਇ ਨ ਵਸਹਿ ਇਕ ਠਾਇ ॥[33]	560

P. 190 ਸੂਰਬੀਰ ਧੀਰਜ ਮਤਿ ਪੂਰਾ ।। 890-891
ਸਹਜ ਸਮਾਧਿ ਧੁਨਿ ਗਹਿਰ ਗੰਭੀਰਾ ।।
ਸਦਾ ਮੁਕਤੁ ਤਾ ਕੈ ਪੂਰੇ ਕਾਮ ।।
ਜਾ ਕੈ ਰਿਦੈ ਵਸੈ ਹਰਿ ਨਾਮ ।।
ਸਗਲ ਸੂਖ ਆਨੰਦ ਅਰੋਗ ।।
ਸਮਦਰਸੀ ਪੂਰਨ ਨਿਰਜੋਗ ।।
ਆਇ ਨ ਜਾਇ ਡੋਲੈ ਕਤ ਨਾਹੀ ।।
ਜਾ ਕੈ ਨਾਮੁ ਬਸੈ ਮਨ ਮਾਹੀ ।।[35]

P. 191 ਕਿਰਤਿ ਕਰਮ ਕੇ ਵੀਛੁੜੇ ਕਰਿ ਕਿਰਪਾ ਮੇਲਹੁ ਰਾਮ ।। 133
ਚਾਰਿ ਕੁੰਟ ਦਹ ਦਿਸ ਭ੍ਰਮੇ ਥਕਿ ਆਏ ਪ੍ਰਭ ਕੀ ਸਾਮ ।।
ਧੇਨੁ ਦੂਧੈ ਤੇ ਬਾਹਰੀ ਕਿਤੈ ਨ ਆਵੈ ਕਾਮ ।।
ਜਲ ਬਿਨੁ ਸਾਖ ਕੁਮਲਾਵਤੀ ਉਪਜਹਿ ਨਾਹੀ ਦਾਮ ।।
ਹਰਿ ਨਾਹ ਨ ਮਿਲੀਐ ਸਾਜਨੈ ਕਤ ਪਾਈਐ ਬਿਸਰਾਮ ।।
ਜਿਤੁ ਘਰਿ ਹਰਿ ਕੰਤੁ ਨ ਪ੍ਰਗਟਈ ਭਠਿ ਨਗਰ ਸੇ ਗ੍ਰਾਮ ।।
ਸ੍ਰਬ ਸੀਗਾਰ ਤੰਬੋਲ ਰਸ ਸਣੁ ਦੇਹੀ ਸਭ ਖਾਮ ।।
ਪ੍ਰਭ ਸੁਆਮੀ ਕੰਤ ਵਿਹੂਣੀਆ ਮੀਤ ਸਜਣ ਸਭਿ ਜਾਮ ।।
ਨਾਨਕ ਦੀ ਬੇਨੰਤੀਆ ਕਰਿ ਕਿਰਪਾ ਦੀਜੈ ਨਾਮੁ ।।[40]

P. 194 ਕ੍ਰਿਪਾ ਨਿਧਿ ਬਸਹੁ ਰਿਦੈ ਹਰਿ ਨੀਤ ।। 712-13
ਤੈਸੀ ਬੁਧਿ ਕਰਹੁ ਪਰਗਾਸਾ ਲਾਗੈ ਪ੍ਰਭ ਸੰਗਿ ਪ੍ਰੀਤਿ ।। ਰਹਾਉ ।।
ਦਾਸ ਤੁਮਾਰੇ ਕੀ ਪਾਵਉ ਧੂਰਾ ਮਸਤਕਿ ਲੇ ਲੇ ਲਾਵਉ ।।
ਮਹਾ ਪਤਿਤ ਤੇ ਹੋਤ ਪੁਨੀਤਾ ਹਰਿ ਕੀਰਤਨ ਗੁਨ ਗਾਵਉ ।।
ਆਗਿਆ ਤੁਮਰੀ ਮੀਠੀ ਲਾਗਉ ਕੀਓ ਤੁਹਾਰੋ ਭਾਵਉ ।।
ਜੋ ਤੂ ਦੇਹਿ ਤਹੀ ਇਹੁ ਤ੍ਰਿਪਤੈ ਆਨ ਨ ਕਤਹੂ ਧਾਵਉ ।।
ਸਦ ਹੀ ਨਿਕਟਿ ਜਾਨਉ ਪ੍ਰਭੁ ਸੁਆਮੀ ।। ਸਗਲ ਰੈਣ ਹੋਇ ਰਹੀਐ ।।
ਸਾਧੂ ਸੰਗਤਿ ਹੋਇ ਪਰਾਪਤਿ ਤਾ ਪ੍ਰਭ ਅਪੁਨਾ ਲਹੀਐ ।।
ਸਦਾ ਸਦਾ ਹਮ ਛੋਹਰੇ ਤੁਮਰੇ ਤੂ ਪ੍ਰਭ ਹਮਰੋ ਮੀਰਾ ।।
ਨਾਨਕ ਬਾਰਿਕ ਤੁਮ ਮਾਤ ਪਿਤਾ ਮੁਖਿ ਨਾਮੁ ਤੁਮਾਰੋ ਖੀਰਾ ।।[41]

P. 195 1. ਪ੍ਰਭ ਜੀ ਮਿਲੁ ਮੇਰੇ ਪ੍ਰਾਨ ।। 716
ਬਿਸਰੁ ਨਹੀ ਨਿਮਖ ਹੀਅਰੇ ਤੇ ਅਪਨੇ ਭਗਤ ਕਉ ਪੂਰਨ ਦਾਨ ।।ਰਹਾਉ।।
2. ਖੋਵਹੁ ਭਰਮੁ ਰਾਖੁ ਮੇਰੇ ਪ੍ਰੀਤਮ ਅੰਤਰਜਾਮੀ ਸੁਘੜ ਸੁਜਾਨ ।।
3. ਕੋਟਿ ਰਾਜ ਨਾਮ ਧਨੁ ਮੇਰੈ

4. ਅੰਮ੍ਰਿਤ ਦ੍ਰਿਸਟਿ ਧਾਰਹੁ ਪ੍ਰਭ ਮਾਨ ।।
ਆਠ ਪਹਰ ਰਸਨਾ ਗੁਨ ਗਾਵੈ ਜਸੁ ਪੂਰਿ ਅਘਾਵਹਿ ਸਮਰਥ ਕਾਨ ।।
5. ਤੇਰੀ ਸਰਣਿ ਜੀਅਨ ਕੇ ਦਾਤੇ ਸਦਾ ਸਦਾ ਨਾਨਕ ਕੁਰਬਾਨ ।।[42]

P. 195 ਦਰਸਨ ਪੇਖਤ ਮਨ ਆਘਾਵੇ ।। 105
ਸਦ ਬਲਿਹਾਰਿ ਜਾਈਐ ਕੁਰਬਾਨਾ ।।
ਜਲਿ ਥਲਿ ਪੂਰਿ ਰਹਿਆ ਮਿਹਰਵਾਨਾ ।।
.....ਰਾਖਿ ਲੀਏ ਸਗਲੇ ਪ੍ਰਭਿ ਆਪੇ ।।
ਉਤਰਿ ਗਏ ਸਭ ਸੋਗ ਸੰਤਾਪੇ ।।
ਨਾਮੁ ਜਪਤ ਮਨੁ ਤਨੁ ਹਰੀਆਵਲੁ ਪ੍ਰਭ ਨਾਨਕ ਨਦਰਿ ਨਿਹਾਰੇ ਜੀਉ ।।[43]

P. 195 ਨਾਨਕ ਸੇ ਅਖੜੀਆ ਬਿਅੰਨਿ ਜਿਨੀ ਡਿਸੰਦੋ ਮਾ ਪਿਰੀ ।।[44] 1100

P. 196 ਤੁਮ ਮਾਤ ਪਿਤਾ ਹਮ ਬਾਰਿਕ ਤੇਰੇ ।। 268
ਤੁਮਰੀ ਕ੍ਰਿਪਾ ਮਹਿ ਸੂਖ ਘਨੇਰੇ ।।
ਕੋਇ ਨ ਜਾਨੈ ਤੁਮਰਾ ਅੰਤੁ ।।
..... ਤੁਮਰੀ ਗਤਿ ਮਿਤਿ ਤੁਮ ਹੀ ਜਾਨੀ ।।
ਨਾਨਕ ਦਾਸ ਸਦਾ ਕੁਰਬਾਨੀ ।।[45]

P. 196 ਤੂੰ ਮੇਰਾ ਪ੍ਰੀਤਮੁ ਤੁਮ ਸੰਗਿ ਹੀਤੁ ।। 181
..... ਤੁਝ ਬਿਨੁ ਨਿਮਖੁ ਨ ਜਾਈ ਰਹਣਾ ।।
ਤੂੰ ਮੇਰੇ ਲਾਲਨ ਤੂੰ ਮੇਰੇ ਪ੍ਰਾਨ ।।
ਤੂੰ ਮੇਰੇ ਸਾਹਿਬ ਤੂੰ ਮੇਰੇ ਖਾਨ ।।
..... ਤੂੰ ਮੇਰੀ ਸੋਭਾ ਤੁਮ ਸੰਗਿ ਰਚੀਆ ।।
ਤੂੰ ਮੇਰੀ ਓਟ ਤੂੰ ਹੈ ਮੇਰਾ ਤਕੀਆ ।।
ਮਨ ਤਨ ਅੰਤਰਿ ਤੁਹੀ ਧਿਆਇਆ ।।
ਮਰਮੁ ਤੁਮਾਰਾ ਗੁਰ ਤੇ ਪਾਇਆ ।।[46]

P. 197 ਕਿਆ ਗੁਣ ਤੇਰੇ ਸਾਰਿ ਸਮਾਲ੍ਹੀ ਮੋਹਿ ਨਿਰਗੁਨ ਕੇ ਦਾਤਾਰੇ ।। 738
ਬੈ ਖਰੀਦ ਕਿਆ ਕਰੈ ਚਤੁਰਾਈ ਇਹੁ ਜੀਉ ਪਿੰਡੁ ਸਭੁ ਥਾਰੇ ।।
ਲਾਲ ਰੰਗੀਲੇ ਪ੍ਰੀਤਮ ਮਨਮੋਹਨ ਤੇਰੇ ਦਰਸਨ ਕਉ ਹਮ ਬਾਰੇ ।। ਰਹਾਉ ।।
..... ਮਿਤ ਨਹੀ ਪਾਈਐ ਅੰਤੁ ਨ ਲਹੀਐ ਮਨੁ ਤਰਸੇ ਚਰਨਾਰੇ ।।[47]

P. 197 ਤੁਧੁ ਬਿਨੁ ਦੂਜਾ ਨਾਹੀ ਕੋਇ ।। ਤੂ ਕਰਤਾਰੁ ਕਰਹਿ ਸੋ ਹੋਇ ।। 723-24

ਤੇਰਾ ਜੋਰੁ ਤੇਰੀ ਮਨਿ ਟੇਕ ।। ਸਦਾ ਸਦਾ ਜਪਿ ਨਾਨਕ ਏਕ ।।
ਸਭ ਊਪਰਿ ਪਾਰਬ੍ਰਹਮ ਦਾਤਾਰੁ ।। ਤੇਰੀ ਟੇਕ ਤੇਰਾ ਆਧਾਰੁ ।। ਰਹਾਉ ।।
ਹੈ ਤੂਹੈ ਤੂ ਹੋਵਨਹਾਰ ।। ਅਗਮ ਅਗਾਧਿ ਊਚ ਆਪਰ ।।
ਜੋ ਤੁਧੁ ਸੇਵਹਿ ਤਿਨ ਭਉ ਦੁਖੁ ਨਾਹਿ ।। ਗੁਰ ਪਰਸਾਦਿ ਨਾਨਕ ਗੁਣ ਗਾਹਿ ।।
ਜੋ ਦੀਸੈ ਸੋ ਤੇਰਾ ਰੂਪੁ ।। ਗੁਣ ਨਿਧਾਨ ਗੋਵਿੰਦ ਅਨੂਪ ।।
ਸਿਮਰਿ ਸਿਮਰਿ ਸਿਮਰ ਜਨ ਸੋਇ ।। ਨਾਨਕ ਕਰਮਿ ਪਰਾਪਤਿ ਹੋਇ ।।
ਜਿਨਿ ਜਪਿਆ ਤਿਸ ਕਉ ਬਲਿਹਾਰ ।। ਤਿਸ ਕੈ ਸੰਗਿ ਤਰੈ ਸੰਸਾਰ ।।
ਕਹੁ ਨਾਨਕ ਪ੍ਰਭ ਲੋਚਾ ਪੂਰਿ ।। ਸੰਤ ਜਨਾ ਕੀ ਬਾਛਉ ਧੂਰਿ ।।[48]

P. 198 ਤੂ ਠਾਕੁਰੋ ਬੈਰਾਗਰੋ ਮੈ ਜੇਹੀ ਘਣ ਚੇਰੀ ਰਾਮ ।। 779
ਤੂੰ ਸਾਗਰੋ ਰਤਨਾਗਰੋ ਹਉ ਸਾਰ ਨ ਜਾਣਾ ਤੇਰੀ ਰਾਮ ।।
ਸਾਰ ਨ ਜਾਣਾ ਤੂ ਵਡ ਦਾਣਾ ਕਰਿ ਮਿਹਰੰਮਤਿ ਸਾਂਈ ।।
ਕਿਰਪਾ ਕੀਜੈ ਸਾ ਮਤਿ ਦੀਜੈ ਆਠ ਪਹਰ ਤੁਧੁ ਧਿਆਈ ।।
ਗਰਬੁ ਨ ਕੀਜੈ ਰੇਣ ਹੋਵੀਜੈ ਤਾ ਗਤਿ ਜੀਅਰੇ ਤੇਰੀ ।।
ਸਭ ਊਪਰਿ ਨਾਨਕ ਕਾ ਠਾਕੁਰੁ ਮੈ ਜੇਹੀ ਘਣ ਚੇਰੀ ਰਾਮ ।।[49]

P. 198 ਜਲ ਬਿਹੂਨ ਮੀਨ ਕਤ ਜੀਵਨ ਦੂਧ ਬਿਨਾ ਰਹਨੁ ਕਤ ਬਾਰੋ ।। 829
ਜਨ ਨਾਨਕ ਪਿਆਸ ਚਰਨ ਕਮਲਨ੍ਹ ਕੀ ਪੇਖਿ ਦਰਸੁ ਸੁਆਮੀ ਸੁਖ ਸਾਰੋ ।।[50]

P. 199 ਸੁਨਹੁ ਬੇਨੰਤੀਆ ਸੁਆਮੀ ਮੇਰੇ ਰਾਮ ।। 547
..... ਬਿਨਵੰਤਿ ਨਾਨਕ ਦਾਸੁ ਹਰਿ ਕਾ ਪ੍ਰਭ ਜੀਅ ਪ੍ਰਾਨ ਅਧਾਰੀ ।।[51]

P. 199 ਪ੍ਰਭ ਜੀ ਮੋਹਿ ਕਵਨੁ ਅਨਾਥੁ ਬਿਚਾਰਾ ।। 1220
ਕਵਨ ਮੂਲ ਤੇ ਮਾਨੁਖੁ ਕਰਿਆ ਇਹੁ ਪਰਤਾਪੁ ਤੁਹਾਰਾ ।।
ਜੀਅ ਪ੍ਰਾਣ ਸਰਬ ਕੇ ਦਾਤੇ ਗੁਣ ਕਹੇ ਨ ਜਾਹਿ ਅਪਾਰਾ ।।
ਸਭ ਕੇ ਪ੍ਰੀਤਮ ਸਰਬ ਪ੍ਰਤਿਪਾਲਕ ਸਰਬ ਘਟਾਂ ਆਧਾਰਾ ।।[52]

P. 200 ਸਤਿਗੁਰ ਆਇਓ ਸਰਣਿ ਤੁਹਾਰੀ ।। 713
ਮਿਲੈ ਸੂਖੁ ਨਾਮੁ ਹਰਿ ਸੋਭਾ ਚਿੰਤਾ ਲਾਹਿ ਹਮਾਰੀ ।।
ਅਵਰ ਨ ਸੂਝੈ ਦੂਜੀ ਠਾਹਰ ਹਾਰਿ ਪਰਿਓ ਤਉ ਦੁਆਰੀ ।। ਰਹਾਉ ।।
ਲੇਖਾ ਛੋਡਿ ਅਲੇਖੈ ਛੂਟਹ ਹਮ ਨਿਰਗੁਨ ਲੇਹੁ ਉਬਾਰੀ ।।
ਸਦ ਬਖਸਿੰਦੁ ਸਦਾ ਮਿਹਰਵਾਨਾ ਸਭਨਾ ਦੇਇ ਅਧਾਰੀ ।।
ਨਾਨਕ ਦਾਸ ਸੰਤ ਪਾਛੈ ਪਰਿਓ ਰਾਖਿ ਲੇਹੁ ਇਹ ਬਾਰੀ ।।[54]

P. 201 ਤੂ ਮੇਰਾ ਪਿਤਾ ਤੂਹੈ ਮੇਰਾ ਮਾਤਾ ।। 1144

ਤੂ ਮੇਰੇ ਜੀਅ ਪ੍ਰਾਨ ਸੁਖਦਾਤਾ ॥
ਤੂ ਮੇਰਾ ਠਾਕੁਰੁ ਹਉ ਦਾਸੁ ਤੇਰਾ ॥
ਤੁਝ ਬਿਨੁ ਅਵਰੁ ਨਹੀ ਕੋ ਮੇਰਾ ॥[55]

P. 201 ਪ੍ਰਭ ਕੀਜੈ ਕ੍ਰਿਪਾ ਨਿਧਾਨ 1321
ਹਮ ਹਰਿ ਗੁਨ ਗਾਵਹਗੇ ॥
.....ਹਮ ਬਾਰਿਕ ਮੁਗਧ ਇਆਨ..... ॥[56]

P. 201 ਸਜਣੁ ਤੂਹੈ ਸੈਣੁ ਤੂ ਮੈ ਤੁਝ ਉਪਰਿ ਬਹੁ ਮਾਣੀਆ ॥ 761
ਜਾ ਤੂ ਅੰਦਰਿ ਤਾ ਸੁਖੇ ਤੂੰ ਨਿਮਾਣੀ ਮਾਣੀਆ ॥
..... ਕਿਤੀ ਲਖ ਕਰੋੜਿ ਪਿਰੀਏ ਰੋਮ ਨ ਪੁਜਨਿ ਤੇਰਿਆ ॥
ਤੂ ਸਾਹੀ ਹੂ ਸਾਹੁ ਹਉ ਕਹਿ ਨ ਸਕਾ ਗੁਣ ਤੇਰਿਆ ॥
ਸਹੀਆ ਤਊ ਅਸੰਖ ਮੰਞਹੁ ਹਭਿ ਵਧਾਣੀਆ ॥[57]

P. 202 ਹਉ ਮਾਗਉ ਤੁਝੈ ਦਇਆਲ ਕਰਿ ਦਾਸਾ ਗੋਲਿਆ ॥ 518
ਨਉ ਨਿਧਿ ਪਾਈ ਰਾਜੁ ਜੀਵਾ ਬੋਲਿਆ ॥
ਅੰਮ੍ਰਿਤ ਨਾਮੁ ਨਿਧਾਨੁ ਦਾਸਾ ਘਰਿ ਘਣਾ ॥
ਤਿਨ ਕੈ ਸੰਗਿ ਨਿਹਾਲੁ ਸ੍ਰਵਣੀ ਜਸੁ ਸੁਣਾ ॥
ਕਮਾਵਾ ਤਿਨ ਕੀ ਕਾਰ ਸਰੀਰੁ ਪਵਿਤੁ ਹੋਇ ॥
ਪਖਾ ਪਾਣੀ ਪੀਸਿ ਬਿਗਸਾ ਪੈਰ ਧੋਇ ॥
ਆਪਹੁ ਕਛੂ ਨ ਹੋਇ ਪ੍ਰਭ ਨਦਰਿ ਨਿਹਾਲੀਐ ॥
ਮੋਹਿ ਨਿਰਗੁਣ ਦਿਚੈ ਥਾਉ ਸੰਤ ਧਰਮ ਸਾਲੀਐ ॥[58]

P. 202 ਪ੍ਰਭ ਇਹੈ ਮਨੋਰਥੁ ਮੇਰਾ ॥ 533
ਕ੍ਰਿਪਾ ਨਿਧਾਲ ਦਇਆਲ ਮੋਹਿ ਦੀਜੈ ਕਰਿ ਸੰਤਨ ਕਾ ਚੇਰਾ ॥ ਰਹਾਉ ॥
ਪ੍ਰਾਤਹਕਾਲ ਲਾਗਉ ਜਨ ਚਰਨੀ ਨਿਸ ਬਾਸੁਰ ਦਰਸੁ ਪਾਵਉ ॥
ਤਨੁ ਮਨੁ ਅਰਪਿ ਕਰਉ ਜਨ ਸੇਵਾ ਰਸਨਾ ਹਰਿ ਗੁਨ ਗਾਵਉ ॥
ਸਾਸਿ ਸਾਸਿ ਸਿਮਰਉ ਪ੍ਰਭੁ ਅਪੁਨਾ ਸੰਤਸੰਗਿ ਨਿਤ ਰਹੀਐ ॥
ਏਕੁ ਅਧਾਰੁ ਨਾਮੁ ਧਨੁ ਮੋਰਾ ਅਨਦੁ ਨਾਨਕ ਇਹੁ ਲਹੀਐ ॥[59]

P. 202 **ਅਰਦਾਸ** [60]

1. ੴ ਵਾਹਿਗੁਰੂ ਜੀ ਕੀ ਫਤਹਿ ॥
2. ਸ੍ਰੀ ਭਗੌਤੀ ਜੀ ਸਹਾਇ ॥
   ਵਾਰ ਸ੍ਰੀ ਭਗੌਤੀ ਜੀ ਕੀ ॥ ਪਾਤਿਸ਼ਾਹੀ 10 ॥

3. ਪ੍ਰਿਥਮ ਭਗੌਤੀ ਸਿਮਰਿ ਕੈ ਗੁਰ ਨਾਨਕ ਲਈਂ ਧਿਆਇ ।।
4. ਫਿਰ ਅੰਗਦ ਗੁਰ ਤੇ ਅਮਰਦਾਸੁ ਰਾਮਦਾਸੈ ਹੋਈਂ ਸਹਾਇ ।।
5. ਅਰਜਨ ਹਰਿਗੋਬਿੰਦ ਨੋ ਸਿਮਰੌ ਸ੍ਰੀ ਹਰਿਰਾਇ ।।
6. ਸ੍ਰੀ ਹਰਿਕ੍ਰਿਸ਼ਨ ਧਿਆਈਐ ਜਿਸੁ ਡਿਠੈ ਸਭਿ ਦੁਖ ਜਾਇ ।।
7. ਤੇਗ ਬਹਾਦਰ ਸਿਮਰਿਐ ਘਰ ਨਉ ਨਿਧਿ ਆਵੈ ਧਾਇ ।।
8. ਸਭ ਥਾਈਂ ਹੋਇ ਸਹਾਇ ।।
9. ਦਸਵੇਂ ਪਾਤਿਸ਼ਾਹ ਸ੍ਰੀ ਗੁਰੂ ਗੋਬਿੰਦ ਸਿੰਘ ਸਾਹਿਬ ਜੀ ਸਭ ਥਾਈਂ ਹੋਇ ਸਹਾਇ ।।

ੳ. ਦਸਾਂ ਪਾਤਿਸ਼ਾਹੀਆਂ ਦੀ ਜੋਤ ਸ੍ਰੀ ਗੁਰੂ ਗ੍ਰੰਥ ਸਾਹਿਬ ਜੀ ਦੇ ਪਾਠ ਦੀਦਾਰ ਦਾ ਧਿਆਨ ਧਰ ਕੇ, ਬੋਲੋ ਜੀ ਵਾਹਿਗੁਰੂ ।।

ਅ. ਪੰਜਾਂ ਪਿਆਰਿਆਂ, ਚੌਹਾਂ ਸਾਹਿਬਜ਼ਾਦਿਆਂ ਚਾਲ੍ਹੀਆਂ ਮੁਕਤਿਆਂ, ਹਠੀਆਂ, ਤਪੀਆਂ, ਜਿੰਨ੍ਹਾਂ, ਨਾਮ ਜਪਿਆ, ਵੰਡ ਕੇ ਛਕਿਆ, ਦੇਗ ਚਲਾਈ, ਤੇਗ ਵਾਹੀ, ਦੇਖ ਕੇ ਅਣਡਿੱਠ ਕੀਤਾ, ਤਿਨ੍ਹਾਂ ਪਿਆਰਿਆਂ, ਸਚਿਆਰਿਆਂ ਦੀ ਕਮਾਈ ਦਾ ਧਿਆਨ ਧਰ ਕੇ, ਖਾਲਸਾ ਜੀ, ਬੋਲੋ ਜੀ ਵਾਹਿਗੁਰੂ।।

ੲ. ਜਿਨ੍ਹਾਂ ਸਿੰਘਾਂ ਸਿੰਘਣੀਆਂ ਨੇ ਧਰਮ ਹੇਤ ਸੀਸ ਦਿਤੇ, ਬੰਦ ਬੰਦ ਕਟਾਏ, ਖੋਪਰੀਆਂ ਲੁਹਾਈਆਂ ਚਰਖੜੀਆਂ ਤੇ ਚੜ੍ਹੇ, ਤਨ ਆਰਿਆਂ ਨਾਲ ਚਿਰਾਏ, ਗੁਰਦੁਆਰਿਆਂ ਦੀ ਸੇਵਾ ਲਈ ਕੁਰਬਾਨੀਆਂ ਕੀਤੀਆਂ, ਧਰਮ ਨਹੀਂ ਹਾਰਿਆ, ਸਿੱਖੀ ਕੇਸਾਂ ਸੁਆਸਾਂ ਨਾਲ ਨਿਬਾਹੀ, ਤਿਨ੍ਹਾਂ ਦੀ ਕਮਾਈ ਦਾ ਧਿਆਨ ਧਰ ਕੇ, ਖਾਲਸਾ ਜੀ ! ਬੋਲੋ ਜੀ ਵਾਹਿਗੁਰੂ ।।

ਸ. ਪੰਜਾਂ ਤਖ਼ਤਾਂ ਅਤੇ ਸਰਬੱਤ ਗੁਰਦੁਆਰਿਆਂ ਦਾ ਧਿਆਨ ਧਰ ਕੇ, ਬੋਲੋ ਜੀ ਵਾਹਿਗੁਰੂ ।।

ਹ. ਪ੍ਰਿਥਮੇ ਸਰਬੱਤ ਖਾਲਸਾ ਜੀ ਕੀ ਅਰਦਾਸ ਹੈ ਜੀ, ਸਰਬੱਤ ਖਾਲਸਾ ਜੀ ਕੋ ਵਾਹਿਗੁਰੂ, ਵਾਹਿਗੁਰੂ, ਵਾਹਿਗੁਰੂ ਚਿੱਤ ਆਵੇ, ਚਿੱਤ ਆਵਨ ਕਾ ਸਦਕਾ, ਸਰਬ ਸੁਖ ਹੋਵੇ ।। ਜਹਾਂ ਜਹਾਂ ਖਾਲਸਾ ਜੀ ਸਾਹਿਬ, ਤਹਾਂ ਤਹਾਂ ਰੱਛਿਆ ਰਿਆਇਤ, ਦੇਗ ਤੇਗ ਫਤਹ, ਬਿਰਦ ਕੀ ਪੈਜ, ਪੰਥ ਦੀ ਜੀਤ, ਸ੍ਰੀ ਸਾਹਿਬ ਜੀ ਸਹਾਇ, ਖਾਲਸਾ ਜੀ ਕੇ ਬੋਲ ਬਾਲੇ, ਬੋਲੋ ਜੀ ਵਾਹਿਗੁਰੂ ।।

ਕ. ਸਿੱਖਾਂ ਨੂੰ ਸਿੱਖੀ ਦਾਨ, ਕੇਸ ਦਾਨ, ਰਹਿਤ ਦਾਨ, ਬਿਬੇਕ ਦਾਨ, ਵਿਸਾਹ ਦਾਨ, ਭਰੋਸਾ ਦਾਨ, ਦਾਨਾਂ ਸਿਰ ਦਾਨ, ਨਾਮ ਦਾਨ, ਸ੍ਰੀ ਅੰਮ੍ਰਿਤਸਰ ਜੀ ਦੇ ਇਸ਼ਨਾਨ, ਚੌਂਕੀਆਂ ਝੰਡੇ, ਬੁੰਗੇ, ਜੁਗੋ ਜੁਗ ਅਟੱਲ, ਧਰਮ ਕਾ ਜੈਕਾਰ, ਬੋਲੋ ਜੀ ਵਾਹਿਗੁਰੂ ।। ਸਿੱਖਾਂ ਦਾ ਮਨ ਨੀਵਾਂ, ਮਤ ਉਚੀ, ਮਤ ਪਤ ਦਾ ਰਾਖਾ ਆਪਿ ਵਾਹਿਗੁਰੂ ।।

ਖ. ਹੇ ਅਕਾਲ ਪੁਰਖ ! ਆਪਣੇ ਪੰਥ ਦੇ ਸਦਾ ਸਹਾਈ ਦਾਤਾਰ ਜੀਓ ! ਸ੍ਰੀ ਨਨਕਾਣਾ ਸਾਹਿਬ ਤੇ ਹੋਰ ਗੁਰਦੁਆਰਿਆਂ ਗੁਰਧਾਮਾਂ ਦੇ ਜਿਨ੍ਹਾਂ ਤੋਂ ਪੰਥ ਨੂੰ ਵਿਛੋੜਿਆ ਗਿਆ ਹੈ, ਖੁਲ੍ਹੇ ਦਰਸ਼ਨ ਦੀਦਾਰ ਤੇ ਸੇਵਾ ਸੰਭਾਲ ਦਾ ਦਾਨ ਖਾਲਸਾ ਜੀ ਨੂੰ ਬਖਸ਼ੋ ।।

ਗ. ਹੇ ਨਿਮਾਣਿਆਂ ਦੇ ਮਾਣ, ਨਿਤਾਣਿਆਂ ਦੇ ਤਾਣ, ਨਿਓਟਿਆਂ ਦੀ ਓਟ, ਸੱਚੇ ਪਿਤਾ, ਵਾਹਿਗੁਰੂ ! ਆਪ ਜੀ ਦੇ ਹਜ਼ੂਰ..........(ਇੱਥੇ ਉਸ ਪਾਠ ਜਾਂ ਕੀਤੀ ਜਾ ਰਹੀ ਅਰਦਾਸ ਲਈ ਯੋਗ ਸ਼ਬਦ ਵਰਤੇ ਜਾਣ) ਦੀ ਅਰਦਾਸ ਹੈ ਜੀ ।

ਙ. ਅੱਖਰ ਵਾਧਾ ਘਾਟਾ ਭੁਲ ਚੁਕ ਮਾਫ਼ ਕਰਨੀ। ਸਰਬੱਤ ਦੇ ਕਾਰਜ ਰਾਸ ਕਰਨੇ। ਸੇਈ ਪਿਆਰੇ ਮੇਲ, ਜਿਨ੍ਹਾਂ ਮਿਲਿਆਂ ਤੇਰਾ ਨਾਮ ਚਿੱਤ ਆਵੇ।

ਚ. ਨਾਨਕ ਨਾਮ ਚੜ੍ਹਦੀ ਕਲਾ ।। ਤੇਰੇ ਭਾਣੇ ਸਰਬਤ ਦਾ ਭਲਾ ।।

ਛ. ਵਾਹਿਗੁਰੂ ਜੀ ਕਾ ਖਾਲਸਾ ।।
ਵਾਹਿਗੁਰੂ ਜੀ ਕੀ ਫਤਹਿ ।।

P. 207 ਤੁਮ੍ ਕਰਹੁ ਦਇਆ ਮੇਰੇ ਸਾਈ ।। 673
ਐਸੀ ਮਤਿ ਦੀਜੈ ਮੇਰੇ ਠਾਕੁਰ ਸਦਾ ਸਦਾ ਤੁਧੁ ਧਿਆਈ ।।[64]

P. 207 ਜਗਤੁ ਜਲੰਦਾ ਰਖਿ ਲੈ ਆਪਣੀ ਕਿਰਪਾ ਧਾਰਿ ।। 853
ਜਿਤੁ ਦੁਆਰੈ ਉਬਰੈ ਤਿਤੈ ਲੈਹੁ ਉਬਾਰਿ ।।[65]

P. 207 ਹਰਿ ਕਿਰਪਾ ਕਰਿ ਕੈ ਬਖਸਿ ਲੈਹੁ ਹਉ ਪਾਪੀ ਵਡ ਗੁਨਹਗਾਰੁ ।।[66] 1416

P. 207 ਜੇਤਾ ਸਮੁੰਦੁ ਸਾਗਰੁ ਨੀਰਿ ਭਰਿਆ ਤੇਤੇ ਅਉਗਣ ਹਮਾਰੇ ।। 156
ਦਇਆ ਕਰਹੁ ਕਿਛੁ ਮਿਹਰ ਉਪਾਵਹੁ ਡੁਬਦੇ ਪਥਰ ਤਾਰੇ ।।[67]

P. 207 ਹਾ ਹਾ ਪ੍ਰਭ ਰਾਖਿ ਲੇਹੁ ।। 675
ਹਮ ਤੇ ਕਿਛੂ ਨ ਹੋਇ ਮੇਰੇ ਸ੍ਵਾਮੀ ਕਰਿ ਕਿਰਪਾ ਅਪੁਨਾ ਨਾਮੁ ਦੇਹੁ ।।[68]

P. 207 ਕਿਰਤਿ ਕਰਮ ਕੇ ਵੀਛੁੜੇ ਕਰਿ ਕਿਰ੍ਪਾ ਮੇਲਹੁ ਰਾਮ ।। 133
ਚਾਰਿ ਕੁੰਟ ਦਹ ਦਿਸ ਭ੍ਰਮੇ ਥਕਿ ਆਏ ਪ੍ਰਭ ਕੀ ਸਾਮ ।।[69]

P. 208 ਹਮ ਮੂਰਖ ਮੁਗਧ ਅਗਿਆਨ ਮਤੀ ਸਰਣਾਗਤਿ ਪੁਰਖ ਅਜਨਮਾ ।। 799
ਕਰਿ ਕਿਰਪਾ ਰਖਿ ਲੇਵਹੁ ਮੇਰੇ ਠਾਕੁਰ ਹਮ ਪਾਥਰ ਹੀਨ ਅਕਰਮਾ ।।[70]

P. 208 ਕੁਚਿਲ ਕਠੋਰ ਕਪਟ ਕਾਮੀ ।। ਜਿਉ ਜਾਨਹਿ ਤਿਉ ਤਾਰਿ ਸੁਆਮੀ ।। 1301
ਤੂ ਸਮਰਥੁ ਸਰਨਿ ਜੋਗੁ ਤੂ ਰਾਖਹਿ ਅਪਨੀ ਕਲ ਧਾਰਿ ।।
ਜਾਪ ਤਾਪ ਨੇਮ ਸੁਚਿ ਸੰਜਮ ਨਾਹੀ ਇਨ ਬਿਧੇ ਛੁਟਕਾਰ ।।
ਗਰਤ ਘੋਰ ਅੰਧ ਤੇ ਕਾਢਹੁ ਪ੍ਰਭ ਨਾਨਕ ਨਦਰਿ ਨਿਹਾਰਿ ।।[71]

P. 208 ਹਉ ਅਪਰਾਧੀ ਗੁਨਹਗਾਰ ਹਉ ਬੇਮੁਖ ਮੰਦਾ।। ਵਾਰਾਂ ਭਾਈ ਗੁਰਦਾਸ ਜੀ
ਚੋਰੁ ਯਾਰੁ ਜੁਆਰਿ ਹਉ ਪਰ ਘਰਿ ਜੋਹੰਦਾ।।
ਨਿੰਦਕੁ ਦੁਸਟੁ ਹਰਾਮਖੋਰੁ ਠਗੁ ਦੇਸ ਠਗੰਦਾ।।
ਕਾਮ ਕ੍ਰੋਧ ਮਦੁ ਲੋਭੁ ਮੋਹੁੰ ਅਹੰਕਾਰੁ ਕਰੰਦਾ।।
ਬਿਸਾਸਘਾਤੀ ਅਕਿਰਤਘਣ ਮੈ ਕੋ ਨ ਰਖੰਦਾ।।
ਸਿਮਰਿ ਮੁਰੀਦਾ ਢਾਢੀਆ ਸਤਿਗੁਰ ਬਖਸੰਦਾ।।[72]

P. 209 ਜਿਹ ਪ੍ਰਸਾਦਿ ਧਰ ਊਪਰਿ ਸੁਖਿ ਬਸਹਿ ।। 267
ਸੁਤ ਭ੍ਰਾਤ ਮੀਤ ਬਨਿਤਾ ਸੰਗਿ ਹਸਹਿ ।।
ਜਿਹ ਪ੍ਰਸਾਦਿ ਪੀਵਹਿ ਸੀਤਲ ਜਲਾ ।।
ਸੁਖਦਾਈ ਪਵਨੁ ਪਾਵਕੁ ਅਮੁਲਾ ।।
ਜਿਹ ਪ੍ਰਸਾਦਿ ਭੋਗਹਿ ਸਭਿ ਰਸਾ ।।
ਸਗਲ ਸਮਗ੍ਰੀ ਸੰਗਿ ਸਾਥਿ ਬਸਾ ।।
ਦੀਨੇ ਹਸਤ ਪਾਵ ਕਰਨ ਨੇਤ੍ਰ ਰਸਨਾ ।।
ਤਿਸਹਿ ਤਿਆਗਿ ਅਵਰ ਸੰਗਿ ਰਚਨਾ ।।
ਐਸੇ ਦੋਖ ਮੂੜ ਅੰਧ ਬਿਆਪੇ ।।
ਨਾਨਕ ਕਾਢਿ ਲੇਹੁ ਪ੍ਰਭ ਆਪੇ ।।[73]

P. 212 ਆਰਤੀ [78] 663

1. ਗਗਨ ਮੈ ਥਾਲੁ
2. ਰਵਿ ਚੰਦ ਦੀਪਕ ਬਨੇ
3. ਤਾਰਿਕਾ ਮੰਡਲ ਜਨਕ ਸੋਤੀ
4. ਧੂਪੁ ਮਲਆਨਲੋ
5. ਪਵਣੁ ਚਵਰੋ ਕਰੇ
6. ਸਗਲ ਬਨਰਾਇ
7. ਫੂਲੰਤ ਜੋਤੀ
8. ਕੈਸੀ ਆਰਤੀ ਹੋਇ
9. ਭਵ ਖੰਡਨਾ ਤੇਰੀ ਆਰਤੀ
10. ਅਨਹਤਾ ਸਬਦ ਵਾਜੰਤ ਭੇਰੀ

11. ਸਹਸ ਤਵ ਨੈਨ
12. ਨਨ ਨੈਨ ਹੈ ਤੋਹਿ ਕਉ
13. ਸਹਸ ਮੂਰਤਿ
14. ਨਨਾ ਏਕ ਤੋਹੀ
15. ਸਹਸ ਪਦ ਬਿਮਲ
16. ਨਨ ਏਕ ਪਦ
17. ਗੰਧ ਬਿਨੁ
18. ਸਹਸ ਤਵ ਗੰਧ
19. ਇਵ ਚਲਤ ਮੋਹੀ
20. ਸਭ ਮਹਿ ਜੋਤਿ
21. ਜੋਤਿ ਹੈ ਸੋਈ
22. ਤਿਸ ਕੈ ਚਾਨਣ
23. ਸਭ ਮਹਿ ਚਾਨਣੁ ਹੋਇ
24. ਗੁਰ ਸਾਖੀ
25. ਜੋਤਿ ਪਰਗਟੁ ਹੋਇ
26. ਜੋ ਤਿਸੁ ਭਾਵੈ
27. ਸੁ ਆਰਤੀ ਹੋਇ
28. ਹਰਿ ਚਰਣ ਕਮਲ
29. ਮਕਰੰਦ ਲੋਭਿਤ
30. ਮਨੋ ਅਨਦਿਨੋ ਮੋਹਿ ਆਹੀ ਪਿਆਸਾ
31. ਕਿਰਪਾ ਜਲੁ ਦੇਹਿ ਨਾਨਕ
32. ਸਾਰਿੰਗ ਕਉ
33. ਹੋਇ ਜਾ ਤੇ ਤੇਰੈ ਨਾਮਿ ਵਾਸਾ

***

BIBLIOGRAPHY

Basic

Ādi Shri Guru Granth Sahibji, Standard 1430 pages, Shri Damdami Bir, Bhai Jawahar Singh Kirpal Singh and Co., Amritsar (Devnagri).

Ādi Granth Shabad Anukramanika: ed. by Gurcharan Singh, Shri Guru Granth Sahib Adhyayan Vibhag, Punjabi University, Patiala, 1971, 2 Volumes (Punjabi).

New Catholic Encyclopaedia, McGraw Hill Book Company, 1967, Vol.V.

Summa Theologica, 2a, 2ae, 1, 2.

Sankshipt Hindi Shabd Sāgar edited by Ramchandra Varma, Nagri Pracharini Sabha, Kashi, 8th edition, 1981.

General

A.J. Ayer: *Language, Truth and Logic*, London, 1946, 2nd edition.

Amar Singh and Shamsher Singh: *Varan Bhai Gurdas ji*, Shiromani Gurdwara Prabandhak Committee, Amritsar, 1977.

A.M. Hunder: *The Gospel According to St. Paul*, London, 1966, cited in *Divine Grace and Human Response*, edited by C. M. Vadakekkara, O.B.S., Asirvanam Benedictine Monastery, Bangalore, 1981.

St. Augustine: *Sermon X on the Words of the Lord.*

Avtar Singh: *Ethics of the Sikhs*, Punjabi University, Patiala, 1970.

'Theory and Falsification' In *The Philosophy of Religion*, Oxford Readings in Philosophy, edited by Basil Mitchell, (O.U.P. 1977 Reprint).

Chinmayananda Swami: (ed.) *The Holy Geeta*, Central Chinmaya Mission Trust, Sandeepany, Sadhanalaya, Bombay.

Canon George D. Smith: (ed.) *The Teachings of the Catholic Church*, Macmillan, New York, 1949, I.17. Cited by Brand Blandshard in his *Reason and Belief*, George Allen & Unwin, 1974.

D.Z. Phillips: *The Concept of Prayer*, Routledge and Kegan Paul, London, 2nd impression, 1968.

Gabriel Marcel: *Being and Having,* tr. by Katharine Farrer, The University Press, Glasgow, 1949.

G. Marcel: *Faith and Reality* (Part II of the *Mystery of Being*), Gateway Edition, 1960.

Ganda Singh: *Sikhs and Sikhism,* Sikh Cultural Centre, Patna, 1968.

George Henrick Von Wright: *Explanation and Understanding,* Ithaca, Cornell University Press, 1971.

Gopal Singh: (translated and annotated) *Sri Guru Granth Sahib,* Gurdas Kapoor and Sons, 1960.

H.D. Lewis: *Our Experience of God,* George Allen and Unwin Ltd., London, 2nd impression, 1962.

Habermas Jurgen: *Knowledge and Human Interests,* tr. Jeremy J. Shapiro, Boston, Beacon Press, 1971.

Hoy, David Courzens: *The Critical Circle: Literature, History and Philosophical Hermeneutics,* University of California Press, 1978. Cited in *Three Faces of Hermeneutics,* Roy J. Howard, University of California Press Ltd., 1980.

K. Barth: *Church Dogmatics,* tr. by G.T. Thomson, Vol. I, Part I, T and T Clark, 1936.

Kirpal Singh: *Prayer, Its Nature and Technique,* The Sant Bani Press, America, Tilton, New Hampshire, 3rd Printing, 1974.

Kirpal Singh: *Naam or Word,* The Sant Bani Press, America, Tilton, New Hampshire, 3rd Printing, 1974.

M. K. Gandhi: *In Search of the Supreme,* compiled and edited by V.B. Kher, Navjivan Publishing House, 1961, Vol. I.

Manmohan Singh: (tr. English and Punjabi), *Sri Guru Granth Sahib,* Shiromani Gurudwara Prabandhak Committee, Amritsar, 1962, 1st impression.

M. K. Gandhi: *An Autobiography or The Story of My Experiments with Truth,* Navajivan Publishing House, Ahmedabad, 1958 reprint.

M. R. Sampat Kumaran: (tr. into English) *The Gitābhasya of Ramanuja,* Vidya Press, Madras, First edition, June 1969.

Newman: *Grammer of Assent,* Longmans, 1947.

Patrick Shanghnessy: tr. 'The Nature of Grace' and 'Union with God' from *The Glories of Divine Grace,* Matthias, J. Scheeben, O.S.B., S.T.D., A Grail Publication, Third Printing, 1948, Part–I.

P. D. Lefevre: *The Prayers of Kierkegaard,* The Univesity of Chicago Press, 1956.

Pritam Singh Gill: *Concepts of Sikhism,* New Academic Publishing Co., Jullundur, 1979.

Pyarelal: *The Last Phase,* Navjivan Press, Ahmedabad, 1958.

R. C. Pandeya: *The Philosophy of Name,* included in *Perspectives on Guru Nanak* (Seminar Papers), edited by Harbans Ṣingh, Department of Religious Studies, Punjabi University, Patiala, 1975.

Rex Warner: tr. *The Confessions of St. Augustine,* A Mentor Omega Book, 1963.

Roy J. Howard: *Three Faces of Hermeneutics,* University of California Press Ltd., 1982.

The Mind of Mahatma Gandhi, compiled and edited by R. K. Prabhu and U. R. Rao: Navajivan Publishing House, Ahmedabad, 1976.

S. K. Langer: *Problems of Art,* Routledge and Kegan Paul, London, 1957.

S.K. Saxena: *Ever Unto God: Essays on Gandhi and Religion,* Indian Council of Philosophical Research, New Delhi, 1988.

Simone Weil: *Gravity and Grace,* Routledge and Kegan Paul, 1972.

Simone Weil: *Waiting on God,* tr. by Emma Craufurd, Collins Fount Paperbacks, 1950.

S. S. Kohli: *A Critical Study of Ādi Granth,* Punjabi Writers' Co-operative Industrial Society Ltd., 1961.

Sher Singh: *Philosophy of Sikhism,* Sterling Publishers, Jullundur, 2nd edition, 1966.

Sören Kierkegaard: *Edifying Discourses,* A Selection, edited by Paul L. Holmer, Harper Torch Books, New York, 1958.

Veer Singh: *Shri Guru Granth Kosh,* Khalsa Tract Society, Amritsar, 1960.

Wazir Singh: *Philosophy of Sikh Religion,* Ess Ess Publications, 1st edition, 1981.

W.F. Zuurdeeg: *An Analytical Philosophy of Religion,* George Allen & Unwin, 1959.

William James: *The Varieties of Religious Experience, A Study in Human Nature,* Collins, Fount Paperbacks, 1960.

W. Owen Cole: *The Guru in Sikhism,* Darton, Longman & Todd, 1st edition, 1982.

W. Owen Cole and Piarā Singh Sambhi: *The Sikhs, Their Religious Beliefs and Practices,* Rupa and Co., 1st edition, 1984.

INDEX